New worlds for old words

The impact of cultured borrowing on the languages of Western Europe

Mundos nuevos para viejas palabras

El impacto de los cultismos en los idiomas de Europa occidental

Edited by

Christopher Pountain
Queen Mary University of London

Bozena Wislocka Breit
Queen Mary University of London

Series in Language and Linguistics

Copyright © 2022 by the authors.

All rights reserved. No part of this publication may be reproduced, stored in a retrieval system, or transmitted in any form or by any means, electronic, mechanical, photocopying, recording, or otherwise, without the prior permission of Vernon Art and Science Inc.
www.vernonpress.com

In the Americas:
Vernon Press
1000 N West Street, Suite 1200,
Wilmington, Delaware 19801
United States

In the rest of the world:
Vernon Press
C/Sancti Espiritu 17,
Malaga, 29006
Spain

 Bridging Languages and Scholarship

Series in Language and Linguistics

Library of Congress Control Number: 2021930171

ISBN: 978-1-64889-386-5

Also available: 978-1-64889-193-9 [Hardback]; 978-1-64889-274-5 [PDF, E-Book]

Product and company names mentioned in this work are the trademarks of their respective owners. While every care has been taken in preparing this work, neither the authors nor Vernon Art and Science Inc. may be held responsible for any loss or damage caused or alleged to be caused directly or indirectly by the information contained in it.

Every effort has been made to trace all copyright holders, but if any have been inadvertently overlooked the publisher will be pleased to include any necessary credits in any subsequent reprint or edition.

Cover design by Vernon Press using elements designed by aopsan / Freepik and Layerace / Freepik.

Copyright © 2022 de los autores.

Todos los derechos reservados. Ninguna parte de esta publicación puede ser reproducida, ni almacenada en un sistema de recuperación de datos, ni transmitida de ninguna forma ni por ningún medio, ya sea electrónico, mecánico, fotocopiado, grabado u otro, sin el permiso previo por parte de Vernon Art and Science Inc.

Los nombres de productos y compañías mencionados en este trabajo son marcas comerciales de sus respectivos propietarios. Si bien se han tomado todas las precauciones al preparar este trabajo, ni los autores ni Vernon Art and Science Inc. pueden ser considerados responsables por cualquier pérdida o daño causado, o presuntamente causado, directa o indirectamente, por la información contenida en él.

Se han hecho todos los esfuerzos posibles para rastrear a todos los titulares de derechos de autor, pero si alguno ha sido pasado por alto inadvertidamente, la editorial se complacerá en incluir los créditos necesarios en cualquier reimpresión o edición posterior.

Diseño de cubierta de Vernon Press usando elementos diseñados por aopsan / Freepik y Layerace / Freepik.

También disponible: 978-1-64889-193-9 [Tapa dura]; 978-1-64889-274-5 [PDF, E-Book]

The book is consistently scholarly and informative, often original, and at times entertaining. Gloria Clavería Nadal hits the nail on the head as to why the topic is of interest: "Old words have actually become the most natural way for modern languages to name these new worlds created on a daily basis" (p.29), most obviously, but not only, in non-linguistic fields such as science and medicine. Thus this book will make clear why 'cultured borrowings' should not be dismissed as irrelevant, as they have tended to be in the past.

Roger Wright
Emeritus Professor of Spanish
University of Liverpool

The issue—what traditionally used to be called "learnèd borrowing"—is an important one also in the light of more recent theoretical contributions that consider language dynamics not just as a homogeneous process of evolution but rather as a differentiated composite history of discursive traditions between "immediacy" and "distance" ... The contact of modern European languages (mainly Spanish, but also other European languages) with classical languages via cultural contact and translation is treated in this volume from a wide range of perspectives: from medieval to contemporary borrowings, from philological, psycholinguistic to didactic approaches and including not only purely lexical, but also morphological aspects. The book is particularly of interest for advanced students and scholars in Romance linguistics.

Dr. Johannes Kabatek
University of Zurich

What is transcendent and makes the present studies a source for further research, is that, in many cases, by process of metaphorization, the lexical piece taken from the classical language becomes a term of the common language, and its oral version. This is the first strength of this publication. The second is that much of the research presented is part of ongoing research, developed not individually, but by team members of recognized quality. The third strength is the origin of the data handled ... Explanations are not ventured but are given with the support of reliable sources. There is a fourth strength, and it is the volume and quality of the bibliographies that each author has provided at the end of their chapter. For the specialized reader, there is a fifth strength: almost all the authors mention that theirs is an open investigation, which will be outlined in future works.

Dr. Emma Martinell
Professor Emeritus
University of Barcelona, Spain

The central idea of the contributed volume ... is that the concept of "learnèd borrowing" ... should be seen as a palpable linguistic consequence of one of the best-documented cultural contacts ever in the history of Western Europe. This idea, as a common thread, (re-)appears cunningly through the book, showing that learned borrowing-regardless of the source and target languages-has been very productive either in earlier or in the present states of the studied languages of Western Europe. Thus, each of the 13 chapters addresses the linguistic as well as the extralinguistic causes and mechanisms contributing to its output, seen from different linguistic perspectives.

Dr. Andrzej Zieliński
Instytut Filologii Romańskiej
Uniwersytet Jagielloński, Krakow, Poland

Table of contents

List of figures	ix
Acknowledgements	xiii
Abbreviations	xv
The authors	xvii
Introduction	xxiii

Chapter 1
Cultured borrowings in the light of dictionaries 1
Gloria Clavería Nadal
Universitat Autònoma de Barcelona

Chapter 2
Learnèd borrowings induced by translation: Paratactic lexical groups as interference phenomena in Medieval and Early Renaissance Romance texts 25
Santiago Del Rey Quesada
Universidad de Sevilla

Chapter 3
Apuntes sobre la integración de un cultismo médico: la historia de la voz *síntoma* 53
Isabel García Ortiz
Queen Mary University of London

Chapter 4
El latinismo en los titulares de la prensa deportiva española 71
Susana Guerrero Salazar
Universidad de Málaga

Chapter 5
Datos psicolingüísticos en torno a la vitalidad y la neologicidad de la composición culta en la prensa escrita en español 91
Carmen Varo Varo
Universidad de Cádiz

Chapter 6
Cultismos en el aula de enseñanza de la secundaria 109
María del Carmen Rodríguez Caballero
I.E.S. "Poeta Claudio Rodríguez", Zamora

Chapter 7
"Classical" and "modern" languages 117
Bozena Wislocka Breit
Queen Mary University of London

Chapter 8
Latinisms as Lexical Substitutes in Late Medieval and Early Modern Spanish 135
Steven N. Dworkin
University of Michigan

Chapter 9
Sustituciones léxicas en los arabismos del reino de Granada (siglos XVI y XVII) 157
Inmaculada González Sopeña
Universidad de Granada

Chapter 10
Cultured borrowing of verbs: the case of the Spanish *-ir* conjugation 173
Christopher J. Pountain
Queen Mary University of London

Chapter 11
The Impact of New Contacts on an Old Pattern: the Modifier–Modified Order in the Formation of Italian Compounds 191
Alessandro Carlucci
University of Bergen

Chapter 12
Los cultismos en una novela dialogada del siglo XVI: un estudio de sociolingüística histórica 211
Rocío Díaz-Bravo y Gael Vaamonde
Universidad de Granada

Chapter 13
Magic, witches and magicians in a semantic and etymological perspective in European languages 231
Ingmar Söhrman
Göteborgs Universitet

Index of topics 257

Index of words in Romance languages, Latin, Greek, Arabic and English 261

List of figures

Figure 1.1. Learnèd consonantal groups (Penny 1991, 92) — 9

Figure 2.1. Linguistic interference between the source text and the target text in translation from Latin — 37

Figure 2.2. Paratactic lexical groups containing at least one learnèd borrowing in the corpus — 38

Figure 2.3. Effects of convergence and divergence in paratactic lexical groups with at least one LB in PGs motivated by the ST — 45

Figure 2.4. Phenomena of Hyper- or Hetero-Latinism (counting non-translated excerpts) vs. Latinism in the corpus — 46

Figura 3.1. Acepciones del Lat. *symptoma* y el Lat. *accidens* en la Database of Latin Dictionaries (DLD) — 59

Figura 3.2. Términos de significación en textos médicos castellanos según *CORDE*. — 63

Figura 3.3. Aumento en la frecuencia de uso de la voz *síntoma* en español según datos del *CDE*. — 66

Figura 4.1. Tabla de latinismos crudos registrados (las formas con asterisco no se consideran correctas) — 88

Figura 5.1. Usos neológicos formales por composición (Fuente: BOBNEO) — 97

Figura 5.2. Neologismos por composición culta registrados (Fuente: BOBNEO) — 98

Figura 5.3. Registro de los elementos compositivos cultos utilizados en el estudio (Fuente: BOBNEO) — 100

Figura 5.4. Datos sobre la relación entre interpretación acertada, familiaridad y esfuerzo de procesamiento — 102

Figura 5.5. Datos sobre la relación entre interpretación errónea, familiaridad y esfuerzo de procesamiento ... 103

Figura 5.6. Datos sobre la relación entre grado de novedad y grado de dificultad ... 104

Figure 7.1. *Classical Latin* and *Ancient Latin* in Google ngram viewer, 1800–2019 ... 119

Figure 7.2. *Classical Greek* and *Ancient Greek* in Google ngram viewer, 1800–2019 ... 120

Figure 7.3. Occurrences of *classic, classick* and *classical* in *EEBO*, 1590–1700 ... 122

Figure 7.4. Characterisations of languages in *EEBO*, 1540–1700 ... 127

Figure 7.5. The principal characterisations of *languages/tongues* in Google ngram viewer, 1700–present. ... 128

Figure 7.6. Characterisations of *languages/tongues* in *EEBO*, 1540–1700 ... 128

Figure 7.7. The principal characterisations of *languages/tongues* in Google ngram viewer, 1700–present ... 129

Figure 7.8. Characterisations of *lengua(s)/idioma(s)* in *CDE*, thirteenth–twentieth centuries ... 129

Figure 7.9. The principal characterisations of *lenguas/idiomas* in Google ngram reader, 1700–present ... 130

Figure 7.10. Characterisations of *lengua(s)/idioma(s)* in *CDE*, thirteenth–twentieth centuries ... 130

Figure 7.11. The principal characterisations of *lenguas/idiomas* in Google ngram viewer, 1700–present ... 131

Figure 10.1. Radical change in the Spanish *-ir* conjugation ... 175

Figure 10.2. Competition between *elegir* and *esleír* in Spanish (*CDE*) ... 178

Figure 10.3. *Intuir, intuición, intuitivo* in *CDE* ... 180

Figure 10.4. *-vertir* verbs in *CDE*	182
Figure 10.5. *adherir* in *CDE*	184
Figure 11.1. Type 3 compounds according to the period of their first recorded occurrence	201
Figure 11.2. Type 3 compounds by decade (1900–2000)	203
Figure 11.3. Type 3 compounds by century and likely model language	204
Figura 12.1. Distribución de personajes según el nivel educativo	214
Figura 12.2. Personajes cultos en *RLA*	215
Figura 12.3. Variedades discursivas en *RLA*, adaptado de Díaz-Bravo (2010, 239; 2019b, 1197)	216
Figura 12.4. Fragmento *tokenizado* y anotado en *LD. Lozana Digital*	217
Figura 12.5. Marcación de cultismos en *LD. Lozana Digital*	218
Figura 12.6. Marcación de tipos discursivos en *LD. Lozana Digital*, clasificación adaptada de Díaz-Bravo (2010, 110)	219
Figura 12.7. Marcación de tipos discursivos en *LD. Lozana Digital*	219
Figura 12.8. Marcación de los rasgos de personajes en *LD. Lozana Digital*	220
Figura 12.9. Distribución de cultismos por personaje	221
Figura 12.10. Distribución de *tokens* por personaje	222
Figura 12.11. Distribución de cultismos por parte de personajes cultos	223
Figura 12.12. Distribución de cultismos según el nivel educativo de los personajes	224
Figura 12.13. Cultismos y no cultismos en personajes cultos y analfabetos	224

Figura 12.14. Distribución de cultismos según el tipo
  discursivo 225

Figura 12.15. Cultismos y no cultismos en discursos de
  distancia e inmediatez comunicativas 226

Acknowledgements

We gratefully acknowledge the OWRI *Language Acts and Worldmaking* project, of which we are members, which provided the funds and administrative help for the Colloquium in which the component Chapters of this book originated as papers. Special thanks are due to Felicity Roberts for all the smooth organisation of the event itself.

We also owe an enormous debt to the goodwill, time and effort of all the peer reviewers involved in offering opinions and advice on each contribution. They must sadly remain anonymous, but their contribution to this book has been significant.

Abbreviations

a.C.	antes de Cristo
ár.clás.	árabe clásico
ár.hisp.	árabe hispánico
ca.	*circa* (about)
cast.	castellano (Castilian)
Cat.	Catalan
CE	Christian Era
cf.	compare
d.	died
d.C.	después de Cristo
e.g.	*exempli gratia* (for example)
Eng.	English
esp. ant.	español antiguo
esp.	español
fem.	feminine
ff.	following
fn.	footnote
Fr.	French
Gasc.	Gascon
Gk./gr.	Greek/griego
i.e./*i. e.*	*id est* (that is/es decir)
ibid.	*ibidem* (in the same place)
ing.	inglés
It.	Italian
Lat./lat.	Latin/latín
leon.	leonés (Leonese)
masc.	masculine
MFr.	Modern French
MSp.	Modern Spanish

n.d.	no date
Occ.	Occitan
OEngad.	Old Engadine
OFr.	Old French
OOcc.	Old Occitan
OSp.	Old Spanish
p./pág.	page/página
p.ej.	por ejemplo
pl.	plural
Port.	Portuguese
Rom.	Romanian
s.v.	*sub voce*
Sard.	Sardinian
sg.	singular
Sp.	Spanish
var.	variant
vol.	volume

The authors

Alessandro Carlucci is a Research Fellow at the University of Bergen, where he is in charge of a project on the role of language contact in the history of the Italian language, as well as an Honorary Fellow of the Faculty of Medieval and Modern Languages at the University of Oxford. He is also a consultant to the *Oxford English Dictionary*. His articles have appeared in *Language Sciences*, *Modern Language Review*, *Zeitschrift für romanische Philologie*, *Rivista italiana di dialettologia*, *Revue Romane*, and several other journals. He is the author of *The Impact of the English Language in Italy: Linguistic Outcomes and Political Implications* (Lincom, 2018) and *Gramsci and Languages: Unification, Diversity, Hegemony* (Brill, 2013; Haymarket, 2015), which was co-winner of the Giuseppe Sormani International Prize for the best monograph on Antonio Gramsci (2017).

Gloria Clavería Nadal is Professor of the Spanish Language at the Universitat Autònoma de Barcelona (UAB). She specialises in the history of the Spanish language, lexicography and historical lexicology and is also interested in the application of computer tools to the historical study of language. Her research is focused on the early stages of the Spanish language, but also covers its modern and contemporary development. Her most relevant publications include the monographs *El latinismo en español* and *De «vacunar» a «dictaminar»: la lexicografía académica decimonónica y el neologismo*, in addition to a number of editions and co-editions of a number of books that reflect her research interests. She was responsible for the CD-ROM edition of the *Diccionario crítico etimológico castellano e hispánico* by J. Corominas and J. A. Pascual (Madrid: RBA-Gredos, 2012). She has been a member of the author team of the *Nueva gramática de la lengua española. Fonética y fonología* of the Real Academia Española (Madrid: Espasa, 2011). Since 1994 she has been the researcher responsible for the Grup de Lexicografia i Diacronia (SGR). She currently directs the research project *Internal History of the Dictionary of the Spanish Language of the Royal Spanish Academy in the 19th Century (1817-1852)*, and collaborates in the project *Osservatorio degli italianismi nel mondo (OIM)* developed for the Accademia della Crusca, in which she deals with the Ibero-Romance area (Spanish and Catalan).

Santiago Del Rey Quesada graduated in Hispanic Philology and Classical Philology from the University of Seville, where he currently teaches and researches after periods spent at the Universities of Tübingen and Munich. At Munich he held a postdoctoral grant from the Alexander von Humboldt Foundation which allowed him to develop a research project on Latin and Romance models in the formation of European Renaissance dialogue. His main areas of research concern the elaboration of the Romance languages from the medieval to the modern periods, historical discourse analysis, variationist linguistics, language contact and the history of translation.

Rocío Díaz-Bravo is a Lecturer in Spanish Linguistics at the University of Granada and a Visiting Researcher at King's College London, where she is a member of the *Loaded Meanings* team, researching cultured borrowings in the *Retrato de la Loçana andaluza*. Her study and critical edition of this work is published by the Modern Humanities Research Association, and together with Gael Vaamonde, she is developing *Lozana Digital*, a digital edition which will enable the linguistic investigation of this Golden Age text. Her doctoral thesis was a linguistic study of the orality of this work. She also holds Master's in both Digital Humanities and in the Teaching of Spanish as a Foreign Language. Her current research is on the application of digital humanities to the Spanish language, the teaching of Spanish and the history and varieties of Spanish.

Steven N. Dworkin recently retired after forty years as Professor of Romance Languages and Literatures and Professor of Linguistics at the University of Michigan. He specialises in Romance and Hispanic diachronic linguistics, with an emphasis on the evolution of the lexicon. His recent publications have dealt with internal structural factors which have led to changes (especially word loss) in the vocabulary of Medieval Spanish, the rivalry in Spanish between Latinisms and inherited vocabulary, and the issue of lexical stability in the history of the Romance languages. He is actively involved in the preparation of the *Dictionnaire Etymologique Roman*, a collaborative international project, for which he has written a number of entries. He has recently published two books with Oxford University Press, *A History of the Spanish Lexicon: A Linguistic Perspective* (2012) and *A Guide to Old Spanish* (2018).

Isabel García Ortiz is a doctoral student at Queen Mary, University of London. Her research focuses on the borrowing and embedding of scientific and medical loanwords from Latin into the Western European languages. She holds a BA in Translation and Interpreting and a MA in Hispanic Linguistics from the University of Granada and is currently also studying for an MA in Compulsory Secondary Education at the University of Almería.

Inmaculada González Sopeña is Assistant Lecturer in Spanish Language in the University of Granada, where she also gained her doctorate in 2019 with the award of a scholarship from the University. She is a member of the research group *Investigaciones Histórico-lingüísticas y Dialectales* (HUM-278) directed by Miguel Calderón Campos, the I+D+i project *HISPANAE TESTIUM DEPOSITIONES. Las declaraciones de testigo en la historia de la lengua española* (FFI2017-83400-P) and the project *Atlas Lingüístico y Etnográfico de Andalucía, S. XVIII. Patrimonio documental y humanidades digitales* (Junta de Andalucía-FEDER, P18-FR-695).

Susana Guerrero Salazar is Professor of Spanish Language at the University of Málaga. She gained the Premio Extraordinario de Licenciatura y de Doctorado and the Premio Nacional de ensayo Leonor de Guzmán. She is director of the *La Hemeroteca Virtual de las Lenguas de España como recurso para la iniciación a la investigación* project at the University of Málaga and of the Spanish Government I+D+i project *El discurso metalingüístico sobre "mujer y lenguaje" en la prensa española: Análisis del debate lingüístico y su repercusión social*. Her main areas of research are lexicology and the discourse analysis of communication. Amongst her publications are *Voces comentadas del español actual* (2001), *La parodia quevediana de los mitos. Mecanismos Léxicos* (2002), *La creatividad en el lenguaje periodístico* (2007), *La prensa deportiva española: sexismo lingüístico y discursivo* (2017) and *Creatividad y juego en el discurso deportivo de la prensa* (2018).

Christopher J. Pountain is a graduate of the University of Cambridge, where he also gained his doctorate, and is Emeritus Professor of Spanish Linguistics at Queen Mary University of London, being also a Life Fellow of Queens' College, Cambridge. He has published over 50 articles in the field of the history of the Romance languages and is the author of *A History of the Spanish Language through Texts* (London: Routledge, 2001) and *Exploring the Spanish Language* (second edition, London: Arnold, 2016), as well as being co-author of several Spanish pedagogical works. He leads the *Loaded Meanings* strand of the AHRC research project *Language Acts and Worldmaking* at King's College London. His current research interests are the impact of Latin on the Romance languages and sociolinguistic variation in the history of Spanish.

María del Carmen Rodríguez Caballero is a graduate in English Philology from the University of Salamanca, where she also studied for her doctorate. She holds TEFL and TESL diplomas from UCLA, the Further and Adult Education Teachers' Certificate from Southampton Technical College, a Certificate in Psychic Disabilities from the Universidad Nacional de Educación a Distancia, and a Certificate in Teaching Spanish to Immigrants from the Menéndez Pelayo International University, Santander. She was a Spanish teacher in Southampton (UK) and Lynwood (California), as well as teaching Spanish for Foreigners at the Pontifical University of Salamanca. She is currently a secondary teacher in Zamora.

Ingmar Söhrman is Professor Emeritus of Romance Languages at the University of Gothenburg. He obtained his doctorate from the University of Uppsala and has held positions at the universities of Alcalá and Umeå. His main linguistic interests are semantics, syntax, history of the language, minority languages, medieval history, Romance and Slavic languages and cultures and cultural contacts.

Gael Vaamonde received his doctorate in Linguistics from the University of Vigo in 2011. He was a member of the European project *Post Scriptum: A Digital Archive of Ordinary Writing* (2012-2017), which has collected a wide range of private letters and made them available for searching in two prepared formats: a critical edition and an annotated corpus. He is currently Lecturer in Spanish Linguistics at the University of Granada and participates in various projects related to corpus linguistics and digital humanities. Since 2018 he has been a member of the Grupo de Investigaciones histórico-lingüísticas y dialectales at the University of Granada (HUM-278). His main areas of research are corpus linguistics, Spanish grammar, digital humanities and the history of Spanish.

Carmen Varo Varo graduated in both Hispanic Philology and Linguistics in 1995 and 1997 respectively and gained her doctorate in Linguistics in 2002. She is Lecturer in General Linguistics at the University of Cádiz, where she is a member of the *Semaínein* research group. She has published a wide range of books, book chapters and journal articles, and has participated in numerous sponsored research projects and Research and Development contracts. She is currently secretary of the Instituto Universitario de Investigación en Lingüística Aplicada (ILA) of the University of Cádiz, and is responsible for coordinating the *Avances en la investigación del procesamiento lingüístico y los trastornos* *del lenguaje* strand for the University's doctoral programme in Linguistics. She is a member of the Editorial Advisory Board of *Pragmalingüística*.

Bozena Wislocka Breit is currently a Lecturer in Technical English at the Polytechnic University of Madrid, following completion of a three-year period as a Post-Doctoral Researcher on the *Language Acts and Worldmaking* project at Queen Mary University of London. She graduated in Spanish at the Jagiellonian University, Cracow, and in English at the Complutense University of Madrid, and holds a PhD in Linguistics as well as a postgraduate Diploma in Translation. She has taught at the Jagiellonian University, Cracow, and at the Instituto Universitario de Lenguas Modernas y Traductores at the Complutense University of Madrid. Her recent research has focused on the impact and presence of cultured borrowings in the contemporary Spanish language. She has presented and published papers on the history of translation, on Spanish, English and Polish oenological languages, on MOOC courses for digital humanities and on cultured borrowings in diverse Spanish historical texts.

Introduction

The subject of this book is the study of what in English is usually termed "learnèd" borrowing, that is, direct borrowing by the languages of Western Europe from the most widely used languages of European antiquity, Latin and Greek (the latter very often via Latin). This process, which we will refer to overall as "cultured borrowing" (though individual authors may use different terminology: see the Index of Topics), may be considered the single most important cultural contact observable in the history of Western Europe, and, moreover, so far from being a matter of purely historical interest, is ongoing. The Romance languages have a particular characteristic in this respect since they have a history of continuous descent from Latin, with the result that the same Latin word may have both inherited and cultured developments: for example, French *froid* 'cold' (popular) and *frigide* (learnèd), which both derive from Latin *frigidus*. Such words of cultured origin are widely shared, and a notable consequence of their wide adoption is that they have brought about some convergence among the Romance languages and indeed with other Western European languages too, especially English: thus to French *frigide* there correspond Spanish and Portuguese *frígido* and Italian *frigido*, as well as English *frigid*. Although originally these words can be seen to have been introduced by a cultured élite in the process of elaboration of vernaculars which needed more specialised vocabulary in order to achieve greater discrimination of meaning, either to label new concepts or for creative literary effect, many have now migrated into everyday usage. This can be illustrated by the borrowing from Greek via Latin of the word *problem*, which as Spanish *problema* is today the 145th commonest word in the language (Davies and Davies 2017).

This has been the theme of one of the six research strands of a major UK languages research project funded by the Arts and Humanities Research Council called *Language Acts and Worldmaking*, directed overall by Professor Catherine Boyle at King's College London. The research questions initially posed by this strand (called *Loaded Meanings*) were deliberately wide ranging and to a large extent original. How did cultured borrowings become embedded in their host language, both socially and linguistically, and how can we detect and quantify their dissemination through society? To what extent do they replace existing words, or, in the event that they represent an "elaboration" of the host language and a gain in semantic discrimination, how were the concepts they denote previously expressed, if at all? How do their meanings change after their first embedding, and how do they become associated with particular linguistic, social and cultural contexts? How do present-day language users and planners exploit cultured sources in creating neologisms or in resurrecting words which have become obsolete?

The project also raises some much wider issues.

The history of the Romance languages has often been construed as the history of the development of spoken Latin, on which cultured influence is seen as being a contamination, an interference in the "natural" processes of linguistic change. For this reason, the ideal subject in the dialect surveys on which the great linguistic atlases were based was an illiterate sexagenarian who had never moved far from his or her place of birth. For the same reason, the initial interest in cultured borrowings was that they provided a rationale for saving the Neogrammarian hypothesis about the regularity of sound change, since cultured borrowings could be discounted as being patently exceptional; the focus was on the date of their first attestation, which is recorded in etymological dictionaries as the occasion on which they were "added" to the language. However, the Romance languages which are usually the prime object of study, and those for which the largest corpus of textual material exists, are the elaborated and now standardised official languages we know as French, Spanish, Portuguese, etc. None has escaped the transforming influence of Latin as they have become vehicles of lawmaking, culture and technical writing, and such elaboration is a characteristic feature of all such *Ausbau* languages, in Kloss's (1967) useful terminology. As such, the influence of Latin is an equally "natural" process in the linguistic evolution of the languages of Western Europe, and cannot be set aside, as neither can the wide range of written registers and styles which is observable in all these languages.

There is also a question about what has been referred to as the "embedding problem" (Weinreich, Labov and Herzog 1968) of how innovating features are diffused and become established in their host language. It has been evident from our researches that the date of the first attestation of a cultured borrowing is by no means evidence of its wide adoption within the language, which may follow only centuries later (if indeed it follows at all). In fact, philological scrutiny of early examples often reveals that a word was still essentially foreign, or being used in a technical way (and that in modern orthographic

Introduction

practice would be likely to have been written in italics or quotation marks). It is for this reason that we have started at the end of the story, as it were (though ongoing tendencies lead us to suppose that it is in fact very far from the end), and focused on the history of cultured borrowings which can now be demonstrated through their frequency in the modern language to have become thoroughly integrated.

Most elusively, there is the question of what is often referred to today as "transnational" influence. Although etymological dictionaries habitually say that cultured borrowings originate in Latin (or Greek, though as already observed, many Hellenisms passed into both Classical Latin and Medieval Latin and were probably borrowed from there, especially prior to the Humanist period when Greek was less well known by the educated), the extent of the shared cultured vocabulary within the Romance languages and English, and even further afield by other Germanic languages, seems to suggest that the borrowing, or encouragement of borrowing, was due to contact among the scholarly communities of their speakers. The actual mechanics of the process, are, however, difficult to trace: for two examples (Eng. *problem* / Fr. *problème* / Sp. and It. *problema*; Eng., Fr. and Sp. *social* / It. *sociale*), see Pountain, Wislocka Breit, Díaz-Bravo and García Ortiz (in press).

Lastly, there is a question which relates to the fundamental concept of the *Language Acts and Worldmaking* project. Since many cultured borrowings have become successfully embedded in their host languages, they appear to label quite basic notions (the words for "easy" and "difficult", Fr. *facile* / Sp. *fácil* / It. *facile* and Fr. *difficile* / Sp.*difícil* / It. *difficile* are obvious examples), while others, in labelling new concepts, such as *apendicitis*, effectively "make worlds". The question therefore arises as to how such concepts were previously expressed, particularly the basic notions which we may assume were always of importance, even if more technical words discriminate genuinely new ideas, conditions and artefacts. This question has been most extensively studied by Dworkin, who explores the theme further in this volume.

In September 2019 an International Colloquium was held in London inviting contributions on these themes, together with invited presentations from world-renowned experts. This book collects together a selection of these papers and assesses their significance for our understanding of the field and its future development. All make an original contribution to knowledge in terms of both the new interpretation of data and the development of new methodological approaches.

Although *Language Acts and Worldmaking* was originally designed with a predominantly Hispanic emphasis, it quickly embraced interest in other languages, as well as in wider concern with the issues its research was raising. This expansion of focus is reflected in this collection of papers: while most are connected with the particular research questions in which members of the home research team were engaged, more general linguistic questions such as the nature and impact of linguistic borrowing, historical sociolinguistics and the history of the expression of basic concepts are also addressed, as is the relevance of cultured borrowings to the teaching of Latin.

It is hoped that this volume will encourage interest in the field of cultured borrowings and open up new directions for further research along these lines.

Synopsis

The majority of Chapters address the question of the processes by which cultured borrowings became established in their host languages.

Gloria Clavería Nadal highlights the ongoing process of cultured borrowing in Spanish from the 18th to the early 21st centuries. She examines the many dictionaries published during this period, assessing the evidence they offer for the introduction of Latinisms and for the impact they made upon the language, especially with regard to the increase of complex consonantal groups and the productivity of compound formations. The problems posed by such borrowings for the spelling system of Spanish are also analysed.

Some particular agents of change are then considered.

Translation from Latin into Spanish has long been considered a vehicle for the introduction of cultured borrowings, as translators strive to find Spanish translation equivalents for Latin words in the Middle Ages and early Renaissance and may simply adapt these words into their vernacular. **Santiago Del Rey Quesada** studies the phenomenon of paratactic lexical groups in which one term appears to explain the other, so that a new word is effectively glossed by an old one, in translations from Latin into French, Italian, Spanish and Portuguese. He reaches the important conclusion that the influence of Latin as a direct result of translation is not as great as might be intuitively suspected.

Introduction

The use of cultured borrowings from Latin and Greek is also apparent in technical discourse, where such words are adopted to name essentially new concepts or distinctions which cannot be so clearly discriminated in existing vernacular words. Attention is called to the role of medical science as a vehicle of borrowing by **Isabel García Ortiz** in a single-word case study of Spanish *síntoma*: she shows that, in addition to the process of borrowing for technical purposes, the more recent diffusion of the word has been brought about by a process of metaphorisation.

The role of the press is examined in two Chapters. **Susana Guerrero Salazar** looks at the exploitation of Latin words and expressions in the headlines of the Spanish sporting press. She shows that while a small number of these have found their way into approved usage, many are to be regarded as quotations from Latin; their use has an intensifying effect and is associated with humour or with the expression of approval or criticism. **Carmen Varo Varo** examines the use of cultured elements in neologistic compounds used by the Spanish press, demonstrating that this is a phenomenon which has recently grown in productivity. She then reports on a psycholinguistic experiment in which speakers were asked to evaluate certain words of this type from the point of view of their newness and complexity.

María del Carmen Rodríguez Caballero reports on how as a teacher of Latin she has been able to call attention to the pervasive presence of Latin words and expressions in everyday use in modern Spanish, especially in the promotion of the Roman origins of her city of Zamora. Finally, **Bozena Wislocka Breit** traces the use of the cultured adjectives Eng. *classical* and *modern* / Sp. *clásico* and *moderno* in a comparative study of their characterisations of languages in English and Spanish. She suggests that they have come to denote a dichotomy between the teaching and learning of Latin and Greek as against living foreign languages, although in the course of time they have had a number of competitors, the majority equally cultured borrowings.

Subsequent Chapters look at the different kinds of impact made by cultured borrowings on modern host languages.

The theme of competition between borrowings and existing words is taken up by **Steven N. Dworkin**, who looks at cases of competition between Latinisms and inherited words in late medieval and early modern Spanish. While the majority of cultured borrowings were, as suggested in earlier Chapters, part of the process of the elaboration of the vernacular and tended to expand its vocabulary, there is a smaller number of cultured borrowings which intriguingly substituted common inherited words which denoted basic concepts, or even substituted previous borrowed forms. **Inmaculada González Sopeña** considers in a similar way the presence of two borrowings from Arabic (*almofía* and *tarquín*) which have currency in 16th and 17th-century Granada, although they have in the long run not prospered. One of these, *almofía*, shows an interesting competition with another word of Arabic origin, *jofaina*.

The next two Chapters are concerned with the possible wider structural impact of cultured lexical borrowing. **Christopher J. Pountain** shows that the extensive cultured borrowing of Latin verbs into the Spanish -*ir* conjugation reinforces what had become a small and unproductive conjugation-type and even added to its morphological complexity with a variation that is still ongoing in the modern language. **Alessandro Carlucci** examines the role of English in the increasing favouring in Italian of compound noun phrases in which the modified element follows the modifier (e.g. *scuolabus*, parallel to Eng. *school bus*). He points out that this order is present in many cultured borrowings such as *termometro* 'thermometer', and establishes a typology of such compounds.

Rocío Díaz Bravo and Gael Vaamonde analyse the presence of cultured borrowings in the speech of characters in the sixteenth-century Spanish novel *La lozana andaluza*, broadly demonstrating the association of such words with educated characters. Their work shows the importance of such literary texts as a source of evidence for historical sociolinguistics, but also the need for philological care in its evaluation. The final Chapter, by **Ingmar Söhrman**, is a very wide-ranging study of words belonging to the semantic field of 'magic' in European languages. It highlights the intriguing question of transnational contact and influence in the process of borrowing.

Christopher J. Pountain and Bozena Wislocka Breit

December 2020

Bibliographical references

Davies, Mark, and Kathy Hayward Davies. 2017. *A Frequency Dictionary of Spanish. Core Vocabulary for Learners*, 2nd ed. London: Routledge.

Kloss, Heinz. 1967. "*Abstand*-Languages and *Ausbau*-Languages." *Anthropological Linguistics* 9: 29–41.

Pountain, Christopher J., Bozena Wislocka Breit, Rocío Díaz-Bravo, and Isabel García Ortiz. In press. "How old words become new (and then old again)". In *Language Acts and Worldmaking: How and why the languages we use shape our world and our lives*, edited by Catherine Boyle et al. London: John Murray Press/Hodder and Stoughton.

Weinreich, Uriel, William Labov, and Marvin I. Herzog. 1968. "Empirical Foundations for a Theory of Language Change". In *Directions for Historical Linguistics: A Symposium*, edited by Winfred P. Lehmann and Yakov Malkiel, 95–189. Austin: University of Texas Press.

Chapter 1

Cultured borrowings in the light of dictionaries[1]

Gloria Clavería Nadal

Universitat Autònoma de Barcelona

Abstract

Latinisms, i.e. lexicon formed by expressions loaned from Latin, have become increasingly more widespread throughout the history of the Spanish language. The process is easily observable from the information amassed in modern Spanish dictionaries, which reflect the kind of language used in the times when they were printed, thus making them excellent records of how a language's lexicon has evolved.

Therefore, lexicographical works will be taken as the starting point for a study of how the history of Latinisms has manifested and unfolded in Spanish. A contrastive analysis of different dictionaries from the eighteenth to the early twenty-first centuries, with special emphasis on those of the nineteenth century, is used to establish the different evolutionary tendencies of Latinism in modern Spanish. It starts by assessing the formal characteristics, related to the processes of accommodating loanwords in the structural properties of the host language, and their treatment in dictionaries. Secondly, attention will be paid to the increased usage of such elements across different editions of dictionaries, not only through the inclusion of new entries, which generally correspond to the neologisms of each era, but also semantic extension through the recording of new meanings for Latinisms that already existed in the language or the inclusion of complex structures made up of such units (for example, the compound terms formed by the noun *ácido* and an adjective).

---

[1] The research required to produce this publication was undertaken with support from grants PGC2018–094768–B–I00 and 2017 SGR1251. I gratefully acknowledge the comments and suggestions of Christopher J. Pountain and the anonymous reviewer.

The overall intention is to contribute to the history of cultured borrowings in modern Spanish, a history that is to a large extent still unexplored.

Resumen

El latinismo, concebido como el componente léxico formado por los préstamos del latín, ha ido adquiriendo una importancia creciente a lo largo de la historia del español. Este proceso resulta fácilmente observable a través de la información atesorada en los diccionarios del español moderno porque en estas obras se refleja el modelo de lengua de la época en la que fueron elaborados y, desde este punto de vista, se erigen como excelentes testimonios de la evolución del léxico de una lengua.

Por esta razón, se tomarán las obras lexicográficas como punto de partida para estudiar cómo se manifiesta y se desenvuelve en ellas la historia del latinismo en español. El análisis contrastivo de diferentes diccionarios, desde el siglo XVIII hasta principios de siglo XXI y con especial incidencia en los del siglo XIX, permitirá establecer las distintas líneas evolutivas de los latinismos del español moderno. Se atenderá, en primer lugar, a sus características formales, relacionadas con los procesos de acomodación de los préstamos a las propiedades estructurales de la lengua de acogida, y al tratamiento de estas en los diccionarios. En segundo lugar, se prestará atención a las líneas de crecimiento de este tipo de elementos a través de distintas ediciones de los diccionarios no solo con la incorporación de nuevas entradas, que corresponden generalmente a neologismos de cada momento, sino también con la ampliación semántica observable en el registro de nuevas acepciones para latinismos ya existentes en la lengua o con la inclusión de estructuras complejas integradas por este tipo de unidades (por ejemplo, los compuestos terminológicos formados con el sustantivo *ácido* y un adjetivo).

Con todo ello, se intentará contribuir a la historia de los préstamos cultos en el español moderno, una historia de la que aún queda una buena parte por indagar.

Keywords

Lexical borrowing, Neologism, Latin, Spanish lexicography, Spanish spelling.

1 The linguistic study of learnèd words from linguistics

In 1935, poet and philologist Dámaso Alonso published *La lengua poética de Góngora,* a book that had won the *Premio Nacional de Literatura* in the memorable year of 1927, when the *Ministerio de Instrucción Pública* held a competition to commemorate the tercentenary of the death of Luis de Góngora. Thanks to Alonso's work, the learnèd word became a matter of major relevance, being the subject of several chapters of his essay, where it is dealt with in both lexical and syntactic terms.

Alonso's monograph begins with a statement that, in my view, is still fully applicable today. The opening section defends the "necesidad del estudio del cultismo" and maintains that it is not possible to produce a suitable study of the learnèd word in Góngora without there also being an "historia del cultismo español desde la aparición de los primeros documentos romances hasta nuestros días" (Alonso 1935, 43). Alonso attributes the lack of such a history to the methodology used in positivist linguistics, with its distinction between popular and learnèd words, and the fact that its focus is on the former, "estudiándolas con todo detenimiento y fijando con exactitud casi matemática las leyes de su evolución", while learnèd words have only been examined "por lo que tenían de excepción a las leyes de la evolución fonética" (Alonso 1935, 43). He goes on to lament how the study of the latter is always conducted in negative terms and wonders whether "no obedecerían ellas también a alguna ley de carácter positivo" (Alonso 1935, 43–4). To support his case, he recurs to none other than a quantitative criterion to justify the importance of this lexical field, namely general monolingual dictionaries: "Ábrase el Diccionario de la Lengua Española, cuéntense los cultismos que contiene y se tendrá inmediatamente la prueba de lo que acabo de decir" (Alonso 1935, 44). He does indeed present the litmus test for the opposition between inherited and learnèd words, since any column of any dictionary provides evidence of the extent of learnèd as opposed to inherited vocabulary in modern language, the latter being basic but vastly inferior in number (Patterson and Urrutibéheity 1975; Pountain 2011, 636–39).

Times have moved on, and in the early twenty-first century, rather than opening a random page of a dictionary, internet searches can instead be performed. Simply using the *DLE* 2014 search engine to find words that begin the letters *me–* produces an alphabetical list that offers the ideal watchtower from which to view Spanish vocabulary with a panchronic perspective. The first entry in the catalogue is a Latin expression, *mea culpa*, while in tenth place there is the noun *meandro*, a Latinism that in turn comes from Greek, and which first appeared in dictionaries in the nineteenth century (*NTLLE*: Domínguez 1853, *DRAE* 1899)[2] but which rarely appeared in texts before the twentieth century (see *CORDE*). In fifteenth place appears the term *meato*, an example of a specialist learnèd word originating from the lexis of medicine and botany. Then there are all the words that start with *mecan-* (*mecánica, mecánicamente, mecanicismo, mecanicista*, etc.), which are a fine example of the presence of large families of learnèd words that have an ample number of derivative forms and compounds. Also, the extensive *medio* family, a word whose peculiar evolution throughout grammatical history has led to much debate over its status as an inherited or learnèd word, has been in constant development since words that can be traced right back to the origins of the language and through to such modern derivatives as *mediatización* (*DRAE* 1936) and *mediático* (*DRAE* 2001). Later on, there is the sizeable *médico* and *medicina* family (Malkiel 1961), with more recent inclusions like *medicalizar* and *medicalización* (*DLE* 2014).

The above examples, in accordance with Alonso's observation, reveal the full complexity of the constitution of Spanish vocabulary and the growing weight of the learnèd word via different routes, including the extremely important role played by inter-linguistic borrowing (e.g. *medicalizar*, from the Fr. *médicaliser, DLE* 2014).

The views that Alonso (1935, 44) used as the starting point for his research led him to defend learnèd words as "hechos idiomáticos (lo mismo que los populares) y deben ser, por tanto, objeto de la lingüística". It is only in a footnote that he makes a bolder stand in support of this genealogical component: "hasta cierto punto debían haber sido objeto preferente. En la mayor parte de los casos tras un cultismo se abre un mundo de posibilidades para el explorador, mucho mayor que en las palabras no eruditas" (Alonso 1935, 44, footnote 2).

---

[2] All dictionaries are cited via the *NTLLE*. Real Academia dictionaries appear with the acronym *DRAE* and the publication year, except for the *Diccionario de autoridades* (1726–39) for which *DAut* is used. In all other cases, the author's name and the year of publication are used preceeded by *NTLLE*, for example, *NTLLE*: Domínguez 1853.

The phenomenon of learnèd words crosses linguistic boundaries (Pountain 2016), so it is no surprise that their intrinsic value for an understanding of the history of Romance languages should also have been defended from the study of other Neo-Latin languages (cf., for example, *DEL*: 5; Reinheimer-Rîpeanu 2004; Sălişteanu-Cristea 2000 and 2017; Serianni 2017, 141).

Therefore, and following Alonso's lead, the goal of this study is to analyse certain characteristic aspects of the development of learnèd words in modern Spanish by drawing upon lexicographic sources.

1.1 Terminological and conceptual matters

Since Alonso's seminal work, much progress has been made in the understanding of this genealogical component, with a concern, among other aspects, for terminology and the inclusion of the concept in linguistic theory. I shall begin with the fundamentally linguistic distinction between "borrowed" and "inherited", claimed by Pountain (2011, 628) and which are more suitable than the traditional "learnèd" and "popular".

Indeed, the concept of borrowing is undoubtedly a more appropriate term for describing the linguistic reality than the opposition between learnèd and popular, which is always interpretable from other points of view (Clavería 1991, 39–41). However, the terminological issue has been widely discussed and there is no need to reopen that debate here (Bustos Tovar 1974, Wright 1989, Clavería 1991, García Valle 1998, Azofra 2006, García Gallarín 2007). In any case, "Latinism" and "learnèd word" are used as technical terms in historical linguistics to describe words borrowed from Latin (cf. Dworkin 2012, 158).[3] Here I will defend the idea, as has been done when tackling the issue in the past (Clavería 1991, 74–78), that every linguistic expression, whether inherited or borrowed from Latin, has its idiosyncrasies, and that individual words and their histories really should be viewed more holistically, and the relationships between the two should be reconstructed from an approach that encompasses the full complexity of the history of language. This should also include the relationship and interdependence between spoken and written language, something that is always necessary when dealing with Latinisms due to the philological aspect that this always entails, something that

---

[3] Note that many Latinisms are, in turn, borrowed from Greek, so the term "cultured borrowing" is especially appropriate.

Serianni (2017, 141) put so succinctly in his observation that "In tutti i casi definire un latinismo comporta in primo luogo risalire ai testi che lo documentano; detto in altri termini: passare dalla lingua alla filologia".

1.2 The borrowing of a "linguistic ancestor" and "relatinisation"

It was Hock who established (1986, 404–7; cf. Clavería 1991 and 2017, 103–4) that Latinisms are, in actual fact, borrowed from a "linguistic ancestor", which implies that the Latin language was involved in two different ways in the history of Romance languages: cf. Burgassi and Guadagnini (2014, 5) and their reference to the "doppio ruolo del latino" or the "two distinct layers" described by Dworkin (2012, 156). This double role is found, on the one hand, in Latin as the common origin of the inherited component of Neo-Latin languages (Pountain 2011, 606–7); and, on the other, in the way that Latin orchestrates and has orchestrated the evolution of these languages from many different perspectives (Pountain 2011, 607), a phenomenon whose outcome has been dubbed "relatinisation" a term first coined in reference to French by Gougenheim (1959) and which Raible (1996), in a more panoramic approach to the phenomenon, extended to the different Romance languages (Pountain 2011, 635).

In terms of Spanish, the phenomenon has been studied by Harris-Northall (1999) and Eberenz (1998 and 2004), amongst others, with particular attention to the lexical shifts of the fifteenth and early sixteenth centuries. However, it is Dworkin who has delved deepest into the matter (for example, 1998, 2002a, 2002b, 2010, this volume, Chapter 8).[4] Following the same train of thought, it was Clavería (1991, 50–1) who noted the existence of formal "remodelación" in the history of Latinisms in accordance with their etymology.

This concept has also been applied to the domain of derivative morphology, a field in which Latin has left a major mark on the derivative resources of Romance languages, as shown by a glance at *DESE*, in which two-thirds of the suffixes relate to learnèd elements (Clavería 2013, 54). This topic is highlighted by Rainer (2002, 124), who views relatinisation as one of the convergence processes involved in the very evolution of the Romance languages.

---

[4] Similar processes can be found in other Romance languages, cf. for Italian Burgassi and Guadagnini 2017a and 2017b.

Such relatinisation is still happening, if not more, in modern Spanish, as shown in the latest research by Pountain (2016 and in press), which emphasises the *transnational* dimension of Latinisms and how these lexical items can become part of everyday usage. These findings clearly suggest that the acquisition of learnèd words, which has been occurring throughout the course of the history of Romance languages, is now snowballing.

1.3 The structural impact of borrowing

The accumulation from the Middle Ages of loanwords of Latin origin, with minimal accommodation to the structural properties of the host language (Pountain 2011, 628–30) and in most cases imported by reading the written form, explains why these borrowed words feature different formal characteristics from those of the inherited vocabulary, and how their structural impact became more widespread with the continual increase in cultured borrowings (Clavería 1991, 52–65; Pountain 2011, 639–43).

These structural impacts are highly visible in present-day linguistic descriptions of Spanish. For example, when forming plurals, the *NGLE* (2009, vol. I, chap. 3) structures its explanation by distinguishing between the general rules (§3.2) and "El plural de las voces de origen no castellano", i.e. Latinisms (§3.3) and words borrowed from other languages (§3.4), which do not follow the general rules.[5]

This structural impact is also evident in the phonological description of learnèd words which include combinations of phonemes that do not exist in inherited vocabulary. For instance, the description of syllables in the *NGLE* (2011) makes a distinction between the "léxico tradicional (voces patrimoniales y voces generadas con reglas de formación de palabras) y léxico ampliado, constituido fundamentalmente por los vocablos procedentes de otras lenguas, entre las que destacan por su número los cultismos o préstamos del latín y del griego" (*NGLE* 2011, § 8.4b). The "léxico ampliado" presents possible combinations that are not part of the "léxico tradicional": in such words, the segments /p, b, t, k, g, x, f, ʧ, m/ can be found in word-final position and /p, b, t, d, k, g, x, f, ʧ/ in syllable-final position within a word (*NGLE* 2011, § 8.7v). Thus, the consonantal sequences that have traditionally been called *learnèd groups*, such as /ps/ in *cápsula*, /bt/ in *obtener*, /kt/ in *efecto* and /gn/ *digno*, are instances of "léxico ampliado" features.

---

[5] Such cases include *campus, axis, júnior, sénior, déficit, álbum,* etc.

2 Learnèd words in the light of dictionaries

2.1 Research framework

The framework for this study consists of a research project focused on the historiography of nineteenth-century lexicography of the Real Academia Española, "Historia interna del *Diccionario de la lengua castellana* de la Real Academia Española en el siglo XIX (1817–1899)", whose objectives are centred on the analysis of the expansion and revision process observed in producing the ten editions of the Academia dictionary published in the nineteenth century. These ten editions are of highly variable importance (*DRAE* 1803, 1817, 1822, 1832, 1837, 1843, 1852, 1869, 1884 y 1899), and as a series constitute the transition towards modern lexicography. The project sought to reconstruct both the history of Academia lexicography and the history of the reception of the vocabulary presented therein through the analytical comparison of each edition with the one that came immediately after.

I shall use the materials obtained from this research project to study the history of Latinisms in modern Spanish, on the assumption that the extensions and changes recorded in the successive editions of the dictionary reflect, always through the filter of the Real Academia, the evolution of Spanish. At least two different aspects of the particular growth of Latinisms can be observed. First, the orthography set out by the dictionary itself, where the treatment of learnèd groups is a good example of the relatinisation process (§2.2). Secondly, the inclusion of new terms and meanings which offer strong evidence of the acceptance of the new vocabulary and the presence of Latinisms in the constitution of modern vocabulary (§2.3).

2.2 Standardised orthography of learnèd words through dictionaries

Mention was made earlier of the major impact of learnèd words on the characteristics of Spanish phonology, to such an extent that two phonological subsystems are apparent: that of inherited words and that of Latinisms, which often overlaps with words borrowed from other languages. One of the characteristic traits of the latter is found in what have traditionally been known as "learnèd consonantal clusters", a phenomenon of such importance that it warranted a section with this title in Penny (1991, §2.6.5), where it is described as one of the phonological shifts in the Middle Ages. Penny notes that "many groups of consonants which had existed in Latin had been reduced to single phonemes during the development from Latin to Old Spanish" (Penny 1991, 91). This comment is exemplified with characteristic evolutions of the inherited vocabulary like *ct* in Lat. *factu* > *hecho*, *gn* in Lat. *pugnu* > *puño* and the Latin letter *x* (/ks/) in Lat. *dīxī* > *dije* (Penny 1991, 91). For learnèd words which the language acquired after its formation, the author notes that "many learnèd words borrowed in the late Middle Ages and (increasingly) in the Golden Age, were adaptations of Latin words which contained such groups, and these groups now posed a phonological problem for Spanish" (Penny 1991, 91).

This "phonological problem" lies in the existence of consonantal sequences which did not exist in the inherited vocabulary (first column, Figure 1.1) and which, when adopted by Spanish, led to copious shifts in form involving the reduction (second column) or conservation of the learnèd group (third column):

ct	efeto	efecto	< Lat. *effectu*
ct (before *i* + vowel)	lición	lección	< Lat. *lēctione*
gn	sinificar	significar	< Lat. *significāre*
x	examen (/ʃ/)	examen (/ks/)	< Lat. *exāmen*
	exercer (/ʃ/)	exercer (/ks/)	< Lat. *exercēre*
xc	ecelente	excelente	< Lat. *excellente*
mn	solene	solemne	< Lat. *sollemne*
pt	acetar	aceptar	< Lat. *acceptāre*
mpt	pronto	prompto	< Lat. *promptu*
nst	istante	instante	< Lat. *instante*
bst	astener	abstener	< Lat. *abstinēre*

Figure 1.1. Learnèd consonantal groups (Penny 1991, 92)

This variation, at least in written language, "was eventually resolved (by the Academy in the late eighteenth century) in favour of the more Latinate forms (those with the consonantal group intact: *efecto, significar*, etc.)" (Penny 1991, 92). Indeed, many studies of linguistic historiography mention the option chosen by the Real Academia Española from its earliest publications, with a preference for the forms of learnèd words that were closest to Latin, as enshrined in the nineteenth century with the dissemination and official acceptance of Academia orthography (Martínez Alcalde 2007; 2010, 61; 2013) and the birth of orthoepy (Satorre 2006 and 2013; Satorre and Viejo 2013).[6] The Academia's dictionaries offer excellent evidence of this process. For instance, *DAut* included some of these variations, as shown by the following examples in which words like *efeto, licion* and *acetar* are offered as alternatives in cross-reference to *efecto, lección* and *aceptar*.

(1)
    a.   EFETO. Vease Efecto (*DAut*).
    b.   LICION. Vease Lección (*DAut*).
    c.   ACETAR. v. a. Vease Aceptar. En la Poesía suele usarse sin la P este verbo, por la precisión del consonante (*DAut*).

Later dictionary versions, until *DRAE* 1817, followed on in a similar fashion, with *DRAE* 1803, for example, adding *solene*[7] and its family (*solenemente, solenizado, solenizar*) and cross-referencing these with the forms using *mn*. However, this method was modified from the sixth edition of the dictionary (*DRAE* 1822) to a far more restrictive, standardised focus, with the prologue to that edition commenting that it had eliminated "alteraciones viciosas, que tanto han perjudicado á la pureza y fijacion del idioma castellano", and illustrates this principle using *probe* (*pobre*), *pusicion* (*posición*) and *licion* (*lección*). In compliance with this instruction, a large number of entries are omitted (more than 2,000: see Clavería 2019), many of which were minor variations of learnèd groups, such as *efeto, licíón* and *acetar*.

Together with this eradication of "non-standard" variants, there was also a change in spelling that had significant consequences both for the history of orthography and for that of learnèd words. This has related to the letter *x*, which appears in Figure 1.1 with two possible approaches: the first is that of *examen*, a word in which Latin /ks/ has been kept in modern Spanish; the second is illustrated with *ejercer*, a Latin borrowing from *exercere* in which /ks/ corresponds to /x/ in modern Spanish, and which must therefore have initially been adapted with the old voiceless palatal fricative /ʃ/.

Two different equivalents of *x* were maintained in Spanish orthography until the early nineteenth century: one was the "inherited" (/ʃ/ > /x/) and the other

---

[6] Not forgetting, however, that the tendency to conserve learnèd groups could be an evolutionary branch that appeared in previous texts, cf. Ramírez Luengo 2011.
[7] It also appears in all previous lexicography, since *NTLLE*: Nebrija 1495. It is maintained after *DRAE* 1822.

was associated with Latinisms (/ks/); hence Alcoba (2007, 23) writes of the *polifonía* of this letter. This double development is clearly alluded to in the description in *DAut*: "En Castellano conservamos el sonido de la *c*, y *s*: como en *Examen, Exótico*; pero el de la *g*, y *s* le convertimos en otro mucho mas fuerte, y gutural, tanto que no la distinguimos de la *j*, ó la *g* fuerte, como en *Xamugas, Exército*" (s.v. *x*).

One of the last major restructurings in the history of Spanish orthography is that included in the *Ortografía* of 1815 with the elimination of the use of *x* for the voiceless velar fricative, which was replaced with *j* or *g* (Esteve Serrano 1982, chap. 15; Martínez de Sousa 1991, 191 ff.; Quilis Merín 2008, 113; 2013, 507 ff.; Martínez Alcalde 2010, 62–63). This orthographic innovation is included for the first time in the Academia's *Ortografía* (1815) and two years later appears in the dictionary (*DRAE* 1817) with all its consequences: (a) modifications to the description of the letter; (b) change of letter and relocation in alphabetical order of words that start with *x*; (c) changes to words that contain the letter *x*, and (d) the generation of certain doublets.

(a) The description of the letter in the dictionary certifies the changes made. The letter *x* is only maintained to represent /ks/ in learnèd words such as those cited as examples in the entry itself:[8]

> X. Vigésima cuarta letra de nuestro alfabeto, y decimanona de las consonantes. Es una de las semivocales y de las paladiales ó guturales, porque se forma con el medio de la lengua arrimada á lo interior del paladar, no del todo apegada, sino acanalada de modo que quede paso á el aliento y espíritu que produce su sonido. Su pronunciacion, tomada de las lenguas latina y griega, equivale á *cs*, como en *examen, exequias, extension, éxtasis, sintaxis*. El sonido gutural que la *x* ha tenido hasta ahora en algunas voces, y nos vino del árabe, debe remitirse en adelante á la *j* y a la *g* en sus casos respectivos… (*DRAE* 1817: s.v. *x*).

(b) The change meant that almost all words that began with *x* now started with *j* or *g* (*xabón* > *jabón, xeringa* > *geringa*). In consequence, in

---

[8] As noted by Pozuelo (1989, 1174 and 1179), Quilis Merín (2010, 113) and Blanco Izquierdo (2018, 197), the article contains "incongruencias" in the description of the letter as a result of the source that was used (López de Velasco, 1582).

contrast to the 173 entries for the letter *x* in the 1803 edition, there were just 20 in the next. Most of these were dialectalisms (for example, *xa* or *xano* identified as Galician forms), because as yet there were no learnèd words in the dictionary starting with *x*, like *xilografía,* which would only begin to appear from the second half of the nineteenth century (*DRAE* 1869).

(c) This shift also affected all words containing *x* with the value of /x/. Hence, words commonly written with an *x*, like *coxear, floxo* or *xeringa* were now written with a *j* or a *g*: *cojear, flojo* and *geringa.*

(d) With these changes, the letter *x* was limited almost exclusively to learnèd words[9] and consequently a few doublets emerged which had thus far been concealed by the polyvalent use of *x*, even though they may have been pronounced differently. Such are the cases with *anexo/anejo, próximo/prójimo* and *complexo/complejo.* In what follows, the lexicographical re-configuration of these elements is examined by comparing *DRAE* 1803 with the following edition (*DRAE* 1817), which includes the new spellings.

In the first case, the entry for *anexo* in the fourth edition (2a) is split into two spellings (*anejo* and *anexo*) and three different articles in the following edition (2b):

(2)

    a. ANEXO, XA. adj. Lo unido á otra cosa con dependencia de ella. *Annexus.*
ANEXO. s. m. El beneficio, ó iglesia que depende de otra, que es su principal, ó cabeza. *Res annexa* (*DRAE* 1803).

    b. ANEJO. s. m. El beneficio ó iglesia que depende de otra que es su principal ó cabeza. *Parochus priori parocho: parochia priori charochiae subjecta.*
ANEJO, JA. adj. Lo mismo que ANEXO.
ANEXO, XA. adj. Lo unido á otra cosa con dependencia de ella. *Annexus* (*DRAE* 1817).[10]

---

[9] However, the *x* did persist in other circumstances (cf. *relox* or *carcax*) for some time.

[10] In this period, word entries were written in capitals and sub-entries repeated the word in small capitals.

It can hence be observed that, according to the dictionary (2b), on the one hand there was *anejo* (noun), and on the other the alternatives *anejo* and *anexo* (adjectives), which suggests the existence of two different pronunciations in the adjectival use. These differences contrast with the rest of this lexical family, where the letter *x* is invariable (*anexación, anexar, anexidades, anexión*).

Something similar occurred with the pair *próximo/prójimo*, although in this case the diacritic circumflex on the vowel *î* was already indicating the pronunciation of *x* as /ks/, unlike the other entries that did not include this mark, and therefore had an *x* corresponding to /x/.[11]

(3)

PRÓXÎMO, MA. adj. Inmediato, cercano, ó allegado. *Proximus*.[12]
PRÓXIMO. s. m. Qualquiera criatura capaz de gozar la bienaventuranza [...].[13]
PRÓXIMO. fest. El asno.
EL HOMBRE NO ES PRÓXIMO. loc. fam. y fest. del juego del hombre [...] (*DRAE* 1803).

In consonance with this distinction, in *DRAE* 1817 the first definition maintains the letter *x* (*próximo*), while the three following entries replace *x* with *j*[14] and therefore constitute a different lexicographical article (*prójimo*).

Finally, note the word *complexo* in which, contrary to what would be expected, there is no change in *DRAE* 1817. It would not be until the eleventh edition that a phonetic and orthographic distinction is made between *complexo* and *complejo* (*DRAE* 1869):

(4)
   a. COMPLEXO. m. El conjunto ó union de dos ó más cosas. ‖ adj. Lo opuesto á simple ó sencillo. ‖ *Anat*. Se aplica á uno de los catorce músculos que hay en la cabeza para sus movimientos (*DRAE* 1869).
   b. COMPLEJO, JA. adj. V. COMPLEXO. ‖ NÚMEROS COMPLEJOS, V. NÚMERO (*DRAE* 1869).

---

[11] This practice is described in the *Orthographía* (1741, 216), but was not always applied.
[12] This definition appeared in *DAut* with the instruction to "pronunciase la *x* como *cs*".
[13] *DAut* commented that "en este sentido se pronuncia la *x* como *j*".
[14] The expression "el hombre no es prójimo" is included in the entry for *hombre* due to the changes in the lemmatisation of complex structures which were introduced in this edition.

In fact, the orthographical innovation that implied the elimination of the letter *x* for the velar /x/ had already been applied beforehand in the excellent dictionary compiled by the Jesuit Esteban de Terreros (*NTLLE*: Terreros 1786–1793), completed before the suppression of the Society of Jesus (Álvarez de Miranda 1992, 560). This publication uses *j* to represent the phoneme /x/, thus resolving the issue of the triple variation of *j, g* and *x* that existed at that time (Martínez Alcalde 2006; Terrón 2019).

This dictionary (*NTLLE*: Terreros 1786–93) also included invaluable notes on pronunciation that help to piece together the history of the adaptation of Latinisms using *x* and to reconstruct the phonetic variability of these elements in the eighteenth and nineteenth centuries. For example, the dictionary reflects the alternation between *anejo* and *anexo* (5a), and the distinction between *prójimo* (5b) and *próximo* (5c).

(5)
- a. ANEJO, o según pronuncian otros, *Anexo*, dandole á la *x* el sonido de *cs*; lo que está unido, ó junto, dependiente, ó hace como parte de una cosa […] Pero se dice siempre *derecho de anexion*, pronunciando la *x* con el sonido *cs* […]
- b. PROJIMO. se dice en jeneral de cada uno de los hombres […] en este sentido lo escribimos en castellano con *j*, porque tiene en nuestra pronunciacion este sonido; lo contrario hacemos cuando se toma por un lugar, ó cosa cercana, pues entonces conserva el sonido de *cs*, y así se escribe con la *x*, que le tiene.
- c. PROXIMO, ma, adj. V. Inmediato, Cercano […]
  PROXIMO, en esta significacion conserva en la *x* del Cast. la pronunciacion de *cs*, al contrario en la de significar á un hombre, &c. y así se escribe prójimo, como se pronuncia: amarás al prójimo como á tí mismo.

These observations arise from the existence of different pronunciations, /ks/ and /x/, as mentioned in the following entries:

(6)
COMPLEJION, ó según otros COMPLEXIóN, con pron. de *cs* en la *x*, disposición naturál de un cuerpo, constitución de los humores…
COMPLEJIONADO, V. Complexionado, que es más comun.

COMPLEXIóN, V. complejión: unos le dan á la *x* en esta voz pronunciacion de *cs*, y otros de *j* (*NTLLE*: Terreros 1786–93).[15]

The coexistence of spellings and pronunciations is also perceived in *relajación–relaxación* and *reflejo–reflexo*,[16] where the Basque Jesuit admits that "en esto acaso habrá varios modos de pensar". His notes also reveal the alternation between /ks/ and /s/: "Algunos escriben *auxiliar*, pero la *x* no tiene aquí sonido alguno de tal, sino de solo *s*, y da motivo á la equivocacion, que vamos a evitar de que la pronuncien como *j*, lo cual sería un absurdo" (*NTLLE*: Terreros 1786–93, s.v. *auxiliado*). Accordingly, the dictionary contains *ausiliar, ausiliado* and *ausilio*, reflecting a widespread pronunciation (García Macho and Pascual 1990), even though the Academia's dictionary never included these variations in spelling.

Unfortunately, other entries have no comments at all, as is the case with the *x/s* variation for *tóxico/toxicado* and *tósigo/atosigado*, in which the former are cross-referenced to the latter. In the dictionaries of the Real Academia, *tóxico* is included in *DAut* with cross-reference to *tósigo*, a situation that is maintained through to *DRAE* 1803; the fifth edition of the dictionary (*DRAE* 1817) omits the entry for *tóxico*, which reappears in *DRAE* 1884 as a technical term used in medicine (together with the compounds *toxicología* and *toxicológico*), as well as an archaic variant of *tósigo*.[17] These points lead to ask how the archaic *tóxico* was pronounced and to the observation of what could probably be called the reincorporation of a learnèd word.

The evidence of Terreros's instructions is the tip of an iceberg regarding the extent of variation in the adaptation of Latinisms with the letter *x*. A retrospective look at such learnèd words, documented from the late Middle Ages, shows evidence of the existence of different outcomes of their treatment. Some were adapted with the voiceless palatal fricative /ʃ/, commonly written as *x*, in parallel with the inherited vocabulary. This process is observed in such Latinisms as

---

[15] However, although *complejo* is written with a *j*, Terreros notes that "en Castellano se suele decir complexo, dandole el sonido de x".

[16] There may be an error in the entry for *reflexo* because it is cross-referenced to *reflexo* rather than *reflejo* (*reflejo*, however, does not appear in Terreros's dictionary).

[17] Note that Salvá's dictionary (*NTLLE*: Salvá 1846) included *tóxico* and *toxicado* as archaic words and *toxicología* as "La ciencia que trata de los venenos". *DECH*, on the other hand, refers to *tóxico* as a late form of "consolidación".

ejército, substitute of *hueste* (Dworkin 2006, 67–68 and 2012, 168; Clavería 2017, 123), *ejercer*, *ejercitar* or *ejercicio*. The same phonetic outcome is shown by *ejecutar, ejecución* and its family; *lujo, lujoso, lujuria* and its family; *relajar, relajación*, etc. In all these cases, the etymological adaptation of *x* as /ʃ/ (later /x/) prevails, with the written form being read in accordance with the inherited vocabulary (cf. Lat. *dīxī* > *dije*). Yet there had been another way of adapting the etymological /ks/ represented by Lat. *x* into the phonological structure of Late Middle Ages Romance, namely as /s/, the /k/ being dropped in syllabic coda. This equivalence can be found in Nebrija's *Vocabulario Romance-Latino* (*NTLLE*: Nebrija 1495) in words like *complision, complisionado, esecutar, esecucion, esecutor, esecutorial, esequias, esento, esencion, esaminar, esamen, esaminador*. These variants are also documented in other texts, both ancient[18] and from the Golden Age (Satorre 1989).

In some cases, words can be found with an even greater degree of fluctuation: for example, the Hellenism *paroxismo* is documented in seventeenth- and eighteenth-century dictionaries as *parocismo* (*NTLLE*: Minsheu 1617; *NTLLE*: Stevens 1706),[19] *parosismo* (*NTLLE*: Minsheu 1617; *NTLLE*: Terreros 1786–93), *parasismo* (*NTLLE*: Vittori 1609; *NTLLE*: Covarrubias and other bilingual dictionaries) and *paroxismo* (*NTLLE*: Vittori 1609; *NTLLE*: Minsheu 1617; *NTLLE*: Bluteau 1721); the latter is also found in *DAut* (*paroxysmo*) along with *parasysmo*, a form that is recognised to be of "uso mas freqüente". There are also the variants *parajismo* and *esparajismo*,[20] which suggest an adaptation with a prepalatal outcome.

To summarise, tracing the history of the letter *x* in dictionaries reveals the complex coexistence through to the early nineteenth century of inherited words and cultured borrowings, and how from then on it was almost entirely

---

[18] For example, and according to data from *DECH*, *complesión* and *complissión* are documented from the *Setenario* (ca. 1250) and Sem Tob (1360); *esaminar* (1330–1343, Juan Ruiz); *esecrar* (1444, Juan de Mena); (*e*)*secutar* and family (documentation from the fifteenth century); *inesausto* (1582, Herrera); *parosismo* (before 1578, Aldana); *tósigo* (1251, *Calila*).

[19] Also in French (*TLFi*, s.v. *paroxysme*).

[20] Cf. *DECH*, s.v. *acedo*. *Parajismo* is found, in *NTLLE*: Pagés 1925 and in *DRAE* 1927, defined as "mueca, visaje, gesticulación exagerada". *Esparajismo* appears in *DRAE* 1925 as "Alb. y León. Aspabiento". In *CORDE esparajismo* is recorded three times in texts by Saint Teresa.

the spellings originating from Latinisms and Hellenisms that survived,[21] which were undergoing constant expansion.

2.3. The evolution of learnèd word families and their reception in dictionaries

The increase in verified nomenclature in each edition of the Real Academia dictionary reflects the presence of learnèd words as one of the main strands of the gestation of modern Spanish. This is a constant that appears to a greater or lesser extent in each new edition depending both on the work of the Real Academia and its standards. The nineteenth-century editions of the dictionary include an ever-increasing number of learnèd words, such as *ácaro, bibliografía, clasificar, compulsivo, espasmódico, fumigación, pugilato, rudimento* (*DRAE* 1817); *abdomen, accéssit, convergencia, estadística, filantropía, lactación, nauseabundo, ostensible, preludiar* (*DRAE* 1822); *absorción, bípede, cúspide, ontología, retentivo, veterinario, zoología* (*DRAE* 1832); *cohesión, detergente, filarmónico, proyectil, remitente* (*DRAE* 1837); *aberración, bronquio, evacuante, impermeable, óbito, seductivo, versatilidad* (*DRAE* 1843); *acústico, dentífrico, fotografía, internacional, obstetricia, típico* (*DRAE* 1852); *aborígenes, decámetro, efectividad, fosforescencia* (*DRAE* 1869); *abscisa, bórico, deflagración, fórceps, hexasílabo,* (*DRAE* 1884); and *albuminoideo, bicóncavo, digitígrado, glúteo* (*DRAE* 1899).[22]

The addition of complex structures and meanings within each article also highlights the evolution of modern Spanish, which is easily perceptible when comparing one edition with the immediately preceding one. For example, *ácido*, a learnèd word that is strongly identified by its proparoxytonic stress, appears in *DAut* with just two definitions, but by the end of the following century it has undergone considerable expansion, basically through its use in syntagmatic compounds that are highly characteristic of scientific language and are used to form adjectives that are, in turn, often words derived from learnèd stems. For instance, *DRAE* 1817 includes *ácido carbónico, muriático, nítrico, sulfúrico* and *vitriólico*. The 1899 edition of the dictionary contains eighteen compounds formed by *ácido* and an adjective (*ácido acético, benzoico, bórico*, etc.). Currently (*DLE* 2014), the entry includes forty-nine

---

[21] Note that this letter is also used nowadays for Native American words, with a variety of pronunciations, cf. *Ortografía* 2010, 158–9.
[22] Examples drawn from *Lemateca del DRAE*, n.d.

similarly formed syntagmatic structures (*acetilsalicílico, acrílico, arsénico, barbitúrico*, etc.). Thus two directions in the growth of cultured borrowings can be observed: on the one hand, scientific and technical vocabulary, highly visible in these forty-nine syntagmatic compounds of *ácido* that are recorded in the dictionary (characterised by thematic abbreviations such as *Quím.* or *Bioquím.*); and on the other the semantic expansion implicit in the new senses generated from already existing words. In the case of *ácido*, the latest edition of the Academia dictionary (*DLE* 2014) includes the following new meanings:

(7)

ácido, da
2. adj. Áspero, desabrido.
3. adj. mordaz (‖ propenso a murmurar).
6. adj. jerg. *Hond.* Dicho de una persona: Experta o que tiene muchos conocimientos sobre algo.
7. m. jerg. LSD.

These new usages clearly show the vitality of the word in the modern language.

Morpholexical families are gradually but incessantly extending, driven by an increasing need for new vocabulary. A fine example of this is *iniciar* and its family, which offers an excellent model for the pattern followed by the spread of Latinisms. This lexical family was found in eighteenth-century dictionaries with a core formed by the verb *iniciarse* and the adjective *inicial*. The recorded semantic values were limited. According to the lexicographical information, the adjective was used to denote initials (as in letters), while the verb was recorded in the context of "recibir las primeras órdenes ú órdenes menóres" (*DAut*). Terreros documents *iniciar* as a forensic term synonymous with "empezar, comenzar" (*NTLLE*: Terreros 1786–1793), which is now its basic meaning, so at some point this word spread beyond technical usage. Meanwhile, the adjective *inicial* shifted from solely being associated with the noun *letra*, shown by the *DRAE* 1884's definition as "Perteneciente al origen ó principio de las cosas. *Velocidad* INICIAL *de un proyectil*. // V. **Letra inicial**". The texts contained in *CORDE* prove that until the eighteenth century, *inicial* was an adjective associated with the noun *letra* and, by extension, with *sonido* or *voz*, but from the nineteenth century, and mainly in the latter part of the century, it frequently appears in scientific texts together with such nouns as *velocidad, posición, fuerza, presión, vena*. At the same time, there was also major growth in the frequency of the adjective.

At the same time, the *iniciar/inicial* family was extended with other lexical elements: the Latin expression *ab initio* was included in *DRAE* 1791; the noun *iniciación* was recorded in Terreros (*NTLLE*: 1786–93) and is found throughout the lexicographical literature of the nineteenth century, but not in the Academia dictionary until the end of the century (*DRAE* 1899); *iniciativo/va* was recorded in the *DRAE* 1803; *iniciador/ra* is documented in the Domínguez dictionary (*NTLLE*: Domínguez 1853) and was later included in the *DRAE* 1899; and *iniciativa* was first made part of the *DRAE* nomenclature in 1843. Meanwhile, the noun *inicio* did not appear until *DRAE* 1956. The dictionaries of the early twenty-first century reveal further growth of this family with the incorporation of five terms, two of them exclusive to the Americas (*inicialar* and *inicialista*, included in *DRAE* 2001 and *DLE* 2014, respectively), another originating from computing (*inicializar,* also recorded in the *DRAE* 2001), as well as *iniciático/ca* in *DRAE* 2001.

The examples cited in this section are only a small illustration of how one of the ways in which modern vocabulary evolved can be traced through its representation in Spanish dictionaries, and shows the strong creative force of learnèd words and their increasing use.

3 Conclusion

In line with Alonso's appreciation of the need for a place for learnèd words in linguistics, given their importance in numbers and taking their presence in the dictionary as the basis, I have taken a short journey through the lexicographical works of the eighteenth and nineteenth centuries to verify how this genealogical class has developed over the years.

It has been demonstrated that, in terms of spelling and phonetics, learnèd words have left a considerable mark on the history of the Spanish language. I have been able to show how, in the history of the standardisation of Spanish, there has been a predominance of the closest forms to the Latin etymology, through continual restructuring that has been overriding, at least in written language, the processes of adaptation to the inherited lexicon. This has led to learnèd groups becoming thoroughly naturalised, and within these, the presence of the letter *x*, albeit with different pronunciations, has been consolidated, as attested by the *DLE* 2014.

Dictionaries also reveal the gradual increase in cultured borrowings, their vitality for creating morpholexical families, their semantic flexibility and their extraordinary capacity for syntagmatic composition. And these processes are not limited to Spanish, but can also be found in the foundations of lexical growth in many other modern languages.

Are the analysed cases "new worlds for old words"? *Old words* have actually become the most natural way for modern languages to name these *new worlds* created on a daily basis, a scenario in which cultured words truly have taken the leading role.

Bibliographical references

Alcoba, Santiago. 2007. "Ortografía y *DRAE*. Algunos hitos en la fijación léxica y ortográfica de las palabras." *Español actual: Revista de español vivo* 88: 11–42.

Alonso, Dámaso. 1935. *La lengua poética de Góngora*. Madrid: S. Aguirre.

Álvarez de Miranda, Pedro. 1992. "En torno al 'Diccionario' de Terreros." *Bulletin hispanique* 94, no. 2: 559–72.

Azofra, María Elena. 2006. "Consideraciones sobre el concepto de cultismo." *Revista de Filología Románica* 23: 229–240.

Blanco Izquierdo, M.ª Ángeles. 2018. "Un proceso significativo de revisión: la definición de las letras." In *El diccionario de la Academia en el siglo XIX: la quinta edición (1817) al microscopio*, edited by Gloria Clavería and Margarita Freixas, 175–202. Madrid: Arco/Libros.

Burgassi, Cosimo, and Elisa Guadagnini. 2014. "Prima dell'*indole*. Latinismi latenti dell'italiano." *Studi di lessicografia italiana* 31: 5–43.

Burgassi, Cosimo, and Elisa Guadagnini. 2017a. *La tradizione delle parole. Sondaggi di lessicologia storica*. Strasbourg: Éditions de linguistique et de philologie.

Burgassi, Cosimo, and Elisa Guadagnini. 2017b. "L'integrazione lessicale di *facile* nel vocabolario italiano: 'prova dei volgarizzamenti' e quadro romanzo." In *"Rem tene, verba sequentur." Latinità e Medioevo romanzo: testi e lingue in contatto*, edited by Elisa Guadagnini and Giulio Vaccaro, 157–177. Alessandria: Edizioni dell'Orso.

Bustos Tovar, José Jesús. 1974. *Contribución al estudio del cultismo léxico medieval (1140–1252)*. Madrid: Anejo XXVIII del *Boletín de la Real Academia Española*.

CORDE = Real Academia Española. *Banco de datos (CORDE). Corpus diacrónico del español*. Accessed 8 August 2020. https://www.rae.es/recursos/banco-de-datos/corde.

DECH = Corominas, Joan, and José Antonio Pascual. 1980–1991. *Diccionario crítico etimológico castellano e hispánico*. Madrid: Gredos. Electronic version on CD–ROM, 2012.

DEL = Reinheimer-Rîpeanu, Sanda (dir.). *Dictionnaire des emprunts latins dans les langues romanes*. Bucharest: Academiei Române.

DESE = Pharies, David. 2002. *Diccionario etimológico de los sufijos españoles*. Madrid: Gredos.

DLE 2014 = Asociación de Academias de la Lengua Española. 2014–. *Diccionario de la lengua española*, 23rd ed. Accessed 8 August 2020. https://dle.rae.es.

DRAE 2001 = Real Academia Española. 2001. *Diccionario de la lengua española*, 22nd ed. Accessed 8 August 2020. http://lema.rae.es/drae2001.

Dworkin, Steven N. 1998. "Lexical Loss and Neologisms in Late Medieval Spanish: Two Case Studies." *Bulletin of Hispanic Studies (Liverpool)* 75: 1–11.

Dworkin, Steven N. 2002a. "La introducción e incorporación de latinismos en el español medieval tardío: algunas cuestiones lingüísticas y metodológicas." In *Pulchre, Bene Recte: Estudios en homenaje al Prof. Fernando González Ollé*, edited by Carmen Saralegui Platero and Manuel Casado Velarde, 421–433. Pamplona: Eunsa.

Dworkin, Steven N. 2002b. "Pérdida e integración léxicas: *aína* vs. *rápido* en el español premoderno." In *Vocabula et vocabularia. Études de lexicologie et de (méta-)lexicographie romanes en l'honneur du 60ᵉ anniversaire de Dieter Messner*, edited by Bernhard Pöll y Franz Rainer, 109–18. Frankfurt: Peter Lang.

Dworkin, Steven N. 2006. "Historia de la lengua y el cambio léxico." *Iberoromania* 62: 59–70.

Dworkin, Steven N. 2010. "Thoughts on the Relatinization of the Castilian Lexicon." *Romance Philology* 64: 273–83.

Dworkin, Steven N. 2012. *A History of the Spanish Lexicon. A Linguistic Perspective*. Oxford: Oxford University Press.

Dworkin, Steven N. 2021. "Latinisms as Lexical Substitutes in Late Medieval and Early Modern Spanish". This volume.

Eberenz, Rolf. 1998. "Dos campos semánticos del español preclásico: 'fácil' y 'difícil'." In *Estudios de lingüística y filología españolas. Homenaje a Germán Colón*, edited by Irene Andrés–Suárez and Luis López Molina, 167–83. Madrid: Gredos.

Eberenz, Rolf. 2004. "En torno al léxico fundamental del siglo XV: sobre algunos campos verbales." In *Historia del léxico español. Enfoque y aplicaciones. Homenaje a Bodo Müller*, edited by Jens Lüdtke and Christian Schmitt, 111–136. Madrid/Frankfurt: Iberoamericana/Vervuert.

Esteve Serrano, Abraham. 1982. *Estudios de teoría ortográfica del español*. Murcia: Universidad de Murcia.

García Gallarín, Consuelo. 2007. *El cultismo en la historia de la lengua española*. Madrid: Parthenon.

García Macho, María Lourdes, and José Antonio Pascual. 1990. "Sobre la lengua de santa Teresa: el valor de sus elecciones gráficas evitadas por fray Luis." *Mélanges de la Casa Velázquez* 26, no. 2: 129–40.

García Valle, Adela. 1998. *La variación nominal en los orígenes del español*. Madrid: CSIC.

Gougenheim, Georges. 1959. "La relatinisation du vocabulaire français." *Annales de l'Université de Paris* 29: 5–18.

Harris-Northall, Ray. 1999. "Re-Latinization of Castilian Lexis in the Early Sixteenth Century." *Bulletin of Hispanic Studies (Liverpool)* 76, 1–12.

Hock, Hans Heinrich. 1986. *Principles of Historical Linguistics*. Mouton de Gruyter: Berlin/The Hague/New York.

Lemateca del DRAE. n.d. Accessed 3 March 2020. https://draesxix.wixsite.com/draesxix/lemateca.

López de Velasco, Juan. 1582. *Orthographia y pronunciacion castellana*, Burgos.

Malkiel, Yakov. 1961. "Etimología y cambio fonético débil: trayectoria iberorrománica de *medicus, medicāmen, medicīna*." *Ibérida* (*Homenagem a Marcel Bataillon*) 6, 127–72.

Martínez Alcalde, María José. 2006. "La codificación lexicográfica de la ortografía: el diccionario de Terreros." In *Nuevas aportaciones a la historiografía lingüística*, edited by Cristóbal J. Corrales, Josefa Dorta, Antonia Nelsi Torres, Dolores Corbella and Francisca del Mar Plaza, 691–703. Madrid: Arco/Libros.

Martínez Alcalde, María José. 2007. "Lexicografía y codificación ortográfica en el siglo XVIII." In *Historia de la lexicografía española*, edited by Mar Campos, Rosalía Cotelo and José Ignacio Pérez Pascual, 111–18. Coruña: Universidade da Coruña.

Martínez Alcalde, María José. 2010. *La fijación ortográfica del español: norma y argumento historiográfico*. Bern: Peter Lang.

Martínez Alcalde, María José. 2013. "Ortografía y prosodia." In *Historia de la pronunciación de la lengua castellana*, edited by María Teresa Echenique and Francisco Javier Satorre, 295–336. Valencia: Tirant Humanidades.

Martínez de Sousa, José. 1991. *Reforma de la ortografía española*. Madrid: Visor Libros.

NGLE 2009 = Real Academia Española. 2009. *Nueva gramática de la lengua española*. Madrid: Espasa Calpe.

NGLE 2011 = Real Academia Española and Asociación de Academias de la Lengua Española. 2011. *Nueva gramática de la lengua española. Fonética y Fonología*. Madrid: Espasa Calpe.

NTLLE = Real Academia Española and Asociación de Academias de la Lengua Española. 2001. *Nuevo Tesoro Lexicográfico de la Lengua Española*. Madrid: Espasa. DVD edition. Accessed 8 August 2020. http://ntlle.rae.es.

Orthographía 1741 = Real Academia Española. 1741. *Orthographía española*, Madrid: Imprenta de la Real Academia Española.

Ortografía 1815 = Real Academia Española. 1815. *Ortografía de la lengua castellana*, octava edición notablemente reformada y corregida, Madrid: Imprenta Real.

Ortografía 2010 = Real Academia Española and Asociación de Academias de la Lengua Española. 2010. *Ortografía de la lengua española*. Madrid: Espasa. Accessed 8 August 2020. http://aplica.rae.es/orweb/cgi–bin/buscar.cgi.

Patterson, William, and Hector Urrutibéheity. 1975. *The Lexical Structure of Spanish*. Mouton: The Hague/Paris.

Penny, Ralph. 1991. *A History of the Spanish Language*. Cambridge: Cambridge University Press.

Pountain, Christopher J. 2011. "Latin and the Structure of Written Romance." In *The Cambridge History of the Romance Languages*, vol. I *Structures*, edited by Martin Maiden, John Charles Smith and Adam Ledgeway, 606–659. Cambridge: Cambridge University Press.

Pountain, Christopher J. 2016. "Learnèd borrowing as a transnational phenomenon." Communication presented to the Conference *Transnational Modern Languages*, The Italian Cultural Institute, London, 2–3 December 2016.

Pountain, Christopher J. In press. "Los cultismos de cada día." In *Actas del XI Congreso Internacional de Historia de la Lengua Española, Lima, 6–10 de agosto de 2018*.

Pozuelo, José María. 1989. "Las primeras descripciones fonéticas de la Real Academia Española." *Estudios Románicos* 5: 1165–84.

Quilis Merín, Mercedes. 2008. "La presencia de los *neógrafos* en la lexicografía del siglo XIX." In *Gramma–temas 3 España y Portugal en la tradición gramatical*, 267–93. León: Universidad de León.

Quilis Merín, Mercedes. 2010. "La articulación de los sonidos en la lexicografía del español (siglos XIX y XX)." *Quaderns de Filologia. Estudis Lingüístics* 15: 97–120.

Quilis Merín, Mercedes. 2013. "La pronunciación del español a través de la lexicografía." In *Historia de la pronunciación de la lengua castellana*. María Teresa Echenique and Francisco Javier Satorre, 491–523. Valencia: Tirant Humanidades.

Raible, Wolfgang. 1996. "Relatinisierungstendenzen." In *Lexikon der Romanistischen Linguistik*, vol. 2, 1, edited by Günter Holtus, Michael Metzeltin and Christian Schmitt, 120–34. Tübingen: Max Niemeyer.

Rainer, Franz. 2002. "Convergencia y divergencia en la formación de palabras de las lenguas románicas." In *Aspectos de morfología derivativa del español*, edited by Joaquín García-Medall, 103–133, Lugo: Tris-Tram.

Ramírez Luengo, José Luis. 2011. "Sobre la historia de los grupos consonánticos cultos: el caso del español de Bilbao en los siglos XVI y XVII." *Oihenart* 26: 455–72.

Reinheimer-Rîpeanu, Sanda. 2004. *Les emprunts latins dans les langues romanes*. Bucharest: Editura Universităţii din Bucureşti.

Sălişteanu-Cristea, Oana. 2000. *Prestito latino – Elemento ereditario nel lexico della lingua italiana. Doppioni e varianti*. Prague: Istituto di Studi Romanzi-Facoltà di Lettere-Università Carolina.

Sălişteanu-Cristea, Oana. 2017. "Alcune considerazioni sui fenomeni allotropici nel lessico italiano: voci ereditarie, voci dotte, voci semidotte." In *"Rem tene, verba sequentur." Latinità e Medioevo romanzo: testi e lingue in contatto*, edited by Elisa Guadagnini and Giulio Vaccaro, 65–101. Alessandria: Edizioni dell'Orso.

Satorre, Francisco Javier. 1989. "Los grupos consonánticos cultos en un texto vallisoletano del Siglo de Oro." *Boletín de la Real Academia Española* 79: 65–89.

Satorre, Francisco Javier. 2006. "Los grupos consonánticos cultos: escritura y pronunciación." In *Rumbos del hispanismo en el umbral del cincuentenario de la AIH*, vol. 8, edited by Patrizia Botta and Sara Pastor, 37–46. Roma: Bagatto Libri.

Satorre, Francisco Javier. 2013. "La codificación de los grupos consonánticos cultos." In *Historia de la pronunciación de la lengua castellana*, edited by María Teresa Echenique and Francisco Javier Satorre, 381–418. Valencia: Tirant Humanidades.

Satorre, Francisco Javier, and María Luisa Viejo. 2013. "Ortología." In *Historia de la pronunciación de la lengua castellana*, edited by María Teresa Echenique and Francisco Javier Satorre, 337–79. Valencia: Tirant Humanidades.

Serianni, Luca. 2017. "Per una tipologia dei latinismi nei testi dei primi secoli." In *"Rem tene, verba sequentur." Latinità e Medioevo romanzo: testi e lingue in contatto*, edited by Elisa Guadagnini and Giulio Vaccaro 125–141. Alessandria: Edizioni dell'Orso.

Terrón, Natalia. 2019. "El sistema ortográfico en el *Diccionario castellano con las voces de ciencias y artes* (1786–1793) de Esteban de Terreros y Pando." *Boletín de la Sociedad Española de Historiografía Lingüística* 13, 277–297.

TLFi = ATILF – CNRS and Université de Lorraine. *Trésor de la Langue Française informatisé*. Accessed 8 August 2020. http://www.atilf.fr/tlfi.

Wright, Roger. 1989. *Latín tardío y romance temprano en España y la Francia Carolingia*. Madrid: Gredos.

Chapter 2

Learnèd borrowings induced by translation: Paratactic lexical groups as interference phenomena in Medieval and Early Renaissance Romance texts[1]

Santiago Del Rey Quesada
Universidad de Sevilla

Summary

This Chapter aims to describe paratactic lexical groups (Del Rey 2017a) in Medieval and Early Renaissance Romance translations from Latin source texts. In the first section I define what is a paratactic lexical group, relating the term to others that have been proposed so far within the Romance tradition (see Pellegrini 1953; Malkiel 1959; Elwert 1959). The corpus of this research, which is constituted by three French, three Italian and three Spanish translations and by two Portuguese translations together with the corresponding Latin source text for each of them, is presented in the second section. The analysis of this corpus is carried out in the next sections, where I discuss the relationship between paratactic lexical groups and linguistic elaboration (Kloss 1978; Pountain 2011) in Romance languages. Latin source texts are observed and compared to the Romance translations in order to quantitatively determine to what extent

---

[1] This paper was written within the framework of the project "Tradicionalidad discursiva, tradicionalidad idiomática, sintaxis del discurso, traducción y cambio lingüístico en la historia del español moderno: prosa (pre-)periodística, prosa (pre-)ensayística y prosa literaria [Discourse Traditionality, Idiomatic Traditionality, Discourse Syntax, Translation and Linguistic Change in the History of Modern Spanish: (Pre-)Journalistic Prose, (Pre-)Essay Prose and Literary Prose] (PGC2018-097823-B-I00)", funded by FEDER/Ministerio de Ciencia e Innovación – Agencia Estatal de Investigación.

convergence and divergence phenomena (Del Rey 2018c) are implicated in the formation of the paratactic lexical groups, whether they incorporate lexical borrowings or not. The conclusions show that direct influence of Latin source texts on Romance translations is not as strong as one could intuitively suspect.

Resumen

Este capítulo se orienta a la descripción de los grupos léxicos paratácticos (Del Rey 2017a) en varias traducciones romances medievales y prerrenacentistas desde textos fuente latinos. En el primer apartado defino qué es un grupo paratáctico, poniendo en relación este término con otros que han sido propuestos en el ámbito romance (cf, Pellegrini 1953; Malkiel 1959; Elwert 1959). Se presenta en el segundo apartado el corpus de este estudio, constituido por tres traducciones francesas, tres italianas, tres castellanas y dos portuguesas junto con los textos fuente correspondientes a cada una de ellas. El análisis del corpus se lleva a cabo en los siguientes apartados, en los que se discute la relación entre los grupos léxicos paratácticos y los procesos de elaboración lingüística en las lenguas romances (Kloss 1978; Pountain 2011). Se comparan los textos fuente y las traducciones romances para determinar cuantitativamente en qué medida los fenómenos de convergencia y divergencia (Del Rey 2018c) se imbrican en la conformación de los grupos léxicos paratácticos, incorporen estos préstamos léxicos o no. Las conclusiones demuestran que la influencia directa de los textos fuente latinos en las traducciones romances no es tan intensa como podría sospecharse.

Keywords

Lexical borrowing, Linguistic elaboration, Translation, Latin, Romance languages.

1 Paratactic groups: definition and structure

The combination of binary structures in the literary texts of Romance languages from their creation to the most recent occurrences not only has received the attention of numerous authors but has also resulted in a number of terminological proposals for this essentially syntactic phenomenon whose appearance, however, is not confined to literary texts. The coordination of lexical units with a (para)synonymous or antonymous meaning[2] is frequent even for discourses typical of communicative immediacy[3] in many Romance varieties and in most European languages. Expressions such as *sain et saif* 'safe and sound', *hot and cold*, *mondo y lirondo* 'plain and simple',[4] *alto e chiaro* 'loud and clear', *branco e negro* 'black and white', etc., evidence survival in the use of coordinate binary units with a varied degree of syntagmatic fixation. In any case, one could dare say that, in the absence of a specific diachronic study, literary texts have been particularly receptive to such combinations throughout the history of Romance languages. Nevertheless, no conclusive explanation has yet been given for their frequent presence in contexts in which communicative distance is inherent, where they are undoubtedly preferred and exploited.[5] This Chapter will place the emphasis on combined lexical units which generally contribute to characterise discourses as belonging to this communicative domain, considering the different functions that they assume within the translation process in which they are involved.

When it comes to twentieth- and twenty-first-century Romance bibliography, this linking of units (usually through copulative coordination) has been given different names. Casares (1992) referred to such linked units as *combinaciones binarias* 'binary combinations' for Spanish. The designation *iterazioni sinonimiche* 'synonymous iterations', coined by Pellegrini (1953) has reached great popularity in Italian. Elwert (1959) labelled them as *Synonymendoppelungen* 'synonymous doublets', an equally successful term in the Germanic tradition. One of the most influential studies is Malkiel (1959), who carried out a thorough formal study, from

---

[2] For a succinct discussion of the synonymous, parasynonymous or antonymous nature of such structures, cf. Del Rey (2017a).

[3] The formulation for the concept of "communicative immediacy", as well as that of "communicative distance", in this work follows the variational space view proposed by Koch and Oesterreicher (2011). According to these scholars, conceptual variation, represented as a continuum between maximum communicative immediacy (conceptual orality) and maximum communicative distance (conceptual scripturality), appears as the main axis of linguistic variation and has a universal nature.

[4] Not only in Spanish (*a tontas y a locas* 'without thinking', *por activa y por pasiva* 'insistently', etc.) but also in most of the European languages where the phenomenon under study has been analysed, the combination of units, above all, those which have reached a high degree of fixation, has a paronomasic effect (cf. Malkiel 1959).

[5] My discussion of the possible interpretations corresponding to this phenomenon as a translation fact is offered in Del Rey (2017a, 120–22; 2021a, §2.4).

an interlinguistic approach, of what he called *binomials*, even though his attention mainly focused on those which already had a high degree of fixation (*irreversible binomials*) in the languages examined by him. In the early 1950s, Alonso (1951) had included the units mentioned here inside the group of *sintagmas no progresivos* 'non-progressive syntagmata', a terminological label which already has a faithful tradition in linguistic and literary works within the Hispanic context.

Terminological options have continued to proliferate from fields such as lexis, syntax, rhetoric or translation, however.[6] Without the shadow of a doubt, the most successful terms have been those which attributed a synonymous nature to the elements involved in these structures.[7] Nonetheless, two questions arise: (a) Are all the lexical or syntagmatic coordinations appearing in literary texts (or, broadly speaking, in texts typical of conceptual scripturality) truly synonymous? (b) Should that not be the case, must they be regarded as a discursive (stylistic) phenomenon whose nature differs from that identified in other types of binary syntagmatic combinations?

As for the first question, the answer obviously depends on what is understood by "synonymy", a problem that will not be analysed in depth here.[8] The corpus presented in §3 clearly documents the coordination of what should be seen as true synonyms from my point of view (*a curer et a guérir* 'to cure and to heal', F1: 173);[9] however, cases exist where it is inappropriate to speak

---

[6] Just for Spanish, I have documented the following in the bibliography (amongst some others left unmentioned because they sometimes only imply small variations): *desdoblamientos léxicos* 'lexical doublets', *pares léxicos* 'lexical pairs', *explanaciones* 'explanations', *dobletes* 'doublets', *binomios sinonímicos* 'synonymous binomials', *términos complementarios* 'complementary terms', *ditologías* 'ditologies', *vocablos sinónimos* 'synonymous words', *tautologías* 'tautologies', *parasinónimos* 'parasynonyms', *parejas sinonímicas* 'synonymous pairs', *duplicaciones léxicas* 'lexical duplications', *geminados léxicos* 'lexical geminates', *traducciones binarias* 'binary translations', *duplicaciones de términos* 'duplications of terms', *desdoblamientos sinonímicos* 'synonymous doublets', *hendíadis* 'hendyadis', *sinatroísmos* 'congeries', *metabolé* 'metabole'. Concerning the classical rhetorical origins of the last three terms, cf. Serés (1997).

[7] Cf., in addition to the references included in the preceding paragraph, Bertolucci (1957), Diekamp (1972), Dembowski (1976), Buridant (1980), Wittlin (1991), Gutiérrez Cuadrado (1993) or Díez de Revenga (2009).

[8] Refer to Del Rey (2021a, §1) for a discussion of this issue.

[9] The key with the correspondence of the abbreviations related to the works contained in the corpus can be found in the bibliographic references section.

about perfect synonymy (if such a thing even exists), but rather about parasynonymy (*justamente e dereitamente* 'fairly and forthrightly', P1: 14). On some occasions, the combinations cannot be considered a connection of synonyms, insofar as the words involved find themselves within a relationship of hyperonymy/hyponymy (*montes e logares* 'mountains and places', S2: 35), of antonymy (*gens lais et clers* 'lay people and clerics', F1: 168) or of semantic continuity (*indagatio atque inventio* 'search and discovery', LP1: 7). Otherwise, very often only semantic proximity can be appreciated (*pace e riposo* 'peace and rest', I1: 12). Since the corpus I am working with comprises translations, numerous excerpts will show cases of *translatio* where a learnèd borrowing (hereinafter LB) is prototypically clarified by means of two words, one highbrow and the other lowbrow (e.g. in *inulto y sin vengança* 'unavenged and without revenge', S3: 119, as a translation of *inultum* 'unavenged' in the original Latin text).

Since this *translatio* technique often becomes visible in translated texts, translation studies have usually opted for the term *doublet*. However, the term *doublet* does not seem completely suitable to me either as far as translation is concerned, either because the pair is sometimes not a binary structure or because these lexical or syntagmatic combinations often appear in contexts which do not stem from a direct translation of the source text (ST). For this reason and from my conviction (in response to the second question posed above) that it would not be convenient to draw a distinction between non-synonymous combinations, or those which are not doublets, and synonymous ones, at least as far as the field of translation is concerned, my final choice was to suggest a new terminological label, *paratactic groups*, to describe the combinations examined here.

Despite having several drawbacks (cf. Del Rey 2017a, 118), this label brings certain advantages which make it operational to define the phenomenon both formally and semantically. Amongst them stand out five advantages which justify the adoption of this term in my study:

(a) When speaking about groups (and not about pairs, bimembrations or ditologies, for instance), the combination of more than two members might be included under this name, e.g. *cobiiçarem honras e imperio e poderios e louvores* 'coveting honor and might and power and praise' (P1: 20).

(b) As opposed to what is usually suggested in numerous descriptions of this phenomenon, the designatory capacity of the noun *group* permits to subsume the combination of segments which do not obligatorily show a morphological identity under the terminological label of *paratactic groups*, e.g. *maravigliose e quasi da non credere* 'marvellous and almost unbelievable' (I1: 19).

(c) On the same grounds, paratactic groups may comprise complex groups, which often happens in cases of parallelism and chiasmus, e.g. *el temor* [1a] *de la fama* [2a] *e reçelo* [1b] *de los dezires* [2b] 'the fear of fame and the misgivings about what people may say' (S2: 30).

(d) Due to my consideration of these groups as non-necessarily synonymous, the different semantic relationships mentioned above, including antonymy, may appear in paratactic groups, e.g. *humanarum divinarumque rerum* 'of things human and divine' (LF1: 10).

(e) 'Group' refers to a combination of elements, but it does not specify the type of relationship existing between them. In this respect, paratactic groups may be formed by units linked through a variety of syntactic procedures, not only positive copulative coordination (which is of course the most common one) but also negative copulative coordination (*serviço maior nem melhor* 'neither greater nor better service', P2: 114), disjunctive coordination (*quant il ordonneroit ou instruiroit ses battailles* 'when he orders or arranges his battles'), F3: 67; *disse questa diceria (ovvero orazione)* '(he) said this word (or sentence)', I1: 28), connection by means of reformulating mechanisms (*a les armes de prudence, ce est a dire de industrie et de engin* '(he) has the arms of wisdom, that is, of skill and artifice'), F2: 50) or juxtaposition (*falso lleno de nemiga* 'false, full of evilness', S1: 6, as the translation for the Latin term *scelerate* 'wicked').

2 Corpus and objectives of this work

The purpose of this research study is to examine the shaping of paratactic groups in target texts (TT) regarding their correspondences in the source text (ST), paying special attention to the attitude shown by translators towards lexical LBs. A range of medieval and Early Renaissance Romance translations (in French, in Italian, in Portuguese, and in Spanish) from Latin were analysed to that end. Note that the corpus is homogeneous in several respects and heterogeneous in others. It is heterogeneous in the sense that the translations examined fit into various textual genres, from poetry to political treatises, including dialogue and epic. Furthermore, the Latin source texts belong to different authors and periods, which surely influences the attitude shown by translators towards the model and which undoubtedly affects the characteristics of the handwritten tradition that would have inspired these interpreters. The results obtained in this study may be partially determined by the heterogeneity of my corpus, but it also allows the drawing of interesting conclusions by virtue of the differences in discourse tradition (genre- or subgenre-related) between texts (cf. Del Rey 2021b).

A particularly high level of heterogeneity stands out in the subcorpus of French translations, amongst which my study dealt with the translation of Boethius's *Consolatio philosophiae* by Jean de Meun (thirteenth century), the translation made by Nicole Oresme (ca. 1320–?) of the medieval Latin translation of Aristotle's *Politics* and the translation provided by Jean de Quesne of one part of Book III of Caesar's *Gallic War* (fifteenth century).[10]

The Italian texts selected were indeed translations of Latin classics: the Ciceronian translation of Brunetto Latini (ca. 1220–1295), *Le tre orazioni di M. T. Cicerone*, the translation of Ovid's *Metamorphoses* by Arrigo Simintendi (fourteenth century) and the *volgarizzamento* of Livy's IV Decade, attributed to Boccaccio (ca. 1313–1375).[11]

The Portuguese subcorpus was confined to two translations of Cicero: the medieval one of *Livro dos Oficios* by Infante D. Pedro (1392–1449) and the translation of *De Senectute* carried out by the Erasmist Damião de Góis.[12]

Another three Spanish translations from the Middle Ages complete the corpus of this work: the translation by Alfonso X "the Wise" (1221–1284) of the Ovidian *Heroides* from Dido to Aeneas (in addition to a part of the one from Ariadne to Theseus), Enrique de Villena's (1384–1434) translation of the *Aeneid* and the translation of the Homeric compendium which is known as *Ilias latina* made by Juan de Mena (1411–1456).[13]

---

[10] Each one of these translations is identified with the abbreviations F1, F2 and F3 respectively in the examples, followed by the page number of the edition used, which can be consulted in the bibliographic references section.

[11] They will be identified with the abbreviations I1, I2 and I3, respectively.

[12] Identified as P1 and P2, respectively.

[13] S1, S2 and S3, respectively.

The homogeneity of my corpus additionally has to do with the treatment of data. None of the aforementioned translations has been fully studied; instead, my decision was to consider some 5,000 words in each one of them with the aim of balancing the length of text analysed. If translations have a known prologue or preface, this was also analysed together with the 5,000 words per translation. The corpus of this work contains a total of 2,068 paratactic groups (PGs), organised by lexical entries (of which there are 4,256). Concerning PGs which contain one or more lexical LBs (those of most interest) a total of 325 were collected, a count which includes PGs found in prologues and those segments which are not directly translated. It is worth highlighting my decision to consider only PGs with LBs in all languages for this group and not to consider what have been termed "semi-learnèd" borrowings (semi-LBs) amongst these.[14] In this respect, note that many PGs from Italian were excluded because they did not meet the criteria followed to select LBs in the other languages. It is widely known that the syllabic structure of Italian (as opposed to other Romance languages) resembles that of Latin to a greater extent; hence both the greater difficulty to identify LBs in Italian and the small number of PGs with LBs in this language that will be recorded through the statistics provided in §4.[15] A monographic study (Del Rey 2021a) that I have

---

[14] On the distinction between learnèd borrowing (LB) and semilearnèd borrowing (semi-LB), cf. Migliorini (1973), Bustos Tovar (1974, 33–37; 2007), Clavería Nadal (1991, 14–18) and Dworkin (2012, 158–159). The criteria adopted to distinguish popular words, semilearnèd borrowings and learnèd borrowings had an essentially graphophonetic nature. I agree with Bustos Tovar (1974, 35) that the determination of LBs and semi-LBs cannot be performed exclusively on the basis of the phonetic outcome. Scavuzzo (1994, 470, n. 5) also suggests that "[i]n molti casi [...] la veste fonetica di una parola non basta da sola per assegnarla con certezza all'una [parole ereditarie] o all'altra categoria [parole dotte]" 'very often, the phonetic appearance of a word alone does not suffice to place it categorically in one category [popular words] or another [learnèd borrowings]'. Even so, since the texts included in this corpus belong to the communicative distance domain, taking cultural or semantic aspects into consideration becomes particularly problematic, in the sense that even inherited words can be used with a special learnèd meaning in some contexts or, on the contrary, learnèd words can be fully integrated in the common use of writers with a high socio-linguistic profile. I refer in this sense to Burgassi and Guadagnini (2014) and to Sălişteanu-Cristea (2017). See also Del Rey (2021a, §4.2) for a more in-depth discussion of this topic.

[15] In accordance with the methodological decisions adopted for this work, numerous semilearnèd words from Italian were removed (e.g. *assettare* 'to organise, to bring order',

carried out with the PGs in my corpus pays attention to different syntactic, semantic, and translation-related parameters which provide a complete picture of these structures in the Romance languages in the Middle Ages.

Furthermore, it seems advisable to highlight the methodological precautions that need to be applied when analysing PGs. Numerous material aspects must be considered when it comes to assessing their presence in medieval translations, such as the use of glossaries which might have been available in the *scriptoria* and which might also account for the regular co-appearance and even the fixation of certain lexical elements present in such works. Likewise, it is necessary to admit that this study did not include an exhaustive analysis of the original texts that translators could look at, probably sprinkled with marginal notes which would explain many of these PGs. In this regard, it should be stressed that the results shown here are provisional and that the study of PGs requires a more in-depth analysis, more detailed and with more philological rigour than can be offered at this stage of my research. It goes without saying that the goal is to achieve an overall understanding of this phenomenon, for which an approach like the one proposed here is essential.

Finally, it must be highlighted, before I proceed to an analysis of the corpus, that the interpretation of PGs cannot be confined to a quantitative study of the convergence and divergence phenomena (cf. §3) which I will identify. They are an aspect of linguistic elaboration (cf. also §3), which cannot be considered independently of the stylistic (relating to authors and/or periods) and discourse-traditional features of a specific corpus: under stylistic factors, for example, it must be borne in mind that some authors are more prone to using Latinisms than others, notably Juan de Mena (S3) and Villena (S2). Historical period is also an important consideration since, for instance, Alphonse X's School of Translators seeks to build its own language style, above all in historiographical texts, where vernacular trends are prioritised over Latinate

---

condizione 'condition' or *autoritade* 'authority', to quote but a few) which, however, could be categorised as denotative LBs (a term also used by Scavuzzo 1994, 481–87). I am well aware of the fact that the graphophonetic criterion assumed to define LBs in this study may turn out to be too strict, and probably insufficient in the case of Italian. My work (Del Rey 2021a), in fact, rethinks controversial methodological issues like this one and operates differently from the approach assumed in this paper as far as the selection of Italian learnèd borrowings within the corpus is concerned.

ones (cf. Del Rey 2016), something which probably does not fully apply to the Humanist authors included in this corpus. Under discourse-traditional factors, for example, the technical-political genre cultivated by Oresme (F2) should be noted. However, I have not yet been able to determine the relevance of such factors in other authors.

3 Convergence and divergence in PGs

This work will primarily deal with PGs made up of LBs, by virtue of the convergence and divergence processes which take place in the TT with respect to the ST. The incorporation of lexical LBs into Romance languages must be regarded as one of the most outstanding phenomena associated with intensive elaboration in these languages.[16] In my opinion, the translation exercise has been rightly understood as one of the forces driving the introduction of LBs in Romance languages and, therefore, as a catalyst for linguistic elaboration (cf. Pountain 2011). My works (cf. Del Rey 2016; 2017b; 2018c) dedicated to the old syntax of Romance languages have revolved around the direct influence exerted by translations from Latin on these processes. My discussion about the importance of calquing in Romance translations takes place within a theoretical approach in which translation is understood as a linguistic contact phenomenon (cf. Haßler 2001; Albrecht 2017; Del Rey et al. 2018). Translated texts thus seem prone to the accumulation of interference phenomena. 'Interference' arises as a key concept in my proposal for translation phenomena which is based on the ideas and arguments contained in Kabatek (1996, 1997).[17]

In order to speak about interference, it must be made clear that the analysis will refer to cases of linguistic variants within a given context. Two types of interference are going to be distinguished in the analysis: positive and the negative. These terms are not being used in the evaluative sense that often appears in their definition, but refer to the presence of marked (+) or non-

---

[16] On the concept of "elaboration", cf. Kloss (1978), as well as Koch and Oesterreicher (2011), who draw a distinction between *intensive* and *extensive* elaboration: the former refers to the development of linguistic material aimed at achieving the latter, which is the capacity of vernacular languages to fill the communicative distance domain that had so far been exclusively reserved to Latin.

[17] This author puts forward his classification of interference phenomena from the ideas of Weinreich (1967) and Coseriu (1977).

marked (−) variants in the TT. Positive interference leads to marked variants in TTs, either because it brings unsystematic results or because it causes quantitatively or qualitatively abnormal results (in the Coserian sense) in the target language (TL). In turn, negative interference triggers non-marked results in TTs, or expressed differently, variants which could not be recognisable in a given text as the fruit of interference unless a comparative context such as that offered by translation or situations of linguistic contact is considered.[18] My proposal for the classification of phenomena between the ST and the TT presents two subtypes as being related to positive interference. On the one hand, what I shall call *trans-position*, which consists in the production of a marked variant in the TT resulting from an ST calque. This is what my study will specifically refer to as *Latinism*. Example (1) presents the LB *expedient* in the French TT explained as a copy of the Latin word *expediens* 'beneficial' in the ST, even though the translator might have used another variant such as *juste* 'fair', an adjective which is documented in the same contexts for this author, even to translate *expediens*:

(1)

    secundum naturam et **expediens** corpori regi ab anima > ce est selon nature et est **expedient** que le corps soit gouverné de l'ame (F2: 53).

    'it is natural and beneficial for the body to be governed by the soul'

The other positive interference phenomenon, which I shall call *hyper-position*, involves the presence of a marked variant in the TT which is not explained by any units calqued from the ST; it instead develops independently from the ST. My proposal in this regard is to distinguish, on the one hand, the notion of *hyper-Latinism*, described as the appearance of a Latinism in the TT which has not been motivated by the ST original, when a translation etymologically coincident with the original Latin word would not have led (at least as regards lexis)[19] to a marked solution in the TT. This is exemplified by (2), where the LB *enarrara* '(he) had told' translates ST *dixerat* '(he) had

---

[18] Or unless the text portion studied is long enough to allow the identification of linguistic patterns which, due to their high incidence within a given corpus, are likely to provide data about the preferred variants in a text.

[19] The use of the verbal ending *-ra* as a calque of Latin pluperfect might indeed be considered a morphologically marked solution in the TT.

said'). I should clarify that the category of *hyper-Latinism* refers here to those cases where a Latinism appears in additions or within non-translation contexts.

(2)

    Dixerat > Aquestas palabras **enarrara** el saçerdote Crysis (S3: 115).

    'The priest Chrysis narrated these things'

Another phenomenon dealt with as a case of hyper-position is what I shall call *hetero-Latinism*, which explains the presence of a Latinism in the TT independently from the ST, with the peculiarity that the variant is the translation of an ST element which could equally have generated a Latinism in the TT. This is what happens in example (3), where Damião de Góis utilises the word *extremo* 'last' instead of *derradeiro* 'last', which not only would have been more normal in Coserian terms but is also employed by this author on other occasions, or *sumo* 'highest', which would have represented a case of Latinism by calque and is documented in his work too:

(3)

    Sophocles ad **summam** senectutem tragoedias fecit > Sófocles, no **extremo** de sua velhice, compunha e fazia tragédias (P2: 113).

    'Sophocles, at the end of his old age, composed and made tragedies'

As for negative interference, a distinction is drawn between another two phenomena: *identity* and *difference*. *Identity* implies an equivalence with the ST that leads to non-marked variants in the TT. Those cases in which a popular word is documented in the TT as a translation of a word etymologically related to the ST form being translated are considered a manifestation of identity in this corpus.[20] This becomes visible in example (4), where *anima* 'soul' from the ST is translated as *alma* 'soul', even though the form *ánima* 'soul' is widely attested as a translation of Latin *anima* in Mena himself:

---

[20] The concept of "identity" turns out to be problematic when considering lexical equivalences between the ST and the TT, mainly because Latin words have very often not left popular derivatives in Romance languages, in which case this typology (that, as highlighted above, concerns effective variants in a specific paradigmatic variation context) would not be applicable (see Del Rey 2021, §4.1). It does become fully functional, from my point of view, in comparative syntactic studies, as I tried to prove in some works (cf. Del Rey 2017b; 2018c). Nonetheless, identity here also raises certain problems associated with the difficulty to define what a variant is in syntax (cf. Del Rey 2018c, 24–25).

(4)
> purpuream vomit ille **animam** cum sanguine mixtam > y aquél vomita el **alma** purpúrea a bueltas con la sangre (S3: 149).
>
> 'and he vomits his purple soul mixed with the blood'

Difference consists in utilising a popular variant to translate a word which could have triggered a Latinism in the TT; hence my decision to call this phenomenon *anti-Latinism*. By way of example, the Italian *volgarizzamento* of Livy (5) allows reading *grandezza* 'greatness' as the translation of *magnitudine* 'greatness', and that despite Italian *magnitudine* being profusely documented by corpora such as *OVI* or *DiVO* (cf. Consiglio Nazionale delle Ricerche, n.d.) in a huge number of medieval Italian texts:

(5)
> **magnitudine** imperii > per la **grandezza** dell'imperio (I3: 18).
>
> 'by the greatness of power'

As summarised in Figure 2.1, both trans-position and identity are convergence phenomena, since they consist in matching the ST, regardless of whether coincidence takes place from marked or non-marked variants. Instead, hyper-position and difference are divergence phenomena that entail a conscious or unconscious detachment from the ST. My next step will be to describe how lexical convergence and divergence become visible in my corpus, specifically referring to those PGs in whose constitution one or more LBs are involved.

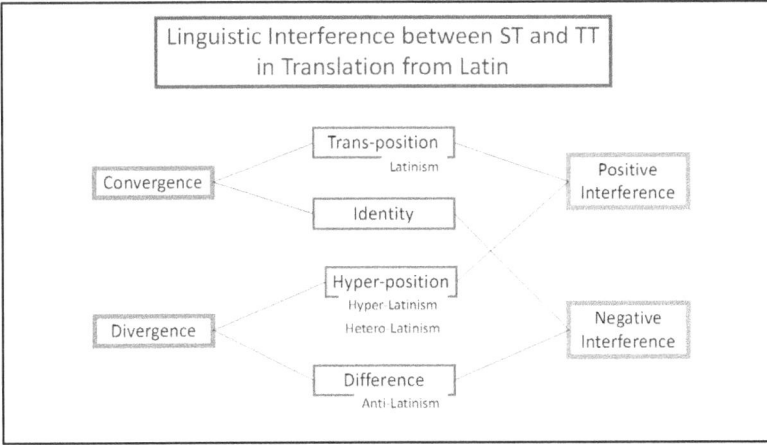

Figure 2.1. Linguistic interference between the source text and the target text in translation from Latin

4 Learnèd borrowings in paratactic groups

The analysis of PGs with LBs that will be performed in this section involves a total of 325 PGs which contain at least one LB, in a different distribution per work, as shown in Figure 2.2:

	PG not translating any elements from the ST	PG translating some element from the ST						TOTAL 325
		no elements within the PG etymologically linked	some element within the PG etymologically linked	(semi-)LB + LB or vice versa		LB + popular word or vice versa		
				etymologically-linked LB	not-etymologically-linked LB	etymologically-linked LB	not-etymologically-linked LB	
F1	9	0	4	3	0	1	0	13
F2	24	15	54	20	16	21	12	93
F3	4	2	14	4	6	1	5	20
I1	0	2	3	0	1	1	3	5
I2	0	0	0	0	0	0	0	0
I3	0	1	0	0	1	0	0	1
P1	1	2	0	0	2	0	0	3
P2	8	14	9	3	12	5	3	31
S1	0	0	0	0	0	0	0	0
S2	59	11	19	8	8	7	7	89
S3	19	10	41	18	2	22	9	70

Figure 2.2. Paratactic lexical groups containing at least one learnèd borrowing in the corpus

A distinction was drawn between a variety of occurrence contexts so that the reader can have a complete overview of the use of LBs in the structures under study. The type of PGs with LBs considered in this paper may not translate any elements from the ST, as it happens in prologues and added or deeply reformulated excerpts. Some translations give a great many results inside this group, as illustrated by that of Oresme (F2) or those carried out by Villena (S2) and Mena (S3). Below can be found a number of examples of such PGs with LBs. Some of these LBs are very strong, especially in Spanish works, as can be seen in the text of Villena (8), where there occur *dinigrasçión, impugnasçión.*

(6)

il convient que il soit menés **par doctrine et par mainte experience** a ce que il viegne a la discrecion et au devisement de biens (F1: 169).

'it is advisable for him to be guided by doctrine and by great experience so that he achieves the discernment and discrimination of gifts'

(7)

Uma causa por que se a velhice **repreende e vitupera** (P2: 111).

'a reason for which old age is scolded and vituperated'

(8)

ya no temiendo la de su fama **dinigrasçión nin otra impugnasçión** alguna (S2: 37).

'no longer fearing the denigration of her reputation or any punishment'

PGs with LBs can also occur as a translation of some ST element, however. Two effectively identified scenarios were distinguished in this respect: (a) none of the PG elements is etymologically related to the ST word or words being translated; or (b) a PG element does have such a relationship. In either case, the PG may include two (or more) LBs or an LB and a popular word (or a combination of elements in variable numbers for PGs with more than two elements). When the PG comprises two or more LBs or is formed by one LB and one semi-LB,[21] one of them may be etymologically linked to the conveyed

---

[21] It must be remembered that the total of forms considered for the occurrences corresponding to each translation in Table 1 is based on the cases of crude LBs and not on those of semi-LBs (cf. §2, especially fn.13 y fn.14). Anyhow, the utilisation of semi-LBs coordinated with LBs is indicative of each translator's stylistic behaviour.

ST word, as shown in example (9), where the LB *conferente* 'beneficial' is a calque of the Latin word *conferens* 'beneficial', while the other LB or semi-LB (i.e. *utile* 'useful') is introduced without there being any motivation in the ST:

(9)

> sermo autem est in ostendendo **conferens** et nocivum > mes parole est en moustrant ou pour moustrer quele chose est **conferente et utile** et quele chose est nuisible (F2: 49).
>
> 'my word serves to show what is beneficial and useful and what is harmful'

A PG formed by two LBs or by one LB and one semi-LB may not have any etymological relationship whatsoever with the ST element being translated. This becomes visible in (10), where neither the LB *ignorantes* 'ignorants' nor the semi-LB *carecem* '(they) lack' are etymologically linked to the Latin word translated in this context, i.e. *insipienti* 'ignorants':[22]

(10)

> nec **insipienti** etiam in summa copia non gravis > Nem aos ***ignorantes, e que carecem de virtude*** [...] per rica e abundosa que seja (P2: 208).
>
> 'neither to the ignorant nor to those who lack virtue, however rich and abundant it may be'

As for PGs made up of an LB and a popular word, or vice versa,[23] cases are also likely to be found where the LB included in the PG is etymologically linked to the ST element being translated; or expressed differently, cases in which trans-position from the ST (or Latinism) unquestionably takes place, as exemplified by (11), where the first PG element clearly stems from the word used in the Latin original. However, as happens in PGs comprising two LBs or one LB and one semi-LB, the LB joined to a popular word in the PG may once again have no etymological relationship whatsoever with the word it translates. This is attested in example (12), where *similitud* 'similarity' coappears with

---

[22] Needless to say, a certain degree of convergence exists in this case regarding the presence of a negative prefix in *insipienti* and in *ignorantes*.

[23] It is sadly impossible to develop the issue of order amongst the constituent elements of a PG here. Refer to Del Rey (2017a, 125–31) for a discussion of the effects caused by PG shaping order.

rastro 'trace' independently from the original *vestigia* 'traces', which constitutes yet another case of hyper-Latinism in this translation by Villena:

(11)
> manifestum quod omnes quidem bonum aliquod **coniecturant** > Et pour ce est il manifeste que tous en faisant communité **conjecturent et entendent a** aucun bien (F2: 45).
>
> 'and for that reason, it is clear that all those constituting a community project and tend towards some good'

(12)
> agnosco ueteris **uestigia** flammae > Ya me paresçe conosçer e sentir el **rastro o similitud** de la antigua d'amor llama (S2: 24).
>
> 'I think I already know the trace or the similarity of an old love flame'

From the different ways in which the LB appears in the corpus, it can be seen that its presence in PGs may not be the result of a servile translation exercise. On the contrary, translations show a considerable degree of versatility in introducing Latinising vocabulary in the structures examined here. Of course, mere calques (even in original Latin PGs which eventually trigger a double LB in the TT) are documented in the corpus as well. An example can be found in (13), where the two lexical LBs *opportune e ydonnne* 'appropriate and suitable' are nothing but a trans-position of the original PG *oportuno atque idoneo* 'appropriate and suitable'. The LB may go beyond copying the lexeme in the TT, however. On some occasions, the calque is likely to resort to the syntactic construction in the ST, even though it diverges from it lexically. For example, (14) keeps the present participle which acts as a Latinism in the Portuguese translation, even though the verbal bases used in each case differ. The units motivating PGs with more than one LB in the TT do not necessarily have to be included in the original PG: the PG may simply render the Latin lexical units which motivate it but which do not form a group in the ST. Thus, *potente y egregio* 'powerful and eminent' in (15) are coordinated as opposed to the uncoordinated syntagm in Latin.

(13)
> loco [...] **oportuno atque idoneo** > en place **oportune et ydonne** (F3: 68).
>
> 'in an appropriate and suitable place'

(14)

    aut iam **urgentis aut** certe **adventantis** senectutis > esta carga dela já **ocorrente, ou** certo **acelerante** (P2: 105).

    'Its burden [old age], which is already arriving and surely hastening'

(15)

    sequitur totidem ratibus Telamonius Aiax, / **egregia** virtute **potens** > con otras tantas naves sigue Ajas Talamonio **potente y egregio** por virtud (S3: 131).

    'with as many vessels, Ajax Telamonius goes on, powerful and eminent in virtue'

As highlighted in Section 1, one of the most notable manifestations of PGs with LBs is where the lexical LB in the PG appears joined to another word which serves as a *translatio* of the learnèd word. This stands out as the combination which has raised the most interest amongst scholars, and obvious examples of it can be found in my corpus too. Within this group, the number of PGs in which the *translatio* takes place by means of a litotes (i.e. through the negation of a form interpreted as the antonym of the translated Latin word) is strikingly high. This happens frequently when a derived adjective corresponds to a (precisely negative) prefix in the ST, as shown by the use of *iniquorum* in (16), split in the trans-posed LB into a Latinism and a litotes formed by *no(n)* 'not' and a popular adjective:

(16)

    scribunt **iniquorum** > ont escript que tel droit est **inique et non juste** (F2: 55).

    '(they) have written that such a right is iniquitous and unfair'

The examples below provide evidence that PGs working as the *translatio* of an LB very often show the disjunctive conjunction (*o*, *ou* 'or') as a linking element. Coordination by means of this conjunction is particularly common in texts of a specialised nature (cf. Sánchez González de Herrero 2013), where I have described them (cf. Del Rey 2018a) as discourse-traditional elements (cf. Koch 1987; Winter-Froemel et al. 2015) which characterise this type of discourse, as well as those PGs whose elements are joined through a reformulating unit (19). This is what happens in my corpus even with non-translated texts, as illustrated by example (20), which reveals how the reformulating mechanism (contrary to what might be expected, since reformulators are explanatory strategies *par excellence*) can also introduce a *translatio* in a non-translational context:

(17)

    a servis et a **domesticis** animalibus > par les serfs et par les bestes **domestiques ou privees** (F2: 54).

    'by the serfs and by the domestic or private animals'

(18)

    devolat in **thalamos** Agamemnonis > boló dentro en los **tálamos o lecho** de Agamenón (S3: 121).

    'flew to Agamemnon's bed'

(19)

    aut tecum malit **contendere** bello > o contigo **contender**, mas guerreando quisiesse, **siquiere la tuya contradezir voluntad**? (S2: 31).

    'or (he) preferred to fight against you by waging war, that is, contradicting your will'

(20)

    el fructo de la doctrina **latente, siquiere cubierta**, en el artifiçioso dezir (S2: 28).

    'the fruit of latent doctrine, that is, hidden, in the affected way of speaking'

My final reference will focus on PGs in which a hyper-Latinism or hetero-Latinism develops; that is to say, PGs in which the LB occurs in the TT without being motivated by the ST. Examples (21), (22) and (23) attest the presence of LBs as hyper-Latinisms in the PGs of TTs:

(21)

    sceleratus > **tres inique et tres pervers** (F2: 48d).

    'iniquitous and very wicked'

(22)

    auxilium > **de profit ou de subside** (F2: 54).

    'fruitful and helpful'

(23)

    et nitidum Titan radiis caput extulit **undis** > el resplandeçiente sol con sus rayos se demostró fuera **de las aguas y del insano emisperio** (S3: 125–27).

    'the shining sun rose with its rays from the waters and from the insane hemisphere'

Even more worthy of attention is the existence of PGs where an LB is joined to a popular word (or vice versa) but where the LB does not represent a calque of the ST word being translated, but just the opposite: the LB is a hyper-Latinism, while it is the popular word that has an etymological connection with the translated term. Evidence of authors' Latinising intention beyond mere calquing can be found in examples (24) and (25):

(24)
> **testudine** facta portas succedunt murumque subruunt > puis ordonnerent ung engien qu'ilz appeloient de son nom **testue ou phalange** (F3: 66).
>
> '(they) subsequently assembled a machine that they called a testudo or phalanx'

(25)
> cum res publica **immortalis** esse debeat > conciossiachè la comunanza di Roma debbia essere **perpetua e senza morte** (I1: 15).
>
> 'since the Roman republic must be perpetual and immortal'

The LBs of PGs in examples (26) and (27) could also be considered hetero-Latinisms, insofar as the LBs which might have resulted from calques of the words in the ST were lexical possibilities available in the language of translators at the time. Other cases (e.g. (28)) show an LB splitting into two, which constitutes a clear example of a hyper-Latinism. In other words, the crude LB, which works as a calque of the ST word, is not explained; instead, another Latinism becomes associated with it, in such a way that the outcome might be regarded as doubly Latinising:

(26)
> Quod si rerum tuarum **immortalium**, C. Caesar, hic exitus futurus fuit > E se questa fosse la fine delle tue **grandi e sempiterne** opere (I1: 17–18).
>
> 'and if this were the end of your large and eternal works'

(27)
> magnifici apparatus vitaeque cultus cum **elegantia et copia** > grandes pareceenças e grandes guarnimentos e em grande **excelencia e avondança** (P1: 20, l. 4–6).
>
> 'bright and colourful appearance and good clothes and plenty of excellence and abundance'

(28)

et nuptialis (innominata enim feminae et viri **coniugatio**) > Et l'autre, ce est assavoir **combination ou conjugacion** de homme et de femme, ne est nommee et peut estre dicte nupcial (F2: 50).

'and the other thing, that is, the union or bond between man and woman, is not mentioned and may be termed nuptial'

	CONVERGENCE BETWEEN ST AND TT		DIVERGENCE OF TT FROM ST	
	Tokens	Percentage	Tokens	Percentage
F1	4	100.0%	0	0.0%
F2	41	59.4%	28	40.6%
F3	5	31.3%	11	68.7%
I1	1	20.0%	4	80.0%
I2	0	0.0%	0	0.0%
I3	0	0.0%	1	100.0%
P1	0	0.0%	2	100.0%
P2	8	34.8%	15	65.2%
S1	0	0.0%	0	0.0%
S2	15	50.0%	15	50.0%
S3	40	78.4%	11	21.6%
TOTAL	**114**	**56.4%**	**88**	**43.6%**

Figure 2.3. Effects of convergence and divergence in paratactic lexical groups with at least one LB in PGs motivated by the ST

Figure 2.3 shows the effects of convergence and divergence in paratactic lexical groups with at least one LB in PGs which translate some ST unit in all the testimonies examined. As shown in the table, the degree of convergence with the ST in this case exceeds the level of divergence, even though this outcome is partly due to the figures associated with Juan de Mena (S3), whose 78.4% of convergence presents him as the most Latinising author amongst those appearing in my corpus.[24] Nevertheless, it becomes obvious that most of the testimonies analysed show a clear tendency to divergence in what regards to the configuration of PGs with LBs. This is what happens in F3, I1, I3, P1, P2 and S2, additionally taking into account that no occurrences of LBs are

---

[24] On Mena's Latinising attitude, cf. Azofra Sierra (2007).

documented in the PGs of I2 and S1. To put it in another way, it deserves to be highlighted that the number of LBs not motivated by the ST exceeds that of motivated ones in many translations.

Adding the PGs with LBs also found in those parts where the PG does not translate any ST elements (Figure 5.4) enables the calculation of the percentages both of Latinism (35.1%) and of hyper- or hetero-Latinism (64.9%) in my corpus. This time, it turns out that Mena's (S3) is the only translation where the percentage of Latinisms remains higher than that of hyper- or hetero-Latinism. Expressed differently, the data collected in my study reveal that most of the LBs appearing in the PGs of texts written by translators are not dependent on the ST.

	LATINISM		HYPER- OR HETERO-LATINISM	
	Tokens	Percentage	Tokens	Percentage
F1	4	30.8%	9	69.2%
F2	41	44.1%	52	55.9%
F3	5	25.0%	15	75.0%
I1	1	20.0%	4	80.0%
I2	0	0.0%	0	0.0%
I3	0	0.0%	1	100.0%
P1	0	0.0%	3	100.0%
P2	8	25.8%	23	74.2%
S1	0	0.0%	0	0.0%
S2	15	16.8%	74	83.2%
S3	40	57.1%	30	42.9%
TOTAL	114	35.1%	211	64.9%

Figure 2.4. Phenomena of Hyper- or Hetero-Latinism (counting non-translated excerpts) vs. Latinism in the corpus

5 Final remarks

This work has revolved around the analysis of a set of paratactic groups in various Medieval and Early Renaissance Romance translations. My main interest focused on studying lexical learnèd borrowings inside these groups, comparing source texts and target texts for the purpose of determining the degree of convergence and divergence which can be established in those translations. It has revealed the need to rethink the direct influence of Latin on lexical elaboration processes, after having verified that the indirect or *ex negativo* influence exerted by Latin appears to be stronger than initially expected. It is thus reconfirmed (cf. Del Rey 2017b; 2018b; 2018c, where I come to the same conclusion regarding syntactic phenomena) that negative interference phenomena (cf. Figure 5.1) play a key role in understanding processes of linguistic elaboration. Or, expressed differently, the analysis presented here gives proof that, also as far as Medieval Romance vocabulary is concerned, one must search for Latin beyond Latin itself.

References

Corpora

[F1] Jean de Meun (thirteenth century). *De consolatione philosophiae de Boèce*. Edited by V. Louis Dedeck-Héry in "Boethius' *De Consolatione* by Jean de Meun", *Mediaeval Studies* 14 (1952), 165–275.

[LF1] Boethius. *Philosophiae consolationis Libri quinque*. Edited by Karl Büchner. Heidelberg: Winter Verlag (1977).

[F2] Nicole Oresme (ca. 1320–?). *Le livre de politiques d'Aristote*. Edited by Albert. D. Menut. In *Transactions of the American Philosophical Society* 60/6. Philadelphia: The American Philosophical Society (1970), 1–392.

[LF2] Aristotelis *politicorum libri octo cum vetusta translatione Guilelmi de Moerbeka*. Edited by Franz Susemihl. Leipzig: Teubner (1872).

[F3] Jean de Quesne (fifteenth century). *La guerre des Gaules livre III*. Edited by Séverine Montigny. In *Traduire César entre Moyen Âge et Renaissance: étude de la "translation" de la Guerre des Gaules par Jean du Quesne (1473–1474) à partir de l'exemple du livre III (édition et commentaire)*. Rapport d'étape de thèse. Paris: Université Paris IV Sorbonne (2007).

[LF3] C. Iulii Caesaris *Commentarii rerum gestarum*, vol. I. In *Bellum Gallicum* Liber III. Edited by Otto Seel. Leipzig: Teubner (1968).

[I1] Brunetto Latini (ca. 1220–1295). *Le tre orazioni di M. T. Cicerone*. Edited by Luigi Maria Rezzi. Milano: Dai Torchi di Ranieri Fanfani (1832).

[LI1] M. Tulli Ciceronis *Orationes* / recognovit brevique adnotatione critica instruxit Albertus Curtis Clark, Gulielmus Peterson. Oxford: Oxford University Press (1987, 2nd ed.).

[I2] Arrigo Simintendi (fourteenth century). *I primi V libri delle Metamorfosi d'Ovidio*. Edited by Ranieri Guasti. Prato (1846).

[LI2] P. Ovidii Nasonis *Metamorphoses*. Edited by Roger J. Tarrant. Oxford: Oxford University Press (2004).

[I3] Giovanni Boccaccio (ca. 1313–1375). *IV Deca di T. Livio*. Edited by Francesco Pizzorno. Savona: Luigi Sambolino (1845).

[LI3] Titi Livi *Ab urbe condita*. Edited by Wilhelm Weissenborn and Moritz Müller. Stuttgart: Teubner (1972).

[P1] Infante D. Pedro (1392–1449). *Livro dos Oficios*. Edited by Joseph M. Piel. Coimbra: Universidade de Coimbra (1948).

[LP1] M. Tulli Ciceronis *De officiis*, recognovit brevique adnotatione critica instruxit, Jonathan Michael Winterbottom. Oxford: Oxford University Press (1994).

[P2] Damião de Góis (1502–1574). *Livro de Marco Tvllio Ciçeram chamado Catam maior ou da velhiçe*. Edited by João José Alves Dias. Lisboa: Biblioteca Nacional de Portugal (2002).

[LP2] M. Tulli Ciceronis *De re publica; De legibus; Cato maior de senectute; Laelius de amicitia*, recognovit brevique adnotatione critica instruxit Jonathan G. F. Powell. Oxford: Oxford University Press (2006).

[S1] Alfonso X (1221–1284). *Estoria de España*. Edited by Pedro Sánchez-Prieto Borja, Rocío Díaz Moreno and Elena Trujillo Belso for *CORDE* (see https://www.rae.es/recursos/banco-de-datos/corde). Accessed 9 March 2020. http://dspace.uah.es/dspace/bitstream/handle/10017/7291/Estoria%20de%20 Espa%C3% B1a%20Y.I.2.pdf? sequence=1>) // *General Estoria*, II y III Parte. Edited by Pedro Sánchez-Prieto Borja and Belén Almeida Cabrejas. Madrid: Biblioteca Castro (2009).

[LS1] P. Ovidii Nasonis *Epistulae Heroidum*. Edited by Heinrich Dörrie. Berlin/New York: De Gruyter (1971).

[S2] Enrique de Villena (1384–1434). *Eneida de Virgilio*. Edited by Pedro M. Cátedra. Madrid: Turner, Biblioteca Castro (1994).

[LS2] P. Vergili Maronis *Opera*. Edited by Roger A. B. Mynors. Oxford: Oxford University Press (1969[1990]).

[S4] Juan de Mena (1411–1456). *Ilias latina*. Edited by Tomás González Rolán, M.ª Felisa del Barrio Vega and Antonio López Fonseca. Madrid: Ediciones Clásicas (1996).

[LS4] Juan de Mena (1411–1456). *Ilias latina*. Edited by Tomás González Rolán, María Felisa del Barrio Vega and Antonio López Fonseca. Madrid: Ediciones Clásicas (1996).

Bibliographical references

Albrecht, Jörn. 2017. "Sprachkontakt – schriftlicher Sprachkontakt – Übersetzung (*lato sensu*) – und Übersetzung (*stricto sensu*) als Fakten der Sprachgeschichte und als Gegenstand der Sprachgeschichtsschreibung." In *Romanische Sprachgeschichte und Übersetzung*, edited by Sarah Dessì Schmid and Heidi Aschenberg, 41–52. Heidelberg: Winter-Verlag.

Alonso, Dámaso. 1951. "Sintagmas no progresivos y pluralidades: tres calillas en la prosa castellana." In *Seis calas en la expresión literaria española*.

(Prosa – Poesía – Teatro), Dámaso Alonso and Carlos Bousoño, 21–41. Madrid: Gredos (1979).

Azofra Sierra, María Elena. 2007. "Latinismos artificiales en el siglo XV." *Boletín de la Real Academia Española* 82 (285): 47–57.

Bertolucci Pizzorusso, Valeria. 1957. "L'iterazione sinonimica in testi prosastici mediolatini." *Studi Mediolatini e Volgari* 5: 7–29.

Burgassi, Cosimo, and Elisa Guadagnini. 2014. "Prima dell'*indole*. Latinismi latenti dell'italiano." *Studi di lessicografia italiana* 31: 5–43.

Buridant, Claude. 1980. "Les binômes synonymiques. Esquisse d'une histoire des couples de synonymes du Moyen Âge au XVIIe siècle." *Bulletin du Centre d'Analyse du discours* 4: 5–76.

Bustos Tovar, José Jesús. 1974. *Contribución al estudio del cultismo léxico medieval (1140–1252)*. Madrid: Anejo XXVIII del *Boletín de la Real Academia Española*.

Bustos Tovar, José Jesús de. 2007. "Semicultismos." In *Ex Admiratione et Amicitia: Homenaje a Ramón Santiago*, edited by Inmaculada Delgado Cobos, Inmaculada and Alicia Puigvert Ocal, 179–91. Madrid: Orto.

Casares, Julio. 1992. *Introducción a la lexicografía moderna*, 3rd ed. Madrid: CSIC.

Clavería Nadal, Gloria. 1991. *El latinismo en español*. Barcelona: Universitat Autònoma de Barcelona.

Consiglio Nazionale delle Ricerche. n.d. "OVI: *Corpus OVI dell'italiano antico*." Accessed 9 March 2020. http://gattoweb.ovi.cnr.it/(S(bdci3o45c44mt0554zpajp55))/CatForm01.aspx.

Coseriu, Eugenio. 1977. "Sprachliche Interferenz bei Hochgebildeten." In *Sprachliche Interferenz: Festschrift für Werner Betz*, edited by Herbert Kolb and Hartmut Lauffer, 77–100. Tübingen: Niemeyer.

Del Rey Quesada, Santiago. 2016. "Interferencia latín-romance en Alfonso X: la traducción como pretexto de la elaboración sintáctica." *La corónica* 44 (2): 75–109.

Del Rey Quesada, Santiago. 2017a. "Grupos paratácticos en la traducción del diálogo renacentista." In *Romanische Sprachgeschichte und Übersetzung*, edited by Sarah Dessì Schmid and Heidi Aschenberg, 115–38. Heidelberg: Winter-Verlag.

Del Rey Quesada, Santiago. 2017b. "(Anti-)Latinate Syntax in Renaissance Dialogue: Romance Translations of Erasmus's *Uxor Mempsigamos*." *Zeitschrift für romanische Philologie* 133 (3): 673–708.

Del Rey Quesada, Santiago. 2018a. "Lenguajes de especialidad, sinonimia y elaboración en la historia de la lengua española." In *Nuevas perspectivas en la diacronía de las lenguas de especialidad*, edited by Xosé A. Álvarez, Jairo J. García, Manuel Martí and Ana M. Ruiz, 343–65. Alcalá de Henares: Servicio de Publicaciones de la Universidad de Alcalá.

Del Rey Quesada, Santiago. 2018b. "Latinismo, antilatinismo, hiperlatinismo y heterolatinismo: la sintaxis de la prosa traducida erasmiana del Siglo de Oro." In *Actas del X Congreso Internacional de Historia de la Lengua Española*, edited by M.ª Luisa Arnal Purroy et al., vol. I, 623–45. Zaragoza: Institución Fernando el Católico.

Del Rey Quesada, Santiago. 2018c. "El *De senectute* de Cicerón en romance (ss. XIV-XVI): un estudio sintáctico contrastivo." *Anuari de Filologia. Estudis de Lingüística* 8: 21–56.

Del Rey Quesada, Santiago. 2021a. *Grupos léxicos paratácticos en la Edad Media romance: caracterización lingüística, influencia latinizante y tradicionalidad discursiva*. Frankfurt a. M. et al.: Peter Lang.

Del Rey Quesada, Santiago. 2021b. "Entre género y tradición discursiva: la estructura de la conversación en el diálogo teatral del Siglo de Oro y de la Edad Moderna." In *Pragmática histórica del español: tratamientos, actos de habla y tradiciones discursivas*, edited by Eugenio Bustos Gisbert and Silvia Iglesias Recuero, In press. Sevilla: Editorial de la Universidad de Sevilla.

Del Rey Quesada, Santiago, Florencio del Barrio de la Rosa and Jaime González Gómez. 2018. "Lenguas en contacto, ayer y hoy. Traducción y variación desde una perspectiva filológica. Introducción." In *Lenguas en contacto, ayer y hoy. Traducción y variación desde una perspectiva filológica*, edited by Santiago Del Rey Quesada et al., 9–24. Frankfurt a. M. et al.: Peter Lang.

Dembowski, Peter F. 1976. "Les binômes synonymiques en ancien français." *Kwartalnik Neofilologiczny* 23 (1–2): 81–90.

Diekamp, Clemens. 1972. *Formelhafte Synonymenhäufungen in der Altpoitevinischen Urkundensprache*. München: Wilhelm Fink.

Díez de Revenga Torres, Pilar. 2009. "La lengua notarial en el contexto social de la Edad Media." *Cuadernos del CEMyR* 17: 39–50.

DiVO = Consiglio Nazionale delle Ricerche. n.d. "DiVO: *Corpus del Dizionario dei Volgarizzamenti*." Accessed 9 March 2020. http://divoweb.ovi.cnr.it/(S(ypx0xo45scfvvj45c0eun345))/CatForm01.aspx.

Dworkin, Steven N. 2012. *A History of Spanish Lexicon. A Linguistic Perspective*. Oxford: Oxford University Press.

Elwert, Wilhelm Theodor. 1959. "Zur Synonymendoppelung als Interpretationshilfe." *Archiv für das Studium der Neueren Sprachen* 195: 24–26.

Gutiérrez Cuadrado, Juan. 1993. "Sobre algunos desdoblamientos léxicos del siglo XV." In *Antiqua et nova Romania. Estudios lingüísticos y filológicos en honor de José Mondéjar en su sexagesimoquinto aniversario*, 331–45. Granada: Servicio de Publicaciones de la Universidad de Granada.

Haßler, Gerda. 2001. "Übersetzung als Sprachkontakt." In *Sprachkontakt und Sprachvergleich*, edited by Gerda Haßler, 153–71. Münster: Nodus.

Kabatek, Johannes. 1996. *Die Sprecher als Linguisten. Interferenz- und Sprachwandelphänomene dargestellt am Galicischen der Gegenwart*. Tübingen: Niemeyer.

Kabatek, Johannes. 1997. "Zur Typologie sprachlicher Interferenzen", In *Neue Forschungsarbeiten zur Kontaktlinguistik*, edited by Wolfgang W. Moelleken and Peter J. Weber, 232–41. Bonn: Dümmler.

Kloss, Heinz. 1978. *Die Entwicklung neuer germanischer Kultursprachen seit 1800*, 2nd ed. Düsseldorf: Pädagogischer Verlag Schwann.

Koch, Peter. 1987. *Distanz im Dictamen. Zur Schriftlichkeit und Pragmatik mittelalterlicher Brief- und Redemodelle in Italien*. Freiburg: Habilitation thesis.

Koch, Peter, and Wulf Oesterreicher. 2011. *Gesprochene Sprache in der Romania: Französisch – Italienisch – Spanisch* (Romanistische Arbeitshefte 31), 3rd ed. Berlin/New York: De Gruyter.

Malkiel, Jacob. 1959. "Studies in irreversible binomials." *Lingua* 8: 113–160.

Migliorini, Bruno. 1973. "Le parole semidotte in italiano." In *Lingua d'oggi e di ieri*, 227–237. Caltanissetta–Roma: S. Sciascia.

OVI = Le Banche dati dell' Opera del Vocabolario Italiano Antico. Accessed March 9, 2020. www.ovi.cnr.it.

Pellegrini, Silvio. 1953. "Iterazioni sinonimiche nella Canzone di Rolando." *Studi Mediolatini e Volgari* 1: 155–165.

Pountain, Christopher J. 2011. "Latin and the structure of written Romance." In *The Cambridge History of the Romance Languages. Volume I: Structures*, edited by Martin Maiden, John Charles Smith and Adam Ledgeway, 606–59. Cambridge: Cambridge University Press.

Sălişteanu-Cristea, Oana. 2017. "Alcune considerazioni sui fenomeni allotropici nel lessico italiano: voci ereditarie, voci dotte, voci semidotte." In *"Rem tene, verba sequentur." Latinità e Medioevo romanzo: testi e lingue in contatto*, edited by Elisa Guadagnini and Giulio Vaccaro, 65–101. Alessandria: Edizioni dell'Orso.

Sánchez González de Herrero, María de las Nieves. 2013. "Explicaciones y desdoblamientos léxicos en testimonios científicos medievales castellanos." *Relaciones. Estudios de historia y sociedad* 34 (135): 13–38.

Scavuzzo, Carmelo. 1994. "I latinismi del lessico italiano." In *Storia della lingua italiana. Volume secondo: Scritto e parlato*, edited by Luca Serianni and Pietro Trifone, 469–94. Torino: Einaudi.

Serés, Guillermo. 1997. *La traducción en Italia y España durante el siglo XV. La «Ilíada en romance» y su contexto cultural*. Salamanca: Ediciones Universidad de Salamanca.

Weinreich, Uriel. 1967. *Languages in contact. Findings and problems*. London/Den Haag/Paris: Mouton & Co.

Winter-Froemel, Esme, Araceli López Serena, Álvaro S. Octavio de Toledo y Huerta and Barbara Frank-Job. 2015. "Zur Einleitung / Introducción." In *Diskurstraditionen, Diskurstraditionelles und Einzelsprachliches im Sprachwandel / Tradiciones discursivas, tradicionalidad discursiva e idiomaticidad en el cambio lingüístico*, edited by Esme Winter-Froemel et al., 1–27. Tübingen: Narr (ScriptOralia 141).

Wittlin, Curt. 1991. *Repertori d'expressions multinominals i de grups de sinònims en traduccions catalanes antigues*. Barcelona: Institut d'Estudis Catalans.

Chapter 3

Apuntes sobre la integración de un cultismo médico: la historia de la voz *síntoma*

Isabel García Ortiz

Queen Mary University of London

Resumen

Las líneas de investigación actuales sobre las voces cultas abordan su estudio desde una perspectiva diacrónica e inciden en la necesidad de analizar su proceso de popularización en las lenguas. Tal perspectiva rompe con los planteamientos clásicos, que priorizan el análisis de la primera datación de los préstamos cultos en las lenguas. Partiendo de la perspectiva actual, el presente estudio explora el análisis diacrónico de los derivados de la voz griega σύμπτωμα como un ejemplo del fenómeno de difusión e integración de las voces cultas en español y otras lenguas de Europa occidental. Su análisis permite dar cuenta de los procesos lingüísticos que han favorecido la integración de esta palabra en las lenguas, así como del contexto histórico en el que se ha producido dicha integración. Los resultados del estudio efectivamente demuestran que la primera documentación de una palabra en la lengua no es prueba suficiente de su integración en la misma, sino que, habitualmente, el proceso de integración de los cultismos denominados "de éxito" se produce en el transcurso de varios siglos, y no es hasta fechas recientes que comienza a observarse una tendencia estadística significativa con respecto a su uso.

Summary

Current lines of research on cultured borrowings address the issue from a diachronic perspective and place the emphasis on the need to analyse their process of popularisation and embedding in their host languages. Such a perspective breaks away from traditional approaches to cultured borrowings, which are primarily concerned with questions related to early documentation. In line with the current perspective, this paper explores the diachronic analysis of the derivatives of Gr. σύμπτωμα as a case study of the process of diffusion and embedding of cultured borrowings in Spanish and other languages of Western Europe. The analysis yields evidence for the linguistic and social processes that have operated in the process of social and linguistic embedding of Gr. σύμπτωμα in the languages under study. These findings effectively show that early attestations of a word in a language do not suffice to demonstrate its embedding in the host language. If anything, it has been observed that the linguistic and social embedding of successful cultured borrowings typically takes place over the centuries and it is not until recent times that they begin to display significant statistical patterns of usage.

Keywords

Lexical borrowing, Linguistic elaboration, Latin, Greek, Spanish, Medicine, Metaphor.

1 Introducción

El análisis del proceso de integración de los derivados de la voz griega σύμπτωμα en castellano y de su situación con respecto a lenguas vecinas como el francés o el inglés pretende ser una aportación a un ámbito de investigación más amplio sobre la integración del cultismo médico en las lenguas de Europa occidental. Dicha investigación se desarrolla dentro del programa de doctorado vinculado a la línea de investigación *Loaded Meanings*, cuyo trabajo se enmarca dentro del proyecto *Language Acts and Worldmaking (LAWM)*.

Hasta épocas recientes, el estudio de las voces cultas se ha caracterizado por el interés en la datación de los préstamos cultos, independientemente de su posterior proceso de integración en la lengua receptora. Las líneas actuales de investigación con respecto al cultismo apuntan, no obstante, en otra dirección. La línea de investigación *Loaded Meanings* tiene por objeto de estudio el análisis de las dinámicas del consabido problema de integración (ing. *embedding problem*) (Weinreich, Labov y Herzog 1968) de los préstamos de origen latino en las lenguas de Europa occidental. Si bien los estudios clásicos inciden en la importancia de las primeras dataciones de dichos préstamos en las lenguas, los estudios derivados de esta línea de investigación pretenden demostrar que las primeras documentaciones de una voz culta en un texto no garantizan su posterior integración léxica. Mediante el estudio diacrónico de un número considerable de los denominados "cultismos de éxito", se pretende dar cuenta de los mecanismos lingüísticos que han propiciado la progresiva integración de dichas palabras en el léxico común y familiar de gran parte de las lenguas de Europa occidental. El presente estudio constituye el estudio de un caso.

2 Consideraciones metodológicas

Dado que la línea de investigación *Loaded Meanings* trabaja con los denominados "cultismos de éxito", es decir, aquellos cultismos que se han popularizado exitosamente hasta convertirse en parte del vocabulario común de una determinada lengua, la plantilla de nuestro corpus de estudio son las listas de frecuencias. Para el análisis de los cultismos médicos más comunes, se ha tomado como referencia el diccionario de frecuencias de Davies y Davies (2017), que contiene las 5.000 palabras más comunes del español actual. La voz castellana *síntoma,* que se ofrece como caso de estudio a continuación, ocupa el puesto 2203 en dicha lista de frecuencias.

Para el análisis diacrónico de la voz *síntoma,* se ha combinado el uso de fuentes lexicográficas de todos los idiomas involucrados (griego, latín, inglés, francés y castellano) con el uso de corpus lingüísticos. De acuerdo con los planteamientos de Rojo Sánchez (2010) con respecto a los beneficios del uso combinado del *Corpus del Español (CDE)* y el *Corpus Diacrónico del Español (CORDE),* se ha recurrido al *CDE* para inferir datos estadísticos con respecto al aumento en la frecuencia de uso de la voz castellana *síntoma,* y a *CORDE* para obtener datos concretos con respecto a las primeras documentaciones y posteriores cambios semánticos de la palabra.

3 Estudio de un caso: la voz griega σύμπτωμα

3.1. Lenguas clásicas

El sustantivo neutro σύμπτωμα, originalmente 'suceso, acontecimiento', se formó en griego antiguo por derivación a partir del verbo συμπίπτω, donde συν– significa 'con' y πίπτω significa 'caer'; es decir, 'caer conjuntamente, concurrir'. Dado que el verbo, de uso frecuente en griego antiguo, se asociaba principalmente a circunstancias negativas, como enfermedades o desgracias, el sustantivo σύμπτωμα significó, principalmente, 'desgracia o infortunio' (*Dicciomed,* s.v. "síntoma").

Pese a que este fue el significado más habitual, la palabra desarrolló varias acepciones en griego antiguo, de las cuales dos tienen un significado médico. *Liddell y Scott* (s.v. "σύμπτωμα") recoge como tercera acepción el significado 'symptom' y, como cuarta acepción, 'falling in, collapse', ya sea en un sentido médico o de un caballo.

La documentación más antigua de la palabra de la que se tiene registro se encuentra en las *Historias* de Tucídides, en el siglo V a.C., concretamente en un pasaje del cuarto volumen, en el que el autor narra la emboscada que los arqueros atenienses tienden al ejército espartano. En el ejemplo (1) se pueden ver tanto la fuente original como la traducción al inglés. El σύμπτωμα de Tucídides, traducido al inglés en este pasaje como *predicament,* denota una situación desventajosa, es decir, aquella en la que se encuentran los espartanos tras caer en la trampa tendida por los atenienses.

(1)
"The Lacedaemonians," Thucydides concludes, "were now assailed on both sides, and to compare a smaller thing to a greater, were in the same **predicament** as at Thermopylae" (καὶ οἱ Λακεδαιμόνιοι βαλλόμενοί τε ἀμφοτέρωθεν ἤδη καὶ γιγνόμενοι ἐν τῷ αὐτῷ **ξυμπτώματι,** ὡς μικρὸν μεγάλῳ εἰκάσαι, τῷ ἐν Θερμοπύλαις, 4.36.3).
The "predicament" here is the *σύμπτωμα* (Holmes 2015, 191–192).

Por tanto, la voz griega *σύμπτωμα* no fue, en su origen, un término médico, sino que esta fue una acepción más tardía de la palabra. Los primeros ejemplos de uso de la palabra en documentos médicos se encuentran en los textos de varios autores post–hipocráticos del siglo III a.C., particularmente en Erasístrato (Holmes 2015, 193); es decir, dos siglos más tarde. En esta fecha, la palabra no solo se caracteriza por su escasa frecuencia en textos médicos, sino también por un alto grado de polivalencia (*ibid*). Tanto la baja frecuencia como la imprecisión semántica son datos que sugieren que se trataba de una palabra no arraigada en el discurso médico.

A la luz de la evidencia textual, esta voz griega llegó al latín en forma de préstamo en torno al siglo V d.C. Según las fuentes escritas, las primeras documentaciones de la palabra se encuentran recogidas en los textos médicos de Celio Aureliano y Teodoro Prisciano, ambos autores procedentes del norte de África (*Dicciomed*, s.v. "síntoma"). Según diversas fuentes lexicográficas (*DLD*, s.v. "symptoma"; *Dicciomed*, s.v. "síntoma"), el primer testimonio de su uso en latín proviene de la siguiente cita de Celio Aureliano (2). No obstante, es cuestionable que el autor esté haciendo aquí un uso genuino de la palabra *symptomata*. Más bien, el autor parece estar recurriendo a una estrategia de traducción por la que más bien estaría creando un calco semántico y no incorporando un préstamo griego a la lengua. La oración podría traducirse como: "llamamos *accidentes de las pasiones* a aquello que los griegos llaman *síntoma*". No se trataría, por tanto, de una documentación temprana de la voz latina *symptoma*, sino más bien de un indicio de extensión semántica de la voz latina *accidentia*, que probablemente desarrolló su acepción médica en torno a esta fecha.[1]

(2)
 Passionum accidentia quae **symptomata** Graece vocaverunt (*Dicciomed*, s.v. "síntoma").

---

[1] Según *Dicciomed* (s.v. "síntoma"; s.v. "accidente"), la acepción médica de la voz latina *accidens* devino en latín tardío como resultado de la confusión entre los dos sentidos médicos del griego σύμπτωμα. Según este supuesto, el sentido amplio de la acepción médica de la voz griega σύμπτωμα como 'manifestación de una enfermedad' se mezcló con el significado médico más restringido de 'colapso', particularmente en las obras de Celio Aureliano y otros autores contemporáneos. A este respecto es conveniente recordar que, aunque los derivados del lat. *accidens* perdieron su significado médico a lo largo del siglo XVIII (Tyrkkö 2006, 240), en algunas lenguas este se ha mantenido con el significado de 'indisposición grave que sobreviene repentinamente y que puede dejar secuelas graves o incluso causar la muerte'. Véase, por ejemplo, la colocación en español *accidente cerebrovascular*. Cabe puntualizar, además, que el origen etimológico del Lat. *accidens* corre paralelo al del gr. σύμπτωμα. *Accidens* es un sustantivo neutro compuesto por *ac(d)* 'con' + *cido/cado* 'caer', estructura esta que imita la del gr. σύμπτωμα. El sustantivo *accidens* también está formado por derivación a partir de un verbo (el verbo *accido*). Los distintos significados que la palabra *accidens* tenía en latín parecen provenir de dos términos griegos: de σύμπτωμα tomó los significados 'suceso accidental' y 'señal o indicio de enfermedad' y, en un sentido más restringido, 'enfermedad concomitante'. La acepción 'atributo', por otra parte, parece ser un préstamo semántico del gr. τὸ σῠμβεβηκός, término heredado de la filosofía aristotélica, según la cual σῠμβεβηκός hace referencia a las cualidades no esenciales o complementarias a la sustancia (Roelli 2013: 327; *OED*, s.v. "accident"). Según el *OED* (s.v. "accident"), la acepción médica de la palabra *accidens* fue uno de sus últimos desarrollos semánticos en latín.

En la Figura 3.1 podemos ver una comparación entre los usos de lat. *symptoma* y lat. *accidens*[2] en varios de los diccionarios que ofrece la *DLD*. Se observa que en los diccionarios del latín incluidos en la *DLD* no se recogen de manera sistemática ni la voz latina *symptoma* ni la acepción médica de la voz latina *accidens* antes del latín medieval. Otros usos de la palabra *accidens*, distintos de su acepción médica, sí parecen haber tenido una trayectoria más amplia en latín, ya que todos los diccionarios de la tabla dan testimonio de su uso fundamentalmente con dos significados: (a) como presente de participio activo del verbo *accido* y (b) con el significado de 'suceso accidental'.

De los diccionarios que recogen los usos del latín correspondientes al período clásico, el diccionario de *Lewis y Short* no recoge ni la palabra *symptoma* ni la acepción médica de la voz *accidens*, mientras que *Forcellini* remite, únicamente, a la mencionada cita de Celio Aureliano. Por otra parte, es sabido que la obra de Celio Aureliano de la que proviene el fragmento del ejemplo (2) y que se cita como referencia en *Forcellini*, es en realidad una traducción que el autor hizo de los fragmentos conservados del texto original escrito en griego por Sorano de Éfeso, que el mismo Aureliano tradujo y más tarde reunió bajo el rótulo *De morbis acutis et chronicis*. También en *Forcellini*, la entrada correspondiente a *accidens* remite a su uso médico según el sentido empleado en Celio Aureliano. Por tanto, no es hasta el latín medieval que los diccionarios comienzan a recoger de manera más sistemática las acepciones médicas de ambas palabras, lo que parece sugerir una gradual integración de estas voces en el discurso médico a lo largo de la Edad Media.

---

[2] En latín existían tanto el sustantivo *accidens* como el sustantivo *accidentia*. Aunque algunas de las lenguas vernáculas tomaron ambas voces en préstamo, con el tiempo estas parecen haber mostrado una preferencia por el uso de *accidens* > *accidente(m)*, mientras que lat. *accidentia* solamente sobrevive con un uso muy especializado en lenguas como el inglés o el francés, que utilizan la voz *accidence* con el significado de 'rama de la gramática que se encarga del estudio de los morfemas flexivos' (*OED*, s.v. "accidence").

		Symptoma		Accidens	
		Méd.	No méd.	Méd.	No méd.
Edad Antigua	*Forcellini*	Cel. Aurel. **Acut.**		Cel. Aurel	✓
	Lewis y Short				✓
Período patrístico	*Blaise Patristic*	Cel. Aurel Teod. Prisc.	✓ HIER. *Tr. in psal.* 90, p. 116, 3 et 11		✓
	Souter	Cel. Aurel Teod. Prisc.	✓ HIER. *Tr. in psal.* 90, p. 116, 3 et 11		✓
Edad Media y posterior	*Blaise Medieval*	? Sintoma "Grande sueur" Poet. lat. II, p. 488		✓ "II. accidentia, f. (cl. et lat. chr.) 1. Maladie, accident"	✓
	Du Cange	✓ "Casus quilibet: sæpius de iis quæ in morbis accident"		✓ "2. Accidentia. Morbus, infortunium"	✓

Figura 3.1. Acepciones del Lat. *symptoma* y el Lat. *accidens* en la Database of Latin Dictionaries (DLD)

3.2 Adopción del préstamo en las lenguas de Europa occidental

3.2.1 Primeras documentaciones

Tanto los derivados de la voz latina *accidens* como los derivados de la voz latina *symptoma* están bien documentados en las lenguas vernáculas de Europa occidental.

Según el *OED* (s.v. "accident"), la voz inglesa *accident* adquirió su significado médico antes del siglo XV, mientras que su cognado francés *accident* no desarrolló una acepción médica hasta 1650 (*FEW*, s.v. "accidens"). En castellano, la voz *accidente* se documenta desde 1376 (*Dicciomed*, s.v. "accidente"). Con respecto a los derivados del latín *symptoma,* los testimonios más antiguos en documentos científicos escritos en lengua vernácula datan de finales del siglo XIV, particularmente en el caso del inglés y el francés (*OED*, s.v. "symptom"; *DMF*, s.v. "symptom"), idiomas en los que la palabra se documenta un siglo antes que en castellano (6).

La documentación más temprana del inglés *symptom* que ofrece el *OED* (s.v. "symptom") es la traducción de Trevisa de la obra *De Proprietatibus Rerum* (3), escrita originalmente en latín por Bartolomeo de Glanville en 1240. Estos datos sugieren que el latín *symptoma* podría haber entrado al inglés directamente a través de las traducciones de textos médicos latinos. Según datos del *OED*, la grafía medieval *synthoma* (3) continuó en inglés hasta el siglo XVI, período en el cual se impuso la forma moderna *symptom*, quizá por influencia del francés (*OED,* s.v. "symptom").

(3)
    Yf the heed be corrupte & dystemperate wyth **Synthoma** of corrupcion of heed ache (*OED*: J. Trevisa, translation of *De Propietatibus Rerum*, 1398).

Estudios anteriores sobre el uso de los términos de significación en inglés han mostrado cómo se produjo la integración la voz *symptom* en el lenguaje médico inglés. En Tyrkkö (2006) se muestra cómo la competición entre las palabras *token* (término vernáculo que data del siglo IX), *signo* (cuya primera documentación se remonta al siglo XIII) y *accident* y *symptom*, ambos préstamos del siglo XIV, se resolvió a favor del término *symptom* en el siglo XVIII. Previamente, la palabra *accident* había sido más frecuente que *síntoma* en el discurso médico inglés. El autor atribuye la gradual disminución en la frecuencia de uso de la palabra *accident* a su especialización semántica, ya que la palabra no amplió su campo semántico de 'enfermedad concomitante' a 'señal o indicio de enfermedad', sino que perdió su significado médico antiguo hacia el siglo XVIII y adoptó el significado actual de 'suceso repentino de índole negativa'.[3]

En francés, las documentaciones más tempranas de la palabra se remontan igualmente al siglo XIV. Las fuentes lexicográficas generalmente citan como

---

[3] Las estadísticas se pueden consultar en Tyrkkö 2006, 253–254.

primera documentación del francés *symptôme* una traducción francesa del tratado de Bernard de Gordon, escrito originalmente en latín hacia el siglo XIII y cuya traducción al francés está fechada entre el 1450 y el 1500, donde aparece en una forma plural *sinthomate(s)* (4). En francés, al igual que sucede en inglés, el canal de difusión de la voz latina *symptoma* parece ser la traducción directa de obras latinas. Además, tal como sucede en inglés, la grafía medieval *sinthome* fue sustituida a finales del siglo XVI por la grafía moderna *symptome/symptôme* (*FEW*, s.v. "symptoma").

(4)
> et s'on faisoit plusieurs eructacions et souvent, elles ne peuent estre bonnes, ains sont **sinthomates** et males, car elles signifient corrupcion (*DMF*, Anónimo, *La Practique de maistre Bernard de Gordon appellee Fleur de lys en medicine*, 1450–1500).

En el ejemplo (4), destacan el uso de desdoblamientos léxicos (*sinthomes et males*) y el uso de perífrasis explicativas (*car elles signifient*), mediante las cuales se indica la enfermedad o causa de que dichos síntomas son indicio; en el ejemplo (4), el eructo es *síntoma* de corrupción, *i. e.* alteración de los humores. El uso de estrategias de traducción de esta índole sugiere que se trataba de un préstamo de reciente incorporación. En el ejemplo de uso (5), que data de aproximadamente la misma fecha, se puede observar una estrategia de traducción similar. Se trata de la traducción francesa de 1478 del tratado de cirugía escrito originalmente en latín por Guido de Cauliaco en el siglo XIV.

(5)
> Suppurer et captaplasmer n'est pas selonc la premiere rayson de la cure des appostemes mais aulcunesfoys mictigacions de **sinthomes**, c'est assavoir de la douleur et des accidens (*DMF*, Panis, Nicolas, *Le Guidon de Guy de Chauliac, traduit en français par Nicolas Panis*, 1478).

El autor recurre al desdoblamiento léxico para definir *sinthome* en términos de las palabras *douleur* y *accidens*, dato que sugiere que esta última era también de uso más común que los derivados de la voz latina *symptoma* en el discurso médico francés del siglo XV.

De las documentaciones más tempranas del préstamo en castellano, el ejemplo (6) constituye un testimonio interesante en tanto que se trata de una traducción del título de la obra *De Egritudine & Sinthomate*, que es originalmente una traducción latina de un compendio de obras de Galeno, entre las que figuran *De Symptomatum causis* y *De symptomatum diferentiis* (McVaugh y Ogden 1997). En la traducción *De la enfermedad & sinthomate o accidente*,[4] el autor recurre (a) a la transcripción de la palabra *sinthomate*, hecho que muestra la intertextualidad existente entre el original y la traducción y que parece indicar que *síntoma* es aún un extranjerismo; y (b) al desdoblamiento léxico, que sugiere que *accidente* es, también en castellano, el término de significación más común en el siglo XV.

(6)

De la flema aquosa & serosa se engendra la apostema aquosa & floxa del todo sin dolor. donde en el .vj. de la enfermedad & **sinthomate** o acidente dize por cierto quando habundan las superfluydades serosas en el cuerpo: se engendra el ydropisis (*CORDE*, Anónimo, *Traducción del Tratado de cirugía de Guido de Cauliaco*, 1493).

En el ejemplo (7) se repite la misma estrategia de traducción. En este caso, se trata de la traducción al castellano de la obra de Bernard de Gordon, escrita originalmente en latín. Estos datos son, además, testimonio del contacto intercultural, ya que los registros textuales más antiguos de que se tiene noticia de los derivados de la voz latina *symptoma* proceden de la traducción de las mismas obras tanto en francés como en castellano. En inglés, aunque no constituye el primer ejemplo de uso, el *OED* también documenta la traducción inglesa de la obra de Gordon (8).

(7)

E el fluxo del vientre tiene quatro tiempos los quales se destinguen cerca delas cosas que salen & cerca delos **sinthomates** id est accidentes. Señales.[5] Quando la disinteria viniere delas partes de arriba entonces es ay

---

[4] La mayoría de ejemplos de uso en textos médicos del siglo XV en *CORDE* remiten a esta misma obra. De hecho, la documentación más temprana de la palabra *síntoma* en *CORDE* procede de un fragmento de la traducción castellana del tratado de Guido de Cauliaco (1493), en la cual la mención *sinthomate* aparece en referencia al título original latino de dicha obra, titulada *De Egritudine & Sinthomate*. Es por esto que interpreto el primer ejemplo de uso del término *síntoma* en *CORDE* como una cita y no como evidencia de su uso en castellano.

[5] Al contrario de lo que sucede con los términos *accidente* o *síntoma*, la voz castellana *señal* es una palabra patrimonial, ya presente en el vocabulario médico de la época

dolor & graueza & la egestion es ansy como vna raedura: o como vna lauadura & la sangre es fuertemente vuelta conla egestion (*CORDE*: Anónimo, *Gordonio*, 1495).

A la luz de las primeras documentaciones en castellano, la voz *accidente* parece haber sido más común en la terminología médica del siglo XV que la voz *síntoma*. Siguiendo la metodología de Tyrkkö (2006), la Figura 3.2 que se presenta a continuación muestra el aumento y la disminución en el número de ejemplos de uso de varios términos de significación en textos médicos castellanos según *CORDE*. Dado que *CORDE*, por diversos factores, no facilita la elaboración de estadísticas, esta tabla no es un resumen de las frecuencias relativas de ninguno de estos términos, al igual que tampoco pretende desvelar ningún tipo de patrón estadístico. Se trata, simplemente, de comparar de manera visual los datos en bruto con respecto a la preponderancia, siglo por siglo, de estos términos en los textos médicos recogidos en *CORDE*.

	Siglo XIII	Siglo XIV	Siglo XV	Siglo XVI	Siglo XVII	Siglo XVIII	Siglo XIX	Siglo XX
Accidente	2	18	697	583	221	31	179	601
Signo	0	3	116	61	6	0	4	467
Síntoma	0	0	39	9	2	2	33	3533

Figura 3.2. Términos de significación en textos médicos castellanos según *CORDE*.[6]

Los datos obtenidos en la Figura 3.2 de nuevo sugieren que la palabra *accidente* era más común en el discurso médico que *síntoma*, al menos entre los siglos XIV y XIX. Estos datos son coherentes con la investigación de Tyrkkö (2006), que sugiere que la voz inglesa *symptom* empezó a superar en frecuencia de uso a la voz *accident* hacia el siglo XVIII. El número de

---

alfonsí (Clavería 2004). La palabra *señal* deriva del adjetivo latino sustantivado *signalis* 'que sirve de signo', y este del latín *signum* (Corominas, s.v. "seña"). Señala el mismo autor que la palabra *señal* "ha usurpado la mayoría de funciones de SIGNUM en todos los romances de occidente" (*ibid*).

[6] Debido a las limitaciones de espacio, se ha excluido de este análisis el estudio de la voz *señal*, término patrimonial de uso muy genérico, como ya se ha mencionado, y que cuenta con abundantes ejemplos de uso en *CORDE*.

resultados obtenidos en *CORDE* para el siglo XVIII es, no obstante, muy bajo para los tres términos consultados, aunque esto puede deberse a las limitaciones en el propio diseño del corpus. En la Figura 3.2, la palabra *signo* aparenta ser más común que *síntoma* en documentos del siglo XV, pero esto es así porque la palabra se utilizaba, fundamentalmente, en textos de carácter astrológico (8). En el siglo XX, el número de resultados que *CORDE* ofrece para *síntoma* sobrepasa en número a los otros dos términos de significación. Además, el aumento en el número de resultados de *signo,* que parece resurgir en la literatura médica a partir del siglo XX, puede deberse a un intento de refinamiento de la terminología médica promovido por la comunidad médica internacional e iniciado en el siglo XIX (*Dicciomed*, s.v. "síntoma"), y que tenía por objetivo distinguir entre el signo objetivo y el síntoma subjetivo (9).

(8)
Entonce conuiene a entrar el sol enel comienço del **signo** de Aries / por la qual razon escaliente el ayre: por que el Sol esta en derecho dela nuestra cabeça & son sus rayos mas fuertes que non enel inuierno que non vienen en derecho de nuestra cabeça (*CORDE*: Anónimo, *Sevillana medicina de Juan de Aviñón*, c 1381–1418).

(9)
La tabes dorsal, en su comienzo, es una polirradiculitis sifilítica, y en tal fase puede persistir largo tiempo, dando lugar a crisis viscerales dolorosas (v. página 263 y a los clásicos dolores fulgurantes tabéticos, que en muchos casos son, durante largo tiempo, el único **síntoma subjetivo** de la enfermedad y no rara vez atribuídos (sic) a las más diversas causas: reumáticas, etc. (*CORDE*: Marañón, Gregorio, *Manual de diagnóstico etiológico*, 1943).

Por último, la Figura 3.2 muestra un aparente descenso en la frecuencia de uso de la palabra *accidente* en textos médicos en el siglo XVII, seguida por un nuevo aumento de frecuencia en el siglo XX. Este posterior aumento de frecuencia coincide en el tiempo con una nueva extensión semántica de la palabra (10), que añadió el significado de "suceso repentino e inesperado que provoca secuelas" (*CED*, s.v. "accident") y que tuvo lugar, no solo en castellano, sino también en otras lenguas como el inglés.

(10)
>   Vómitos en la dilatación aguda del estómago – Constituyen el síntoma principal de este grave **accidente**: vómitos intensos, sin esfuerzo, no fecaloideos, con rápida deshidratación, con enorme meteorismo alto, sin dolor de vientre marcado, sobrevenidos después de una laparotomía o en el curso de una infección aguda, etcétera (*CORDE*: Marañón, Gregorio, *Manual de diagnóstico etiológico*, 1943).

Al igual que sucedió con los términos de significación con los que la palabra *síntoma* competía, esta última también estuvo sujeta a cambios semánticos a lo largo del tiempo. Si bien en los primeros siglos tras la primera documentación de la palabra en castellano esta se utiliza fundamentalmente en su sentido restringido de 'enfermedad concomitante', conforme su uso se asienta en el discurso científico, esta amplía su significado y comienza a designar, en un sentido más general, 'señal o indicio de enfermedad'. Aunque hay pocos ejemplos de uso de la palabra *síntoma* en *CORDE* entre los siglos XVI y XIX, los ejemplos de uso del siglo XIX muestran que esta ampliación de significado ya está consolidada (11).

(11)
>   Lo mismo que con el cólera pasa con todas las virulentas, que consisten en la alteración de la sangre, obran por contacto, como el ácido exanhídrico. Los coléricos presentan todos los **síntomas** de un envenenamiento (*CORDE*, Orduña Rodríguez, Tomás, *Manual de higiene privada*, 1881).

3.2.2. Metaforización

Hacia el siglo XVII ya empiezan a aparecer usos figurados de la palabra, como este que vemos en el ejemplo (12), lo que parece sugerir que la palabra amplió su significado médico antes del siglo XIX y que fue el proceso de metaforización lo que permitió su consiguiente uso en otros géneros textuales.

(12)
>   Sin embargo, lejos de contener el mal tan legítimos y saludables preservativos, insulta indiferentemente médicos y enfermos, y lo que antes se recelaba **síntoma** de mortal letargo, hoy se celebra como decretorio de apacible sueño (*CORDE*: Isla, José Francisco de, *Historia del famoso predicador Fray Gerundio de Campazas alias Zotes*, 1758).

En el ejemplo (13), el sentido de la palabra parece ser metonímico más que metafórico. No obstante, en el ejemplo (14), que data de finales del siglo XVIII, ya se puede observar un uso plenamente metafórico, incluso poético.

(13)
> La tierra no siente los funestos síntomas del invierno, ni el aire está expuesto a la intolerable variedad de las estaciones; en la tierra reina una perpetua primavera y en el aire un continuado estío, al cual se acostumbran fácilmente sus habitantes; pero el continuo sudor de sus cuerpos y las frutas con que en todo tiempo les regala la tierra, los exponen a varias enfermedades que no se conocen en otros países. (*CORDE*: Clavijero, Francisco Javier, *Historia Antigua de México*, 1780).

Las fechas que ofrece *CORDE* con respecto a los primeros usos figurados de la palabra coinciden con las fechas propuestas para otras lenguas, lo que constituye una muestra de contacto intercultural y apunta nuevamente a la existencia de una dinámica transnacional. En el caso del inglés, el *FEW* (s.v. "symptoma") sugiere que el proceso de metaforización de la palabra se produjo antes que en otras lenguas de Europa occidental, y propone las fechas de 1722 para el sustantivo *symptom* y 1751 para el adjetivo *symptomatic*. El *TLFi* (s.v. "symptôme") sugiere unas fechas similares con respecto al francés *symptome*. Las fuentes lexicográficas del castellano, por otra parte, no recogen la acepción metafórica de la palabra hasta el siglo XIX. El diccionario de Salvá (1846) es el primero en recoger la definición "met(afórico). Señal, indicio, presagio".

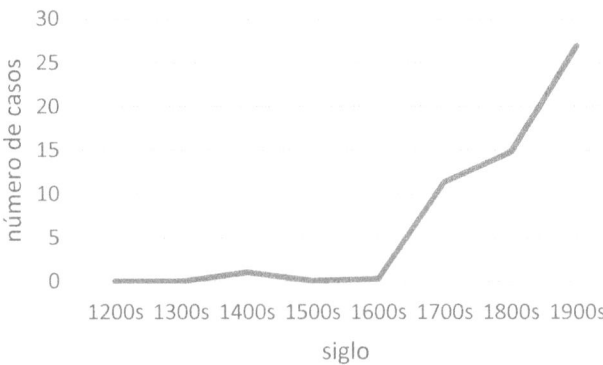

Figura 3.3. Aumento en la frecuencia de uso de la voz *síntoma* en español según datos del *CDE*.

Esta apertura semántica que fue resultado de los procesos de metaforización descritos arriba puede al mismo tiempo explicar el aumento en la frecuencia de uso de la palabra *síntoma* que se produjo a partir del 1600s en castellano, tal y como muestra la Figura 3.3, en el que vemos cómo la palabra aumenta drásticamente su frecuencia, particularmente en el siglo XVIII.

4 Conclusiones

De este análisis con respecto a la difusión de la voz griega σύμπτωμα, primero en latín y, más tarde, en las lenguas de Europa occidental, se desprenden tres conclusiones fundamentales. En primer lugar, el estudio diacrónico de la palabra *síntoma* demuestra que entre el primer ejemplo de uso de la palabra y su integración lingüística pueden mediar siglos de diferencia. En segundo lugar, la labor de los traductores en la comunidad científica internacional fue decisiva para la transmisión de la palabra a las lenguas vernáculas, hecho que explica que *síntoma* sea hoy día una palabra compartida por las distintas lenguas de Europa occidental. Finalmente, el proceso de integración de la palabra en la lengua fue paulatino y en él intervinieron procesos lingüísticos cuya acción puede observarse a través del estudio de los corpus históricos. En el caso de la palabra *síntoma*, los factores lingüísticos decisivos para su integración parecen ser (a) el refinamiento de su significado, que puso fin a la ambigüedad y la polivalencia del término; (b) una ampliación semántica que permitió que la palabra se difundiera a otros registros textuales y (c) su consiguiente metaforización.

Referencias bibliográficas

Diccionarios

Blaise Medieval = Blaise, Albert. 1975. *Lexicon latinitatis medii aevi*. Turnhout: Brepols. Fecha de consulta agosto 2020. http://clt.brepolis.net.libproxy.kcl.ac.uk/dld/pages/QuickSearch.aspx.

Blaise Patristic = Blaise, Albert. 1967. *Dictionnaire latin-français des auteurs chrétiens*. Turnhout: Brepols. Fecha de consulta agosto 2020. http://clt.brepolis.net.libproxy.kcl.ac.uk/dld/pages/QuickSearch.aspx.

CED = *Cambridge English Dictionary*. Cambridge: Cambridge University Press. Fecha de consulta agosto 2020. https://dictionary.cambridge.org/.

Corominas = Corominas, Joan, y José Antonio Pascual. 1980–1991. *Diccionario crítico etimológico castellano e hispánico,* 6 vols. Madrid: Gredos.

Davies, Mark, y Kathy Hayward Davies. 2017. *A Frequency Dictionary of Spanish. Core Vocabulary for Learners*, 2ª ed. Londres: Routledge.

Dicciomed = Cortés Gabaudán, Francisco. 2012–. *Diccionario médico-biológico, histórico y etimológico*. Salamanca: Universidad de Salamanca. Fecha de consulta agosto 2020. https://dicciomed.usal.es/.

DMF = Nancy, ATILF/Nancy-Université y Centre National de la Recherche Scientifique. *Dictionnaire du Moyen Français*. Fecha de consulta agosto 2020. http://www.atilf.fr/dmf/.

Du Cange = Du Cange, Charles du Fresne. *Glossarium mediae et infimae latinitatis*. *1883–1887*. Niort: L. Favre. Fecha de consulta agosto 2020. http://clt.brepolis.net.libproxy.kcl.ac.uk/dld/pages/QuickSearch.aspx.

Etymonline = Douglas, Harper. 2001–. *Harper Douglas Online Etymology Dictionary*. Fecha de consulta agosto 2020. https://www.etymonline.com/.

FEW = Wartburg, Walter von. 1922–2002. *Französisches Etymologisches Wörterbuch. Eine Darstellung des galloromanischen Sprachschatzes*. Bonn/Heidelberg/Leipzig/Berlín/Basilea: Klopp/Winter/Teubner/Zbinden. Fecha de consulta agosto 2020. https://apps.atilf.fr/lecteurFEW/.

Forcellini = Forcellini, Egidio et al. 1940. *Lexicon Titius Latinitatis*. Padua: Typis seminarii. Fecha de consulta agosto 2020. http://clt.brepolis.net.libproxy.kcl.ac.uk/dld/pages/QuickSearch.aspx.

Lewis y Short = Lewis, Charlton Thomas and Charles Short. 1879. *A Latin Dictionary*. Oxford: Clarendon Press. Fecha de consulta agosto 2020. http://www.perseus.tufts.edu/hopper/text?doc=Perseus:text:1999.04.0059.

Liddell y Scott = Liddell, Henry, Scott, Robert, and Henry S. Jones. 1843–. *The Online Liddell-Scott-Jones Greek-English Lexicon*. Fecha de consulta agosto 2020. http://stephanus.tlg.uci.edu/lsj/#eid=1.

OED = Simpson, John, and Edmund Weiner. 1989–. *Oxford English Dictionary*. Oxford: Oxford University Press. Fecha de consulta agosto 2020. https://en.oxforddictionaries.com/.

Salvá, Vicente. 1846. *Nuevo diccionario de la lengua castellana*. París: Garnier Hermanos. Fecha de consulta agosto 2020. http://buscon.rae.es/ntlle/SrvltGUILoginNtlle.

Souter = Souter, Alexander, 1957. *A glossary of Later Latin to 600 A.D.* Oxford: Clarendon Press. Fecha de consulta agosto 2020. http://clt.brepolis.net.libproxy.kcl.ac.uk/dld/pages/QuickSearch.aspx.

TLFi = ATILF – CNRS and Université de Lorraine. *Trésor de la Langue Française informatisé*. Fecha de consulta agosto 2020. http://www.atilf.fr/tlfi.

Corpus y bases de datos

CDE = Davies, Mark. 2002–. *Corpus del Español: 100 million words, 1200s–1900s*. Fecha de consulta agosto 2020. http://www.corpusdelespanol.org.

CORDE = Real Academia Española. *Banco de datos (CORDE). Corpus diacrónico del español.* Fecha de consulta agosto 2020. http://www.rae.es.

DLD= Brepols Publishers. 2001–. *Database of Latin Dictionaries.* Fecha de consulta agosto 2020. http://apps.brepolis.net/BrepolisPortal/default.aspx.

Otras referencias

Clavería, Gloria. 2004. "Aproximación a los inicios de la lengua de la medicina: la terminología patológica en la lengua alfonsí." En *Revista de Investigación Lingüística*, 7, 71–90.

Holmes, Brooke. 2015. "Medicine and Misfortune: *Symptōma* in Greek Medical Writing." En *The Frontiers of Ancient Greece. Essays in Honor of Heinrich von Staden*, editado por Brooke Holmes y Klaus-Dietrich Fischer, 191–209. Berlín / Múnich / Boston: Walter de Gruyter.

McVaugh, Michael R., y Margaret S. Ogden. 1997. *Inventarium Sive Chirurgia Magna. Volume Two: Commentary* (Leiden/Nueva York/Colonia: Brill).

Roelli, Philipp. 2013. "Globale Untersuchung zum Sondervokabular des Thomas von Aquin." En *Archivum latinitatis medii aevi: Bulletin du Cange*, 71, 323–344.

Rojo Sánchez, Guillermo. 2010. "Sobre codificación y explotación de corpus textuales: otra comparación del *Corpus del Español* con el *CORDE* y el *CREA*." En *Lingüística* 24: 11–50.

Tyrkkö, Jukka. 2006. "From Tokens to Symptoms: 300 Years of Developing Discourse on Medical Diagnosis in English Medical Writing." En *Diachronic Perspectives on Domain–Specific English*, editado por Irma Taavitsainen y Marina Dossena, 229–254. Berna: Peter Lang.

Weinreich, Uriel, William Labov, y Marvin I. Herzog. 1968. "Empirical Foundations for a Theory of Language Change." En *Directions for Historical Linguistics: A Symposium,* editado por Winfred P. Lehmann y Yakov Malkiel, 95–189. Austin: University of Texas Press.

Chapter 4

El latinismo en los titulares de la prensa deportiva española

Susana Guerrero Salazar

Universidad de Málaga

Resumen

Este trabajo se centra en un aspecto relevante que aún no ha sido atendido: el uso del latinismo en los titulares de la prensa deportiva española. El corpus analizado consta de 3000 titulares extraídos de los cuatro diarios deportivos de pago más leídos en España (*Marca*, *As*, *Mundo Deportivo* y *Sport*), en un marco temporal que abarca desde 2008 a 2019. El objetivo es responder a las siguientes preguntas de investigación: qué latinismos aparecen en la titulación deportiva, cómo, en qué tipo de titulares y con qué función. Se trata de una investigación descriptiva y analítica con un enfoque pragmático, donde interesa el latinismo crudo en un contexto de uso concreto (el titular deportivo). Tras el análisis realizado, se demuestra que el 4,8% de los titulares presentan un latinismo instalado en la lengua (la mayoría de ellos sancionados por el diccionario de la Real Academia Española), que, en algunos casos, se escribe de manera errónea o presenta fluctuaciones ortográficas u ortotipográficas; que puede llegar a constituir por sí solo un titular (incluso de portada), bien de tipo expresivo y/o creativo, y, en menor media, apelativo. El 47% de los casos constatados son unidades fraseológicas latinas desautomatizadas semántica y/o formalmente, sobre todo por sustitución o adición de algún elemento ajeno. El latinismo es, por tanto, un recurso de intensificación, cuya función es producir humor, ironía o evaluar algún hecho o a alguna persona del ámbito deportivo de manera positiva o claramente tendenciosa.

Summary

This work focuses on a relevant aspect that has not yet been addressed: the use of Latinisms in the headlines of the Spanish sports press. The analysed corpus consists of 3000 headlines extracted from the four most-read paid sports newspapers in Spain (*Marca*, *As*, *Mundo Deportivo* and *Sport*), in a time frame that covers from 2008 to 2019. The objective is to answer the following research questions: what Latinisms appear in the sports title, how, in what type of headlines and with what function. It is a descriptive and analytical research project with a pragmatic approach, where the focus of interest is the raw Latinism in a concrete context of use (the sports headline). After analysis, it is shown that 4.8% of the headlines present a Latinism which is embedded in the language (most of them sanctioned by the Real Academia Española dictionary) and which, in some cases, is written incorrectly or presents orthographic or orthotypographic fluctuations; and that the Latinism can by itself constitute a headline (even on a front page), which can be either of an expressive and/or creative type, or, to a lesser extent, appellative. 47% of the cases found are Latin phraseological units which are manipulated semantically and/or formally, mainly by the replacement by or addition of some other element. Latinisms are, therefore, a resource of intensification, whose function is to produce humour, irony or to evaluate some fact or some person in the field of sport in a positive or clearly tendentious way.

Keywords

Latin, Journalism, Sport, Linguistic humour, Spanish.

1 Introducción

Los pocos trabajos que existen sobre el uso del cultismo en el periodismo actual en lengua española han puesto de manifiesto el alto porcentaje de latinismos que se emplean en la prensa. Entre ellos, el estudio de Truneanu (2005), que versa sobre la prensa venezolana y destaca las vacilaciones ortográficas, los problemas con los plurales y acentos, y los cambios entre el significado literal de la expresión y su significado en el contexto. Así mismo, los trabajos de Campos Vargas (2010, 2012 y 2014) se centran en la prensa costarricense, donde se advierte también la presencia continua de latinismos procedentes de distintos ámbitos.

Varios son los estudios sobre la prensa española, como el de Otaola Olano (2005), quien muestra el elevado número de formas latinas que se registran en todas las secciones del diario *El País* (muchas no sancionadas por los diccionarios). Sánchez Vidal (2013) ha realizado –además de una propuesta didáctica con los latinismos que aparecen en las viñetas gráficas de distintos periódicos españoles (Sánchez Vidal 2012)– un estudio sobre el acatamiento que hace la prensa a las normas académicas que atañen a la escritura de estas formas cultas.

Relacionado también con la adecuación a las normas académicas destaca el trabajo de Hourani Martín (2012), que se ocupa del tratamiento ortográfico, ortotipográfico y lexicográfico de los extranjerismos crudos (entre ellos, los latinismos), no solo en periódicos sino también en revistas. Entre las conclusiones, destaca que los latinismos ocupan el segundo puesto en frecuencia de uso (11,2%) —después de los anglicismos (68,5%)—, que aparecen fundamentalmente en los ámbitos científico y técnico y, que, en general, presentan un alto grado de corrección ortográfica (90%).

Ninguno de estos estudios se centra en la prensa deportiva, ni siquiera incluye periódicos deportivos en su corpus de análisis, a pesar de que una característica del discurso deportivo es la alternancia de diferentes registros lingüísticos y su heterogeneidad, pues, junto al léxico técnico, conviven el argótico, el coloquial, e incluso el vulgar, así como neologismos, enlaces arcaizantes y latinismos (Guerrero Salazar 2018c, 39–41).

Por ello, he decidido centrarme en este ámbito y analizar un aspecto que aún no ha sido atendido: el uso del latinismo en los titulares deportivos. El objetivo es responder a las siguientes preguntas de investigación: qué latinismos se emplean en la titulación deportiva, cómo aparecen ortográfica y ortotipográficamente, en qué tipo de titulares y con qué función.

Presento una investigación descriptiva y analítica con un enfoque pragmático, ya que me interesa el latinismo crudo en un contexto de uso concreto (el titular deportivo). Me baso para el estudio en el concepto de *intensificación*, pues, como se demuestra en Guerrero Salazar (2017b), los titulares deportivos se sustentan fundamentalmente en esta categoría pragmática, pues, a través de la intensificación, se realza la actitud del periodista, cuya finalidad es persuadir y manifestar abiertamente el acuerdo o desacuerdo hacia un hecho, equipo o personaje concreto. La hipótesis de partida es que el latinismo funciona en el titular deportivo, sobre todo, como un recurso intensificador, al igual que los extranjerismos o los neologismos cuando se utilizan con función estilística (Guerrero Salazar 2018a, 2018b, 2020).

El corpus analizado consta de un total de 3.000 titulares extraídos de los cuatro diarios deportivos de pago más leídos en España (*Marca*, *As*, *Mundo*

Deportivo y *Sport*),[1] en sus ediciones digitales, en un marco temporal que abarca desde 2008 a 2019. Para su clasificación, he seguido la taxonomía propuesta por López Hidalgo (2001, 48–56),[2] quien constata siete tipos de titulares, de los cuales solo tres aparecen en el corpus: expresivos (manifiestan sentimientos), creativos (llaman la atención mediante juegos de palabras ingeniosos o estéticos) y, en menor medida, apelativos (tratan de modificar o reforzar las actitudes de los lectores, sobre todo para suscitar su emotividad).

2 Análisis del corpus

Como ha señalado Martino (2012, 365–368), el latín, con su aura de prestigio, consigue destacar entre otros mensajes y dar un toque de esnobismo, incluso cuando se une a la ironía. Muchas frases latinas son sentencias que comparten características estructurales comunes con el titular (también con el eslogan publicitario), como, por ejemplo, la brevedad, la concisión y la capacidad de impactar e imprimirse en la memoria.

Así mismo, el titular es un microtexto en el que la información tiene que estar muy condensada y donde el cultismo ha de servir de reclamo para animar a la lectura. A pesar de la brevedad que lo caracteriza, en el titular pueden convivir cultismos y expresiones coloquiales, como sucede en el siguiente ejemplo con *rara avis* ("persona o cosa conceptuada como singular excepción de una regla cualquiera", *DLE*)[3] y la expresión *empeinazo total*; en esta se unen dos recursos intensificadores característicos de la titulación deportiva, el sufijo *-azo* y el adjetivo *total* pospuesto al sustantivo (Guerrero Salazar 2017b y 2018b):

(1)
    El gol más "**rara avis**" de Beckham fue al Levante: ¡"**empeinazo total**"! (as.com, 7 de septiembre de 2017).

---

[1] Según el EGM, en 2018, el diario *Marca* ha sido el diario impreso más leído en España; el tercer lugar lo ocupa el diario deportivo *As*; el octavo, *Mundo Deportivo* y el décimo, *Sport*. Consulta realizada el 18 de noviembre de 2019 en http://reporting.aimc.es/index.html#/main/diarios.

[2] En dicha clasificación se basa Guerrero Salazar (2017a).

[3] Las palabras y locuciones latinas se escriben como aparecen en el diccionario académico (cito como *DEL*), de donde se toman las definiciones (Real Academia Española 2014). En los titulares se respeta la escritura tal como aparece en el periódico.

Los latinismos registrados en el corpus son préstamos lexicalizados, esto es, palabras y expresiones consagradas que pertenecen al acervo colectivo y que actúan a modo de clichés; se emplean a sabiendas de que son fácilmente entendibles, de ahí que, en su mayoría, estén sancionados por el diccionario académico, como sucede en los ejemplos con *sine die* ("sin plazo fijo, sin fecha. Se utiliza generalmente con referencia a un aplazamiento"), *in memoriam* ("en memoria, en recuerdo") o *primus inter pares* ("primero entre sus iguales, más destacado e importante entre otras personas o cosas de la misma condición o dignidad"):

(2)
La rusa Ekaterina Glazyrina, suspendida "**sine die**" por sospechas de dopaje (marca.com, 10 de febrero de 2017).

(3)
Bernardo Salazar, "**in memoriam**" (as.com, 4 de noviembre de 2018).

(4)
Gales, Francia e Inglaterra, "**primus inter pares**", los favoritos (marca.com, 31 de enero de 2013).

El adjetivo *invictus* (no registrado en el *DLE*) convive con la forma castellana *invicto*, normalmente en titulares expresivos de carácter hiperbólico:

(5)
a. Los "**invictus**" Warriors sobreviven al Curry más terrenal (marca.com, 10-XI-15).
b. El reto del **Invicto** Barça (marca.com, 19 de marzo de 2018).

Los latinismos de origen religioso constatados son unidades fraseológicas o vocablos que se emplean comúnmente en el lenguaje cotidiano, como sucede con *vía crucis* (con el sentido coloquial de "calvario") o con la locución sustantiva *mea culpa*, que, en el ámbito deportivo, se repite con frecuencia cuando se aceptan los errores de la derrota:

(6)
El **vía crucis** particular del "mesías verdiblanco" (sport.es, 25 de septiembre de 2010).

(7)
Giménez entona el **mea culpa**: "De los errores se aprende" (as.com, 31 de octubre de 2015).

El término *réquiem* ("composición que se canta con el texto litúrgico de la misa de difuntos, o parte de él", *DLE*) ha sido constado en siete ocasiones. A veces se emplea con un sentido recto, como despedida u homenaje a personas fallecidas, como sucede en (8a), que hace alusión a los veintitrés jugadores internacionales del fútbol zambiano que se estrellaron en avión. Este latinismo se usa también para anunciar que algo ha desaparecido definitivamente, bien con un sentido irónico o incluso tendencioso (como sucede en el (8b) con el estilo de juego del Barça), o simplemente lúdico (como en (8c), que hace alusión a unas zapatillas deportivas).

(8)
    a. **Réquiem** por Zambia (marca.com, 8 de febrero de 2012).
    b. **Réquiem** por el estilo (marca.com, 23 de mayo de 2019).
    c. Kipchoge y Kosgei, ¿el **réquiem** de las Nike Vaporfly Next%? (marca.com, 13 de octubre de 2019).

En el siguiente titular el latinismo *páter*, utilizado con sentido hiperbólico, se emplea metafóricamente con el significado de individuo que ejerce una gran potestad sobre un grupo, acepción que no está sancionada en el *DLE*, que recoge *páter* únicamente con el significado religioso de "sacerdote":

(9)
    ¿Qué fue de Carlos Marchena? El "pater" de la Selección (as.com, 1 de septiembre de 2017).

Destacan también las expresiones provenientes del ámbito jurídico, como *modus operandi* ("manera especial de actuar o trabajar para alcanzar el fin propuesto"), *in situ* ("en el lugar, en el sitio"), *sui géneris* ("dicho de una cosa: De un género o especie muy singular y excepcional"), o *motu proprio* ("libre y voluntariamente, por iniciativa propia"):

(10)
    Cristiano Ronaldo vio "**in situ**" el partido de Portugal (marca.com, 14 de noviembre de 2009).

(11)
    El **modus operandi** de Pep evitó que Gabriel Jesús fuera al Madrid (as.com, 6 de febrero de 2017).

(12)

　　La retirada "**sui géneris**" de Chema Martínez (sport.es, 24 de octubre de 2017).

(13)

　　Abelardo explota "**motu proprio**" por el trato arbitral (marca.com, 6 de abril de 2015).

Del ámbito académico he registrado *alma mater*, que no se utiliza con el sentido que recoge el *DLE* ("f. U. para designar a la universidad"), sino para referirse a una persona que actúa como impulsora de algo (24a–b), y *cum laude* ("dicho de la calificación de ciertas notas: máxima", *DLE*):

(14)

　　La LFP le da un "**cum laude**" a Williams (mundodeportivo.com, 27 de mayo de 2019).

De las expresiones y frases históricas se constatan cinco: *alea iacta est*,[4] *veni, vidi, vici*,[5] *mens sana in corpore sano*,[6] *carpe diem*[7] y *annus horribilis*.[8]

---

[4] Según el *DLE*: "expr. U. en determinadas situaciones para indicar que ya no es posible volver atrás". Según Herrero Llorente (1985, 43): "*La suerte está echada* (Suet., *Caes.* 32). Frase atribuida a César en el momento de atravesar el Rubicón y marchar con su ejército contra Roma. En realidad, es la traducción al latín de un verso de Menandro. Suele emplearse cuando se toma una decisión importante".

[5] Herrero Llorente (1985, 395): "*Llegué, vi y vencí*. Famoso y lacónico parte por el que César comunica al Senado la rapidez de su victoria sobre Farneces, rey del Ponto, el año 47 a. de C. (Suet., *Caes.* 37, 2). Se usa para expresar la facilidad y rapidez con que se ha llevado a cabo una empresa".

[6] Herrero Llorente (1985, 219): "*Mente sana en cuerpo sano* (Iuv. 10, 356). Dice el poeta que el hombre verdaderamente sabio no pide al cielo más que la salud del alma y la del cuerpo: *orandum est ut sit mens sana in corpore sano*. Sin embargo, suele citarse esta expresión para indicar que la salud del cuerpo es condición indispensable para la salud del alma".

[7] Herrero Llorente (1985, 73): "*Goza del día presente, disfruta de lo presente* (Hor., *Od.* 1, 11, 8)". *DLE*: "Exhortación a aprovechar el presente ante la constancia de la fugacidad del tiempo".

[8] La frase se utilizó en 1891 para describir al año 1870, momento en que la Iglesia Católica Romana definió el dogma de la infalibilidad del papa. Sin embargo, debe su popularidad a la Reina Isabel II en el discurso de Guildhall el 24 de noviembre de 1992, el 40 aniversario de su coronación. Según Otaola Olano (2005, 311), a raíz de entonces

Como comprobaremos más adelante, la prensa deportiva suele desautomatizar muchas de estas unidades fraseológicas, casi siempre con función lúdica:

(15)
> **Mens sana in corpore sano** (marca.com, 4 de septiembre de 2011).

Hay casos en los que, junto al cultismo, se aporta la traducción (16a); en otras ocasiones aparece exclusivamente la traducción castellana (16b), incluso modificada (42a–d):

(16)
  a. Como dijo Julio César al cruzar el Rubicón: "**Alea iacta est**" (la suerte está echada) (marca.com, 19 de abril de 2010).
  b. **La suerte está echada**: ¡a por ellos! (sport.es, 15 de febrero de 2019).

El cultismo puede constituir por sí solo un titular (17), incluso de portada (18–19), en titulares de tipo expresivo donde destaca el carácter hiperbólico:

(17)
> **Statu quo** (mundodeportivo.com, 29 de marzo de 2017).

(18)
> **Invictus** *(Mundo Deportivo*, 30 de abril de 2018, portada).

(19)
> **In extremis** (*Sport*, 15 de septiembre de 2013, portada).

2.1 Vacilaciones ortográficas y ortotipográficas

En cuanto al modo en que aparecen escritos los latinismos, se aprecia bastante fluctuación, ya que unas veces se emplean comillas, otras no, a veces se mantiene el acento (*álter ego*), otras se incorpora un guion (*alter-ego*):

(20)
  a. Los **alter-ego** de Rafa Nadal (mundodeportivo.com, 9 de junio de 2010).
  b. Márquez tendrá su "**alter ego**" de cera en el Museo de Madrid (mundodeportivo.com, 20 de abril de 2016).

---

se ha empezado a usar en el habla española. El *DLE* lo registra como "Año de gran infortunio".

c. Keylor se luce ante su **álter ego** (mundodeportivo.com, 22 de junio de 2018).

A pesar de que la norma de la Real Academia Española dice que los latinismos deben escribirse en cursiva, el hecho de que estén tan instalados en la lengua favorece el que aparezcan sin ningún tipo de marca:

(21)
Florentino debería ser **persona non grata** en el Camp Nou (marca.com, 20 de junio de 2011).

(22)
Se mantiene el **statu quo** en el top 20 (mundodeportivo.com, 23 de mayo de 2016).

Todas estas fluctuaciones tienen que ver, en parte, con los cambios académicos, pues con anterioridad a la publicación de la *Ortografía de la lengua española* (Real Academia Española y Asociación de Academias de la Lengua Española 2010), a los latinismos se les daba el tratamiento de voces españolas, por lo que debían acentuarse (de hecho, *réquiem* siempre aparece acentuado en el corpus). Tras su publicación, se equiparan en el tratamiento a los extranjerismos de las lenguas vivas, con lo que deben mantener su forma original y escribirse en cursiva o entrecomillados. Como ha demostrado Sánchez Vidal (2013), el grado de incumplimiento de la norma académica es bastante elevado en la prensa en general.

En cuanto a los errores que afectan a los cultismos, se detecta que la locución latina *grosso modo* aparece sistemáticamente mal escrita, pues aparece precedida de la preposición *a*:

(23)
Los Redtails o caos a **"Grosso" modo** (as.com, 1 de mayo de 2013).

Se advierte también la vacilación en cuanto a la concordancia en la expresión *alma mater*, que debe escribirse en femenino, sin tilde y en cursiva, pues, como explica la Fundéu: "La norma de cambiar *la* por *el* ante palabras femeninas que comienzan con *a* tónica solo afecta a sustantivos (*el alma contenta*, *el aula espaciosa*), pero en esta locución latina *alma* es un adjetivo que significa 'que alimenta', tal como indican los diccionarios de latín":[9]

---

[9] https://www.fundeu.es/recomendacion/la-alma-mater-no-el-alma-mater-1563/. Consulta realizada el 16 de septiembre de 2019.

(24)
    a. El "**alma mater**" de Tim Duncan silencia al anotador español del futuro (marca.com, 10 de diciembre de 2016).
    b. Alexis Sánchez, la "**alma mater** gunner" (mundodeportivo.com, 2 de noviembre de 2016).

Otro error es la expresión *non grato*, en lugar de *persona non grata* ("persona rechazada por un Gobierno u otra institución", *DLE*), pues, como explica la Fundéu: "Las expresiones españolas *ciudadano no grato* o *persona no grata* y la latina *persona non grata* son las adecuadas para aludir a alguien que es rechazado por un Gobierno o una institución, pero nunca *non grato*, que mezcla latín y español":[10]

(25)
    Emery se gana el título de "**non grato**" en Mestalla (mundodeportivo.com, 10 de mayo de 2019).

En cuanto a la locución *contra natura*, adaptación de la latina *contra naturam*, "se escribe en dos palabras, ya tenga función adjetiva (*alianza/unión contra natura*) o adverbial (*es contra natura*)";[11] sin embargo, se detecta en el corpus su escritura en una sola palabra:

(26)
    Rivalidad **contranatura** (mundodeportivo.com, 7 de julio de 2019).

La locución *rara avis* es ambigua en cuanto al género, es decir, que admite su uso en masculino y femenino, sin que ello implique cambios de significado (de hecho, aparece en tres ocasiones concertando en femenino y en dos en masculino):

(27)
    a. Así se transformó Anthony Davis en una "**rara avis**" monstruosa en la NBA (marca.com, 27 de febrero de 2018).
    b. Rodri, un "**rara avis**" en el Nàstic (mundodeportivo.com, 18 de septiembre de 2017).

---

[10] https://www.fundeu.es/recomendacion/non-grato-es-una-expresion-incorrecta-952/. Consulta realizada el 16 de septiembre de 2019.
[11] https://www.fundeu.es/recomendacion/contra-natura-en-dos-palabras/. Consulta realizada el 16 de septiembre de 2019.

2.2 Desautomatización de unidades fraseológicas latinas

El discurso deportivo se caracteriza por la utilización constante de unidades fraseológicas (UF), entendidas en sentido amplio (locuciones, colocaciones, enunciados fraseológicos, citas, dichos, frases célebres, títulos de obras literarias, películas, series televisivas, eslóganes publicitarios...), siempre y cuando gocen de cierto grado de institucionalización y sean reconocidas e interpretadas sin dificultad.[12]

Uno de los rasgos creativos más característicos del discurso deportivo son los juegos léxicos que se producen mediante la desautomatización de dichas unidades. Se trata de un proceso de intensificación lingüística que consiste en creaciones individuales y conscientes mediante las cuales se persigue la sorpresa, pues se experimenta, por un lado, la agradable sensación de lo conocido y, por otro, la originalidad de la modificación llevada a cabo tanto en el plano del contenido como en el de la expresión, ya que la desautomatización puede ser semántica y/o formal,[13] e incluso combinar distintos procedimientos de ruptura que afectan a la estructura de la frase, como pueden ser la sustitución, la supresión, la adición, la modificación, la alteración del orden, el cambio de modalidad oracional y la fusión (Guerrero Salazar 2017a).[14] En el corpus analizado, destacan la sustitución y/o la adición de elementos extraños a la estructura originaria, procedimientos que sirven para vincular el cultismo al contexto deportivo.

Como se constata, la UF, aunque no esté formalmente modificada, queda desautomatizada si se introduce con su forma canónica en un contexto distinto al usual. Mediante este proceso, se consigue la reliteralización de la expresión. En este sentido, la desautomatización viola la máxima de la cualidad de Grice (que sea verdadero), ya que se ofrece un significado falso (Timofeeva 2009, 251), el que surge en la nueva situación comunicativa en que la UF ha quedado

---

[12] Al igual que Alvarado Ortega (2010), Corpas Pastor (2013) o Zamora Muñoz (2014), entendemos la fraseología como un modelo dinámico, en el que se incluyen unidades fraseológicas prototítipas y no prototípicas.

[13] Según Mena Martínez (2003a), para que se considere desautomatizada una UF, debe cumplir tres requisitos: 1. La modificación debe ser producto de un cambio ocasional, voluntario e intencionado. 2. Debe desviarse lo suficiente para que el cambio pueda ser percibido. 3. La forma base debe ser reconocible con ayuda de los elementos conservados e inalterados, o mediante el contexto.

[14] Otras taxonomías clásicas son la de Corpas Pastor (1996), Mena Martínez (2003a, 2003b y 2003c) y García-Page (2008).

inmersa. La incongruencia entre el significado original y el que surge del contexto genera un efecto normalmente lúdico:

(28)
    a.   El "**carpe diem**" de Ferrari (marca.com, 10 de julio de 2012).
    b.   **Annus horribilis** en el Madrid (as.com, 4 de diciembre de 2015).

En (29a) se establece un juego dilógico entre la interpretación literal de *carpe diem* (en el sentido de "disfrute") y el nombre propio del Club, como se explica en el cuerpo de la noticia (29b):

(29)
    a.   **Carpe Diem** para las sirenas del equipo español de natación sincronizada (mundodeportivo.com, 3 de agosto de 2013 [titular]).
    b.   El equipo nacional de natación sincronizada celebró las esperadas siete medallas del Mundial de Natación de Barcelona en el **Carpe Diem** Lounge Club, del Port Olímpic de Barcelona (mundodeportivo.com, 3 de agosto de 2013 [cuerpo]).

En los dos titulares siguientes, el término *réquiem* forma parte de una UF, concretamente el título de una película estadounidense (*Requiem for a Dream*).[15] En (30a) solo hay desautomatización semántica, producida al introducir la unidad en un contexto deportivo con la intención de magnificar la derrota sufrida por el Barça, la cual ha frustrado su deseo de jugar la final de la Champions. En (30b), se produce, además, una desautomatización formal, ya que se introduce un sustantivo ajeno al título de la película (*campo*) mediante el que se alude al estadio Vicente Calderón:

(30)
    a.   **Réquiem** por un sueño (sport.es, 8 de mayo de 2019).
    b.   **Réquiem** por un campo de sueño (marca.com, 26 de mayo de 2017).

La actualización de la UF latina puede producirse a través de un vocativo, normalmente referido a un personaje del ámbito deportivo. Es lo que sucede en el siguiente titular con el tenista Rafael Nadal, a quien se aplica la frase *Totus tuus* ("todo tuyo"), lema del pontificado de Juan Pablo II, con el que el papa expresaba su entrega a la Virgen María:

---

[15] Llevada al cine en el año 2000, esta película está basada en la novela homónima de Hubert Selby Jr (1978).

(31)
   Totus tuus, Nadal (marca.com, 14 de septiembre de 2010).

Algo similar sucede con la frase latina *quo vadis* ("¿a dónde vas?"), vinculada también a la tradición cristiana,[16] que se utiliza como pregunta retórica claramente tendenciosa, pues, a través de ella, se cuestiona el propósito de una determinada acción. El ejemplo siguiente pone en tela de juicio la actuación del equipo español de rugby en el campeonato de Europa de Naciones:

(32)
   Quo vadis, España? (marca.com, 22 de marzo de 2013).

Tres titulares registrados en el corpus se conforman con la fórmula de salutación latina *Ave* (y un vocativo referido al ámbito deportivo), que alude a la frase *Ave, Caesar, morituri te salutant*;[17] este recurso se utiliza, no tanto como fórmula de apelación, sino más bien para manifestar la admiración hacia el deportista y dignificarlo:

(33)
   Ave Messi (marca.com, 20 de marzo de 2012).

En los casos en que la UF es una máxima o frase con autoría, la ruptura semántica se produce al adjudicarla a un personaje o equipo deportivo; es lo que sucede con las palabras atribuidas a Julio César en (34a–b), referidas a los entrenadores Gregorio Manzano y Rudi García, respectivamente. La frase *veni, vidi, vici* es recurrente en los ámbitos más variados, de hecho, es el latinismo más repetido en los titulares analizados. Esto se debe a que, como ha señalado

---

[16] Según Herrero Llorente (1985, 324): "Según una leyenda, contada por San Ambrosio (*Contra Auxentium*), San Pedro, huyendo de Roma, se encontró en la vía Apia con la figura de Cristo llevando la cruz, y le dirigió tales palabras; Cristo le replicó: 'A Roma, a ser de nuevo crucificado'. San Pedro había usado las mismas palabras con Cristo (*Vulg.*, Joan. 13, 36). Con el título de *Quo vadis?* escribió el famoso novelista polaco Enrique Sienkiewicz una novela basada en la antigüedad cristiana que ha pasado a ser clásica; ha sido traducida a más de treinta lenguas e incluso se la ha llevado a la pantalla. Anteriormente fue llevada al teatro por E. Cain con música de J. Nougués y estrenada en París en 1909". Es el título también de una famosa película estadounidense de 1951 basada en una obra literaria homónima.

[17] Según Herrero Llorente (1985, 61): "Dios te guarde, César, los que van a morir te saludan. Saludo ritual que los gladiadores romanos dirigían al emperador antes de comenzar el combate (Suet., *Claud*. 21, 6)."

Martino (2012, 369), gracias a la estructura de tres miembros asindéticos, la similidesinencia, el isosilabismo y la aliteración, comunica eficazmente la idea de rapidez. En (34c), la frase se actualiza al ser adjudicada al ciclista Aaron Gwin y al añadir la referencia al lugar de la carrera (Lourdes). En (34d) la desautomatización por sustitución (*veni* por *Vini*) se basa en un juego onomástico, pues *Vini* es el acortamiento de *Vinicius,* nombre del deportista.

(34)
    a. Manzano: **Veni, vidi, vici** (marca.com, 31 de mayo de 2017).
    b. Rudi García, **veni vidi vici** (sport.es, 28 de octubre de 2013).
    c. Aaron Gwin: **Veni, vidi, vici** en Lourdes (mundodeportivo.com, 10 de abril de 2016).
    d. **"Vini", vidi, vici** (*Marca*, 26 de julio de 2018, portada).

Cuando la desautomatización se produce por sustitución, en principio, el sustituto debe establecer una conexión entre el significado literal o idiomático del cultismo y el contexto en el que se introduce, como sucede en (35a), donde, aunque se ha permutado el sustantivo *annus* (de *annus horribilis*) por *semana,* seguimos dentro del mismo campo semántico. Sin embargo, a veces, el elemento sustituido no posee nada en común con el referente (35b).

(35)
    a. Renfroe certifica la semana **"horribilis"** del Estu a 1,5" del final (as.com, 30 de septiembre de 2018).
    b. El cuarto **"horribilis"** de los Cavaliers: ¡Ni una canasta de dos! (marca.com, 28 de diciembre de 2017).

El miembro sustituto puede ser el antónimo (como sucede en (36), donde *pares* se cambia por *impares*), lo que produce una ruptura inesperada, pues invierte el sentido de la unidad fraseológica primigenia:

(36)
    Primus inter impares (as.com, 14 de octubre de 2011).

En algunos casos, cuando el miembro sustituido no guarda ninguna relación semántica con el sustituto, el titular se convierte en un enigma que solo se resuelve con la continuación de la lectura; así, en los ejemplos siguientes las palabras sustitutas solo coinciden con las sustituidas en algunos fonemas finales: en (37a), en vez de *Homo Erectus,* aparece *Homo Robustus* (por la escasa estatura del velocista Coleman); y en (37b), en vez de *Homo Sapiens, Homo Champions* (por las cinco Champions de balonmano que el jugador Rutenka ha ganado):

(37)
    a. "**Homo Robustus**" Coleman se ratifica como heredero de Bolt (mundodeportivo.com, 28 de septiembre de 2019).[18]
    b. Rutenka, el nuevo "**Homo** Champions" (mundodeportivo.com, 29 de mayo de 2014).[19]

Lo que se consigue con estos juegos es una unión paradójica de ideas y de palabras que pone de manifiesto la inusual relación establecida. Es lo que sucede con la fórmula latina *Habemus papam* (con la que se informa de la elección de un nuevo pontífice). En los titulares deportivos se emplea frecuentemente modificada mediante la sustitución del término *papam* por otro del contexto deportivo. Para Campos Vargas (2012, 54), se trata de un calco del latín eclesiástico que se emplea para ridiculizar una situación particular. El titular de (38b) está condicionado por un hecho histórico del momento, ya que el 13 de marzo de 2013 fue elegido el papa Francisco, tras la renuncia al cargo de Benedicto XVI.

(38)
    a. ¡Quiniela **habemus**! (marca.com, 17 de febrero de 2011).
    b. **Habemus** Málaga (*Marca,* 14 de marzo de 2013, portada).

La expresión *coitus interruptus* nos lleva al campo semántico del erotismo, muy relevante en el ámbito deportivo, donde se usan palabras muy explícitas relacionadas con el acto sexual (Guerrero Salazar 2018b, 71–72). Como comprobamos en (39a–c), los sustantivos que sustituyen a *coitus* se alejan del campo de la sexualidad para concretarse en el deportivo:

(39)
    a. Mourinho, Ancelotti, Blatter... ellos también sufrieron una rueda de prensa "**interruptus**" (marca.com, 2 de octubre de 2015).
    b. Los Lakers se llevan el partido "**interruptus**" más húmedo (marca.com, 18 de octubre de 2015).
    c. Hezonja, el genio perdido del Barça, dibuja la asistencia "**interruptus**" de la temporada (marca.com, 27 de diciembre de 2017).

La locución *Magister dixit* ("Lo ha dicho el maestro")[20] se utiliza en la titulación deportiva en sentido irónico; se trata de una fórmula rutinaria de

---

[18] Se le llama *robustus* por su estatura, pues mide 20 centímetros menos que el velocista Usain Bolt.
[19] Ha ganado cinco Champions de balonmano.

aseveración, establecida convencionalmente para realizar determinados actos de habla. Como ha señalado Martino (2012, 380), a través de la figura retórica de la ironía se ponen en relación los textos latinos con el mundo contemporáneo; de este modo, al sustituir la palabra *magister* por un nombre propio del ámbito deportivo, se cuestiona la autoridad del personaje aludido. En estos casos, el uso de latinismos paródicos que imitan la estructura empleada en esta lengua sirve para la expresión de máximas con función lúdica (Campos Vargas 2012, 45):

(40)
    Cruyff **dixit**: Un paloma no hace verano (sport.es, 22 de septiembre de 2016).

Algo similar sucede en el titular siguiente; se trata de un híbrido, ya que se mantiene un elemento de la frase latina que se empleaba para saludar a César (*Ave,* vid. (33)); sin embargo, el resto es la traducción castellana, actualizada mediante la sustitución por el nombre del club vasco (*Bidasoa*):

(41)
    "**Ave** Europa, el Bidasoa te saluda" (marca.com, 26 de agosto de 2019).[21]

Por último, hay un grupo de titulares en los que la desautomatización afecta a un cultismo totalmente *in absentia*, ya que lo que aparece es su traducción. Es el caso de la frase *llegué, vi y vencí*, que alude a *Veni, vidi, vici*, latinismo que está en la base de los titulares de portadas de (42a–c). En los tres casos se sustituye el último de los verbos para adecuarlo al contexto deportivo, al que antecede la conjunción copulativa; el último ejemplo combina, además, la sustitución de los verbos (*venció* por *bebió*) con la adición de un sustantivo (*champán*). A veces la desautomatización es más atrevida, pues pueden sustituirse varias palabras, como sucede en el titular (42d); no obstante, se mantienen el tiempo verbal y la estructura trimembre, que nos permite reconocer la frase latina implícita.

---

[20] Según Herrero Llorente (1985, 209): "Con estas palabras los escolásticos de la Edad Media pretendían citar como un argumento sin réplica la opinión del Maestro (Aristóteles), imitando a los discípulos de Pitágoras. Hoy día estas palabras se aplican, por extensión, a todo jefe de una escuela, de una doctrina o de un partido".
[21] Se trata de un eslogan publicitario de la campaña de abonados para la Liga de Campeones 2019/20.

(42)
    a. Benzema llegó, vio y mojó (*Marca*, 29 de julio de 2009, portada).
    b. Llegó, vio y marcó (*Marca*, 28 de julio de 2015, portada).[22]
    c. Llegó, vio y bebió champán (*Marca*,15 de marzo de 2010, portada).[23]
    d. Salió marcó y ganó (*Marca*, 24 de septiembre de 2009, portada).[24]

Por último, destacan dos titulares de portada que remiten, mediante un calambur, a la frase *vade retro* ("Loc. Lat.; literalmente 'vete atrás, retrocede'; 1.loc. interj. U. para rechazar a alguien o algo", *DLE*),[25] fórmula expresiva de recusación. Se establece, además, un juego fónico basado, de una parte, en el parecido del imperativo latino *vade* y el presente del verbo *ir* (*va*) más la preposición española (*de*); de otra, en la sustitución de términos parónimos (*reto* y *récords* en lugar del latinismo *retro*):

(43)
    a. Va de retos (*Mundo deportivo*, 16 de noviembre de 2010, portada).
    b. Va de récords (*Sport*,14 de octubre de 2014, portada).

3 Conclusiones

Tras el análisis presentado, la hipótesis de partida queda demostrada: el latinismo funciona como un recurso de intensificación en los titulares de los diarios deportivos más leídos en España. Así mismo, he dado respuestas a las preguntas de investigación formuladas (qué latinismos aparecen, cómo, en qué tipo de titulares y con qué finalidad) y que resumo a continuación.

De los 3.000 titulares que componen el corpus, 146 (el 4,8%) presentan un latinismo instalado en la lengua (la mayoría de ellos sancionados por la Real Academia Española), que puede llegar a constituir por sí solo el titular (incluso de portada), bien de tipo expresivo y/o creativo, y, en menor media, apelativo. Se trata de términos o expresiones instaladas en la lengua y reconocidas fácilmente, aunque, en algunos casos, se escriben de manera errónea o presentan fluctuaciones ortográficas u ortotipográficas.

---

[22] Se refiere al futbolista James.
[23] Se refiere al piloto Fernando Alonso.
[24] Se refiere a Cristiano Ronaldo, que metió el primer gol nada más comenzar el partido.
[25] Según Herrero Llorente (1985: 393): "Se emplea para rechazar una oferta tentadora. Son palabras que Cristo dirige a Pedro cuando este se atreve a reprenderle: *Vade retro, Satana* 'retírate Satanás' (Vulg., *Marc.* 8, 33)".

El 47% de los casos son unidades fraseológicas latinas que se presentan desautomatizadas semántica y/o formalmente, sobre todo por sustitución o adición de algún elemento ajeno a la frase primigenia. Se trata de invenciones idiolécticas para dar un toque de humor, expresar ironía o evaluar algún hecho o a alguna persona relacionada con el ámbito deportivo, ya sea de manera positiva o claramente tendenciosa.

Si eliminamos las ocurrencias repetidas, nos encontramos con un total de 33 latinismos distintos que presentamos en la Figura 4.1.

álter ego, "alter ego", alter-ego (5)	mens sana in corpore sano (1)
alma mater (11)	modus operandi (3)
alea iacta est (3)	motu proprio (3)
annus horribilis (10)	in memoriam (2)
ave (3)	persona non grata /*non grato (3)
carpe diem (8)	primus inter pares (3)
coitus interruptus (5)	quo vadis (2)
contra natura(m), *contranatura (4)	rara avis (5)
cum laude (10)	réquiem (7)
grosso modo, *a grosso modo (5)	sine die (2)
habemus papam (5)	sui géneris (2)
homo sapiens (2)	statu quo (3)
in extremis (3)	totus tuus (1)
in situ (2)	vade retro (5)
invictus (4)	veni, vidi, vici (12)
magister dixit (2)	via crucis (2)
mea culpa (8)	

Figura 4.1. Tabla de latinismos crudos registrados (las formas con asterisco no se consideran correctas)

Referencias bibliográficas

Alvarado Ortega, M.ª Belén. 2010. *Las fórmulas rutinarias del español: teoría y aplicaciones*. Frankfurt: Peter Lang.

Campos Vargas, Henry. 2010. "Latinismos en la prensa costarricense: latín jurídico versus otros registros". *Káñina. Revista de Artes y Letras*, 34, 31–35.

Campos Vargas, Henry. 2012. "Algunos latinismos empleados en la prensa escrita costarricense". *Káñina. Revista de Artes y Letras*, 36, 45–55. Fecha de consulta junio de 2020. https://revistas.ucr.ac.cr/index.php/kanina/article/download/2321/2280.

Campos Vargas, Henry. 2014. "Latín jurídico, etimologías y algo más: el latín en nuestra prensa". *Revista de Filología y Lingüística de la Universidad de Costa Rica*, 40:2, 181–193.

Corpas Pastor, Gloria. 1996. *Manual de fraseología española*. Madrid: Gredos.

Corpas Pastor, Gloria. 2013. "Detección, descripción y contraste de las unidades fraseológicas mediante tecnologías lingüísticas". En *Fraseopragmática*, editado por Inés Olza y Elvira Manero, 335–373. Berlín: Frank & Timme.

DLE = Asociación de Academias de la Lengua Española. 2014–. *Diccionario de la lengua española*, 23ª ed. Madrid: Espasa. Fecha de consulta junio de 2020. https://dle.rae.es/.

García-Page Sánchez, Mario. 2008. *Introducción a la fraseología española. Estudio de las locuciones*. Barcelona: Ánthropos.

Guerrero Salazar, Susana. 2017a. "La desautomatización de las unidades fraseológicas en los titulares deportivos". *Verba. Anuario Gallego de Filología*, 44, 99–131.

Guerrero Salazar, Susana. 2017b. "La intensificación como estrategia comunicativa en los titulares de las portadas deportivas". *ELUA*, 31, 187–209.

Guerrero Salazar, Susana. 2018a. "La formación de neologismos mediante elementos compositivos en los titulares deportivos de la prensa española". *Hispania*, 101:1, 89–98.

Guerrero Salazar, Susana. 2018b. "Neologismos estilísticos en los titulares de la prensa deportiva española: "NP + -*azo*/-*ada*". *Círculo de lingüística aplicada a la comunicación*, 75, 155–172.

Guerrero Salazar, Susana. 2018c. *Creatividad y juego en el discurso deportivo de la prensa: aportaciones léxico-semánticas*. Madrid: Arco-Libro.

Guerrero Salazar, Susana. 2020. "Principales sufijos en la creación de neologismos tendenciosos en los titulares deportivos de la prensa española". *Neologica*, 14, 185–202.

Herrero Llorente, Víctor José, 1985. *Diccionario de expresiones y frases latinas*, 2ª ed. Madrid: Gredos.

Hourani Martín, Dunia. 2012. "El tratamiento ortográfico, ortotipográfico y lexicográfico de los extranjerismos crudos en la prensa escrita española". *Normas. Revista de Estudios Lingüísticos Hispánicos*, 2, 125–56.

López Hidalgo, Antonio. 2001. *El titular. Manual de titulación periodística*. Sevilla: Comunicación Social.

Martino, Delio de. 2012. "El latín publicitario". *Pensar la Publicidad*, 6:2, 365–80.

Mena Martínez, Florentina. 2003a. "En torno al concepto de desautomatización fraseológica: aspectos básicos". *Tonos digital. Revista Electrónica de Estudios*

Filológicos, 5, 1–12. Fecha de consulta junio de 2020. https://www.um.es/tonosdigital/znum5/estudios/H-Edesautomatizacion.htm.

Mena Martínez, Florentina. 2003b. "Los efectos semánticos producidos por la desautomatización de las unidades fraseológicas". En *Homenaje al profesor Estanislao Ramón Trives,* coordinado por Agustín Vera Luján, Ramón Almela Pérez, José María Jiménez Cano y Dolores Anunciación Igualada Belchí, vol. 2, 501–518. Murcia: Universidad de Murcia.

Mena Martínez, Florentina. 2003c. "Modificaciones fraseológicas y tipología textual: los textos publicitarios". *Paremia*, 12, 97–106. Fecha de consulta junio de 2020. https://cvc.cervantes.es/lengua/paremia/pdf/012/009_mena.pdf.

Otaola Olano, Concepción. 2005. "Los latinismos en el discurso periodístico actual de la prensa española". En *Ad amicam amicissime scripta. Homenaje a la profesora M. José López de Ayala y Genovés*, coordinado por J. Costas Rodríguez, vol. 2, 299–317. Madrid: UNED.

Real Academia Española y Asociación de Academias de la Lengua Española. 2010. *Ortografía de la lengua española.* Madrid: Espasa. Fecha de consulta junio de 2020. https://www.rae.es/recursos/ortografia/ortografia-2010.

Sánchez Vidal, Óscar. 2012. "De *in dubio pro feo* a *habeas corpus*: latinismos en las viñetas gráficas". *Thamyris*, 3, 123–136. Fecha de consulta junio de 2020. http://www.thamyris.uma.es/Thamyris3/VIDAL.pdf.

Sánchez Vidal, Óscar. 2013. "El empleo de las nuevas normas ortográficas sobre los latinismos y locuciones latinas en la prensa española". *Thamyris*, 4, 33–45. Fecha de consulta junio de 2020. http://www.thamyris.uma.es/Thamyris4/OSCAR_SANCHEZ.pdf.

Timofeeva, Larissa. 2009. "La desautomatización fraseológica: un recurso para crear y divertir". En *Estudios de Lingüística. Investigaciones Lingüísticas en el Siglo XXI,* editado por Juan Luis Jiménez Ruiz y Larissa Timofeeva, 249–271. Alicante: Universidad de Alicante. Fecha de consulta junio de 2020. https://rua.ua.es/dspace/bitstream/10045/15289/1/ELUA_monografico_2009_10.pdf.

Truneanu, Valentina. 2005. "De *rara avis* a *referéndum*: El fenómeno de los latinismos en la prensa venezolana". *Telos: Revista de Estudios Interdisciplinarios en Ciencias Sociales*, 7:3, 412–425. Fecha de consulta junio de 2020. https://www.redalyc.org/pdf/993/99318837006.pdf.

Zamora Muñoz, Pablo. 2014. "Los límites del discurso repetido: la fraseología periférica y las unidades fraseológicas pragmáticas". *Verba. Anuario Gallego de Filología*, 41, 213–236.

Chapter 5

Datos psicolingüísticos en torno a la vitalidad y la neologicidad de la composición culta en la prensa escrita en español[1]

Carmen Varo Varo
Universidad de Cádiz

Resumen

La composición culta manifiesta una creciente vitalidad en las lenguas modernas, como queda patente en las creaciones neológicas sustentadas en este procedimiento y presentes en los diversos ámbitos comunicativos, entre los que destaca el periodístico, donde llegan a trascender su motivación inicial, ya sea expresiva o apelativa, y adquieren una potente proyección social. Teniendo en cuenta la propia naturaleza de los elementos compositivos cultos, a medio camino entre afijo y palabra, y, por consiguiente, la convivencia en las formaciones neológicas en las que participan de procesos semántico-

---

[1] Este trabajo forma parte de la investigación sobre neología y neologismos desarrollada por el nodo neológico de la Universidad de Cádiz (NEOUCA), integrado en la Red de Observatorios de Neología del Castellano (NEOROC), coordinada por el Observatori de Neologia del Institut de Linguistica Aplicada (IULA) de la Universitat Pompeu Fabra. Asimismo, responde a las líneas del Gabinete de Industrias de la Lengua del Instituto de Lingüística Aplicada de la Universidad de Cádiz y el grupo de excelencia del Plan Andaluz de Investigación *Semaínein* (HUM 147). En concreto, se vincula con los objetivos de: (a) determinar las tendencias predominantes en distintas lenguas de los procesos de formación de nuevas unidades léxicas; (b) profundizar en los procesos psicolingüísticos y los mecanismos neurocognitivos que explican la producción e interpretación de las nuevas unidades, y (c) analizar la creatividad léxica en los diferentes tipos de lenguaje.

conceptuales y morfosintácticos, este trabajo se concentra en la reflexión sobre la innovación léxica por composición culta desde la perspectiva psicolingüística. Para ello, hemos contrastado los datos sobre el estatus actual de la composición culta en la prensa en español, atendiendo a su progresiva consolidación en las últimas décadas, con los datos derivados de un estudio exploratorio *off-line* del procesamiento de estas formaciones, centrado en el sentimiento de neologicidad que generan y el grado de complejidad cognitiva atribuido por el receptor. Respecto a los resultados obtenidos, el acercamiento a los procesos de identificación y reconocimiento de usos neológicos nos ha permitido constatar la versatilidad de los elementos compositivos cultos, mediada por estrategias cognitivas basadas en el equilibrio entre memoria y atención, que se traducen en procesos lingüísticos como la analogía y el enriquecimiento contextual, que repercuten en el esfuerzo cognitivo de procesamiento y que explican la productividad léxica de las lenguas.

Summary

Compound cultured borrowings are showing a growing vitality in modern languages, as is clear from the neologistic creations which have introduced by this process, and are present in various communicative contexts, foremost among which is journalism. Here, these words transcend their initial denotational or expressive motivation and acquire powerful social projection. While taking into account the intrinsic nature of the component elements of these compounds (halfway between affix and word), as well as the combination of semantic and morphosyntactic processes in which they participate, this Chapter focuses on this kind of lexical innovation from a psycholinguistic perspective. To this end I have contrasted data on the present status of compound cultured borrowings in the Spanish-language press, tracing their progressive consolidation in recent decades, with data derived from an exploratory off-line study of how these forms are processed, which concentrates on the sense of newness which they generate and the degree of cognitive complexity which readers/hearers attribute to them. Understanding these processes of identification and recognition of neologistic usage has allowed me to establish the versatility of the component cultured elements, mediated by cognitive strategies which are based on the balance between memory and attention; these can be translated into linguistic processes such as analogy and contextual enrichment, which impact on the cognitive effort of processing and explain lexical productivity in languages.

Keywords

Lexical compounds, Neologism, Latin, Journalism, Psycholinguistics, Spanish.

1 Introducción

La composición culta manifiesta una creciente vitalidad en las lenguas modernas, como se aprecia en las creaciones neológicas sustentadas en este procedimiento y presentes en diversos ámbitos comunicativos, entre los que destaca el periodístico, donde llegan a trascender su motivación inicial, ya sea expresiva o apelativa, y adquieren una potente proyección social. Teniendo en cuenta la propia naturaleza de los elementos compositivos cultos, a medio camino entre afijo y palabra, y, por consiguiente, la convivencia en las formaciones neológicas en las que participan de procesos semántico-conceptuales y morfosintácticos, este trabajo se centra en la innovación léxica por composición culta desde la perspectiva psicolingüística, partiendo en este caso de su actual estatus en la prensa escrita en español.

La apelación al enfoque psicolingüístico, conducente al análisis de los procesos de codificación y descodificación de estas unidades neológicas, no sólo se justifica por el interés del parámetro psicológico como uno de los criterios manejados en la investigación de la neología para la identificación de tales usos, contribuyente a la diferenciación entre usos novedosos (o de habla) y usos consolidados (o de lengua), sino, sobre todo, porque hace posible ampliar el marco teórico explicativo de este fenómeno, al incluir las principales teorías sobre el procesamiento léxico elaboradas hasta el momento e incluir la reflexión sobre la actuación de distintas estrategias cognitivas basadas en el equilibrio entre memoria y atención, que repercuten notablemente en el tiempo de procesamiento y que explican la productividad léxica de las lenguas.[2] Partiendo de este marco, consideramos la difusión masiva de estas formaciones a través de la prensa escrita como un recurso de gran efectividad para la irradiación, a través de un discurso generalmente accesible al público general, tanto de estructuras analógicas como de asociaciones semánticas y conceptuales. Asimismo, la

---

[2] Sobre el funcionamiento de los procedimientos de neología, Alvar Ezquerra (2002, 11) señala "una tendencia de doble signo, aparentemente contradictoria, pues a la vez se utiliza el código lingüístico y hay una subversión contra él, se reconoce la norma y se transgrede, se crean palabras con arreglo a unas reglas pero esa creatividad cambia las propias reglas."

perspectiva psicolingüística resulta de suma utilidad para la delimitación de la composición culta frente a otros mecanismos de creación léxica en español por plantear nuevos enfoques de acercamiento.

En cuanto a la metodología seguida, tras una somera reflexión sobre la singularidad de la composición culta y las repercusiones de su integración en el discurso periodístico, hemos contrastado los datos cuantitativos sobre el estatus actual de estas formaciones en la prensa en español, atendiendo a su progresiva consolidación en las últimas décadas, con los datos derivados de un estudio exploratorio *off-line* del procesamiento de enunciados que las incluyen. En particular, analizaremos la relevancia de la familiaridad y la frecuencia frente a la transparencia semántica, el grado de complejidad cognitiva atribuida y el sentimiento de neologicidad que generan en el receptor.

2 Sobre la singularidad de la composición culta

La composición culta constituye una de las modalidades más destacadas de la composición, a su vez incluida en el amplio espectro de la denominada neología formal o de forma (Chériguen 1989),[3] referida tanto a la creación de significantes nuevos como a la creación conjunta de significantes y significados nuevos, de gran interés en las lenguas indoeuropeas, donde el alcance de los procesos morfológicos queda de relieve en el predominio de las palabras polimorfémicas sobre las monomorfémicas (Rey-Debove 1984). En el caso que nos ocupa, como es sabido, las nuevas unidades se conforman a partir de elementos preexistentes procedentes de las lenguas griega y latina, llamados bases compositivas cultas, que se combinan entre sí o con elementos léxicos patrimoniales (lo que se denomina *composición semiculta*). A este respecto, deben señalarse algunas observaciones.

---

[3] La *neología de forma, formal u ordinaria* se suele contraponer a la *neología de sentido, de contenido o semántica* (Bastuji 1974; Pottier Navarro 1979). Otros autores añaden, como tercer tipo, la *neología por préstamo* (Auger y Rousseau 2003). A diferencia de esta última, las dos primeras se apoyan en elementos lingüísticos preexistentes en la lengua, frente a otros tipos de innovación léxica entre los que encuentran, además de los préstamos, las creaciones por acronimia (p.ej. *basuraleza*), por abreviación o abreviamiento (p.ej. *trans*), *siglación* (p.ej. *3D*), o *ex nihilo* (p.ej. *yuyu*). Por otra parte, en tanto que la neología semántica manifiesta mayor dependencia del contexto, la neología formal se apoya especialmente en la competencia gramatical del individuo.

En primer lugar, como advierte *NGLE* (pág. 782), "Muchas de estas raíces se usan de manera general en el vocabulario científico y técnico, pero otras también en la lengua común." Abarca, pues, no sólo la neonimia (Rondeau 1984), del tipo *videoendoscopia* o *bioeconomía*, ligada a una motivación expresiva y destinada, por tanto, a cubrir necesidades terminológicas, sino también, como respuesta a un tipo de motivación bastante diferente, la neología espontánea (Cabré et al. 2002), muchas veces de intención meramente apelativa,[4] como en los ejemplos *bicifobia* o *gastroagenda*. Son numerosos los autores que se han ocupado de analizar la interrelación entre prensa y neología en español (Alvar Ezquerra 1998, García Platero 1999, Guerrero Salazar 2007, Méndez Santos 2011, Díaz Hormigo 2020, entre otros). A propósito del caso específico de la composición culta, especialmente aquella de índole terminológica, Guerrero Ramos y Pérez Lagos (2012, 27) han resaltado la relevancia de la modalidad textual periodística en los procesos de renovación y divulgación del léxico: "pensamos que cuando un término se usa en un contexto de divulgación, sufre un proceso de vulgarización, de banalización que supone la aceptación de una nueva unidad en dicho contexto."

En segundo lugar, pese a la categorización de la composición culta como modalidad de neología de forma, la perspectiva semántica no puede quedar fuera de consideración. Ciertamente, pese a algunos notables empeños en adoptar un enfoque prioritariamente semántico en el estudio de la formación de palabras (Bally 1965; Coseriu 2003, entre otros),[5] en las sistematizaciones

---

[4] Así pues, el análisis de la prensa escrita, como apunta, Díaz Hormigo (2020, 4), "[...] arroja siempre, sea cual sea el tipo de estudio, nuevos resultados, de interés y actualidad, pues, entre otros aspectos, da cuenta de la vitalidad presente de la lengua; de los recursos de creación léxica más productivos para la renovación y la actualización del léxico de la lengua; de las nuevas tendencias en esta revitalización del léxico; de la adopción e importación, con adaptación o no a los rasgos y las características propias de la lengua receptora, de voces de otras lenguas, algunas incluso para la denominación de realidades de la cultura foránea inexistentes en el ámbito cultural de la lengua admisora [...]."

[5] Coseriu, que vincula esta cuestión con los problemas de tomar simultáneamente expresión y contenido y la falta de delimitación entre hechos de significado y hechos de designación, prioriza la perspectiva del contenido sobre la expresión por dar cuenta, además, de la génesis de tales procesos, e incluye la formación de palabras en el campo de las relaciones paradigmáticas secundarias (frente a las primarias, campo y clase léxica) a las que asigna una función de *gramaticalización* del léxico primario, que permite someter a este léxico a

de la formación de palabras se terminó imponiendo el criterio morfológico. Sin embargo, desde el punto de vista del proceso creativo, este se inicia indiscutiblemente con la selección del significado. Cuestión distinta es cómo se realiza la selección de ese significado y cómo se proyecta sobre una posible estructura formal. Por otra parte, junto a los mecanismos formales empleados, son destacables los procesos de reajuste y asociación semántica que resultan de la interacción de los elementos compositivos que constituyen estas formaciones. Lüdtke (2011, 21) sintetiza perfectamente la necesidad de combinar ambas perspectivas, morfológica y semántica:

> "El tomar como punto de partida la forma —es lo que se entiende por el llamado 'enfoque morfológico'— no puede conducir a una descripción que refleje la configuración de la formación de palabras de una lengua, ya que la forma sólo sirve a la expresión del contenido. Un enfoque exclusivamente semántico por cierto tampoco promete una solución para todos los problemas: si una forma puede expresar contenidos diversos, un contenido puede ser expresado por formas diversas." [6]

Una tercera cuestión tiene que ver con la naturaleza de los elementos compositivos cultos. De entrada, la propia delimitación entre derivación y composición en las lenguas ha sido asiduo objeto de discusión en la bibliografía sobre la creación léxica, dando origen a distintas visiones interpretativas de la diferencia entre ellos. Así, en ocasiones nos encontramos con la limitación de la derivación a la sufijación y la consecuente inclusión de la prefijación entre los tipos de composición. Sirva de ejemplo el primer tratado específico sobre la formación de palabras en español, de Alemany (1920, 152): "La derivación consiste, como sabemos en formar palabras nuevas por medio de sufijos que se añaden al radical de un vocablo que tiene existencia independiente en la lengua, como *fabulista*, de *fábula*." A su vez, desde la perspectiva diacrónica la derivación se ha contemplado como composición desgastada y consolidada a través de la analogía (Wartburg 1951). También desde un enfoque funcional del

---

procesos de naturaleza gramatical y posteriormente ser devueltas de nuevo al léxico (Coseriu 2003, 183).

[6] En su propuesta este autor, partiendo de un enfoque semántico de la formación de palabras, se manifiesta a favor de incorporar los niveles del lenguaje, universal, idiomático o histórico y discursivo o individual (Lüdtke 2011, 47).

contenido, donde la composición se ha abordado como relación entre dos objetos, la derivación queda integrada en esta interpretación. En esta línea, Coseriu (1978) distinguía la composición lexemática de la denominada composición prolexemática, donde se ven implicadas proformas relativas a clases gramaticales genéricas como *hombre* o *cosa*. En lo que particularmente atañe a la composición culta, debe señalarse el singular carácter híbrido de los elementos compositivos cultos, entre palabras y afijos. De cualquier forma, aunque algunos de estos elementos cultos han sido asimilados con frecuencia a pseudoprefijos o pseudosufijos, como señala *NGLE* (pág. 784), mantienen ciertos aspectos diferenciales, como la posibilidad de ocupar distintos puestos en el marco de la palabra, la presencia de relaciones argumentales (o entre un elemento nuclear y su complemento) en las formaciones en las que participan, y su comportamiento habitual próximo a palabras en el discurso cotidiano, que redunda en la productividad de su explotación tanto léxica como gramatical.

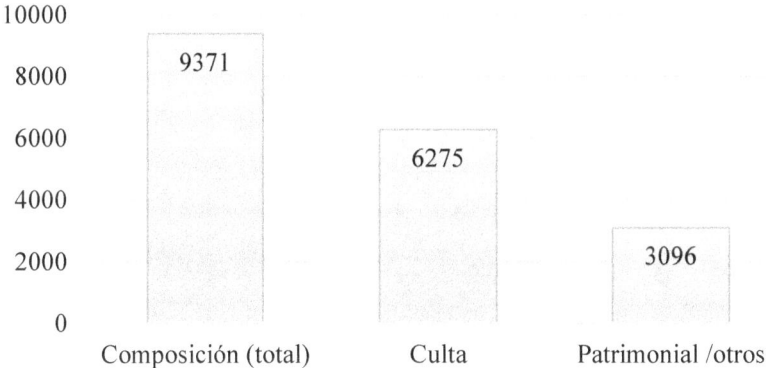

Figura 5.1. Usos neológicos formales por composición (Fuente: BOBNEO)

Si atendemos a los casos de neología consignados a través de la plataforma BOBNEO del Observatori de Neologia del IULA,[7] y relativos los últimos diez años (periodo 2010–2019), que nos sirven de forma orientativa para conocer el

---

[7] La plataforma BOBNEO del Observatori de Neologia del IULA (https://www.upf.edu/web/obneo, fecha de consulta 8 de agosto 2020), permite la extracción semiautomática (desde 1988) de distintos medios comunicación escritos y orales en español y catalán (http://obneo.iula.upf.edu/bobneo/index.php, fecha de consulta 8 de agosto 2020).

estatus actual de la composición culta en la prensa en español[8] (véase Figura 5.1), observamos un claro predominio de la composición culta y semiculta sobre la patrimonial.

Por otra parte, el registro comparativo correspondiente a las últimas décadas parece indicar un aumento progresivo del número de estas formaciones (véase Figura 5.2). Estos datos revelan el creciente protagonismo en español de elementos en principio restringidos a las lenguas de especialidad (Economía, Biología, Medicina, Derecho, etc.) en la lengua común. En todo caso, a pesar de su enorme difusión, muchos hablantes desconocen el significado exacto de estos elementos, por lo que su correcta interpretación se apoya principalmente en estrategias basadas en el enriquecimiento pragmático y la analogía estructural.

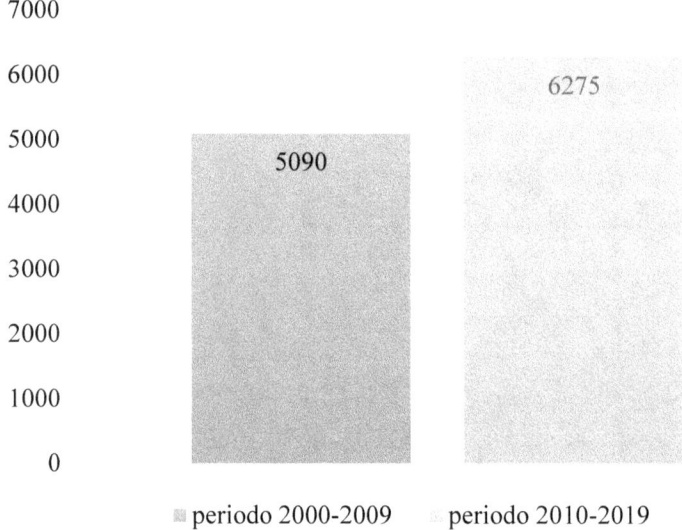

Figura 5.2. Neologismos por composición culta registrados (Fuente: BOBNEO)

---

[8] Los datos cuantitativos ofrecidos en BOBNEO para el periodo 2010-2019 indican la preferencia por la derivación frente a la composición en español, con 16.011 registros para la primera, frente a los 9.371 de la segunda. Sobre esta cuestión, Lüdtke (2011, 344) aduce: "El predominio de la derivación en las lenguas románicas es una herencia latina: la deficiencia de la composición, comparada con la griega, fue sentida como parte de la pobreza de la lengua latina […]."

En este cambio entran, sin duda, en juego aspectos como, de un lado, la marca de prestigio, que en el discurso periodístico puede amplificarse cuando trasciende el contexto especializado, aunque igualmente puede llegar a trivializarse (Adelstein 1998; Guerrero Ramos y Pérez Lagos 2012), y, de otro, el impacto atencional patente especialmente en la composición semiculta. Obsérvese, por ejemplo, la diferencia entre la formación culta *necrobiosis* ('muerte natural de la célula') y la semiculta *necroturismo* ('turismo de cementerios').

3 Datos psicolingüísticos relativos al procesamiento de algunos compuestos cultos del español

3.1 Propuesta metodológica

Con objeto de cotejar la progresiva consolidación de la composición culta a través de la prensa escrita en español en las últimas décadas con los datos psicolingüísticos, hemos tomado como referencia cuatro casos representativos de usos neológicos por composición culta recogidos en el Banco de neologismos del Centro Virtual Cervantes.[9] En ellos participan los elementos compositivos cultos *agro-* (del gr. ἀγρο- 'campo'), *auto-* (del gr. αὐτο- 'por uno mismo'), *-cidio* (del lat. *-cidium,* de la raíz de *caedĕre* 'acción de matar'), *crono-* (del gr. χρονο- 'tiempo') y *-fago* (del lat. *-phăgus,* y este del gr. φαγο- 'que come'). En particular, se ha realizado un estudio exploratorio *off-line* del procesamiento léxico, fundamentalmente centrado en el sentimiento de neologicidad que generan y el grado de complejidad cognitiva atribuido por el receptor. Para ello, estos ejemplos fueron presentados en sus correspondientes contextos periodísticos a través de un cuestionario dirigido a un total de 50 participantes, alumnos de segundo curso del Grado de Lingüística y lenguas aplicadas de la Universidad de Cádiz.

---

[9] El Banco de neologismos del Centro Virtual Cervantes (https://cvc.cervantes.es/lengua/banco_neologismos/default.htm, fecha de consulta 8 de agosto 2020) se apoya en los datos de NEOROC (red creada en 2004 con la participación de las universidades españolas de Alicante, Cádiz, Málaga, Murcia, País Vasco, Salamanca y Valencia) y de Antenas Neológicas (red creada en 2003 con las universidades latinoamericanas de Argentina, Chile, Colombia, Cuba, México, Perú y Uruguay).

Enunciados usados en el cuestionario:
1. Sanidad autoriza la venta en farmacias del equipo de **autodiagnóstico** del VIH (*El País*, España, 2018).
2. Desde el banco chino ICBC, Agustín Ibarguren, gerente de **agronegocios**, señaló que tuvieron consultas firmes por un monto de 500 millones de pesos (*La Nación*, Argentina, 2018).
3. "Somos unos **cronófagos**", define. "¿Qué pasa? Que a los hombres no nos interesa la igualdad. Por muy majo que seas, prefieres tener ventajas, principalmente, más tiempo que las mujeres" (*El País*, España, 2018).
4. El **sincericidio** de Fede Bal: "Volvería a estar con todas mis parejas" (*La Nación*, Argentina, 2019).

Los dos primeros, *autodiagnóstico* 'diagnóstico de un mismo' y *agronegocios* 'negocios agrarios' se distinguen por su mayor transparencia semántica y por presentar, desde la perspectiva funcional, una estructura atributiva (atributo-objeto). Por su parte, *cronófago* 'consumidor de tiempo' y *sincericidio* 'revelación imprudente' aluden a una interpretación alejada de la composicionalidad y, por tanto, poco transparente, además de presentar una estructura funcional predicativa (objeto-acción).

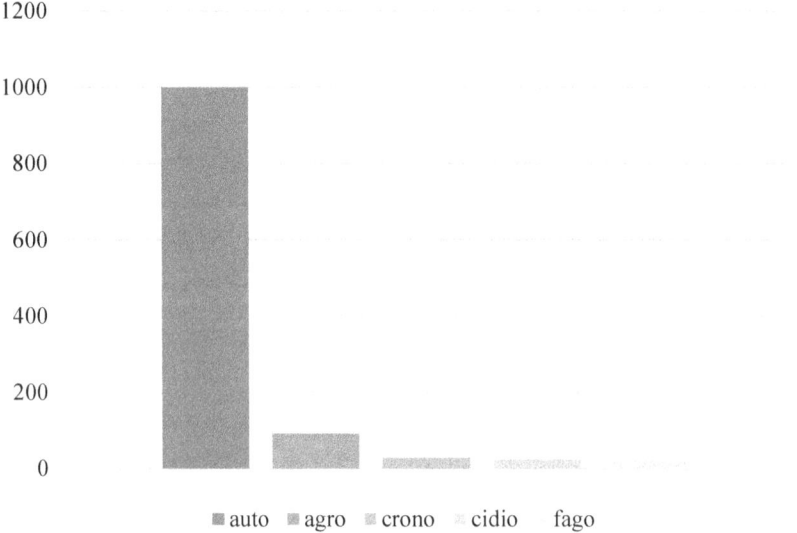

Figura 5.3. Registro de los elementos compositivos cultos utilizados en el estudio
(Fuente: BOBNEO)

Para las consideraciones derivadas del estudio se tomó también como referencia la cantidad de registros en BOBNEO de los elementos compositivos implicados en estas formaciones (véase Figura 5.3), donde sobresale *auto* sobre las otras cuatro.

Además de datos personales como edad, sexo, lengua/s materna/s y nivel de español (sólo para alumnos no nativos de español), se solicitó la siguiente información para cada uno de los enunciados propuestos:

1. Explique brevemente el sentido que tiene en ellos la palabra destacada en negrita. ¿Puede indicar algún sinónimo?
2. Indique si la ha oído o leído antes.
3. ¿Ha tenido que leer el texto más de una vez para entender esa palabra? SÍ / NO
4. ¿Ha utilizado la información contextual para entenderla? SÍ / NO
5. Grado de dificultad de esa palabra: 1 (muy baja)   2 (baja)   3 (media)   4 (alta)   5 (muy alta)
6. Grado de novedad: 1 (muy baja)   2 (baja)   3 (media)   4 (alta)   5 (muy alta)

3.2 Datos obtenidos

Las dos primeras cuestiones de la prueba (véanse las Figuras 5.4 y 5.5) nos permitieron recabar información sobre la relación entre el grado de familiaridad de cada creación léxica y la frecuencia de los elementos compositivos cultos considerados. Debe destacarse en los resultados obtenidos en el caso de la formación *agronegocios* la gran distancia entre el porcentaje de acierto (el mayor de los cuatro, 88,8%) y la familiaridad (relativamente baja, 22%). En el caso de *autodiagnóstico*, otro dato significativo es que, pese a obtener un alto porcentaje relativo al conocimiento previo de la formación (76%), sólo un 46% de los participantes en la tarea identificó de manera acertada el sentido. A partir de estos datos podría inducirse, pues, que, desde el punto de vista de la configuración formal, la familiaridad con el uso neológico tiene menor peso que la frecuencia de los elementos compositivos en otras formaciones y la apelación a procesos analógicos. Ello se ve refrendado, igualmente, por los porcentajes obtenidos por *cronófago*, en los que, aun siendo menores, se muestra de nuevo la distancia entre aciertos en la identificación del sentido (31,1%) y la familiaridad con la formación (apenas un 6,6%).

En términos de esfuerzo cognitivo (cuestiones 3 y 4), como para las otras dos cuestiones anteriores, *agronegocios* (35,5% lectura reiterada y 37% uso del contexto) y *autodiagnóstico* (33% lectura reiterada y 53% uso del contexto) muestran los porcentajes más bajos (véase Figura 5.5), pese a que se trata de formaciones vinculadas a discursos de especialidad (Economía y Medicina), frente a las otras dos, de motivación marcadamente apelativa. La mayor recurrencia a la información contextual en el caso de *autodiagnóstico* (53% frente al 37% de *agronegocios*) podría relacionarse con el carácter polisémico de la expresión *auto*, donde confluye, junto al significado primigenio de la lengua griega 'por uno mismo', el acortamiento de la forma *automóvil*, también presente en múltiples usos neológicos (*autorruta*, *narcoauto*, *automodelismo*, entre otras). En este sentido, pese a su mayor ocurrencia en formaciones neológicas análogas, la falta de univocidad parece añadir cierto grado de complejidad a *autodiagnóstico* frente a *agronegocios*.[10]

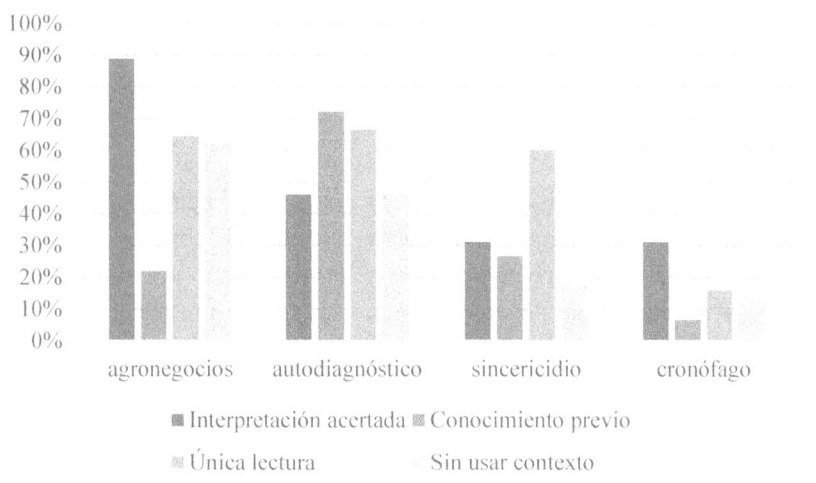

Figura 5.4. Datos sobre la relación entre interpretación acertada, familiaridad y esfuerzo de procesamiento

Respecto a los compuestos *sincericidio* y *cronófago*, al mayor número de errores interpretativos se suma la mayor complejidad cognitiva revelada por

---

[10] Aunque en *agro* existe confluencia homonímica con la voz derivada del latín *acer, acris* 'agrio', apenas compiten en el caso de creaciones neológicas por composición culta.

Datos psicolingüísticos en torno a la vitalidad y la neologicidad 103

los porcentajes correspondientes a la lectura reiterada y el apoyo en la información proporcionada por el contexto. Es evidente que en ambos casos la incongruencia semántica surgida de la combinación creada obliga a recurrir a estrategias de asociación semántica e integración contextual que pueden llegar a ralentizar el procesamiento. Por otra parte, *sincericidio* manifestó menor porcentaje en cuanto a la lectura reiterada, por la familiaridad con la voz patrimonial *sinceridad*, que indudablemente facilitó el proceso interpretativo requerido en esta tarea.

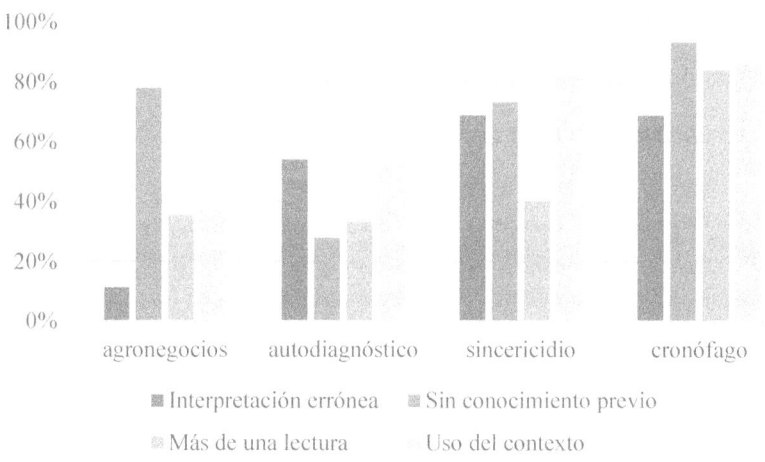

Figura 5.5. Datos sobre la relación entre interpretación errónea, familiaridad y esfuerzo de procesamiento

A la luz de las respuestas proporcionadas para las dos últimas cuestiones que se plantearon en la tarea (véase gráfico 4.6), neologicidad y dificultad cognitiva parecen ir de la mano. *Cronófago* obtiene la puntuación más alta, seguido de *sincericidio*. La confluencia en ambas de un menor grado de transparencia semántica puede, de nuevo, considerarse un factor determinante en este sentido. Respecto a las otras dos formaciones, la menor puntuación de *autodiagnóstico* se puede vincular, además de con la mayor transparencia semántica, con el mayor número de ocurrencias de *auto* en otras formaciones, que convierten a este compuesto en el menos novedoso. De este modo, puede decirse que en tanto que la analogía estructural contribuye decisivamente en la difusión de la composición culta, en un sentido inverso repercute en la pérdida del sentimiento de neologicidad, que se nutre tanto de los constantes reajustes semánticos del hablar como de la innovación combinatoria.

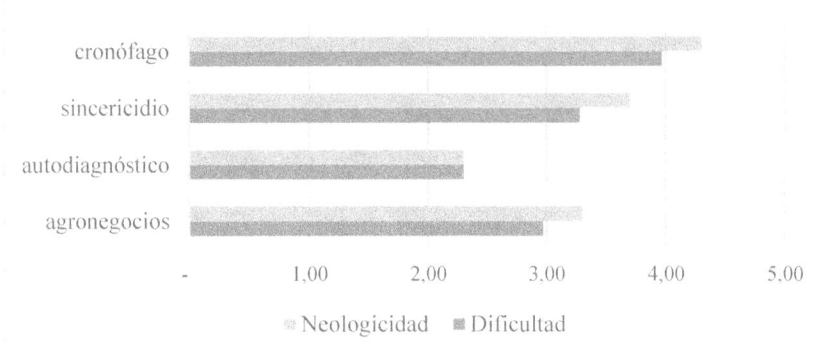

Figura 5.6. Datos sobre la relación entre grado de novedad y grado de dificultad

3.3 Reflexión en torno a los resultados

Los resultados de esta aproximación experimental, que evidentemente necesita ampliar en el futuro el corpus de casos y la muestra de hablantes, es consistente con el enfoque neurocognitivo basado en la existencia de redes asociativas del conocimiento lingüístico sustentadas en la fuerza de las conexiones neuronales (Lamb 1999; Pulvermüller 2005), como fundamento de la plasticidad y el aprendizaje. Este enfoque admite, además, la intervención de funciones mentales como la memoria y la atención.

La ocurrencia de los elementos compositivos cultos en gran número de formaciones permite explicar la eficacia en los procesos de creación y reconocimiento léxico, como parte integral de los mecanismos lingüísticos de abstracción, generalización y combinación simbólica. Este hecho, como se ve en los resultados de este experimento, se refleja en los porcentajes relativos a la identificación acertada del sentido de los compuestos propuestos y su correlación con la frecuencia de los constituyentes en otras creaciones, en tanto que la familiaridad con el uso neológico en cuestión muestra menor peso. Esto evidencia que el léxico es sensible a la composición morfológica de las palabras durante el curso temporal del procesamiento (Meunier y Longtin 2007) y que existe una clara vinculación entre la frecuencia de los constituyentes de la palabra y los tiempos de reconocimiento (Colé et al. 1989).[11]

---

[11] En todo caso, se han aducido diferencias entre lenguas respecto a los mecanismos de acceso y reconstrucción léxica, dependiendo de sus preferencias tipológicas (Waksler 1999).

Por otro lado, tal y como se ha mostrado a través de la comparación entre compuestos con distinto grado de transparencia semántica y diferente estructura argumental, el poder apelativo de estas creaciones neológicas conduce a la búsqueda de rutas semánticas alternativas a las ya presentes para el procesamiento. De este modo, la incompatibilidad surgida entre los elementos compositivos origina la activación de nuevas asociaciones conceptuales[12] como parte de una estrategia atencional relacionada con la búsqueda de relevancia semántica. Puede hablarse, por tanto, en líneas generales de un modelo multifactorial que integra de manera simultánea un sistema de reconstrucción morfológica y léxica y otro de análisis semántico-conceptual, donde cabe la complementariedad entre ambos.

En síntesis, aunque la composición culta, por su caracterización en el contexto de la formación de palabras, parece ajustarse atendiendo a un enfoque psicolingüístico a una estrategia de acceso múltiple cimentada en representaciones tanto léxicas como morfológicas que guían desde el punto de vista estructural la interpretación de la nueva unidad (Varo Varo, Díaz Hormigo y Paredes Duarte, 2009), de acuerdo con los datos de procesamiento obtenidos, también precisa de la actuación de una estrategia de asociación semántica-conceptual sobre todo en aquellos casos en los que no hay una interpretación componencial. De ahí que la posible neologicidad de estas formaciones derive no sólo de su organización interna y su relación con otras creaciones análogas, sino también de sus propiedades semánticas y su interacción con los contextos de uso.

Por último, la proliferación de la composición culta en contextos ajenos a la comunicación especializada, como ocurre en la prensa escrita puede tomarse como prueba de que la formación de palabras en lenguas románicas como el español tiende a una mayor complejidad respecto a las lenguas clásicas (Lüdtke 2011, 427), materializada en una mayor explotación de los mecanismos formales y semánticos y de la interacción entre estos.

---

[12] Los datos de la investigación neurocientífica sobre el lenguaje reconocen una red semántica altamente distribuida, que incorpora tanto áreas heteromodales, ubicadas en el lóbulo temporal y parte del córtex parietal inferior, como áreas del procesamiento motor y sensorial, además de estructuras relacionadas con el control ejecutivo situadas en la región prefrontal izquierda (por ejemplo, Ullmann 2004 y 2006; Federmeier, Kutas y Dickson 2016).

4 Conclusiones

El acercamiento a los procesos de identificación y reconocimiento de usos neológicos nos ha permitido constatar la gran versatilidad de los elementos compositivos cultos, mediada por estrategias cognitivas basadas en el equilibrio entre memoria y atención, que se traducen en procesos lingüísticos como la analogía y el enriquecimiento contextual, que repercuten en el esfuerzo cognitivo de procesamiento y que explican la productividad léxica de las lenguas. Asimismo, las conclusiones alcanzadas hacen posible el establecimiento de delimitaciones frente a otros mecanismos de creación léxica en español.

En suma, la experiencia sensorial, episódica y verbal volcada en el fenómeno de la neología se erige como un mecanismo esencial para construir nuevos moldes para la producción e interpretación del discurso, que ponen a prueba a las lenguas a través de la imaginería mental y los cambios y reajustes semánticos y combinatorios. En este marco, en el que es especialmente constatable el dinamismo en los procesos de innovación léxica, ganan creciente protagonismo los elementos compositivos cultos, por desplegar una enorme versatilidad que conjuga las dimensiones semántica y estructural de los sistemas lingüísticos implicados.

Referencias bibliográficas

Adelstein, Andreína. 1998. "Banalización de términos con formantes de origen grecolatino." En *Actas del V Simposio Iberoamericano de Terminología*, 12–17. México: RITerm.

Alemany, José de. 1920. *Tratado de la formación de palabras de la lengua castellana. La derivación y la composición. Estudio de los sufijos y los prefijos empleados en una y otra*. Madrid: Librería de Victoriano Suárez.

Alvar Ezquerra, Manuel. 1998. "Palabras nuevas en los periódicos de hoy." En *La lengua española a finales del milenio*, coordinado por Antonio Álvarez Tejedor, 13–44. Burgos: Caja de Burgos.

Alvar Ezquerra, Manuel. 2002. *La formación de palabras en español*. 5ª ed. Madrid: Arco/Libros.

Auger, Pierre, y Louis-Jean Rousseau. 2003. *Metodología de la Investigación Terminológica*. Edición y traducción de Gloria Guerrero Ramos y Juan María Bermúdez Fernández. Málaga: Universidad de Málaga.

Bally, Charles. 1965. *Linguistique générale et linguistique française.* Berna: Francke.

Bastuji, Jacqueline. 1974. "Aspects de la néologie sémantique." *Langages* 36: 6–19.

Cabré, María Teresa, M. Rosa Bayà, Elisenda Bernal, Judit Freixa, Elisabet Solé, y Teresa Vallès. 2002. "Evaluación de la vitalidad de una lengua a través de la neología: a propósito de la neología espontánea y de la neología planificada." En *Lèxic i neología*, editado por María Teresa Cabré, Judit Freixa, y Elisabet Solé, 159–201. Barcelona: Universitat Pompeu Fabra, Institut Universitari de Lingüística Aplicada, Observatori de Neologia.

Chériguen, Foudil. 1989. "Typologie des procédes de formation du lexique." *Cahiers de Lexicologie* 55(2): 53-59.

Colé, Pascale, Cécile Beauvillain, y Juan Segui. 1989. "On the Representation and Processing of Prefixed and Suffixed Derived Words. A Differential Frequency Effect." *Journal of Memory and Language* 28: 1–13.

Coseriu, Eugenio. 1978. "La formación de palabras desde el punto de vista del contenido." *Gramática, semántica, universales. Estudios de lingüística functional*, 239–264. Madrid: Gredos.

Coseriu, Eugenio. 2003. "Los procedimientos semánticos en la formación de palabras." *Odisea* 3: 179–189.

Díaz Hormigo, María Tadea. 2020. "Neología y prensa escrita. claves de unas interrelaciones necesarias." *Tonos Digital* 38(1): 1–38.

Federmeier, Kara, Marta Kutas, y Danielle Dickson. 2016. "A common neural progression to meaning in about a third of a second." En *Neurobiology of Language*, editado por Gregory Hickok y Steven L. Small, 557–567. Londres: Academic Press, Elsevier.

García Platero, Juan Manuel. 1999. "Los medios de comunicación ante la neología." En *Léxico y voces el español*, editado por Manuel Alvar Ezquerra y Gloria Corpas, 55–72. Málaga: Universidad de Málaga.

Guerrero Ramos, Gloria, y Fernando Pérez Lagos. 2012. "¿Es la composición culta, en la actualidad, el procedimiento más productivo para la creación de neologismos?" *Terminàlia* 6: 26–36.

Guerrero Salazar, Susana. 2007. *La creatividad en el lenguaje periodístico*. Madrid: Cátedra.

Lamb, Sidney, 1999. *Pathways of the brain. The neurocognitive basis of language*. Ámsterdam/Philadelphia: John Benjamins.

Lüdtke, Jens. 2011. *La formación de palabras en las lenguas románicas: su semántica en diacronía y sincronía*. México: El Colegio de México.

Méndez Santos, M. Carmen. 2011. *Los neologismos morfológicos del español en el lenguaje de la prensa. Estudio de la lexicogénesis del español a través de la prensa del español actual*. Madrid: Editorial Académica Española.

Meunier, Fanny, y Catherine-Marie Longtin. 2007. "Morphological decomposition and semantic integration in word processing." *Journal of Memory and Language* 56: 457–471.

NGLE = Real Academia Española, 2009. *Nueva gramática de la lengua española*. 2 vols. Madrid: Espasa Libros, SLU.

Pottier Navarro, Huguette. 1979. "La néologie en espagnol contemporain." *Les langues néolatines* 229-230: 148-172.

Pulvermüller, Friedemann. 2005. *The neuroscience of language*. Reimpr. Cambridge: Cambridge University Press.

Rey-Debove, Josette. 1984. "Le domaine de la morphologie lexicale." *Cahiers de Lexicologie* 45: 3-19.

Rondeau, Guy. 1984. *Introduction à la terminologie*. Québec: Gaëtan Morin.

Ullmann, Michael T. 2004. "Contributions of memory circuits to language: the declarative/procedural model." *Cognition* 92: 231–270.

Ullmann, Michael T. 2006. "Language and the brain." En *An Introduction to Language and Linguistics*, editado por Jeffrey Connor-Linton y Ralph Fasold, 235-274. Cambridge: Cambridge University Press.

Varo Varo, Carmen, María Tadea Díaz Hormigo, y María Jesús Paredes Duarte. 2009. "Modelos comunicativos y producción e interpretación neológicas." *Revista de Investigación Lingüística* 12 "Investigaciones en neología. Codificación y creatividad en lenguas romances": 185-216.

Waksler, Rachelle. 1999. "Cross-Linguistic Evidence for Morphological Representation in the Mental Lexicon." *Brain and Language* 68: 68–74.

Wartburg, Walther von. 1951. *Problemas y métodos de la lingüística*. Madrid: CSIC.

Chapter 6

Cultismos en el aula de enseñanza de la secundaria

María del Carmen Rodríguez Caballero[1]

I.E.S. "Poeta Claudio Rodríguez", Zamora

Resumen

El propósito de este artículo es estudiar los dobletes, cultismos, palabras patrimoniales y latinismos que aparecen en la lengua española cotidiana. Se ha llevado a cabo en el aula de secundaria en España con presencia de alumnos migrantes, algunos no provenientes de lenguas romances, con lo que transformamos el aula en un espacio intercultural. Se ha adoptado una metodología basada en el análisis del discurso: cada texto está enmarcado en un discurso, y el alumno, para comprender un texto, necesita conocimientos lingüísticos, referenciales y socioculturales.

Summary

The aim of this article is to study the doublets, learnèd words, inherited words and Latinisms which appear in everyday Spanish. It has been carried out with a secondary school class in Spain attended by pupils who are migrants, some of whose mother tongue is not a Romance language, so the class has been transformed into an intercultural space. I adopt a methodology based on discourse analysis: every text is framed in a particular discourse, and to understand the text pupils need linguistic, referential and sociocultural knowledge.

---

[1] Se trata de una redacción de la charla que dio Carmen Rodríguez en el Coloquio, a la que he añadido información de fondo (CJP).

Keywords

Latin, Lexical borrowing, Teaching of Latin, Discourse analysis, Spanish, English.

1 Introducción

El currículo y la ordenación de la etapa de secundaria dispuestos en la Ley Orgánica 8/2013 de 9 de diciembre[2] posibilitan la respuesta a las diferentes motivaciones e intereses del alumnado, contribuyendo, por tanto, a lograr una mejor calidad en la educación que pueda traducirse en éxito para toda la comunidad educativa. En el bloque 3 del currículo de Lengua Castellana y su Literatura se mencionan los aspectos socioculturales y sociolingüísticos y el estudio de cultismos en la lengua. En la Orden ECD/ 65/2015 de 21 de enero[3] se establece que la materia de Cultura Clásica va a contribuir al desarrollo de las competencias básicas en ciencia, tecnología y matemáticas, ya que muchos de los principios y teoremas que se emplean actualmente fueron desarrollados por los matemáticos griegos. También muchas de las ciencias tuvieron su primer desarrollo en la Antigüedad, como la geografía, la zoología, la botánica o la astronomía. Además, el conocimiento de étimos grecolatinos presentes en el lenguaje matemático ayuda a mejorar la comprensión de conceptos, enunciados y otros contenidos científicos y matemáticos.

2 Objetivos

Por medio de la Cultura Clásica los alumnos aprenden a:

- Apreciar manifestaciones culturales y artísticas en general, por ejemplo, festividades como antruejos, fiestas de romanos, Navidad y Semana Santa.
- Valorar hechos culturales, como la mitología, que forma parte de nuestra civilización.
- Ampliar su visión del mundo con visitas a museos, al teatro y a conciertos.

---

[2] https://www.boe.es/buscar/doc.php?id=BOE-A-2013-12886, fecha de consulta 3 de noviembre 2020.
[3] https://www.boe.es/buscar/pdf/2015/BOE-A-2015-738-consolidado.pdf, fecha de consulta el 3 de noviembre 2020.

- Tolerar y respetar las diferencias y el diálogo como base de los acuerdos. El alumnado adquiere estas destrezas, entre otras, gracias al papel mediador de Grecia y Roma.
- Formular hipótesis sobre contenido y contexto.
- Identificar cultismos, dobletes y palabras patrimoniales en la lengua cotidiana.
- Inferir y formular hipótesis sobre significados a partir de la comprensión de elementos significativos, lingüísticos y paralingüísticos.
- Estudiar la pertinencia de estos términos.

3 La deuda del español con las lenguas clásicas

El español no solo es una evolución del latín, sino que tomó prestadas numerosas palabras del latín (y del griego, en muchos casos por medio del latín) como consecuencia de los contactos renacentistas que tuvo con la cultura clásica, en común con otras lenguas de Europa occidental. Muchas de estas palabras se han incorporado a la lengua cotidiana, y los alumnos pueden apreciar fácilmente que en las lenguas modernas existen numerosos latinismos y helenismos que ya conocen, como *cosmética* (del adjetivo griego κοσμητικός 'relativo al adorno'), *técnico* (gr. τεχνικός / lat. *technĭcus* 'profesor de un arte') y *físico* (gr. φυσικός / lat. *physĭcus* 'relativo a la naturaleza'). Además, contamos con un amplio grupo de helenismos surgidos en el ámbito científico-técnico ante la necesidad de nombrar nuevos instrumentos y descubrimientos. Algunos de estos neologismos, presentes en las distintas lenguas modernas, ya están plenamente integrados en el habla común, como son *átomo* (del adjetivo griego ἄτομος 'que no se puede cortar' / lat. *ătŏmus*), *telégrafo* (gr. τηλε- 'a distancia' + -γράφος 'que escribe') y *dermatólogo* (gr. δερματο- 'piel' + -λογος 'estudioso').

A continuación comento las actividades pedagógicas mediante las cuales se puede despertar la curiosidad de los alumnos y fomentar su interés en las lenguas clásicas.

3.1 Estudio de textos

Los alumnos observan los diferentes textos donde aparecen expresiones clásicas como son:
- *lorem ipsum*: el texto pseudo-latino basado en un pasaje de Cicerón que suelen utilizar los tipógrafos para demostrar distintas fuentes tipográficas.

- *ipso facto*: en el sentido de 'por el hecho mismo, inmediatamente, en el acto' (*DLE*), se emplea en determinados estilos de habla:

(1) ¿Me haría el favor de ir y decirle que el inspector Fumero le envía recado urgente de que acuda **ipso facto** al mercado de la Boquería a comprar veinte duros de garbanzos hervidos [...]? (*CORPES XXI*: Carlos Ruiz Zafón, *La sombra del viento* (Barcelona: Planeta), 2003).

- *ultimátum, ¿Quo vadis?*: expresiones bastante corrientes en la prensa:

(2)
   a. **Ultimátum** de Johnson a Europa para renegociar el plan del 'brexit'.
   b. **¿Quo vadis** Ciudadanos? (titulares del *Diario de León*, 6 de mayo 2019).

- *ecológico*: compuesto técnico procedente de los elementos griegos οἰκο- 'casa' + -λόγος 'estudioso', de acuñación relativamente reciente (la primera instancia que se da en *CORDE* es de 1926). Los alumnos conocerán esta palabra en la biología, y es además tema de gran interés actual.

A los alumnos se les pide que hagan una clasificación de estas palabras latinas y griegas y su uso cotidiano. Es muy importante la apreciación del contexto discursivo en que se emplean (registros coloquiales, periodísticos, científicos y técnicos, etc.).

3.2 La música

Otro aspecto que tratamos con ellos es el papel de la música en la vida cotidiana. Sabemos que la música formaba parte de la vida de los romanos. Junto con el departamento de música, los alumnos analizan el Epitafio de Sícilo, una de las composiciones musicales más antiguas que se ha conservado, lo que los lleva a preguntar qué es un epitafio, a quién está dirigido y qué es lo que se canta.

3.3 Orígenes de palabras comunes

Trabajamos étimos griegos en palabras comunes del español, como son *biblioteca* (lat. *bibliothēca*, del gr. *βιβλιοθήκη*) y *farmacia* (del gr. *φαρμακεία*).

3.4 Festividades y tradiciones locales

En las festividades y tradiciones de Castilla y León hay muchas referencias a la civilización romana: véase, por ejemplo, la recreación de un campamento romano que es tema de un informe del *Diario de León* del 5 de julio de 2019.[4] Es más, varios establecimientos de Zamora tienen nombres latinos, aprovechando el pasado romano de la región: *Bar Dativo, Bar Viriato,* y *Ocellum Durii,* nombre de un asentamiento prerromano mencionado por Plinio el Viejo que se ha identificado con la actual ciudad de Zamora, utilizado como nombre por varias empresas zamoranas.

3.5 El cambio semántico

Estudiamos el cambio semántico, y procesos como la ampliación y restricción referencial en la evolución de palabras del latín al castellano. Algunos ejemplos son:

- En la palabra española *éxito* 'resultado feliz' se ve una restricción del sentido del lat. *exĭtus,* que significó una noción más general de 'salida'.
- Lat. *fortis*, además de 'fuerte', significaba 'valiente'.
- Lat. *metĭcŭlōsus* significaba 'medroso, miedoso, tímido' (Blánquez Fraile, 1985, 963). Esp. *meticuloso* se tomó del latín en el siglo XV, originalmente en el mismo sentido; en el castellano moderno, sin embargo, se usa fundamentalmente con el significado de 'concienzudo, detallista'. El enlace se aprecia en su uso en el latín tardío, cuando ya aparece con la acepción de 'cuidadoso por miedo a equivocarse'. Todavía en el siglo XIX tenía un sentido despectivo (3a), y es solo en el siglo XX cuando vemos un valor positivo, tal vez, como lo demuestra (3b), por la asociación de la meticulosidad con el método científico y la salud:

(3)
    a. La reforma doctrinal, ejercida por una crítica estrecha y **meticulosa**, á fuerza de encarecer la llaneza y la claridad, y de hacer estribar una parte muy principal del valor poético en el respeto á amaneradas formas y á clasificaciones arbitrarias, acarreó á la poesía la mayor de las desventuras (*CORDE*: Leopoldo Augusto de Cueto, *Bosquejo histórico-crítico de la poesía castellana*, 1869).

---

[4] https://www.diariodeleon.es/articulo/provincia/pueblo-ejercitos-roma-toman-villa/201907050400011903550.html, fecha de consulta 3 de noviembre de 2020.

b. Gracias a la higiene **meticulosa**, y a la existencia ordenada, y a la sobrealimentación, podían fingir una apariencia de vida (*CORDE*: Wenceslao Fernández Flórez, *Volvoreta*, 1917–1945).

- El sentido de lat. *misericordia* 'compasión, lástima, piedad' (también esp. *misericordia*) se amplió por asociación a significar la pieza, a modo de repisa, situada debajo de los asientos de los coros de las catedrales, colegiatas y monasterios. Mientras los respaldos, baldaquinos y antebrazos de la sillería reproducían escenas o motivos religiosos edificantes, las misericordias se reservaban para tallar en ellas temas profanos, fantásticos o grotescos, en correspondencia muchas veces con la parte del cuerpo a la que la misericordia iba destinada, para dar alivio, o "compadecerse" de los frailes durante los oficios largos.

3.6 Expresiones latinas

Reparto entre alumnos tarjetas con tópicos latinos y comentarios o preguntas sobre la expresión que tendrán que relacionar. Son expresiones que se ven con cierta frecuencia en la literatura e incluso en el habla culta de hoy en día. Los relacionan por parejas y explican su significado aplicándolo a la vida diaria. Buen ejemplo es *carpe diem*, que también aparece en el *DLE*: este tópico se ha utilizado en literatura con sentidos diversos y significa 'Vive el momento (porque has de morir)': proviene de unos versos que el poeta latino Horacio dedicó a Leucónoe *(Odas,* I, IX).

(4)

[...] **carpe diem**, dijo Tomás, eso se llama **carpe diem**. Sí, **carpe diem**, repitió Alfredo, la de cosas que se aprenden y se olvidan, **carpe diem**, toma otro vaso, el último, ya se ha acabado la botella (*CORPES XXI*: J.A. Bueno Álvarez, *El último viaje de Eliseo Guzmán*. Madrid: Alfaguara, 2001).

Otras expresiones bastante conocidas son:

- *noctuas Athenas afferre* 'llevar lechuzas a Atenas', es decir, llevar algo que es inútil por la abundancia que ya existe (corresponde al modismo castellano *ir a vendimiar y llevar uvas de postre*)
- *audentes fortuna iuvat* 'la suerte ayuda a los valientes'
- *ars gratia artis* 'el arte por el arte mismo'
- *dura lex sed lex* 'la ley es dura, pero es la ley'.

3.7 Recursos en línea

Los alumnos pueden trabajar con los diversos recursos disponibles en línea. Empiezan con cuatro definiciones en forma de códigos QR que definen los términos *palabra patrimonial* ('Términos procedentes del latín hablado que han sufrido cambios fonéticos y semánticos', como, por ejemplo, *agua*), *cultismo* ('Vocablos que penetraron desde el latín escrito a partir del s.XV y apenas han sufrido transformaciones fonéticas o semánticas', como *epístola*), *doblete* ('Par de palabras que poseen la misma etimología; una es patrimonial y otra, culta', como *plano/llano* y *lidiar/litigar*) y *latinismo* ('Expresiones tomadas directamente del latín', como *superávit* y *addendum*). Entonces buscan estas palabras en los diccionarios de la Real Academia Española,[5] en la Fundéu (Fundación del Español Urgente, asesorada por la Real Academia Española),[6] y en el Centro Virtual Cervantes.[7] De esta forma aprecian la deuda del español con el latín y el proceso de asentamiento de los préstamos y los neologismos; también aprenden las normas de escribirlos. Por ejemplo, la Fundéu explica que las locuciones latinas, estén o no asentadas en el uso, deben tratarse como el resto de los extranjerismos y escribirse tal y como se hacía en la lengua original, por tanto sin acentuación gráfica y en cursiva o entre comillas. Así es que mientras *ipso facto* se escribe en cursiva, la preposición *versus* no necesita destacarse con cursiva por considerarse palabra del español;[8] *currículo* se escribe con tilde, mientras que *curriculum vitae* no se acentúa. También hay que tener en cuenta la morfología de estas formas; el plural de *superávit* es *superávits*, y el plural de *ultimátum* es *ultimátums*: el DPD[9] señala que los términos que proceden de otras lenguas y que terminan en *-m* hacen el plural añadiendo una *-s*.

3.8 El leonés

Una comparación de palabras castellanas y leonesas no solo permite una apreciación del cambio fonético sino que también pone al alumno en contacto

---

[5] https://www.rae.es/, fecha de consulta 3 de noviembre 2020.
[6] https://www.fundeu.es/, fecha de consulta 3 de noviembre 2020.
[7] https://blogscvc.cervantes.es/martes-neologico/indice-entradas/, fecha de consulta 3 de noviembre 2020.
[8] https://www.fundeu.es/recomendacion/locuciones-latinas-latinismos-errores-frecuentes-621/, fecha de consulta 3 de noviembre 2020.
[9] https://www.rae.es/dpd/, fecha de consulta 3 de noviembre de 2020.

con su entorno y su herencia cultural. Hay palabras, que aún existen en la zona de Castilla y León, que contrastan con sus cognados castellanos, como:

- leon. *forca* / cast. *horca* (del lat. *furca*). La *f-* inicial del latín se conservó en leonés, pero en castellano se transformó en *h-*, y luego desapareció en la lengua estándar.
- leon. *llar* / cast. *lar* (del lat. *lar*). La *l-* inicial latina se transforma en /ʎ/ en leonés.
- leon. *güechu* / cast. *ojo* (del lat. *ŏcŭlus*). La *ŏ* acentuada del latín se transforma en el diptongo *ue* tanto en castellano como en leonés, pero en castellano este cambio no se produce antes de una consonante palatal (el grupo latino *-c'l-* se convirtió en /ʒ/ en castellano y en /ʎ/ o /tʃ/ en leonés).

4 Conclusiones

A modo de conclusión, se puede decir que por medio del legado lingüístico del latín y del griego en el español moderno se propone a los alumnos una serie de actividades basadas en la comunicación lingüística y cultural que les conciencia de la presencia de elementos clásicos en textos de distintos géneros. Estas actividades se centran en el habla cotidiana, algunos tipos de cambio lingüístico, el cómo los préstamos y los neologismos se asientan en el idioma y lo que se considera la utilización correcta del español. Aprenden también a manejar importantes recursos lingüísticos digitales.

Referencias bibliográficas

Blánquez Fraile, Agustín. 1985. *Diccionario Latino-Español Español-Latino*, 3 tomos. Barcelona: Sopena.

CORDE = Real Academia Española. *Banco de datos (CORDE). Corpus diacrónico del español*. Fecha de consulta 16 de agosto 2020. http://www.rae.es.

CORPES XXI = Real Academia Española. *Banco de datos (CORPES XXI). Corpus del español del siglo XXI*. Fecha de consulta 16 de agosto 2020. https://www.rae.es/recursos/banco-de-datos/corpes-xxi.

DLE = Asociación de Academias de la Lengua Española, 2014–. *Diccionario de la lengua española*, 23rd ed. Madrid: Espasa. Fecha de consulta 16 de agosto 2020. https://dle.rae.es/.

DPD = Real Academia Española. 2005. *Diccionario panhispánico de dudas*. Madrid: Real Academia Española / Asociación de Academias de Lengua Española. Fecha de consulta 16 de agosto 2020. https://www.rae.es/recursos/diccionarios/dpd.

Chapter 7

"Classical" and "modern" languages

Bozena Wislocka Breit

Queen Mary University of London

Summary

I sketch the evolution of the words Eng. *classical* / Sp. *clásico* and Eng. *modern* / Sp. *moderno* as descriptive terms for languages. These words are cultured borrowings (Sp. *cultismos*), borrowed directly from Lat. *classĭcus* and *mŏdernus* (and in the case of Spanish not inherited direcrly from Latin as its parent language). The evolution of Eng. *classical* / Sp. *clásico* is examined in the context of the associated terms Eng. *ancient* / Sp. *antiguo* and Eng. *learnèd* / Sp. *sabio*, and that of Eng. *modern* / Sp. *moderno* in the context of Eng. *vulgar* / Sp. *vulgar*, Eng. *vernacular* / Sp. *vernáculo* and Eng. *foreign* / Sp. *extranjero*. I also explore what would appear to be the idiosyncratic development of the English doublet *classical/classic*, a distinction which is not made in Spanish. I then examine the contrast and competition between these and other words when collocated with Eng. *language(s)* and *tongue(s)* and Sp. *lengua(s)* and *idioma(s)*, concluding with some speculations on the reasons for their favouring at different times.

Resumen

Esbozamos la evolución de las palabras ing. *classical* / esp. *clásico* e ing. *modern* / esp. *moderno* como términos descriptivos aplicados a las lenguas. Estas palabras son cultismos tomados directamente de lat. *classĭcus* y *mŏdernus* (y en el caso del español no heredadas del latín, la lengua patrimonial). Estudiamos la evolución de ing. *classical* / esp. *clásico* en el contexto de los términos relacionados ing. *ancient* / esp. *antiguo* e ing. *learnèd* / esp. *sabio*, y la de ing. *modern* / esp. *moderno* en el contexto de ing. / esp. *vulgar*, ing. *vernacular* / esp. *vernáculo* e ing. *foreign* / esp. *extranjero*. También exploramos lo que parece ser el desarrollo idiosincrásico del doblete inglés *classical* / *classic*, distinción ajena al español. Luego examinamos cómo estas palabras contrastan y compiten con otras en su combinación con ing. *language(s)* y *tongue(s)* y esp. *lengua(s)* e *idioma(s)*, concluyendo con algunas observaciones especulativas sobre las posibles razones por las que se veían favorecidas de una época a otra.

Keywords

Lexical borrowing, Lexical competition, Teaching and study of modern languages, Teaching and study of classical languages.

1 Characterisations of languages

I begin with a consideration of how distinctions in types of languages have been perceived by scholars over the ages. The dichotomy between "classical" and "modern" languages is only one of many possible classifications, and appears to be based primarily on cultural prestige: from a Eurocentric perspective, Greek and Latin as the languages of the Greek and Roman culture transmitted to Western Europe in the Renaissance represent much that underpins the educational traditions of present-day societies. The same distinction is also used in relation to individual "modern" languages themselves, where it is very clearly associated with cultural excellence (implicit, as will be seen, in the etymology of this word and its cognates): see, for example, Cobbin's (1834) explicit title *The Classical English Vocabulary, Containing a Selection of Words Commonly Used by the Best Writers*. But the classical/modern dichotomy also intersects with other commonly used distinctions. It relates to medium: language in its cultured written manifestations, which are of necessity the only source of knowledge of the Greek and Latin of these times, as opposed to the spoken, or vernacular, developments of them which are the basis of the present-day Romance languages and Modern Greek. (This does not mean that Ancient Greek and Latin did not have corresponding spoken languages, but they are sometimes distinguished from the written medium, as, for example, in the vexed term "Vulgar" Latin: see, for example, Lloyd 1979). "Classical" may also refer to a particular period of a "modern" language that is considered to exhibit such excellence (so, for example, *español clásico* is sometimes taken to be the Spanish of the Golden Age, see Cano Aguilar 1984; Serradilla Castaño 2004), and the same is true of Latin, where Classical Latin is contrasted with such terms as Early Latin, Late Latin, Low Latin and Medieval Latin. There is also a relation with the use of "sacred" as opposed to "profane": Latin has such a "sacred" status as the language of the Roman Catholic liturgy, Classical Arabic as the language of the Qur'an. The notion of "modern" interacts with official status (it is usually only standard official languages which are taught and hence constitute the academic subject of "modern languages") and with the mode of learning ("modern languages" implies foreign or non-native languages seen from the perspective of the country in which the teaching is taking place). A further consideration is that of universality, a status to which Latin, French and English might at various times lay claim. Thus the conceptualisations underlying these dichotomies and distinctions are often arbitrary and not always mutually exclusive, as can clearly be seen from the case of Latin, which is at once "classical" both in the sense of pertaining to Roman civilisation, excellent because it was a vehicle of influential literature, history and thought (and in these connections "dead"), but also the spoken language of the Roman Empire living on both in its evolution to the present-day Romance languages, which in an important sense are "neo-Latin" (Wright 2004, 6), and in its use as a universal second language of the Western church and Western European culture.

It is also worth pointing out how preferred usage is essentially arbitrary and is subject to change. In modern English it is usual to speak of "Classical Latin" but of "Ancient Greek", yet, as can be seen from Figures 7.1 and 7.2, which show the frequency of these terms in English texts from 1800–2019 according to Google ngram viewer as against the terms "Ancient Latin" and "Classical Greek", while "Ancient Greek" has remained dominant into the 21st century, the parallel collocation "Ancient Latin", while favoured in the nineteenth century, subsequently declined in favour of the present-day usage.

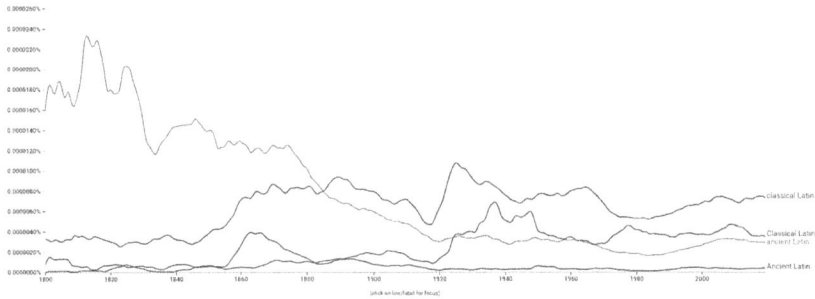

Figure 7.1. *Classical Latin* and *Ancient Latin* in Google ngram viewer, 1800–2019[1]

---

[1] The *y* axis in this and all the graphs generated by the Google ngram viewer show for each bigram (collocation) its percentage within all bigrams; such graphs serve to indicate the frequency of occurrence of a number of bigrams relative to one another.

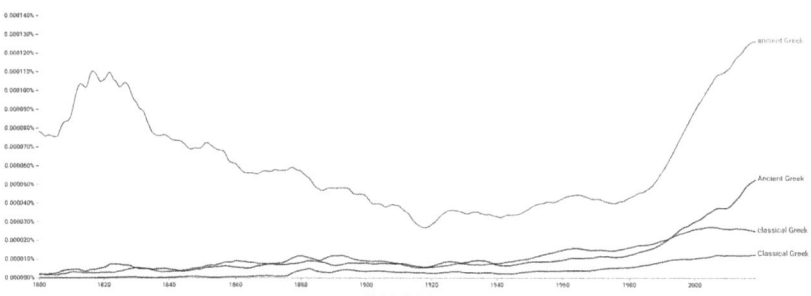

Figure 7.2. *Classical Greek* and *Ancient Greek* in Google ngram viewer, 1800–2019

2 Origins

2.1 Eng. *classical* ~ *classic* / Sp. *clásico*

As already mentioned, these words are clear cultured borrowings which are first attested in their host languages towards the end of the sixteenth century. The first examples in *OED*[2] and *CORDE* are shown in (1a-c); (1b) and (1d) are the first examples of Eng. *classic(al)* and Sp. *clásico* applied to a language.

(1)
    a. The whych myracles, are not fayned of late yeares, but were wrytten, many hundred yeares agone, & that by **classicall** and auncient wryters (*OED*: W. Peryn, *Thre Serm.* (new ed.) iii. sig. K.viiiv, 1546).

    b. Since pedling Barbarismes gan be in request, Nor **classicke** tongues, nor learning found no rest (*OED*: Bp. J. Hall *Virgidemiarum*: 1st 3 Bks. ii. iii. 34, 1597).

    c. Tanta honra era el ser uno soldado que no admitían a qualquiera para serlo, sino sólo a los ciudadanos **clássicos**, que eran los más ricos y honrados (*CORDE*: Gaspar Gutiérrez de los Ríos, *Noticia general para la estimación de las artes*, 1600).

    d. Que ningún idioma hay **clásico** que no haya comenzado también vulgar (*CORDE*: Fray Hortensio Paravicino, *Oración fúnebre a Fray Simón de Rojas*, 1624).

What may be regarded as the stem-form of Eng. *classic(al)* / Sp. *clásico*, Eng. *class* / Sp. *clase*, is attested rather earlier (*OED* 1533, *CORDE* as early as

---

[2] Alphabetically ordered dictionaries are referenced without page numbers.

1400) and has a higher frequency. Both these words are very widely adopted in the languages of Western Europe, and transnational contact is likely to have played a part in such diffusion, although the detail of this is impossible to establish (*OED* in this and many other such cases hedges its bets by suggesting that the word is of multiple origins, partly a borrowing from Latin and partly a borrowing from French). Lat. *classis*, the ultimate origin of Eng. *class* / Sp. *clase*, was originally related to the notion of people assembled or called together (cf. Lat. *clamo* 'to call') and denoted the divisions of the Roman people established by Servius Tullius in the sixth century BC; by extension it referred to a body of citizens called to arms, either as a land army or as a fleet; in post-Augustan Latin it developed the more general meaning of 'group', with which it has settled in modern host languages (Lewis and Short 1879, s.v. "clamo"). Lat. *classĭcus* originally referred to the fifth and most wealthy class of Roman citizens, and eventually came to mean 'of the highest rank, of a superior standard'. This is the sense that is preserved in modern English *classic*, and it can also be seen in such Spanish examples as:

(2)
    ¿Hay arte más sabida ni doctrina más **clásica** en la escuela dellas? (*CORDE*: Antonio de Eslava, *Noches de invierno*, 1609).

I have been able to find no evidence of *classĭcus* being used as a characterisation of "language" in Latin. It is also difficult to know exactly what the meaning of Eng. *classical ~ classic* / Sp. *clásico* is in some early examples: cf. (1b) and (1d) above, where the meaning may be 'regarded as excellent' rather than 'pertaining to Greek and Latin' (except by implication). Similarly, in English, *classic(al)* does not seem to be readily associated with language at first. Indeed, Percyvall (1591) omits *clásico* from his bilingual Spanish-English dictionary, and while Cotgrave (1611) provides a number of translations of French *classique* ('classical, formall, orderlie'; 'approued, authentical' and 'chiefe, principall') there is no explicit mention of *classic(al) writers* or *classic(al) languages*.

However, by the eighteenth century, the specific association with Greek and Latin is clear (3a), and Eng. *classical* appears in collocation with *Latin* and *Greek* already in the seventeenth century (3b–c).

(3)
   a. It is surprising, that without any knowledge of the **classical** languages, he attained to a perfect acquaintance with the French (*OED*: *Biogr. Gallica* II. 123, 1752).
   b. 'Tis as remarkable for the litle sise as the good matter contained in it, and the authentick and **classicall Latin** (*OED*: Sir T. Browne *Let. 25 Feb.* in *Wks.* (1852) III. 442, ?1676).
   c. We are not to expect to meet always with **Classical Greek** there, or with words, always in the sense of Classical Authors (*OED*: T. Baker, *Refl. Learning* xvi. 199, 1699).

As signalled above, English, unlike Spanish, has two words deriving from Lat. *classĭcus*, *classic* and *classical* (*-al* being an analogically added adjectival suffix, cf. *lyric/lyrical*), which in the modern language are discriminated semantically, *classic* having the meaning of 'excellent, prestigious, archetypical, representative of an acknowledged standard' while *classical* is associated with reference to Greek and Latin Antiquity, as well as referring to comparable stages of other languages (e.g. *Classical Arabic*, *Classical Chinese*, *Classical French*). Comparing usage decade by decade, the joint number of occurrences of *classic* and *classick* occurrences is generally significantly smaller than those of *classical*, as shown in Figure 7.3.

	1590	1600	1610	1620	1630	1640	1650	1660	1670	1680	1690
classic(k)	0	0	0	0	1	19	31	36	28	32	54
classical	5	3	2	1	0	33	170	61	83	84	54

Figure 7.3. Occurrences of *classic*, *classick* and *classical* in *EEBO*, 1590–1700

The overlapping meanings of *classic* and *classical* have resulted in numerous lexicographical cross-references signalled in *OED*, mainly related to collocations other than those with *language* (see, for example, Kaunisto 2007). The ongoing split into two adjectives means that it is possible to combine *classic(al)* in its sense of 'excellent' with *modern*, so English exhibits such collocations as *modern classical music, classic modern fiction*.

2.2 Eng. *modern* / Sp. *moderno*

Like Eng. *classical* ~ *classic* / Sp. *clásico*, these words are also cultured borrowings (from Lat. *mŏdernus* 'modern, of the present'), as are their base forms Eng. *mode* / Sp. *modo* (from Lat. *mŏdus* 'measure; manner'): once again the *OED* mentions the involvement of French. The first examples in *OED* and

CORDE[3] (4a–b) are rather earlier than those of Eng. *classical ~ classic* / Sp. *clásico*; in Spanish, it seems to be regularly used in contexts, such as (4b), in which it is counterposed to the antonym *antig(u)o*, and perhaps this antonymic relationship was one of the factors involved in encouraging its diffusion.

(4)
    a. Gif a man proponis [etc.]... he suld suere... yat jt is sa suthely, be alde doctouris. Bot be the opynioun of the doctouris oure maisteris **modernis**... he suld say he traistis fermly jt be sa (*OED*: G. Hay *Bk. Law of Armys* (2005) 250, c.1485).

    b. este libro. prouado por los mejores antigos medicos & **modernos** discretos que podieren ser aujdos por tal que a todos ssea autentico (*CORDE*: Estéfano de Sevilla, *Visita y consejo de médicos*. Biblioteca Nacional de Madrid, MS. 18052, before 1400).

Application of this adjective to languages appears to be first attested in works by scholars writing about language. In English, there are a number of examples from Sir Francis Bacon's *The Advancement of Learning* (5a) while in Spanish the first cases I have been able to find are from the following century, including an extended example by Fray Martín Sarmiento (5b):

(5)
    a. Wherein though men in learnèd tongues do tie themselves to the ancient measures, yet in **modern** languages it seemeth to me as free to make new measures of verses as of dances (Sir Francis Bacon, *The Advancement of Learning*, 1605).

    b. Este lenguaje [of the Strasbourg Oaths] se parece mas al Castellano antiguo, que el Francés **moderno**, al Castellano **moderno**; y se parece mas al Latin, que los dos idiomas **modernos** y vulgares: luego en el siglo nono, aunque el Latin barbarizado hiciese ya, como idiomas distintos, el Romance Francés, y el Romance Español, se prueba en su mayor antigüedad, que no eran lenguas antiguas, sino corrupciones de la Romana (*CORDE*: Fray Martín Sarmiento (Pedro José García y Balboa), *Memorias para la Historia de la poesía y poetas españoles*, c 1745).

---

[3] The apparent fourteenth-century examples in *CORDE* from the *Libro de Cifar* are in fact from a much later copy of this text (see CORDEMÁFORO).

In both these examples there is valuable evidence of relationships with other words: in (6a) *modern* is opposed to *learnèd* (and, to a lesser extent, *ancient*, while in (6b) *moderno* contrasts with *antiguo*; *moderno* is also associated with *vulgar*.

The use of Eng. *modern* to characterise contemporary languages as opposed to Latin and Greek is well established in the seventeenth century (6a). However, *modern* does not yet appear to be in a dichotomous relationship with *classic(al)*: rather, it contrasts with *ancient* (6b).

(6)
  a. [...] have also refin'd our Language to that height, that, for elegance, for fluency, and hapinesse of expression, I am perswaded it gives not place to any **Modern** Language, spoken in *Europe*; scarcely to the Latin and Greek themselves." (Edward Phillips, *The new World of English Words: Or, a General Dictionary*, Preface b31658, 1658. https://books.google.co.uk/books?id=RR9lAAAAcAAJ&source=gbs_navlinks_s, 4 December 2019).
  b. [...] if he [Sir William Temple] means, that we cannot make a new Grammar of a dead Language, whose Analogy has been determined almost Two Thousand Years, it is what can admit of no Dispute. But if he means, that **Modern** Languages have not been Grammatically examined; at least, not with that Care that some **Ancient** Tongues have been; that is a Proposition which may, perhaps, be very justly questioned (William Wotton, *Reflections upon Ancient and Modern Learning*, 1694, pp. 57–58. https://babel.hathitrust.org/cgi/pt?id=mdp.39015074712558&view=1up&seq=7, 9 November 2020).

2.3 Eng. / Sp. *vulgar*

I now look at two other cultured borrowings which have been used to express some of the characterisations of language mentioned in §1.

I noted in respect of (5b) that Sp. *vulgar* was used as a near synonym of *moderno*. Eng. / Sp. *vulgar* derive from Lat. *vulgāris* 'belonging to the *vulgus*, the great mass or multitude, the public' (Lewis and Short 1879, s.v. "vulgus"). The first attested examples in both languages (7a-b) are from the late fourteenth or early fifteenth century. While English clearly exhibits the broader meaning of 'common, customary, ordinary', and the first example given by *OED* of applicability to language is later on in the fifteenth century

(7c), the early Spanish examples are mostly to do with language, although ((7b) is strictly speaking a nominal usage of the adjective; probably from somewhat later is (7d).

(7)
    a. The same manere maistow worke to knowe the quantite of the **vulgar** nyht (*OED*: G. Chaucer *Treat. Astrolabe* (Cambr. Dd.3.53) (1872) ii. §9. 22, c. 1400).
    b. "Non minor est uirtus quam que sunt parta tueri" que quiere tanto dezir en **vulgar**: "Non est menor o chica virtut defender las cosas guanyadas." (*CORDE*: Anon., *Gestas del rey don Jayme de Aragon*, before 1396).
    c. hath desired & required me to trāslate & reduce this said book out of frenssh in to our **vulgar** englissh (*OED*: Geoffroy de La Tour Landry, *Knight of the Tower*, 1484).
    d. el qual vino al enfermo e luego fablole en lengua **vulgar** que es nuestra lengua (*CORDE*: Clemente Sánchez de Vercial, *Libro de los exemplos por A. B. C.*, c.1400–c.1421, but dated by CORDEMÁFORO at potentially any time in the fifteenth century).

Phrases such as Eng. *(our) vulgar tongue* / Sp. *lengua vulgar* refer to English and Spanish (Castilian) respectively and are often explicitly opposed to Latin, as in (7b).

2.4 Eng. *vernacular* / Sp. *vernáculo*

These words, also cultured borrowings, derive from Lat. *vernācŭlus* 'home-born (slave)' and first of all have the general meaning of 'indigenous'. In the earliest Spanish examples (8a) *vernáculo* is used nominally with this meaning but is soon strongly associated with the notion of 'indigenous (i.e. local) language', also in a nominal use (8b). In English, the earliest example cited by *OED* already has this nuance (8c).

(8)
    a. el rey Darío hizo una çena y un grand convite a todos sus **vernáculos** y a todos los magistrados de Media y de Persia (*CNDHE*: Sebastián de Horozco, *Libro de los proverbios glosados*, 1570-1579).
    b. Yo, aunque me parece muy ingeniosamente pensado, no creo que sea verdad, sino que quizás más bien sea un nombre griego, de los cuales se conservan muchos ejemplos en el **vernáculo** (*CORDE*: Sebastián

de Covarrubias, *Suplemento al Tesoro de la lengua española castellana*, c.1611).

c. A **vernaculer** pen-man... hauing translated them into English (OED: Bp. W. Barlow Def. Protestants Relig. 2, 1601).

3 Competition and contrast

Despite these early attestations, the use of these words is for some time by no means frequent, and the cultured borrowings appear to be in competition with one another (Eng. *modern* not only with *vulgar* and *vernacular* but also with *foreign*, Sp. *moderno* similarly not only with *vulgar* and *vernáculo* but also with *extranjero*) as well as with other words which express related concepts (Eng. *ancient* and *learnèd* with *classic(al)*, Sp. *antiguo* and *sabio* with *clásico*). Antonymic relations must also be borne in mind: Eng. *modern* / Sp. *moderno* is directly opposed to Eng. *ancient* / Sp. *antiguo*, while Eng. *foreign* / Sp. *extranjero* is the opposite of Eng. *native* / Sp. *materno* (none the less, with regard to this latter contrast, the study of a language which is not one's native language or the official language of a particular country is today characterised as Eng. *modern languages* or *(modern) foreign languages* / Sp. *lenguas modernas* or *lenguas extranjeras*, which ironically excludes the native language (also objectively a "modern language") from this area of study. It is also, of course, in this sense that Eng. *modern language* / Sp. *lengua moderna* contrasts with Eng. *classical language* (Sp. *lengua clásica*).

Some indication of the rise and fall in preferred collocations can be gleaned from the evidence available in historical corpora. For English I have used the Early English Books Online (*EEBO*) database for the period 1475–1700, and for 1700 to the present day the data accessible through Google ngram reader, searching for the combinations *classic(al) / learned / ancient language(s) /tongue(s)* and *modern / foreign / vulgar / vernacular language(s) / tongue(s)*. For Spanish I have used the Corpus del Español (*CDE*), afforced similarly by Google ngram reader, searching for the parallel *lengua(s) / idioma(s) clásico/a(s) / antiguo/a(s) / sabio/a(s)* and *lengua(s) / idioma(s) moderno/a(s) / extranjero/a(s) / vulgar(es) / vernáculo/a(s)*.[4] Since the complete set of results

---

[4] Without going into a detailed critique which is beyond the scope of this essay, suffice it to say that all these corpora have their obvious limitations: *EEBO* represents exclusively published books; *CDE* is an eclectic collection of digitised texts, and

obtained via Google ngram reader is not easy to assemble in an economical way,[5] I have limited my attention to presenting the most frequently occurring combinations in the plural.

Looking first at English, it can be seen how in the sixteenth and seventeenth centuries *classic(al)* is scarcely used as a characterisation of *language(s) / tongue(s)*, *learnèd* and *ancient* being strongly preferred (Figure 7.4)

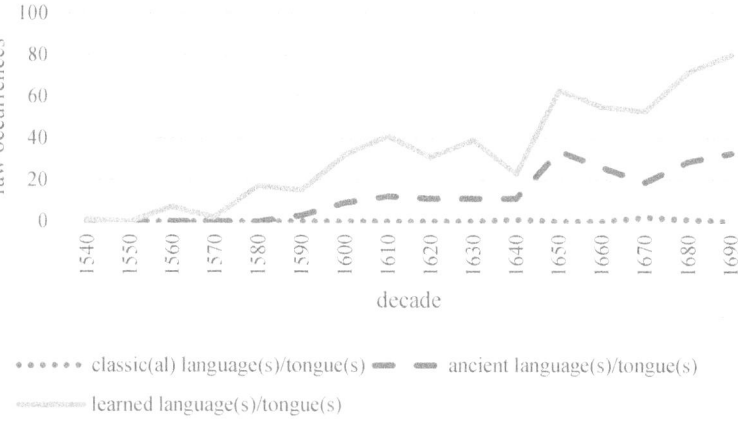

Figure 7.4. Characterisations of languages in *EEBO*, 1540–1700

After this date, the three commonest collocations in the Google corpus show changing fortunes (Figure 7.5). *Learnèd languages* continues to be strongly favoured in the first half of the nineteenth century before declining sharply in favour of *ancient* and *classical languages*; today these two collocations appear to be more or less equally maintained.

Google ngram viewer is similarly those books which have been digitised by Google. None the less, all allow a statistical comparison of different historical periods.
[5] Searches are limited to a number of characters and variants such as inflected gender and number forms have to be specified; data cannot be extracted in a straightforward numerical format.

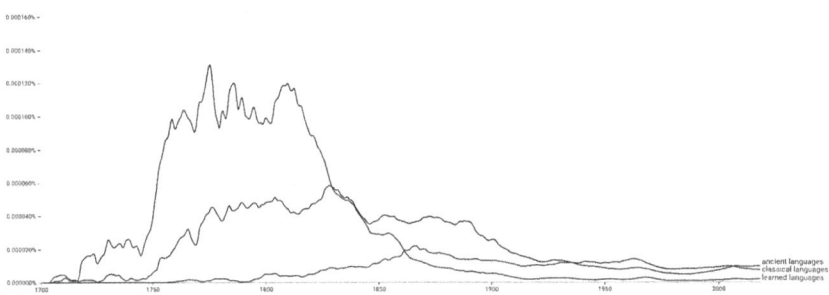

Figure 7.5. The principal characterisations of *languages/tongues* in Google ngram viewer, 1700–present.

Modern itself begins to rise in frequency only from the mid-sixteenth century, and it lags significantly behind *foreign* and *vulgar* (the generalisations in Figure 7.6 hide the fact that *vulgar tongues* is by some margin the most frequent collocation of all). *Vernacular* is scarcely attested.

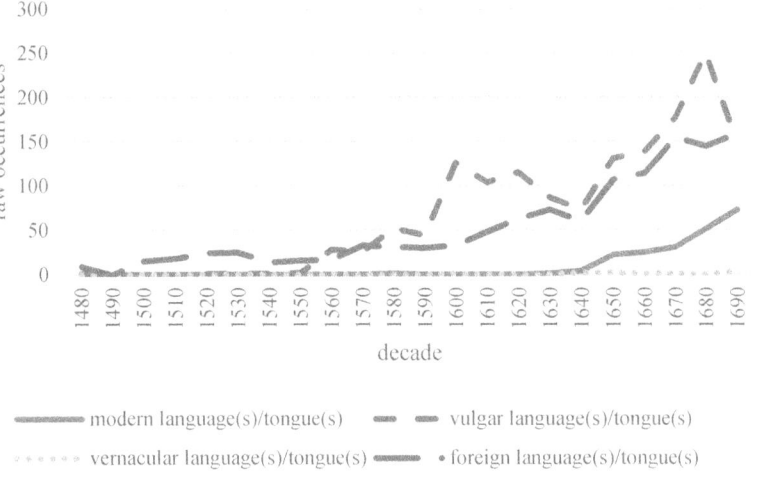

Figure 7.6. Characterisations of *languages/tongues* in *EEBO*, 1540–1700

Modern enjoys greatest popularity in the later eighteenth and nineteenth centuries (Figure 7.7), but in the twentieth century is eclipsed by *foreign* (both now in combination with *languages*, which decisively displaces *tongues* over the same period).

"Classical" and "modern" languages 129

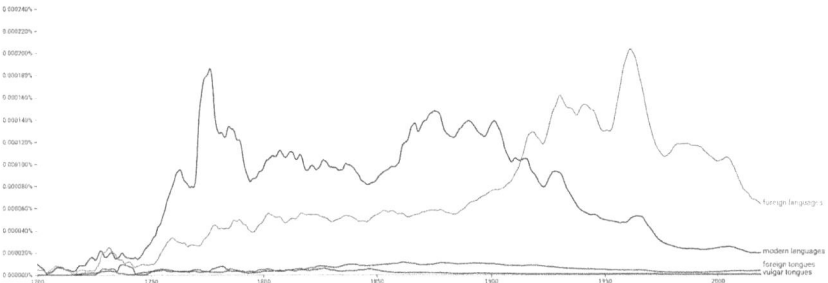

Figure 7.7. The principal characterisations of *languages/tongues* in Google ngram viewer, 1700–present

Turning now to Spanish, the broader sweep given by the century-by-century statistics available from *CDE* shows that the use of *clásico* (almost exclusively with *lengua(s)*) increases significantly in the nineteenth and twentieth centuries (Figure 7.8), and that although *antiguo* also has a substantial attestation, it is not as frequent, while *sabio* has today declined to the point of insignificance. These tendencies are confirmed by the Google corpus (Figure 7.9).

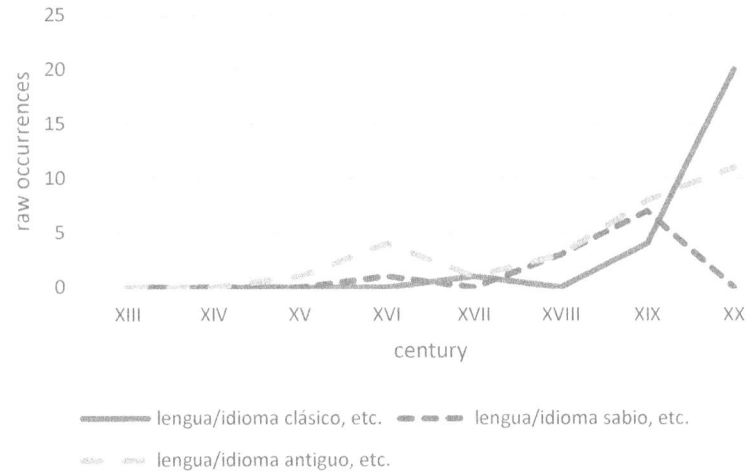

Figure 7.8. Characterisations of *lengua(s)/idioma(s)* in *CDE*, thirteenth–twentieth centuries[6]

---

[6] Although *CDE* does permit the calculation of relative frequencies century by century, I have presented the raw occurrences in these graphs in parallel with the English language data given.

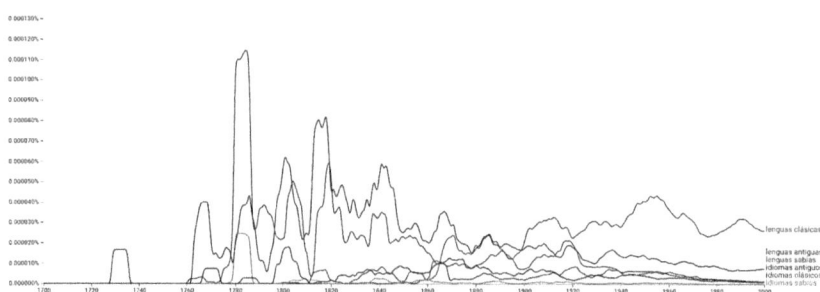

Figure 7.9. The principal characterisations of *lenguas/idiomas* in Google ngram reader, 1700–present

Among the competitors of *moderno*, there is in *CDE* what may be considered a surprising rise in frequency of *vernáculo* in the twentieth century; however, on closer inspection this is entirely due to its favouring in the now discontinued Encarta Encyclopedia, which is one of its principal academic register sources.

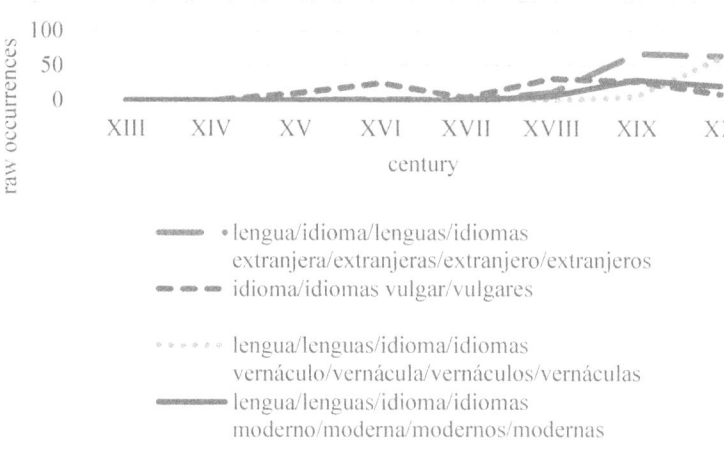

Figure 7.10. Characterisations of *lengua(s)/idioma(s)* in *CDE*, thirteenth–twentieth centuries

The Google corpus, on the other hand, shows that *extranjeras*, *modernas* and *vivas* are the most common characterisations of *lenguas* in recent times. Similar figures are not returned for *idiomas*, but since both words continue to be common in Spanish, I have also obtained data for the three adjectives in combinations with *idiomas* too (Figure 7.11). This shows a strong general preference for *extranjeras* with *lenguas modernas* and *lenguas vivas* showing favouring at different times.

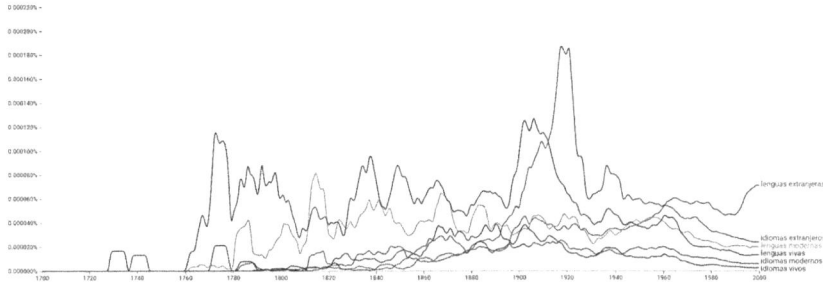

Figure 7.11. The principal characterisations of *lenguas/idiomas* in Google ngram viewer, 1700–present

The present-day dichotomous use of Eng. *classical/modern* and Sp. *clásico/moderno* to contrast Greek and Latin with currently spoken languages is clear from an inspection of the contexts in which these characterisations are predominantly used. Some examples are:

(9)
- a. [...] they stress the inherent educational value of such subjects as **classical** languages (Greek and Latin) (*BNC*: Sander Meredeen, *Study for survival and success* (London: Paul Chapman), 1988).
- b. [...] where they appeared to threaten the hegemony of existing disciplines, as English and **modern** languages did with classics (*BNC*: G. Squires, *First degree: the undergraduate curriculum* (Milton Keynes: Open University Press), 1990).
- c. catedrático emérito de Filología Griega y experto internacional en lenguas **clásicas** (*CORPES XXI*: *El País*, 2004).
- d. Para mí que cada vez utilizaba menos libros en latín y más en lenguas **modernas** (*CORPES XXI*: César Fernández García, *El e-mail del mal* (Madrid: Alfaguara), 2007).

Native languages as well as foreign languages are included in this notion of "modern" while the notion of "classical" is usually restricted to Latin and Greek. To discriminate between non-native languages and a native language, the term *modern foreign languages / lenguas modernas extranjeras* is sometimes used, and in the world of language teaching even finer distinctions are currently made (e.g. Eng. *lesser-studied languages*).

4 In conclusion

I end with a brief tentative speculative account of the reasons for the changing fortunes of the cultured borrowings whose evolution I have been tracing. (It is beyond the scope of this essay to do more than make inferences, the proving of which is probably in any case not feasible.) Their adoption in both English and Spanish as characterisations of language may be seen in the first place to respond to a *prise de conscience* of the need to distinguish living languages of everyday communication from languages which had been used formerly in the cultural atmosphere of medieval Western Europe where Latin had continued to be cultivated for certain special purposes (academic and ecclesiastical). Awareness of this must always have been clear in a non-Romance-speaking context and had been recognised in a Romance-speaking context since Romance began to be written in a different way from Latin: compare the designations of vernaculars as *romana lingua* and *teudisca lingua* in the Strasbourg Oaths of 842 CE and such medieval distinctions as Sp. *latín/romance*. The first most usual characterisation of the former was predominantly Eng./Sp. *vulgar*, which expressed the everyday, commonly used, nature of these languages, while such terms as Eng. *learnèd* / Sp. *sabio* were preferred for the latter. Humanism exalted the vernaculars as worthy of study and use, and it is during the later Renaissance that a rise in the frequency of several characterisations can be seen as a result of the growing importance of, and interest in, the distinction. The present-day dichotomy between Eng. *classical / modern* and Sp. *clásico / moderno* is perhaps due to the distinguishing of non-native languages within the academic curriculum, the academic study of "modern" languages having generally been cloned on the longstanding study of the "classical" (see Pountain, 2017, 256–7). The favouring of "modern" over "vulgar" reflects the greater importance given to the academic study of modern languages in recent times by comparison with the classics. This is still, however, a shifting area: "foreign" is often favoured to distinguish the study of modern non-native languages from native languages, but in a multicultural environment where many students of "foreign" languages are also native speakers or heritage speakers, the term "foreign" appears disparaging, and is avoided: thus in the world of teaching English to non-native speakers the formerly standard term "English as a Foreign Language" (EFL) has been replaced by "English for Speakers of Other Languages" (ESOL).

Cultured borrowings have thus been drawn upon to systematise, through differential labelling, the perception of a major difference in category between languages. This is far from the only use of Eng. *classical / modern* and Sp. *clásico / moderno*, but it has played a part in their greater diffusion in recent times and their firm embedding in their host languages, both linguistically and socially. At the same time, the fact that English and Spanish have proceeded to a certain extent in parallel suggests the likelihood that such labellings were the result of transnational contact and influence.

A fuller investigation of such speculations awaits further study.

References

Corpora

BNC = Bodleian Libraries, University of Oxford. 2007. *British National Corpus*. Accessed 11 November 2020. https://www.english-corpora.org/bnc/.

CDE = Davies, Mark. 2002–. *El corpus del español, Genre / Historical*. Accessed 11 November 2020. https://www.corpusdelespanol.org/

CNDHE = Real Academia Española. n.d. *Corpus del Nuevo Diccionario Histórico del Español*. Accessed 4 December 2019. http://web.frl.es/CNDHE.

CORDE = Real Academia Española. n.d. *Banco de datos (CORDE). Corpus Diacrónico del Español*. Accessed 11 November 2020. http://corpus.rae.es/corde net.html.

CORPES XXI = Real Academia Española. n.d. *El Corpus del Español del Siglo XX*. Accessed 11 November 2020. https://www.rae.es/banco-de-datos/corpes-xxi.

EEBO = *Early English Books Online* (n.d.). https://search.proquest.com/eebo

Google LLC. Google Books ngram viewer. n.d. Accessed 15 January 2020. https://books.google.com/ngrams.

Bibliographical references

Cano Aguilar, Rafael. 1984. "Cambios de construcción verbal en español clásico." *Boletín de la Real Academia Española*, 44, 231–232: 203–255.

Cobbin, Ingram. 1834. *The Classical English Vocabulary, Containing a Selection of Words Commonly Used by the Best Writers*. London: Frederick Westley.

CORDEMÁFORO = Rodríguez Molina, Javier, and Octavio de Toledo y Huerta, Álvaro. 2017. "Acceso a la base de datos CORDEMÁFORO." *Scriptum Digital*, 6. Accessed 3 September 2019. http://www.scriptumdigital.org/documents/Octavio-Molina-Base-de-datos-Scriptum.xlsx.

Cotgrave, Randle. 1611. *A Dictionarie of the French and English tongues*. London: Adam Islip. Accessed 4 December 2019. https://books.google.co.uk/books?id=IOhMAAAAcAAJ&hl=es&source=gbs_navlinks_s.

Kaunisto, Mark. 2007. *Variation and Change in the Lexicon. A corpus-based analysis of adjectives in English ending in -ic and -ical*. Amsterdam: Rodopi.

Lewis, Charlton Thomas and Charles Short. 1879. *A Latin Dictionary*. Oxford: Clarendon Press. Accessed 13 March 2020. https://www.latinitium.com/latin-dictionaries.

Lloyd, Paul M. 1979. "On the definition of Vulgar Latin: the eternal return." *Neophilologische Mittteilungen*, 80: 110–22.

OED = Simpson, John, and Edmund Weiner. 1989–. *Oxford English Dictionary*. Oxford: Oxford University Press. Accessed 21 December 2019. https://www.oed.com/.

Percyvall, Richard. 1591. *Bibliothecae hispanicae pars altera: containing a dictionarie in Spanish, English, and Latine ...* London: Iohn Iackson. Accessed 4 December 2019. https://hdl.handle.net/2027/ucm.5326526284.

Pountain, Christopher J. 2017. "The Three Ls of Modern Foreign Languages: Language, Linguistics, Literature." *Hispanic Research Journal*, 18:3, 253–271.

Serradilla Castaño, Ana. 2004. "Superlativos cultos y populares en el español clásico." *Edad de Oro*, 23, 95–133.

Wright, Roger. 2004. "Latin and English as world languages." *English Today*, 20.4, 3–13. https://doi.org/10.1017/S026607840400402X. Accessed 1 December 2020.

Chapter 8

Latinisms as Lexical Substitutes in Late Medieval and Early Modern Spanish

Steven N. Dworkin

University of Michigan

Summary

The introduction and incorporation of Latinisms, understood as borrowings from the written Latin of classical antiquity, has characterised the history of the Spanish lexicon from the time of the first texts. The steady stream of Latinisms documented in such thirteenth-century writers as Gonzalo de Berceo and Alfonso X "the Wise" became a flood in the fifteenth and sixteenth centuries. Most Spanish Latinisms resulted from contact at the level of the written language. These learnèd neologisms filled lexical gaps in the vocabulary of Hispano-Romance as part of its elaboration as a language of creative literature, scholarship, and government on a functional par with Latin. Such Latinisms were additions to the lexicon and did not displace already existing words or phrases.

This Chapter will examine that smaller group of Latinisms that displaced existing vernacular signifiers in medieval and early modern Hispano-Romance. These neologisms can be subdivided into Latinisms that replaced over time genetically unrelated words (e.g., the substitution of *ejército* 'army' and *rápido* 'quickly' for orally-transmitted *hueste* and *aína*) and Latinisms that ousted their orally-transmitted doublets (e.g., the replacement of OSp. *preigar* 'to preach', *envidar* 'to invite' and *mascar* 'to chew' by *predicar*, *invitar* and *masticar*, all reflecting vernacular and Latinate routes of transmission of Lat. *praedĭcare*, *invītare* and *mastĭcare*).

Resumen

Desde la época de los primeros textos, la introducción e incorporación de latinismos, préstamos del latín escrito, ha marcado la historia del léxico de las variedades del español. La corriente de tales neologismos, ya documentados en escritores del siglo XIII como Gonzalo de Berceo y Alfonso X «el Sabio», se convirtió en un aluvión en los siglos XVI y XVII. La mayoría de tales latinismos resultan del contacto al nivel de la lengua escrita y llenan huecos en el léxico como parte del proceso de elaboración de la lengua vernácula como vehículo lingüístico apto para fines científicos, culturales y administrativos. Estos neologismos no desplazaron otros vocablos ya presentes en el léxico.

Este Capítulo estudia ejemplos escogidos de un grupo más reducido de latinismos, los que acabaron por desplazar en las épocas medievales y premodernas significantes ya presentes en la lengua. Se subdividen estos latinismos en dos categorías: los que han desalojado a contrincantes no relacionados (p. ej. el triunfo de *ejército* y *rápido* sobre esp. ant. *hueste* y *aína*) y los que han desplazado a su propio doblete de origen popular (p. ej. la eliminación de *envidar, mascar, preigar* a favor de sus dobletes cultos *invitar, masticar, predicar* < Lat. *invītāre, mastĭcāre, praedĭcāre*.

Keywords

Lexical borrowing, Lexical competition, Linguistic elaboration, Latin, Spanish.

1 Latinisms: a brief introduction

The Latin component of the Spanish lexicon (or that of any other Romance language) falls, from a diachronic perspective, into two distinct categories. The first constitutes the historical core of the Spanish lexicon, the *palabras patrimoniales*, those Latin words inherited through uninterrupted oral transmission from the various regional and social varieties of Latin spoken in the Iberian Peninsula when this territory formed part of the Roman Empire. The second group consists of the many words that entered the language as deliberate borrowings on the part of some members of the literate minority from written Latin. Such words are usually labelled as Latinisms or learnèd words (Sp. *latinismos, palabras cultas*), and in the modern language may outnumber those elements that constitute the inherited lexicon. Many of the same Latinisms are found in the five national Romance languages (see Reinheimer-Rîpeanu 2004). Two features facilitate their identification. These lexical items did not participate in the sound changes that characterise the evolution of spoken Latin into the several regional varieties of Hispano-Romance. In addition, many Latinisms are not first attested in Spanish sources until the late fourteenth or fifteenth centuries, a period of great change in the composition of the Spanish lexicon (cf. Dworkin 2004; 2012, chapter 8). Although there are hundreds of Latinisms documented earlier (see Bustos Tovar 1974 for the period prior to 1250), many are found only in a handful of texts, doubtless introduced independently by such writers as Gonzalo de Berceo (ca. 1195–1264) and the scholars active at the court of Alfonso X "the Wise" (1221–1284), and appear not to have become widespread in the written language of literature, scholarship, and administration until they were reintroduced in the fifteenth century as part of the relatinisation of the Spanish lexicon that marks the late medieval and early modern periods (Harris-Northall 1999, Dworkin 2010). Burgassi and Guadagnini (2014, 2017b) have labelled such items (nouns for the most part) "latent Latinisms". The same Latinism may have been repeatedly and independently "reborrowed" by different writers at this time before coming integrated into the written language. It is worth noting that many Latinisms first appear in the Iberian Peninsula in texts coming from the Crown of Aragon, notably (though not exclusively) in the writings produced in the last decades of the fourteenth century in the scriptorium of Juan Fernández de Heredia (d. 1396), many of which are "translations" (in the medieval sense) into a form of literary Aragonese of French, Catalan, Greek, Italian and Latin texts. Some such Latinisms appear for the first time in texts translated from Italian and sometimes even in Italianate garb, as are the cases of (infrequent) *débile, difícile, fácile, útile*. The possible role of Italian as an intermediary in the transmission into the Crown of Aragon and thence into Castile of Latinisms requires further detailed study. Could one argue that, from the perspective of a word's immediate etymology, some alleged Latinisms are really Italianisms? It is worth noting that many of Heredia's manuscripts were acquired by the Marqués de Santillana, one of the first poets who introduced a significant quantity of Latinisms into his writings.

There is a residue of words that formal criteria such as sound change do not allow the analyst to determine with certainty whether they represent *palabras patrimoniales* or *latinismos*. Since Latin tonic /e:/, /i:/, /o:/ and /u:/ consistently entered Spanish as /e i o u/ and /-r-/ and /-n-/ remained intact, Sp. *veneno* 'poison' (discussed below), *pino* 'pine', *vino* 'wine' *corona* 'crown', *duro* 'hard, solid' and *puro* 'pure' lend themselves to interpretation both as orally-transmitted outcomes of Lat. *vĕnēnum, pīnum, vīnum, cŏrōnam, dūrum* and *pūrum* or as Latinisms. The concrete meanings of *duro, pino, vino,* as well as their frequent use in thirteenth-century texts, seem to point to popular transmission while the more abstract meaning of *puro*, combined with its relatively low frequency in the same century, may point to a Latinism.

Throughout the history of Spanish, the introduction of loanwords or borrowings can result from contact both at the level of oral speech or written texts (the latter a source unavailable for loans from the pre-Roman languages or Visigothic). By their very nature, almost all Latinisms result from the deliberate borrowing from written Latin texts to which the relevant Spanish writers had access. Although Latin was not a spoken vernacular in medieval Spain, its oral use in certain ecclesiastic, legal, and academic circles may have been the source of some Latinisms. I shall offer here two possible examples. Specialists agree that the final -*s* of Sp. *Dios* 'God' reflects the Latin nominative *dĕus* rather than the accusative *dĕum*, which would have given *dió*, a form found in the late-eleventh century *Glosas Silenses*, and in some pre-Expulsion (1492) texts written in Spanish by and for Jews. Given the use of Lat. *dĕus* as both a nominative and vocative in the Bible and in the Liturgy (possibly read out loud as [djós]), the form in -*s* may have integrated itself through aural means. The history of Sp. *cruz* 'cross' may constitute a second case of oral transmission of a Latinism. The regular evolution of Lat. *crŭcem* should have yielded OSp. *croz (cf. Fr. *croix*, It. *croce*). Could aural reception of the Latin form in ecclesiastical contexts have impacted on its development in Spanish? The sermons of fifteenth- and sixteenth-century preachers, which abound in Latinisms, may have played a role in the diffusion of such forms. This question is quite complicated, as there are numerous other examples of Latin bases with tonic short /u/ that yielded Sp. /u/ rather than the "regular" /o/. e.g. *iŭgum* > *yugo* 'yoke', *mŭndum* > *mundo* 'world', *nŭmquam* > *nunca* 'never' (Lloyd 1987, 182; Malkiel 1983). However, the overwhelming majority of Latinisms that entered Spanish between ca. 1400–1650 are borrowings from written sources. A very high proportion of these learnèd neologisms have survived to the present day. Although many are known only to a highly educated segment of the population, others have become highly used lexical items. The borrowing of words documented in a language's historical ancestor is not a regular phenomenon in language history. Possible parallels are offered by Sanskrit borrowings in Hindi, Classical Greek loans in Modern Greek, and Biblical Hebrew lexical items in modern Israeli Hebrew.

For the most part writers had recourse to Latinisms to fill conceptual gaps in the lexicon of the vernacular as part of the process of elaboration designed to render Hispano-Romance a tool equal to Latin for use as a language of scholarship and religion. The majority of Latinisms did not displace a previously existing signifier in the Romance vernacular. This Chapter will examine selectively that much smaller group of Latinisms that displaced existing vernacular signifiers in medieval and early modern Hispano-Romance. These neologisms can be subdivided into Latinisms that replaced over time genetically unrelated words (e.g., the substitution of *ejército* 'army' and *rápido* 'quickly' for vernacular *hueste* and *aína*) and Latinisms that ousted their orally-transmitted doublets (e.g. the replacement of OSp. *preigar* 'to preach', *envidar* 'to invite', and *mascar* 'to chew' by *predicar, invitar*, and *masticar*, all three pairs reflecting vernacular and Latinate descendants of Lat. *praedĭcare, invītare*, and *mastĭcare*). One must keep in mind that many of the older words displaced by Latinisms did not necessarily disappear completely from the language. As the reader will see in the lexical vignettes that follow, a number of the relevant items live on in regional varieties of the language. Others are recorded in contemporary dictionaries without being labelled as archaic or obsolete, sometimes with a narrower semantic scope, although their use in modern spoken and written Spanish is infrequent.

2 Replacement of inherited vocabulary by unrelated Latinisms

I shall begin with selected examples of the replacement by Latinisms of earlier genetically unrelated signifiers. This survey makes no claims to being complete. As appropriate, references will be made to previous studies of these rivalries in which relevant textual examples can be found. In some instances the earlier Old Spanish term displayed a high degree of polysemy, which may have contributed to a feeling of semantic vagueness. Writers who were striving to transform the vernacular into a written communicative instrument on the same level of Latin may have felt that the vocabulary found in the texts from classical Rome offered a higher degree of semantic precision and richness, traits that Latinisms could bring to Spanish. I shall start with a series of substitutions involving adjectives.

To express the notion 'easy', the medieval language employed the Gallicism *ligero* (< OFr. *legier*), which could also mean 'light; quickly', as well as, though less frequently, *liviano*, and the Arabism *rafez/rahez/refez, rehez*. The perceived semantic imprecision of polysemous *ligero* may have motivated the introduction of *fácil* < Lat. *făcĭlem*, borrowed a century earlier in Catalan, and Italian (where *fàcil* and *facile* took over from *leuger* and *leggero/agevole* respectively; see Burgassi and Guadagnini 2017a and Clavería Nadal and

Torruella 2016). The same holds true for the notion 'difficult', expressed principally in Old Spanish by *grave (*var. *grieve*, found frequently in the Alfonsine *General estoria*), which could also mean 'heavy, burdensome', prior to the introduction and incorporation of *difícil* in Castilian texts, also in the first half of the fifteenth century.[1] Whereas *difícil* appears (in varying orthographic guises) in the late-fourteenth century writings from the scriptorium of Juan Fernández de Heredia, the adjective *fácil* is absent from that corpus (which offers isolated examples of the noun *facilidat* in the *Crónica de los conquiridores* (Mackenzie 1984, 48, 65). Neither Latin adjective at issue here seems to have left vernacular reflexes in any Romance variety.

Medieval Hispano-Romance turned to *feble*, a Gallicism, and *flaco* to express the notion 'weak'. In all likelihood, *endeble*, rarely found in medieval texts (*Fuero de Béjar*, late thirteenth century) is a borrowing from medieval Gallo-Romance. The Latinism *débil* first appears in the writings of the Aragonese Heredia, and in a handful of Castilian texts in the mid-fifteenth century. It took firm root only in the early modern language. Nebrija's Latin-Spanish (1492) and Spanish-Latin (ca. 1495) dictionaries do not record *débil* as a gloss or as a lemma, whereas it is found in bilingual dictionaries from the second half of the sixteenth century. Over time *feble* fell into disuse and *flaco* began to acquire the meanings 'thin, skinny' alongside 'weak'. Except for some Gallo-Romance forms (e.g., OFr. *end[i]eble*), Lat. *dēbīlem* appears not to have left vernacular descendants in the Romance languages.

The medieval language contained several adjectives whose semantic range included 'last': *cabero, çaguero, derradero, trasero*, and especially *postremero / postrimero / postrero* (the last a compressed variant of its predecessors). *DPD* (s.v. *postrero*) describes *postrero* as "voz literaria que rara vez se emplea hoy fuera de textos escritos". The *CORDE* database records the Latinism *último* in the phrase *último testamento* in a series of fourteenth century wills and testaments before its initial documentation in fifteenth-century texts. The first

---

[1] For a detailed discussion, with abundant examples from fifteenth-century Castilian sources, of the introduction and incorporation of *fácil* and *difícil*, see Eberenz (1998). Clavería Nadal and Torruella (2016) and Burgassi and Guadagnini (2017) describe respectively the introduction of Cat. *fàcil* and It. *facile*. These Latinisms did not take hold in Romanian. The Latin bases *făcĭlem* and *diffĭcĭlem* left no orally-transmitted descendants in the Romance languages.

writer who used this adjective in literary texts was Enrique de Villena (d. 1434) in his translation (ca. 1430) of the first three Books of the *Aeneid*. Examples abound in the mid-fifteenth century *Vergel de los príncipes* of Rodrigo Sánchez de Arévalo. Nebrija admitted *último* into his Latin-Spanish dictionary (1492) in which it glosses Lat. *ultimus* and *extremus*. The Latin adjective left no vernacular progeny in the Romance languages.

The medieval language did not possess signifiers that clearly expressed the meanings 'useful' and 'unique, only'. For the former, writers (and speakers) turned to various (clumsy) periphrases such as *tener pro, mío pro, la pro de la cosa, ser aprovechable cosa*. A sole unintegrated example of *útil* turns up in the thirteenth-century Aragonese legal compilation *Vidal Mayor* modifying the noun *sennyorío* 'dominion'. Elsewhere in this text the translator retained the Latin *utilis*. The Latinism *útil* appeared in Aragon in the late fourteenth-century writings of Heredia before showing up in texts from fifteenth-century Castile (with abundant examples in Villena's rendering of the *Aeneid* and in the *Suma de política* (ca. 1455) of Rodrigo Sánchez de Arévalo. The adjective did not find a place in Nebrija's aforementioned dictionaries. Except for the twelve instances of the phrase *fijo único* 'only son', referring to Jesus Christ, in the fourteenth-century *Mostrador de justicia* of the convert Alfonso de Valladolid (born Abner de Burgos), *único* is rarely documented before 1500. Earlier translations of the Vulgate rendered Lat. *ūnĭcum* by such periphrases as *auer más daquel; ser más daquel*.[2] Neither Latin adjective discussed here left orally-transmitted descendants in other Romance varieties.

Two competing sets of sound changes transformed the Latin adjective *răpĭdum* 'swiftly-flowing (of water); rapid' into *rabio* (preserved only in toponyms such as *Fuenterabia, La Rabia*) and *rabdo/raudo*, form found in the Alfonsine *General estoria* and the *Estoria de Espanna*, and which lives on as part of the Spanish poetic vocabulary. The Latinism *rápido*, today a common lexical item, is first documented in the "versos al lector" added to the second edition (Toledo 1500) of the *Tragicomedia de Calisto y Melibea* or *La Celestina* by the corrector, the humanist Alonso de Proaza, who may be

---

[2] For examples and references to texts containing *débil, último, único, útil*, see Dworkin (2002a, 426–431).

responsible for the introduction of this adjective into the literary language.[3] In the passage in question, *rápido* is employed in its Latin sense of 'swiftly-flowing water'. The textual evidence shows that *rabdo/raudo* was not the main signifier for 'quick, swift'; that role was filled principally by the Gallicism *ligero* and by the adverb *aína* as well as by *festino, presto, pronto, toste*. Whereas *ligero* has retained this meaning in some varieties of Spanish, *aína* has fallen into disuse in the standard language, (although it lives on in Asturian (García Arias 2017, 277–278), and elsewhere in northern Spain. *Rápido* did not become fully integrated until the seventeenth century, a period of the influx of various proparoxytonic adjectival Latinisms in -'*ido* (e.g., *árido, ávido, límpido, nítido, túrbido*). Unlike many of the adjectives discussed in this section, Lat. *răpĭdum* left scattered orally-transmitted reflexes in the Romance languages; witess OFr. *rade*, It. *ratto*, Sard. *rattu*, Cat. *rabeu*.

It is not surprising that Latinisms entered the medical vocabulary of late medieval Spanish, displacing older signifiers. I shall present three cases here. Although there is an isolated example of *estéril*[4] in the Alfonsine *Libro de los iudizios de las estrellas*, this adjective shows little vitality in the written record until the fifteenth century. In the medieval language the dominant signifier for the meaning 'sterile' was (etymologically obscure) *mañero*, which was used in reference to humans, animals and agricultural land. Far less frequent were OSp. *escosso* (usually found as fem. *escossa*) and *machorra*, the latter recorded in Nebrija's Latin-Spanish dictionary (ca. 1495). Sixteenth-century sources offer examples of *mañero* equated with *mañoso* 'full of skill, cunning', a derivative of *maña* 'skill, art, wile'. I have proposed (Dworkin 1998) that association by speakers of *mañero* with the unrelated and semantically distinct family of *maña* may have led to its demise and to the introduction of the Latinism *estéril*, processes that overlap chronologically.[5] Meyer-Lübke (1935, entry 8246) lists vernacular reflexes of Lat. *stĕrĭlem* in various Italian dialects, Sardinian, Romansh, and Occitan (*esterle*).

---

[3] In like fashion, Fr. *rapide*, first documented in the early sixteenth century, ousted OFr. *rade*, the orally-transmitted reflex of Lat. *răpĭdum*.

[4] The copyist of the Royal Scriptorium manuscript of the *Libro de los Iudizios* was clearly unfamiliar with this word, as it also appears as *esterle* and *esterlas* in the same codex. Was he familiar with OOcc. *esterle*?

[5] For examples with text locations of these adjectives, see Dworkin (1998, 1–4).

The Arabism *gafo* (var. *gaho*) was by far and away the most common designation in the medieval language for 'leprous', a function that it shared with less frequent *malato* and *mesiello*, both of which could mean 'sick, ill'. The strong dread and stigma associated in the past with leprosy would have saddled the above adjectives with strong negative connotations, a factor that can play a role in lexical loss. It is not unreasonable to speculate that in multilingual medieval Spain speakers might have recognised negatively tinged *gafo* as an Arabism deserving to be ousted from the language. With regard to medical and scientific terminology and the lexicon of various trades and professions, the early modern period in Spain witnessed a Latinisation of the technical and professional lexicon at the expense of Arabisms in various fields. Although there are scattered examples in earlier texts (as far back as the early thirteenth-century *Fazienda de Ultramar*), *leproso* begins to appear with some regularity only in the Aragonese Heredia and then in fifteenth-century Castile.

The adjective *pálido* 'pale, colourless' first appears in three late fifteenth-century medical texts (Herrera 1996), in two of which it modifies *orina* 'urine'. In the early sixteenth-century *Crónica de Amadrón*, *pálido* is used to modify *rostro* 'face' and is coupled with its synonym *descolorido*: "rostro descolorido y pálido". As in the case of *rápido*, examples of *pálido* are rare until the end of the sixteenth century.[6] The adjective functions neither as a gloss nor as an entry in Nebrija's Latin-Spanish and Spanish-Latin dictionaries, nor did it find a place in Covarrubias (1611), the first monolingual dictionary of Spanish. The medieval language expressed the notions implied in 'pale' with the colour term *amarillo* 'yellow', and the set *descolorado*, and (with less frequency), *descolorido*, of which the primary meaning was 'lacking colour'. The polysemy of *amarillo* as both a specific colour term and as a signifier for the lack of colour in one's complexion may have paved the way for the entry of a Latinism viewed as a more specific technical term. In modern Spanish, *descolorido* continues to persist alongside *pálido*.

The preceding paragraphs have dealt with the replacement of vernacular adjectives by Latinisms. I shall summarise here three cases involving nouns,

---

[6] In contrast, OFr. *pasle* (MFr. *pâle*) is first documented in the second half of the eleventh century (Rey 2000, s.v. *pâle*), and It. *pàllido* in the second half of the thirteenth century (Cortelazzo and Zolli 1999, s.v. *pallido*).

the replacement of OSp. *hueste* 'army', *poridad* 'secret' and *po(n)çoña* 'poison' by *ejército*, *secreto* and *veneno* respectively.

Despite still unresolved questions concerning its formal and semantic history, specialists still derive *poridad* (as well as OPtg. *poridade/puridade*) from Lat. *pūrĭtātem* 'cleanliness, without admixture, purity'. Regular evolution of the base ought to have yielded **purdad*. Only in Spanish and Portuguese did the vernacular reflexes of Lat. *pūrĭtātem* acquire the meaning 'secret'. Various renowned specialists have seen in this semantic development a calque on an Arabic phraseological model (for bibliography and discussion see Dworkin 2006: 35–38). Although far outnumbered by *poridad*, the Latinism *secreto* (< Lat. *sēcrētum* 'separated, alone', past participle of *sēcernĕre* 'to separate, keep apart') appears in scattered thirteenth-century texts (the poetry of Berceo, *Libro de Alexandre*, *Libro de los doze sabios*, the Alfonsine *Picatrix*, *Vidal Mayor*). As is often the case, the Latinism begins to dominate in the second half of the fourteenth century and triumphs definitively in the fifteenth. The variant *puridad* begins to appear alongside *poridad*, which lives on in the fixed phrase *en poridad* 'secretly; frankly'. Portuguese *segredo* shows vernacular development of Lat. *sēcrētum*.

In the medieval language *hueste* dominated as the main signifier for the concept 'army'. The local descendant of Lat. *hŏstem* first faced competition from *exército* (MSp. *ejército*) in the second half of the fourteenth century. This Latinism first appears with considerable frequency in the texts prepared by Heredia, although *hueste* continues to dominate in his writings, a situation that continues until the end of the fifteenth century. Nebrija's Latin-Spanish dictionary (1492) employs *hueste* to gloss Lat. *exercĭtus*; only *hueste* merits an entry in his Spanish-Latin dictionary in the form *ueste de gentes*, glossed by Lat. *exercitus* and *copiae* 'large number of men'. The decline of *hueste* is confirmed by its inclusion in the list of obsolete words in the humanist Gonzalo Argote de Molina's edition (1575) of the fourteenth-century *Conde Lucanor* and Covarrubias's (1611) tagging of *hueste* as being from the "antigua lengua castellana" (for details and citations see Dworkin 2005, 67–68). The *DLE* continues to record *hueste* as a plural noun with two meanings, 'ejército en campaña' and 'conjunto de los seguidores o partidarios de una persona o de una causa'. One further point concerning the introduction of *ejército* requires brief mention here. It is reasonable to posit that Heredia (or his court translators) were responsible for the introduction of this neologism. Lat. *exercĭtum* also came into Italian as the Latinism *esercito* which first meant 'crowd, multitude' (so used by Dante) before it displaced *oste* as the signifier for 'army' in the fourteenth century (Cortelazzo and Zolli 1999, s.v. *esercito*). As a result of its commercial and political presence in the Mediterranean basin, the Crown of Aragon played a major role in the transmission of Italianisms into the Iberian Peninsula. Since *esercito* appears in Italian at least a century before its initial documentation in Spanish, the possibility that the Italian noun played a role in the history of Sp. *ejército* cannot be discarded. The Latinism at issue seems not to have taken root in Old or Middle French. Wartburg (1949, 292b) records one example of OFr. *exercite* 'army'. The presence of the related noun *exercite* 'exercise, practice, military training' may have blocked the incorporation of the Latinism based on *exercĭtum*.

Both *poçoña/ponçoña* and *veneno* (var. *venino*) enjoyed considerable vitality in the medieval language to denote 'poison'. The former represents oral transmission of Lat. *pōtĭōnem*, whereas *veneno*, on formal grounds, could be explained as a popular reflex of Lat. *vĕnēnum* or as a Latinism. Prior to 1400, examples of *venino* far outnumber those of *veneno*. The earliest cluster of examples of *veneno* turns up in the writings of Heredia. The medieval record also documents the Latinism *tóssico* (var. *tóssigo*), of which almost all thirteenth-century examples are found in the Alfonsine *Lapidario* (ca. 1250), alongide *tossigoso* and *tossigamiento* (which might imply the undocumented verb **tossigar*). The *DLE* includes *ponzoña*, glossed as 'poison' in both its literal and figurative senses. Elsewhere, orally-transmitted reflexes of Lat. *pōtĭōnem* live on in Fr. *poison*, Occ. *pozon*, OEngad. *puschun*.

3 Ordinal numerals in Spanish: a special case

The series of Spanish ordinal numerals, syntactically adjectives, shows an almost complete replacement by Latinisms of the forms inherited from Latin. The ordinals 'first' through 'fifth' continue their Latin sources: *primero / primo* < Lat. *prīmum/prīmārĭum*, *segundo* < Lat. *secundum*, *tercio / tercero* < Lat. *tertĭum / tertārĭum*, *cuarto / quarto* < Lat. *quartum*, *quinto* < Lat. *quintum*. Old Spanish also formed ordinals with the suffix *-eno*, a continuation of the Latin distributive *-ēnus* (usually found in the plural *-ēni*, e.g., *septēni* 'seven each', *nŏvēni* 'nine each', *dŭŏdēni* 'twelve each'): *doseno* 'second', *treseno* 'third',[7] *cuarteno* / *quarteno* 'fourth', *cinqueno* 'fifth', *seseno* 'sixth', *seteno* 'seventh', *ocheno* (alongside more frequent *ochavo* < *octavum*) 'eighth', *noveno* 'ninth', *dezeno* 'tenth', *onzeno* 'eleventh', *dozeno* 'twelfth', *trezeno* 'thirteenth', *catorzeno* 'fourteenth', *quinzeno* 'fifteenth', *dicesseno* / *diez y seseno* 'sixteenth', *diez y seteno* 'seventeenth', *diez y ocheno* 'eighteenth', *veinteno* 'twentieth', *treinteno* 'thirtieth', *cuarenteno* 'fortieth', *cinquanteno* 'fiftieth', *sesenteno* 'sixtieth', *setenteno* 'seventieth', *ochenteno* 'eightieth'.

Although the replacement of the Old Spanish ordinals in *-eno* by Latinisms in *-ésimo* began in the medieval language, the vernacular forms dominated through the end of the fifteenth century. The following overview is based principally on the materials found in the *CORDE* database. Instances of *sexto* 'sixth' far outnumber those of *seseno* for the period 1200–1500, after which examples of *seseno* are almost non-existent.[8] There are scattered examples of the Latinism *séptimo* 'seventh' in thirteenth-century texts (the poetry of Berceo, *Fuero Juzgo*, the writings of Alfonso X), but very few in the fourteenth. Although *séptimo* increased in frequency in the following century, numerous examples of *seteno*, now a minority option, are found through the early modern period. Instances of Latinate *octavo* outnumber *ochavo* in medieval sources. Both *noveno* and the Latinism *nono* have come into the modern language as the ordinal 'ninth'. Beyond 'ninth' the Latinate ordinals in *-ésimo* (< *-ēsĭmum*) are rare in the medieval language; instances of *dezeno, onzeno, dozeno, trezeno, catorzeno, quinzeno*[9] far outnumber cases of *décimo, undécimo, duodécimo, tredécimo, quatrodécimo*. The *CORDE* database provides no medieval examples of learnèd *décimocuarto, décimoquinto*

---

[7] Standalone examples of *doseno* and *treseno* are rare. They are almost always found in such combinations as *veynte doseno, treynta doseno, veynte treseno*. For an overview with discussion of the rivalry between vernacular and Latinate ordinals in Spanish see García Gallarín (2007, 135–150).

[8] I have found no examples of an ordinal **siesto/siesta* sixth' < Lat. *sextum/sextam*; the feminine *siesta* in the phrase *sexta hora* 'at the sixth hour' has been substantivised as the noun *siesta* 'afternoon nap'. OSp. *siesto* 'position' is unrelated to this word family (see Dworkin 1976).

[9] Some of the Old Spanish ordinals have survived as nouns: *primo* 'cousin' *ochavo* 'type of coin', *decena* 'about ten', *docena* 'dozen', *veintena* 'a score', *cuarentena* 'period of forty days; quarantine'.

alongside *catorzeno, quinzeno*. Very rare are forms such as *séptimo décimo* 'seventeenth', found once each in the Alfonsine *General estoria* and in the *Fuero de Plasencia*, and *diez y octavo* 'eighteenth'. One example each of feminine *quartodécima, decimosexta* and *decimonona* appear in the Royal Scriptorium manuscript of the Alfonsine *Libro de las cruzes* (Kasten and Nitti 2002). The *CORDE* data indicate that such Latinate ordinals as *vigésimo*, 'twentieth', *trigésimo* 'thirtieth', *cuadragésimo* 'fortieth', *quincuagésimo* 'fiftieth', etc., were almost unknown in medieval Spanish, first appearing, for the most part, in the second half of the sixteenth century. An exception is *uicésimo*, which is found in two Alfonsine texts from the Royal Chancellery (*Libro de las cruzes, General estoria, cuarta parte*) and in a handful of fifteenth-century sources. Today ordinals above 'ten' are used only in higher oral and written registers.

4 Rivalry between vernacular and Latinate doublets

Students of Spanish diachronic lexicology have long been familiar with the phenomenon of doublets (Sp. *dobletes*), those Latin bases that first came into Hispano-Romance through oral transmission and then later as outright borrowings from written Latin. Speakers would have not perceived the genetic relationship between each member of the relevant semantically-differentiated set, e.g. *fraguar* 'to forge' and *fabricar* 'to manufacture' < Lat. *făbrĭcāre*, *rezar* 'to pray' and *recitar* 'to recite' < Lat. *rĕcĭtāre*. In these cases the Latinism does not oust its vernacular counterpart from the lexicon. A second category of lexical substitution involving Latinisms consists of cases where an orally-transmitted reflex of a Latin base gives way to its Latinate counterpart and falls into disuse (or at least obsolescence). A number of such cases occurred within the medieval language. In the following list of selected examples, the first Spanish form is the medieval vernacular reflex of the Latin base, while the second is the Latinism that displaced it. I have divided the material into two groups, verbs and nouns/adjectives:

aorar ~ *adorar* 'to adore' < Lat. *ădōrāre, batear* ~ *bautizar* 'to baptise' < Lat. *baptīzāre, gemer* ~ *gemir* 'to groan' < Lat. *gĕmĕre, enfeñir* ~ *fingir* 'to pretend' < Lat. *fingĕre, envidar/convidar* ~ *invitar* 'to invite' < Lat. *invītāre, esleer* ~ *elegir* 'to choose, select' < Lat. *elĭgĕre, mascar* ~ *masticar* 'to chew' < Lat. *mastĭcāre, nodrir/nodrecer* ~ *nutrir* 'to feed, nourish' < Lat. *nūtrīre*, *preigar* ~ *predicar* 'to preach' < Lat. *praedĭcāre*, *ruir* ~ *rugir* 'growl, grumble' < Lat. *rŭgīre* *cosso* ~ *curso* 'course' < Lat. *cursum*, *cutiano* ~ *cotidiano* 'daily' < Lat. *quŏtīdĭānum*, *melezina* ~ *medicina* 'medicine' < Lat. *mĕdĭcīna*, *viesso* ~ *verso* 'verse' < Lat. *versum*, *yente* ~ *gente* 'people, nation' < Lat. *gentem*

In some pairs, the use of Latin in oral and written ecclesiastical and liturgical contexts would have favoured the triumph of the Latinate doublet. Although *aorar* appears frequently in the *Fazienda de Ultramar* (ca. 1200) and in the Alfonsine historical writings (*General estoria* and *Estoria de Espanna*),[10] it was completely supplanted by *adorar* by the end of the thirteenth century. The same holds true for vernacular *preigar*, found in the Alfonsine *Lapidario* and the contemporary Vulgate-based Bible translation preserved in Escorial manuscript i-j-6 vis-à-vis the Latinism *predicar*. Elsewhere vernacular reflexes of Lat. *praedĭcāre* have thrived: Fr. *prêcher*, OOcc. *prezicar*, OGen. *prichar*, Sard. *preikare/preigare*. Numerous examples of *batear* turn up in the Alfonsine *Primera Partida* (also known as the *Libro de las leyes*), in the writings of Heredia, and as late as the mid-fifteenth century *Atalaya de las corónicas* of the Arcipreste de Talavera. The *CORDE* data indicate that both verbs co-existed in the medieval language, with *bautizar* enjoying a slight numerical superiority before its definitive triumph by the end of the fifteenth century, after which examples of *batear* are exceedingly rare. However, *batear* continues to be recorded in dictionaries in the early modern period (see Nieto Jiménez and Álvar Ezquerra 2007, Vol. 2, s.v. *batear*).

Not surprisingly, Latinisms often triumphed over vernacular rival doublets in the field of medicine. Oral transmission of Lat. *mĕdĭcīna* seems to have yielded in Old Spanish *melezina*, a form whose evolution still raises some questions regarding the origin of the *-l-* (sporadic sound change or lexical blend?) and the preservation of the intertonic vowel. The Latin base yielded OPtg. *meezinha*. The *CORDE* data records for the period 1200–1500 hundreds of examples of both forms, with *melezina* showing a numerical superiority.

---

[10] Forms reflecting both *aorar* and *adorar* appear in both sources. Are the instances of *adorar* Latinate spellings that mask the vernacular pronunciation? OFr. *aorer*, OOcc. *azorar*, OCat. *aorar* bespeak oral transmission of the Latin base (see Meyer-Lübke 1935, entry 191).

Both Nebrija's Spanish-Latin dictionary (ca. 1495) and Covarrubias's *Tesoro* (1611) register only *medicina*. In the fifteenth century the Latinism *médico* 'doctor' took firm root and ousted other medieval designations such as *fís(s)ico/fís(s)igo*, the Arabism *alfaquim* and the less frequent Gallicism *me(t)ge*. Could the introduction and consolidation of *médico* have played a role in the triumph of *medicina* over *melezina*? The *DLE* marks *melecina* as obsolete.

In some instances both reflexes of the same Latin base have survived into the modern language, but the popularly-transmitted member of the set has undergone a sharp reduction in its semantic scope or is found only in regional dialects. To judge by the available evidence, the medieval language opted for *mascar* 'to chew' until Latinate *masticar* began to appear in texts (as the participle *masticado*) only in the second half of the sixteenth century, after which it displaced the vernacular verb. Nebrija employed *mascar* as one of the Spanish glosses for Lat. *conmandūco* in his Latin-Spanish dictionary (1492). The verb is found in numerous bilingual dictionaries of the sixteenth and seventeenth centuries prepared outside Spain; *mascar* is labelled "término vulgar" in Covarrubias's *Tesoro de la lengua castellana o española* (1611). It has survived in Aragonese (Nagore 1999, s.v. *mascar*) and in Asturian as *mazcar* (García Arias 1999, 263) and is recorded without any diatopic or diastratic qualifications in the *DLE*.

The few medieval instances of *envidar* 'to invite', the vernacular reflex of Lat. *invītāre*, found in the Alfonsine corpus (Kasten and Nitti 2002, s.v. *invitar*), are outnumbered by those of *convidar* < Lat. *convitare, a verb modelled on the noun *convīvĭum* and whose reconstruction is supported by Fr. *convier*, It. *convidare*. The *CORDE* database offers two examples of the gerund *invitando* from Enrique de Villena's *Tratado de la consolación* (1424). Indeed, *invitar* continues to be sparsely attested in the period 1500–1700. The verb does not merit an entry in Covarrubias's *Tesoro* (1611), but seems to appear in the entry for *embidar*: "Cuasi *invitar* porque el que envida está convidando al compañero con quien juega con el dinero ..." (my italics). Although *invitar* is recorded in several seventeenth- and early eighteenth-century bilingual dictionaries prepared outside Spain, it seems to be absent from the Academy's pioneering *Diccionario de autoridades* (1726–39); see Nieto Jiménez and Álvar Ezquerra (2007, vol. 6, s.v. *invitar*).

Oral transmission of Lat. *fingĕre* yields OSp. *feñir*, which appears in the prefixed form *enfeñir* 'to pretend' in thirteenth-century texts. Although it appears in Heredia, the Latinate doublet *fingir* first appears in Castilian sources in the early fifteenth century in the *Libro de los enxemplos por A.B.C.* of Clemente Sánchez de Vercial and in the writings of Enrique de Villena, after which it definitively replaces its vernacular counterparts as a verb expressing the meaning 'to pretend'. Before 1400 such forms as *enfengir/enfingir* show the gradual Latinisation of the earlier forms. Very early in its history, the unprefixed *feñir* had come to signify 'to knead' (so attested in the mid-thirteenth-century Bible translation preserved in Escorial MS i-j-8 [ca. 1400]), and has survived as *heñir* with this meaning into the modern language. A similar semantic split is seen in Cat. *fenyer* alongside *fingir*.[11]

To judge by the medieval record, the vernacular reflex of Lat. ēlĭgĕre, OSp. *esleer* (var. *esleír*) 'to choose, elect' enjoyed tremendous vitality until the second half of the fourteenth century, during which its use became increasingly infrequent. Nebrija did not record the verb in his pioneering bilingual dictionaries. In his *editio princeps* (Seville, 1575) of don Juan Manuel's fourteenth-century *Conde Lucanor* Argote de Molina included *esleír* in his list of the archaic words found in that text. Covarrubias (1611) also recorded *esleír*, labelling it as obsolescent, as did Lorenzo Franciosini's Spanish-Italian dictionary (1620) and the Real Academia's first dictionary, the so-called *Diccionario de autoridades* (1726–1739), both quoted in Nieto Jiménez and Álvar Ezquerra (2007, s.v. *esleír*). The Latinism *elegir* began to flourish in the second half of the fourteenth century. The two examples of *elegir* in a *carta real* dated 1253 from the court of Alfonso X dealing with the election of an abbess may reflect a failed early attempt to introduce Lat. ēlĭgĕre into a Romance document. Romance texts of the thirteenth century offer examples of learnèd *electo* (never **elecho*) and the related noun *elección*. As is the case with many Latinisms, *elegir* first appears with some frequency in Aragonese sources, e.g. Heredia (alongside *esleer/esleír*) before taking firm root in Castilian in the fifteenth century (for details, see Dworkin 2006, 32–34).

Examples of vernacular *cutiano* far outnumber those of *cotidiano* until the fifteenth century, prior to which the latter is found sporadically in some legal texts such as the *Vidal Mayor, Fueros de la Novenera* (both of Navarrese or Aragonese origin), and the *Fuero de Plasencia*. *CORDE* gives two texts with

---

[11] For a detailed and rigorous discussion, with numerous textual citations, of the dual development of Lat. *fingĕre* in Hispano-Romance, see Harris-Northall (1992–93).

cutiano for the period 1500–1700. Abundant examples of both *cosso* and *curso* are found in medieval sources. Nebrija's Spanish-Latin dictionary (ca. 1495) contains an entry "cosso do corren el toro", glossed with Lat. *harena* 'sand', and Covarrubias, *Tesoro* (1611) defines *coso* as "la plaza o campo donde lidian los toros, cuasi corso, porque los corren allí". A similar definition is found in the *DLE*, which also records the meaning 'calle principal en algunas ciudades'.

The extinction of *viesso* 'verse' by the end of the fourteenth century coincides with the rise and integration of its Latinate counterpart *verso*. Competition between *viesso* and *verso* is observable in OSp. *vierso*, found in some Alfonsine texts from the Royal Chancellery (Kasten and Nitti 2002, s.v. *verso*), and as late as the mid-fifteenth century translation of the Rule of Saint Benedict. The rivalry between these doublets is observable in the textual tradition of the fourteenth-century collection of exempla known as *El Conde Lucanor* (ca. 1335) of don Juan Manuel. The author uses the noun *viessos* to refer to the short verse summaries at the end of each tale, but Argote de Molina's 1575 edition consistently replaces *viessos* with *versos*. This substitution is not surprising. In the late medieval and early modern periods, men of letters would be familiar with Latinate literary terminology and the average illiterate speaker would have no need for a word meaning 'verse'. To what extent was *viesso* known by the average speaker in medieval Spain?

5 Three unclear cases

There are some instances in which the status of the neologism as a Latinism is open to question. I shall present three examples here. Instances of *ruir* 'to roar, groan' are rare; the vernacular reflex of Lat. *rŭgīre* turns up in the late-thirteenth century Aragonese *Vidal Mayor*, in the Alfonsine *General estoria* (Kasten and Nitti 2002, s.v. *rugir)*), the fourteenth-century *Libro de la caça* of don Juan Manuel, and once in the *Etimologías romanceadas de san Isidoro* (a text that may go back to the thirteenth century, although preserved in a unique fifteenth-century manuscript). The Latinism *rugir* (var. *rogir*) first appears in the fifteenth century. Although *ruir* failed to survive, the related noun *ruido* (< Lat. *rŭgītum*) 'noise' has enjoyed tremendous vitality throughout the entire history of the language. Given the meaning of the verb in question, might phonosymbolic considerations have played a role in the selection of the variant with the voiced palatal affricate represented by -*g*-? One might argue that *rugir* was a conservative earlier vernacular variant of *ruir* and not a deliberate borrowing from written Latin. Would the speech community have turned to a Latinism to express the notion 'roar'? The same question arises with regard to Sp. *mugir* 'to moo' < Lat. *mūgīre*. The record provides no evidence for the existence of orally-transmitted *muir. Like *rugir*, *mugir* is first documented in the fifteenth century, in the writings of Enrique de Villena. It is not surprising that words for 'moo' do not appear frequently in medieval texts. The Alfonsine corpus offers several instances of *mudiar*, so used (Kasten and Nitti 2002, s.v. *remudiar*).

In the cases of *emer/gemir* 'to groan' and *yente/gente* 'people, nation', the innovation may be a Gallicism rather than a Latinism. A handful of cases of *emer* (alongside forms reflecting *gemer/gemir*) are found in the Alfonsine *General estoria*. Although examples of *gemir* begin to abound in the fifteenth century, a handful of instances of this verb turn up such thirteenth-century texts as the *Calila e Dina* (preserved only in two fifteenth-century manuscripts) and the Sixth Part of the *General estoria*. Texts from the same century furnish examples of the noun *gemido* 'groan' (alongside *yemdo* < Lat. *gĕmĭtum* 'id.'), a form that presupposes the existence of the corresponding verb.[12] In all these cases it is possible that *gemir* results from scribal alteration in the manuscripts that have preserved these texts. It is difficult to determine with any degree of certainty whether *gemir* is an early Latinism or a Gallicism. Oral transmission of Lat. *gentem* yielded OSp. *yente*, for which the *CORDE* database records over 900 examples in the thirteenth century alone. For that same century *CORDE* records an almost equal number of instances of *gente*. *Yente* virtually disappears from the written record at the beginning of the fourteenth century. It seems reasonable to posit that the frequency of *gente* in thirteenth-century texts speaks in favour of viewing this noun as a borrowing from neighbouring Gallo-Romance. Latinisms rarely appear with such frequency. One may legitimately ask whether the many examples of OSp. *gent* reflect local apocope of the *-e* or point to the borrowing of Gallo-Romance *gent*.

---

[12] The paroxytonic stress of *gemido* points to derivation from the verb by means of the sound suffix *-ido* (see Craddock and Georges 1963) rather than a learnèd adaptation of Lat. *gĕmĭtum*.

6 Conclusion

The introduction and incorporation of Latinisms in the late medieval and early modern periods (1400–1700) changed radically the makeup of the Spanish lexicon. The entry of neologisms as loanwords is an instance of language change resulting from linguistic contact. Borrowings from Latin differ in certain key aspects from words taken from other languages with which Spanish has been in contact over its history. Whereas contact with living languages with long literary traditions such as French, Italian, Portuguese, Catalan, and, most recently, English, took place on the levels of both oral and written language, almost all Latinisms came from the written registers of Latin, accessible only to an elite minority of speakers. Most such borrowings first entered written Hispano-Romance, a linguistic vehicle of a very small portion of the population. As is the case with most loanwords, the majority of Latinisms served to fill gaps in the lexicon. They were borrowings motivated by necessity as part of creating an elaborated written language, and did not replace lexical items already present in the language. These items functioned as necessary loans.

This Chapter has focused selectively on the much smaller group of Latinisms that, over time, replaced earlier signifiers for the notions and concepts at issue. Most of these neologisms also came into the language in the late medieval period, first entering the written language of individual authors, in many cases at the outset, independently. At the time they enjoyed little diffusion at the oral level in the speech community as a whole. Some, such as *débil, pálido, rápido, útil*, do not appear with any degree of frequency until well into the early modern period. The paucity of derivatives that they produced may bespeak later integration into the language. Indeed, forms such as *facilidad, dificultad, debilidad* are probably Latinisms rather than internally-created derivatives o the type *palidez* and *rapidez*. Various factors may have influenced the choice of a Latinism over a vernacular rival or its popular doublet. In the late medieval period, Latin continued to enjoy greater prestige as a language of scholarship, science, religion and administration. Latin boasted a richer lexicon and was perceived as having a higher degree of semantic precision. Except for the clumsy periphrases employed to express the notions 'useful' and 'unique, only', the vernacular rivals seem not to be burdened with internal structural defects that rendered them inadequate as signifiers for the notions and concepts at issue.

The adage "Each word has its own history", attributed (perhaps inaccurately) to the early twentieth-century Swiss-French pioneer of dialect geography, Jules Gilliéron (d. 1926), was coined to describe the vagaries of sound change. It applies equally well to lexical change. There is no one overarching cause for the use of Latinisms as lexical substitutes. Each case merits separate examination to determine whether lexical internal structural conditions or external factors played the decisive role in the eventual triumph of a specific Latinism. This study has only scratched the surface of the question raised by the use of Latinisms as lexical substitutes. It has focused on the initial moments of their presence in the Spanish lexicon. Can one next trace the ways in which these learnèd neologisms passed over time from the written language of a literate minority to the general language of the community? Another relevant topic worthy of close study is the rivalry between vernacular reflexes of Latin suffixes and prefixes and their Latinate counterparts.[13] Much work remains to be done.

Bibliographical references

Burgassi, Cosimo, and Elisa Guadagnini. 2014. "Prima dell'*indole*. Latinismi latenti dell'italiano." *Studi di lessicografia italiana* 31: 5–43.

Burgassi, Cosimo, and Elisa Guadagnini. 2017a. "L'integrazione lessicale di *facile* nel vocabolario italiano: 'prova dei volgarizzamenti' e quadro romanzo." In *"Rem tene, verba sequentur." Latinità e Medioevo romanzo: testi e lingue in contatto*, edited by Elisa Guadagnini and Giulio Vaccaro, 157–177. Alessandria: Edizioni dell'Orso.

Burgassi, Cosimo, and Elisa Guadagnini. 2017b. *La tradizione delle parole. Sondaggi di lessicologia storica*. Strasbourg: Éditions de linguistique et de philologie.

Bustos Tovar, José Jesús. 1974. *Contribución al estudio del cultismo léxico medieval (1140–1252)*. Madrid: Anejo XXVIII del *Boletín de la Real Academia Española*.

Clavería Nadal, Gloria, and Joan Torruella. 2016. "La introducción de las familias léxicas de *fàcil* y *difícil* en catalán a partir de un corpus histórico." *Scriptum Digital* 5: 65–83.

Cortelazzo, Manlio, and Paolo Zolli. 1999. *Dizionario etimologico della lingua italiana*, 2nd ed. Bologna: Zanichelli.

Covarrubias, Sebastián de. 1611. *Tesoro de la lengua castellana o española*. Edited by Felipe C. R. Maldonado. Madrid: Castalia, 1994.

---

[13] For some examples and a very preliminary discussion, see Dworkin (2012, 172).

Craddock, Jerry R., and Emanuel S. Georges. 1963. "The Hispanic Sound-Suffix -*ido*." *Romance Philology* 17: 87–107.

DPD = *Diccionario panhispánico de dudas*. 2005. Madrid: Real Academia Española.

Dworkin, Steven N. 1976. "The Etymology of Old Spanish *siesto*: A Return to the Family of SEDERE." *Romance Philology* 30: 118–123.

Dworkin, Steven N. 1998. "Lexical Loss and Neologisms in Late Medieval Spanish: Two Case Studies." *Bulletin of Hispanic Studies (Liverpool)* 75: 1–11.

Dworkin, Steven N. 2002a. "La introducción e incorporación de latinismos en el español medieval tardío: algunas cuestiones lingüísticas y metodológicas." In *Pulchre, Bene Recte: Estudios en homenaje al Prof. Fernando González Ollé*, edited by Carmen Saralegui Platero and Manuel Casado Velarde, 421–433. Pamplona: Eunsa.

Dworkin, Steven N. 2002b. "Pérdida e integración léxicas: *aína* vs. *rápido* en el español premoderno." In *Vocabula et vocabulaire: Études de lexicologie et de (méta)-lexicographie romanes en l'honneur du 60e anniversaire de Dieter Messner*, edited by Bernard Pöll and Franz Rainer, 109–118. Frankfurt: Peter Lang.

Dworkin, Steven N. 2004. "La transición léxica en el español bajomedieval." In *Historia de la lengua española*, coordinated by Rafael Cano Aguilar, 643–656. Barcelona: Ariel.

Dworkin, Steven N. 2005. "Historia de la lengua y el cambio léxico." *Iberoromania* 62: 59–70.

Dworkin, Steven N. 2006. "Cambio léxico en el Medioevo tardío: La pérdida del esp. ant. *esleer* y *poridad*". *Revista de Historia de la Lengua Española* 1: 31–43.

Dworkin, Steven N. 2010. "Thoughts on the Relatinization of the Castilian Lexicon." *Romance Philology* 64: 273–83.

Dworkin, Steven N. 2012. *A History of the Spanish Lexicon: A Linguistic Perspective*. Oxford: Oxford University Press.

Eberenz, Rolf. 1998. "Dos campos semánticos del español preclásico: 'fácil' y 'difícil'." In *Estudios de lingüística y filología españolas: Homenaje a Germán Colón,* edited by Irene Andrés-Suárez and Luis López Molina, 167–183. Madrid: Gredos.

García Arias, Xosé Lluis. 2009. *Propuestes etimolóxiques (4)*. Oviedo: Academia de la Llingua Asturiana.

García Arias, Xosé Lluis. 2017. *Diccionariu etimolóxicu de la llingua asturiana, I: A–B*. Oviedo: Universidad de Oviedo and Academia de la Llingua Asturiana.

García Gallarín, Consuelo. 2007. *El cultismo en la historia de la lengua española*. Madrid: Parthenon.

Harris-Northall, Ray. 1992–93. "Learnèd Borrowings in Spanish in the 14th and 15th Centuries: The Case of the Descendants of FINGERE." *Journal of Hispanic Research* 1: 289–313.

Harris-Northall, Ray. 1999. "Re-Latinization of Castilian Lexis in the Early Sixteenth Century." *Bulletin of Hispanic Studies (Liverpool)* 76: 1–12.

Herrera, María Teresa. 1996. *Diccionario español de textos médicos antiguos*, 2 vols. Madrid: Arco/Libros.

Kasten, Lloyd A. and John Nitti. 2002. *Diccionario de la prosa castellana de Alfonso X*, 3 vols. New York: Hispanic Seminary of Medieval Studies.

Lloyd, Paul M. 1987. *From Latin to Spanish. Vol. 1: Historical Phonology and Morphology of the Spanish Language.* Philadelphia: American Philosophical Society.

Mackenzie, Jean Gilkison. 1984. *A Lexicon of the 14th-Century Aragonese Manuscripts of Juan Fernández de Heredia.* Madison: Hispanic Seminary of Medieval Studies.

Malkiel, Yakov. 1983. "Alternatives to the Classic Dichotomy/ Family Tree / Wave Theory? The Romance Evidence." In *Language Change*, edited by Irmengard Rauch and Gerald F. Carr, 192–256. Bloomington: Indiana University Press.

Meyer-Lübke, Wilhelm. 1935. *Romanisches Etymologisches Wörterbuch*, 3rd ed. Heidelberg: Winter.

Nagore Lain, Francho. 1999. *Endize de bocables de l'aragonés seguntes os repertorios lesicos de lugars y redoladas de l'Alto Aragón*, 4 vols. Huesca: Instituto de Estudios Altoaragoneses.

Nebrija, Elio Antonio de. 1492 [1979]. *Diccionario latino-español (Salamanca 1492).* Preliminary study by Germán Colón and Amadeu-J. Soberanas, 1979. Barcelona: Puvill.

Nebrija, Elio Antonio de. ca. 1495. *Vocabulario español-latino.* Facsimile edition, 1951. Madrid: Real Academia Española.

Nieto Jiménez, Lidio, and Manuel Álvar Ezquerra. 2007. *Nuevo tesoro lexicográfico del español (s. XIV–1726)*, 11 vols. Madrid: Arco Libros.

Reinheimer-Rîpeanu, Sanda. 2004. *Dictionnaire des emprunts latins dans les langues romanes.* Bucharest: Editura Academiei Române.

Rey, Alain, dir. 2000. *Dictionnaire historique de la langue française*, 3 vols. Paris: Dictionnaires Le Robert.

Wartburg, Walther von. 1949. *Französisches Etymologisches Wörterbuch. Eine Darstellung des galloromanischen Sprachschatzes.* Vol. 3, D–F. Tübingen: J.C.B. Mohr.

Chapter 9

Sustituciones léxicas en los arabismos del reino de Granada (siglos XVI y XVII)[1]

Inmaculada González Sopeña

Universidad de Granada

Resumen

Este objetivo del presente estudio se centra en el análisis histórico-lingüístico de dos arabismos léxicos adscritos a campos léxico-semántico distintos del reino de Granada durante la etapa inmediatamente posterior a la conquista cristiana (siglos XVI y XVII): *almofía* y *tarquín*. Para ello se parte de un corpus de documentos administrativos y municipales vinculados a algunos de los territorios que conformaban el reino de Granada (actuales provincias de Málaga, Granada y Almería). En este espacio geográfico y en dicho período cronológico la variedad de español que se desarrolla se caracteriza por el mantenimiento, e incluso se incorporación, de préstamos léxicos tomados del árabe en contra de la tendencia general de pérdida que se observa en otras zonas hispanohablantes debido al particular contexto histórico, político y social allí desarrollado. Con todo, los arabismos seleccionados evidencian posibles sustitutos léxicos de origen latino con los que compitieron en el uso.

Summary

The objective of this study focuses on the historical-linguistic analysis of two lexical Arabisms from different lexical-semantic fields linked to the everyday life of the Kingdom of Granada during the period immediately after the

---

[1] Este estudio ha sido realizado dentro del marco del proyecto de investigación "Hispane Testium Depositiones", con referencia FFI2017-83400-P del Ministerio de Economía y Competitividad (España) y del proyecto "Atlas Lingüístico y Etnográfico de Andalucía, S. XVIII. Patrimonio documental y humanidades digitales" (Proyectos I+D+i Junta de Andalucía-FEDER, P18-FR-695).

Christian conquest (16th and 17th centuries): *almofía* and *tarquín*. To do that, a corpus of administrative and municipal documentation related to the territories that composed the Kingdom of Granada (current provinces of Málaga, Granada and Almería) has been elaborated. In this geographical space and in the said chronological period, the variety of Spanish that is developed is characterised by the maintenance, and even incorporation, of lexical loanwords taken from the Arabic language. That situation contrasts with the general trend of loss of Arabisms observed in other Spanish-speaking areas due to the specific historical, political and social context developed there. The selected Arabisms show possible lexical substitutes of Latin origin with which they competed in use.

Keywords

Lexical borrowing, Lexical competition, Arabic, Spanish.

1 Introducción

El elemento árabe se erige como uno de los componentes más importantes del léxico de la lengua española (Lapesa 2008, Giménez Eguibar 2016). Su importancia quedó manifestada desde las primeras décadas tras la invasión musulmana de la Península en el 711, a la que dieron el nombre de al-Ándalus. Rápidamente, se impuso "una supraestructura religiosa y política de corte islámico, y una infraestructura económica y social que los habitantes fueron progresivamente adoptando" (Corriente 2004, 185). Existen bastantes estudios que confirman la progresiva arabización de la península ibérica a lo largo de ocho siglos (Steiger 1967, García González 2008). Esta situación contrasta con la que se halla a finales del siglo XV y, sobre todo, en el siglo XVI, en la que los arabismos se vieron sometidos a un proceso de pérdida, sustitución u obsolescencia a favor de otros términos de origen romance o latino (Giménez-Eguibar 2016): "el árabe pasó a estar en una situación de deslizamiento o pérdida en favor de las lenguas romances" (García González 2008, 679).

El objetivo de este trabajo se centra en el análisis histórico-lingüístico, lexicográfico, de una serie de arabismos a través de un corpus de documentos administrativos vinculados al antiguo reino de Granada, a saber: *almofía* y *tarquín*. Estos términos evidencian posibles sustitutos léxicos romances entre los que se establece una competencia léxica en el uso. Estas voces cuentan con un uso mayor en los territorios que conformaban el reino de Granada (actuales provincias de Málaga, Granada y Almería), la zona peninsular de más tardía castellanización, en contraste con lo que sucedía en otras regiones hispanohablantes en las que casi de forma total, el arabismo se ha visto desplazado por otro término, quedando, por tanto, obsoleto o arrinconado a áreas rurales en dialectos específicos.

El siglo XVI se presenta como un momento de decadencia en la incorporación de léxico de origen árabe (Walsh 1967, Giménez Eguibar 2011, González Sopeña 2019). El nuevo discurso renacentista del siglo XVI refleja una mentalidad de rechazo hacia la religión musulmana, y con ello, su lengua como razón fundamental que impedía una conversión verdadera al cristianismo. Partiendo del estrecho vínculo e influencias existentes entre los cambios históricos y los cambios léxicos,[2] determinados acontecimientos de la época marcaron el declive en la introducción de arabismos, los cuales contaban con plena vigencia hasta entonces. Paralelamente, dichos factores externos también guiaron el rumbo y expansión del español como lengua de cultura que, de forma progresiva, fue ocupando todos los espacios funcionales de la vida.

La conquista final del reino de Granada se produjo en 1492, mismo año en el que comenzó la colonización de Hispanoamérica y fue, además, el año en el que se publicó la primera gramática castellana de Antonio de Nebrija. Conviene recordar que la toma de Granada, último enclave musulmán en la Península, se llevó a cabo mediante la firma de un pacto que se materializó en las *Capitulaciones*. Ese pacto respetaba la permanencia de los musulmanes que vivían en el reino de Granada, así como su libertad religiosa, sus leyes y sus costumbres (González Jiménez 2000, 470–472). Dicho documento garantizaba la conservación de los bienes y propiedades de los musulmanes y se traspasaron determinadas instituciones nazaríes administrativas y fiscales (Galán Sánchez y Peinado Santaella 2006). Esa aparente tolerancia pronto se vio alterada y se pretendió una asimilación progresiva de la comunidad musulmana al nuevo orden cristiano a través de la traducción de los textos religiosos al árabe y de la escuela. Con la llegada del cardenal Cisneros al

---

[2] Partiendo de los estudios de Baldinger (1985), así como de Álvarez de Miranda (1992) o García-Godoy (2012), entre otros. En el caso de los arabismos esta cuestión es fundamental: "gran parte de las palabras de origen árabe deben su existencia en la lengua española a factores extralingüísticos, esto es, a la introducción de nuevas realidades en la vida material" (Lörinczi 1969, 65).

reino de Granada a finales del siglo XV, se pusieron en marcha una serie de medidas que contravenían con todo lo dispuesto en las *Capitulaciones*, generando enorme malestar entre la comunidad musulmana. La revuelta musulmana que se originó en 1499 tuvo como consecuencia "la empresa de conversión forzosa dirigida hacia los seguidores del islam" (Domínguez Ortiz y Vincent 1978, 19), pasando a ser denominados "moriscos".

A partir de la primera década de 1500, se promulgaron diferentes cédulas reales cuyo objetivo principal fue "destruir las peculiaridades de la cultura morisca" (Domínguez Ortiz y Vincent 1978, 21). En ellas, se establecieron, por ejemplo, la prohibición de hablar árabe para las transacciones comerciales, la expropiación de bienes y tierras, la imposición de tributos adicionales, la vigilancia inquisitorial para garantizar la auténtica conversión al cristianismo, así como las penas y castigos en caso de contravenirlas. De ello se conservan un sinfín de documentos: "Y algunos que estavan rebeldes y pertinaçes [el cardenal] haze prender y echar en cadenas y prisiones, hasta que venian en conosçimiento e de su voluntad pedian el agua de baptismo" (Barrios Aguilera 2002, 78).

No obstante, a pesar del rechazo hacia cualquier aspecto susceptible de ser vinculado con la religión musulmana, la documentación municipal y administrativa granadina de los siglos XVI y XVII que sirve de base para este estudio está impregnada de arabismos relacionados con diferentes ámbitos de la vida cotidiana y social; algunos solo han tenido recorrido dentro de los límites geográficos de dicho reino, mientras que otros términos consiguieron encontrar una vía de expansión hacia otras zonas.

Muchos de los arabismos documentados en el corpus elaborado han quedado finalmente obsoletos (González Sopeña 2019). No obstante, siguen faltando estudios que se detengan en el análisis específico de cada caso, con el fin de establecer los usos de los arabismos, su pérdida, la actitud lingüística hacia ellos, su tratamiento lexicográfico o la distribución dialectal actual que presentan (Giménez Eguibar 2011, 52).

2 El mantenimiento de arabismos en el reino de Granada y la competencia léxica

El particular contexto histórico, social y político desarrollado en los antiguos territorios que conformaban el reino de Granada tuvo como consecuencia, en el plano lingüístico del español, el mantenimiento de arabismos léxicos en un volumen mayor del que se observa en otras áreas hispanohablantes hasta, por lo menos, el siglo XVII (González Sopeña 2019, 65). La conquista cristiana de Granada en 1492, como se ha expuesto, no supuso una ruptura radical e inmediata con el régimen nazarí anterior. Administrativamente, estructuras e instituciones heredadas de los musulmanes se traspasaron al nuevo contexto cristiano. Este hecho es una de las razones principales que explica el mantenimiento de una parcela léxica de vocablos árabes muy específicos en la documentación granadina.

Este estado de cosas se contrapone al nuevo discurso renacentista, que promovía la vuelta al mundo clásico grecolatino y amagaba por la total eliminación de cualquier elemento de corte musulmán, en consonancia con las aspiraciones políticas de los Reyes Católicos. No solo existe documentación estrictamente histórica al respecto, también, las autoridades lingüísticas de la época dejaron por escrito la pésima opinión que les merecía el uso de arabismos, como Martín de Viciana (Giménez Eguibar 2011, 94). A ello, debe unirse otra razón más que explica el mantenimiento de voces de origen árabe, como lo es la permanencia de población morisca en territorio peninsular hasta el siglo XVII: "Mientras los moriscos permanecieron en España, su vestido, costumbres y usos tenían valor de actualidad; desde su expulsión quedaron solo como recuerdo" (Lapesa 2008, 138).

El empuje de ambos hechos (el traspaso de instituciones nazaríes y otros elementos junto con la permanencia de población morisca, por un lado, y el horizonte ideológico renacentista, por otro lado) derivó, en el plano lingüístico, en una competencia léxica en el uso entre arabismos y voces de otro origen, como el latín, el griego, el francés o el italiano, por pasar a ser consideradas lenguas prestigiosas. A pesar de los escasos estudios sobre la pérdida de arabismos en español, existen datos relativos al uso de arabismos en el siglo XVI, casi totalmente restringidos al reino de Granada (Walsh 1967, 314–340).

Sobre la competencia léxica que se observa en los arabismos, los escasos estudios existentes se limitan, casi de forma exclusiva, a los presentados por Giménez Eguibar (2011, 2016a, 2016b), quien ha establecido distintas motivaciones por las cuales muchos arabismos bien han quedado obsoletos y solo puede decirse de ellos que tienen un uso histórico, bien han sufrido un proceso de peyorización semántica o bien han quedado vinculados a dialectos específicos de forma anecdótica.

3 El corpus del reino de Granada como corpus base de estudio

Para el análisis histórico-lingüístico de los arabismos seleccionados y sus sustitutos léxicos se parte de un corpus de estudio compuesto de documentación de corte administrativo y municipal vinculada al reino de Granada, previamente editada por historiadores y paleógrafos. Entre los tipos de documentos se han escogido inventarios de bienes fundamentalmente, y documentación administrativa de algunas localidades del antiguo reino granadino. Cronológicamente, el documento más antiguo de este corpus data de 1553, mientras que el más moderno es de 1671, es decir, el corpus se cimenta con documentación administrativa correspondiente a la etapa inmediatamente posterior a la conquista cristiana.[3]

Además, se han establecido otros corpus de control para cotejar los datos y precisar el análisis. Por un lado, se han consultado los datos de los corpus del español general, concretamente, el *Corpus diacrónico del español* (*CORDE*) y el *Corpus del Nuevo diccionario histórico del español* (*CNDHE*). También se ha consultado la información disponible en el *Corpus Léxico de Inventarios* (*CorLexIn*), por estar compuesto de documentos similares a los empleados para el corpus base en el mismo marco cronológico. No obstante, la documentación de *CorLexIn* se vincula a localidades de toda la Península y ello ha ayudado a constatar si alguno de los términos de estudio tuvo algún tipo de uso en otras zonas.

Por otro lado, se ha consultado de forma sistemática un amplio repertorio de obras lexicográficas con el objetivo de poder trazar el tratamiento que los arabismos seleccionados han tenido a lo largo de los siglos y dar cuenta de su evolución, sus variantes gráficas, su etimología, sus cambios semánticos y sus marcas de uso según los autores de diversas épocas: el *Diccionario crítico etimológico castellano e hispánico* (*DCECH*), *Diccionario de arabismos y voces afines* (Corriente 2008), el *Nuevo tesoro lexicográfico de la lengua española* (*NTLLE*), el *Diccionario histórico de la lengua española* (*DHLE*) y algunos diccionarios específicos del español medieval (Alonso 1986, Müller 1987).

---

[3] En el apartado correspondiente a la bibliografía se pueden consultar los documentos empleados en esta investigación junto con la clave bibliográfica escogida para cada uno de ellos, para facilitar la lectura.

Para comprobar si existe algún caso actual de los arabismos en comparación con sus sustitutos léxicos se ha empleado la información del *Diccionario de la lengua española* (*DLE*) en su edición más moderna, así como la información léxica del *Atlas lingüístico y etnográfico de Andalucía* (*ALEA*) y del *Tesoro lexicográfico de las hablas andaluzas* (*TLHA*), los cuales han permitido constatar la supervivencia de algún arabismo, aunque de forma muy escasa.[4]

4 Análisis histórico-lingüístico de los arabismos seleccionados y sus sustitutos léxicos

4.1 *Almofía, jofaina* y *vasija*

El arabismo *almofía* se define como 'vasija semejante a un barreño o una jofaina, que sirve para uso de cocina, para lavarse o para otros fines' (*DHLE*, *s.v.*) cuyo origen etimológico está en el ár. hisp. *almuxfiyyah*, literalmente 'oculta' (Corriente 2008, *s.v.*). Cabe resaltar que el *DLE* remite a la entrada lexicográfica de *jofaina*, como voz sinónima definida como 'vasija en forma de taza, de gran diámetro y poca profundidad, que sirve principalmente para lavarse la cara y las manos'.

Almofía se incorporó a finales del siglo XV[5] al español en vocabularios para definir la voz latina *catinum*, un "vaso de barro para tener cozina o manjar o enfriar vino, como escudilla grande grial hondo o lo que los andaluzes por vocablo arauigo llaman almofía" (Santaella 1499, véase *NTLLE*). Como puede apreciarse, Santaella apunta el uso del préstamo en Andalucía, lugar donde permanecieron durante más tiempo los musulmanes. Casi un siglo más tarde, Guadix (1593 [2005]) *s.v. almofía* restringe el uso de esta voz geográficamente, sin especificar zona: "Llaman en algunas partes d'España a vna conqueta o escudilla algo grandezuela".

A pesar de que para Santaella (1499) *almofía* sea una palabra andaluza, es posible localizarla en otros lugares peninsulares como Asturias y Portugal,

---

[4] Asimismo, se han cotejado los resultados con otros corpus dedicados al español más actual, como el *Corpus de referencia del español* (*CREA*) o el *Corpus del español* de Davies (*CDE*). También, se ha comprobado la información de otros atlas lingüísticos: *Atlas lingüísticos de los dominios catalanes* (*ALDC*).
[5] La primera documentación disponible para esta voz es de finales del siglo XV: "Catinum. dizen vaso torneado o **almofía** bernegal", 1490, Alfonso de Palencia, *Universal Vocabulario en latín y en romance* (Alonso 1986, *DCECH, DHLE*).

único lugar donde sobrevive (*DCECH*, *s.v.*). En Salamanca y Badajoz, *almofía* adquiere matices semánticos derivados del original: (a) en Salamanca *almofía* designa a una 'bacía de barbero' y (b) en Badajoz a una 'cazuela de barro donde ser sirven habichuelas y judías' (*DHLE*, *s.v. almofía*, 2ª y 3ª acep.). El corpus base de estudio proporciona algunos casos más de este arabismo desde la segunda mitad del siglo XVI:

- 1553, Sínodo, 269: y un espejo y dos **almofías** y dos redomas[6] de plata, todo lo cual le da él por su grandeza.
- 1556, Boticas, 385: Vna **almofria** blanca.
- 1568, Inventarios, 262: Una calabaça y una **almofía**.
- 1671, Arquitectos, 395: una **almofía** grande blanca para el pie de la cruz de la torre de la Cruz.

El arabismo *almofía* aparece registrado en inventarios de bienes del siglo XVII en otras zonas, como Cáceres, León o Ávila.[7] Estos datos confirman que no fue únicamente una voz andaluza, sino que estuvo extendida por todo el occidente (Morala 2012, 85). El uso de esta voz se restringe a los siglos XVI y XVII, tal como se observa en el corpus elaborado y en los inventarios de bienes consultados. Los corpus de la Real Academia documentan este arabismo hasta el siglo XVII, principalmente en textos literarios de Francisco Delicado y Miguel de Cervantes para caracterizar a personajes andaluces.[8]

Con respecto a su tratamiento lexicográfico, en el siglo XVII la nómina de autores que registran esta voz aumenta: Palet (1604), Oudin (1607), Vittori (1609), Covarrubias (1611), Rosal (1611), Minsheu (1617), entre otros (véase *NTLLE*). La lexicografía académica define este arabismo como 'jofaina' desde *Autoridades* (1726) (véase *NTLLE*) hasta la última edición del *DLE*. Otra característica sobre la forma de esta vasija se observa en Eguílaz y Yanguas (1886 [1974]) *s.v.*: 'escudilla grande tendida y no honda'.

---

[6] 'Vasija de vidrio ancha en su fondo que va estrechándose hacia la boca', *DLE*, *s.v. redoma*.
[7] El *CorLexIn* recupera varios de esos inventarios: [1652 Badajoz] vna **almofia** blanca y otra pintada; [1661 Cáceres] Vna **almofia** blanca, en un real; [1648 Cáceres] Vna **almofia**, en vn real y seis maravedis; [1651 Ávila] Vna **almofia** grande, dos morillos; [1648 León] una fuente de barro vasta y dos escudillas y vna **almofia** pequeña.
[8] "Os hará una **almofía** llena", 1528, Francisco Delicado, *La lozana andaluza*; "y la **almofía** de tener agua bendita", 1613, Miguel de Cervantes, "Rinconete y Cortadillo", *Novelas ejemplares* (*CNDHE*).

Conviene señalar que la voz *almofía,* aparte de convivir en sinonimia con *vasija,* general en el español actual, pudo competir léxicamente con *(al)jofaina,* otro arabismo que gozó de mayor uso según los datos de los corpus académicos.[9] Se trata de otro tipo de competencia léxica, más escasa en español (González Sopeña 2019, 314): la que se produce entre dos arabismos.

Actualmente, puede afirmarse que *almofía* no tiene uso. Solo existe un ejemplo en *CREA* vinculado a la artesanía[10] en el que *almofía* mantiene su sentido de 'vasija de barro'. *ENCLAVE* nos proporciona frecuencias absolutas ateniéndose a los datos de los corpus académicos: se observa que *vasija* cuenta con documentación desde el siglo XIV al siglo XXI (su mayor frecuencia se produce en el siglo XIV, con 34,72 casos por millón de palabras, disminuyéndose dicha frecuencia progresivamente hasta la actualidad), mientras, *almofía* tiene uso solo en los siglos XVI y XVII (con frecuencias que no superan el 0,27 casos por millón), para, posteriormente, ser relevado por *jofaina* en los siglos XVIII y XIX fundamentalmente, con frecuencias algo mayores (1,52 y 1,27). Cabe apuntar la existencia de otra voz de origen latino con un significado muy afín: *escudilla.*[11] Esta palabra, al igual que *vasija,* está presente en los corpus desde el siglo XIII y su uso llega hasta hoy, si bien con frecuencias menores.[12]

4.2 *Tarquín, cieno y lodo*

El *DLE* define *tarquín* como 'légamo que las aguas estancadas depositan en el fondo, o las avenidas de un río en los campos que inundan'. Su origen se encuentra en el ár.hisp. *tarkím,* y este del ár.clás. *tarkīm,* 'amontonamiento' (Corriente 2008, *s.v.*). No obstante, esta etimología ha sido objeto de controversia dado que han sido varias las que se han propuesto: del aranés *tarküm* 'lodo' (Borao 1859 [2009]); del árabe *tanqīya* (Dozy y Engelmann

---

[9] El *CNDHE* suma casi 300 ejemplos de *(al)jofaina* frente a los 27 casos que se obtienen para *almofía.*
[10] "Y la **almofía** (puchero para cocer castañas)", 1997, Natacha Seseña, *Cacharrería popular. La alfarería de basto en España* (*CREA*).
[11] 'Vasija ancha y de forma de media esfera, que se usa comúnmente para servir en ella sopa o caldo', *DLE, s.v.*
[12] En el siglo XIII *escudilla* presenta una frecuencia de 8,17 casos por millón de palabras, en el siglo XX la frecuencia disminuye hasta 2,67 casos por millón (*ENCLAVE*).

1869); del árabe *ṭarḥîn (Eguílaz y Yanguas 1886 [1974]). La etimología se encuentra finalmente resuelta desde el *Diccionario* de la Real Academia Española de 1884 en el árabe *tarkim*, la misma defendida por Corriente.

A pesar de que es posible constatar ejemplos de esta voz desde el siglo XIV, la inmensa mayoría se corresponde con un nombre propio, a excepción de un caso de la *Traducción de las Vidas paralelas de Plutarco*.[13] A partir de 1600 aparece documentado este arabismo con el significado de 'lodo' en España[14] y en Ecuador.[15]

Lexicográficamente, no hay registros de *tarquín* en los diccionarios del español medieval consultados en este estudio. *DCECH* documenta este término en Covarrubias (1611) (véase *NTLLE*) y se señala que es voz poco extendida en castellano.[16] La lexicografía académica incluye este arabismo desde el *Diccionario de autoridades* de 1739. El corpus elaborado aporta un solo caso más:

- 1574, Albaicín, 462: por tener las açequias açoruadas, llenas de çieno y **tarquín**, no teniendo paso las aguas por las açequias para se de auer de regar la dicha Uega.

Posiblemente, como se observa en la documentación aportada, este arabismo quedó arrinconado ante otros términos de origen latino, como *cieno*, *lodo* o *fango*;[17] voces que vienen a significar exactamente lo mismo que *tarquín*.

---

[13] "Despues deuallo vna grant quantidat de **tarquin**, el qual religo todas las cosas ensemble", 1379-1384, Juan Fernández de Heredia, *Traducción de las Vidas paralelas de Plutarco*, CNDHE.

[14] "Un ministro de Caco me entró en una escudilla un poco de potage, digo, de **tarquín** frió, en quien nadavan los bofes de una oveja", 1626, Gonzalo de Céspedes y Meneses, *Varia fortuna del soldado Píndaro*, CNDHE.

[15] "A fin que se precipite al fondo toda la lama y **tarquín** que tiene", 1774, Francisco Requena, *Descripción de Guayaquil*, CNDHE.

[16] El *DCECH* aporta voces derivadas de *tarquín*: *atarquinar*, *entarquinar*, *desentarquinar*. Un documento granadino de 1524 constata la presencia de uno de los verbos derivados a través de la adición de un prefijo, *intarquinar*: "Yten, con condición que saquéis los vancales a la ranbla, los cavallonéis e los **intarquinéis** y gozéis dellos el tiempo de vuestro arrendamiento" (Segura del Pino 2000, 312).

[17] *Cieno* y *fango* cuentan con más de 1000 ejemplos en el *CNDHE*; para el latinismo *lodo* existen más de 4000 casos. Mientras, para el arabismo *tarquín* solo existen 27 ejemplos en este corpus. Los mapas lingüísticos constatan el uso mayoritario de la voz

Actualmente, el *CNDHE* ofrece para España casos documentados de *tarquín* durante el siglo XX, en ámbitos de especialidad relacionados con la geografía y la meteorología.[18] Dialectalmente, *tarquín* se ha conservado en los antiguos territorios que conformaban el reino de Granada. En Granada y Almería, *tarquín* sobrevive como 'lodo', 'cieno', 'fango', 'arena', 'tierra', 'polvareda', 'barrizal', 'sedimento de agua' entre otros sinónimos (*TLHA*). Para Alvar (1997, 33) la voz *tarquín* es voz propia de Andalucía oriental, si bien otros autores defienden un área dialectal más extensa en el este peninsular que también incluiría Murcia, Aragón[19] e incluso zonas fronterizas de las comunidades catalana y valenciana (*ALDC* vol. V, *Topografía*, mapa 717).[20] Puede establecerse que las voces más empleadas son las que vienen del latín (*cieno*, *lodo*)[21] y el catalanismo *fango*, mientras que *tarquín* tiene un uso muy localizado el este peninsular.

---

fango (*ALEA* vol. IV, mapa 904) y *cieno* (*ALEA* vol. IV, mapa 905) en casi la totalidad del territorio andaluz.

[18] Aparecen ejemplos de esta voz en el *CDE* como nombre propio de persona, cuyo origen etimológico está en el latín *Tarquinius*, por el rey romano Tarquinius Superbus: "No deje de escribir querido **Tarquin**" (enladrillovisto.blogspot.com.es/2013/04/lo-que-el-viento-no-pudo-llevarse.html, fecha de consulta agosto 2020.). A estos casos se suman otros con sentido de 'lodo': "No es que esté embarrado, está de **tarquín** hasta las orejas" (https://www.lamentiraestaahifuera.com/2012/06/27/y-t-que-le-diras-a-un-et/, fecha de consulta agosto 2020)

[19] El arabismo *tarquín* se encuentra incluido en diccionarios de aragonesismos (Borao 1859 [2009], Pardo Asso 1938, *s.v.*). Actualmente, la presencia de esta voz en la zona oriental de Andalucía es un ejemplo más de la huella léxica catalano-aragonesa que caracteriza a esta zona desde el inicio de la reconquista y posterior repoblación: "Tampoco ahora es extraña la presencia de tanto elemento oriental: esta compleja región fue reconquistada en el siglo XIII" (Alvar 1997, 46).

[20] El mapa dedicado al concepto 'lodo' del *ALDC* refleja claramente que en la línea fronteriza entre Aragón y Cataluña se registra el arabismo *tarquín*, con una especial presencia en la franja fronteriza entre Tarragona, Castellón y Teruel.

[21] *Lodo* es la voz que presenta más casos por millón en *ENCLAVE* desde el siglo XII, 37,76 es la más alta. *Cieno* también presenta frecuencias elevadas, aunque menores a las de *lodo* (10,94 la más alta). *Fango* presenta unas frecuencias menores a las anteriores desde el siglo XVIII. Todas estas voces superan la frecuencia del arabismo, que no llega al caso por millón en dicha herramienta.

Conclusiones

Tras el análisis expuesto, pueden determinarse las siguientes conclusiones. Los arabismos *almofía* y *tarquín* presentan voces equivalentes o sinónimas de otros orígenes, por lo común, de origen latino. No obstante, es posible establecer ciertas diferencias en cuanto al uso e integración que han tenido estos arabismos.

Almofía es actualmente voz muy residual. Su período de mayor uso se establece entre los siglos XVI y XVII. El término ha quedado distribuido dialectalmente a favor de *vasija* y *escudilla* principalmente, las cuales son palabras de uso general. Además, la competencia léxica se amplía a otros arabismos, como *(al)jofaina*, cuyo uso y vitalidad es mayor que el de *almofía*, si bien ambos arabismos son dialectales y residuales.

Tarquín se presenta como un arabismo mucho más residual. A los pocos casos documentales se suma el escaso tratamiento lexicográfico que ha recibido. Los términos sinónimos de origen latino se han impuesto en el uso actual: *barro, cieno, lodo*. De forma dialectal se hallan ciertos vestigios del arabismo a lo largo del este peninsular, en zonas limítrofes entre la comunidad valenciana y catalana, y hasta el sudeste de Andalucía.

El reino de Granada se presenta como un espacio geográfico significativo en el mantenimiento de arabismos, especialmente en textos vinculados a la administración, como los inventarios. La lectura de este tipo de textos revela el mantenimiento parcial de arabismos léxicos en comparación con otras zonas. Se ha podido constatar que ambos arabismos tuvieron un área de uso mayor, al occidente y al oriente peninsular. Conviene resaltar que ni *almofía* y ni *tarquín* portan marcas de uso en la edición más actual del diccionario académico.

Por último, puede apreciarse la tendencia general a la obsolescencia de los arabismos estudiados a favor de términos de otro origen. Los arabismos seleccionados se encuentran distribuidos actualmente de forma dialectal en localidades específicas, entre las que destacan las andaluzas por ser territorios en los que la huella lingüística del árabe ha sido más intensa dadas las peculiaridades históricas anotadas.

Referencias

Documentos del corpus base de estudio y clave bibliográfica

Albaicín = Barrios Aguilera, Manuel. 1996. "El Albaicín de Granada sin moriscos. Memoriales para su restauración." *Chronica Nova*, 23: 439–463.

Arquitectos = Galera Mendoza, Esther. 2014. *Arquitectos y maestros de obras en la Alhambra (siglos XVI–XVIII): artífices de cantería, albañilería yesería y forja*. Granada: Comares.

Boticas = De la Obra Sierra, Juan María, María José Osorio y Amparo Moreno Trujillo. 2009. "Familia y negocios: las boticas de los Ripa en la Granada del Quinientos." *Chronica Nova*, 35: 371–401.

Inventarios = Martínez Ruiz, Juan. 1972. *Inventarios de bienes moriscos del reino de Granada (siglo XVI)*. Madrid: CSIC.

Sínodo = Gallego Burín, Antonio y Alfonso Gámir Sandoval. 1996. *Los moriscos del Reino de Granada según el sínodo de Guadix de 1554 (ed. facs.)*. Granada: Universidad de Granada.

Referencias bibliográficas

ALDC = Veny, Joan, y Lídia Pons I Griera. 2010. *Atles lingüístic del domini català*. Barcelona: Institut d'Estudis Catalans.

ALEA = Alvar, Manuel. 1961–1973. *Atlas lingüístico y etnográfico de Andalucía*. Granada: Universidad de Granada–CSIC.

Alonso, Martín. 1986. *Diccionario medieval español: desde las Glosas Emilianenses y Silenses (S.X) hasta el siglo XV*. Salamanca: Universidad Politécnica de Salamanca.

Alvar, Manuel. 1997. "Acercamiento al léxico andaluz." *Demófilo*, 22: 29–47.

Álvarez de Miranda, Pedro. 1992. *Palabras e ideas: el léxico de la ilustración temprana en España (1680–1760)*. Madrid: Anejos del BRAE.

Baldinger, Kurt. 1985. "Lengua y cultura: su relación en lingüística histórica." *Revista Española de Lingüística*, 15: 247–276.

Barrios Aguilera, Manuel. 2002. *Granada morisca: la convivencia negada*. Granada: Comares.

Borao, Gerónimo. 1859. *Diccionarios de voces aragonesas*. Reimpreso. Zaragoza: Imprenta y librería de Calisto Ariño, 2009.

CDE = Davies, Mark. 2002–. *Corpus del Español: 100 million words, 1200s–1900s*. Fecha de consulta agosto 2020. http://www.corpusdelespanol.org.

CNDHE = Real Academia Española. *Corpus del Nuevo Diccionario Histórico del Español*. Fecha de consulta agosto 2020. http://web.frl.es/CNDHE/.

CORDE = Real Academia Española. *Banco de datos (CORDE). Corpus diacrónico del español*. Fecha de consulta agosto 2020. https://www.rae.es/recursos/banco-de-datos/corde.

CorLexIn = Morala Rodríguez, José Ramón. *Corpus léxico de inventarios*. Fecha de consulta agosto 2020. http://web.frl.es/CORLEXIN.html.

Corriente, Federico. 2004. "El elemento árabe en la historia lingüística peninsular: actuación directa e indirecta. Los arabismos en los romances peninsulares." En *Historia de la lengua española*, coordinado por Rafael Cano Aguilar, 185–205. Barcelona: Ariel.

Corriente, Federico. 2008. *Dictionary of Arabic and Allied Loanwords*. Leiden: Brill.

CREA = Real Academia Española. *Corpus de referencia del español actual*. Fecha de consulta agosto 2020. https://www.rae.es/recursos/banco-de-datos/crea.

DCECH = Corominas, Joan, y José Antonio Pascual. 1980–1991. *Diccionario crítico etimológico castellano e hispánico*, 6 vols. Madrid: Gredos.

DHLE = Real Academia Española. 1960–1996. *Diccionario histórico de la lengua española*. Fecha de consulta agosto 2020. https://www.rae.es/recursos/diccionarios/diccionarios-anteriores-1726-1992/diccionario-historico-1960-1996.

DLE = Asociación de Academias de la Lengua Española. 2014. *Diccionario de la lengua española*. 23ª edición. Madrid: Espasa. Fecha de consulta agosto 2020. https://dle.rae.es/.

Domínguez Ortiz, Antonio, y Bernard Vincent. 1978. *Historia de los moriscos. Vida y tragedia de una minoría*. Madrid: Revista de Occidente.

Dozy, Reinhart Pieter Anne, y Willem Herman Engelmann. 1869. *Glossaire des mots espagnols et portugais dérivés de l'arabe*. Leiden: Brill.

Eguílaz y Yanguas, Leopoldo. *Glosario de las palabras españolas de origen oriental (árabe, hebreo, malayo, persa y turco)*. Granada: La Lealtad, 1886. Reimpreso. Madrid: Atlas, 1974.

ENCLAVE = Real Academia Española. 2018. *ENCLAVE*. Fecha de consulta agosto 2020. http://www.enclave.rae.es.

Galán Sánchez, Ángel, y Rafael Peinado Santaella. 2006. "De la *madīna* musulmana al *concejo* mudéjar." En *Fiscalidad de estado y fiscalidad municipal en los reinos hispánicos medievales*, coordinado por Manuel Sánchez Martínez y Denis Menjont, 197–237. Madrid: Casa Velázquez.

García Godoy, María Teresa. 2012. "La lengua de las primeras constituciones hispánicas: el cambio léxico-semántico." En *Actas del IX Congreso Internacional de Historia de la Lengua Española*, coordinado por Teresa Bastardín Martín y Manuel Rivas Zancarrón, 107–132. Madrid: Iberoamericana / Vervuert.

García González, Javier. 2008. "Viejos problemas desde nuevos enfoques: los arabismos en el español medieval desde la perspectiva de la sociolingüística." En *Discurso y sociedad II: nuevas contribuciones al estudio de la lengua en contexto social*, coordinado por José Luis Blas Arroyo, Manuela Casanueva Avalos, Mónica Velando Casanova y Javier Vellón Lahoz, 671–684. Valencia: Universidad Jaume I.

Giménez-Eguíbar, Patricia. 2011. *Arabismos en el campo semántico de los oficios: de la competición léxica a la pérdida léxica.* PhD diss., University of Wisconsin.

Giménez-Eguibar, Patricia. 2016a. "Ni contigo ni sin ti. El arabismo 'albéitar' en el léxico peninsular." En *Etimología e historia en el léxico del español*, coordinado por Mariano Quirós García, José Ramón Carriazo Ruiz, Emma Falque Rey y Marta Sánchez Orense, 303–318. Madrid: Iberoamericana/Vervuert.

Giménez-Eguibar, Patricia. 2016b. "Attitudes towards lexical Arabisms in sixteenth century Spanish texts." En *Spanish Language and Sociolinguistics Analysis*, editado por Sandro Sessarego y Fernando Tejero-Herrao, 8: 363–380. Ámsterdam/Philadelphia: John Benjamins.

González Jiménez, Manuel. 2000. "La guerra final de Granada." En *Historia del reino de Granada*, coordinado por Manuel Barrios Aguilera, vol. 1, 453–476. Granada: Universidad de Granada.

González Sopeña, Inmaculada. 2019. *Los arabismos en el reino de Granada a través de la documentación archivística (finales del siglo XV–siglo XVII).* Granada: Universidad de Granada.

Guadix, Diego de. *Recopilación de algunos nombres arábigos.* 1593. Edición y estudio de Felipe Maíllo Salgado y Elena Bajo Pérez. Gijón: TREA, 2005.

Lapesa, Rafael. 2008. *Historia de la lengua española.* Edición revisada. Madrid: Gredos.

Lörinczi, Marinella. 1969. "Consideraciones semánticas acerca de las palabras españolas de origen árabe." *Revue Roumaine de Linguistique*, 14: 65–75.

Morala Rodríguez, José Ramón. 2012. "Arabismos en textos del siglo XVII escasamente documentados." *Revista de Investigación Lingüística*, 15: 77–102.

Müller, Bodo. 1987. *Diccionario del español medieval.* Heidelberg: Winter.

NTLLE = Real Academia Española and Asociación de Academias de la Lengua Española. 2001. *Nuevo Tesoro Lexicográfico de la Lengua Española.* Fecha de consulta agosto 2020. https://www.rae.es/recursos/diccionarios/diccionarios-anteriores-1726-1992/nuevo-tesoro-lexicografico.

Pardo Asso, José. 1938. *Nuevo diccionario etimológico aragonés.* Zaragoza: Imprenta del Hogar Pignatelli.

Segura del Pino, María Dolores. 2000. *Agua, tierra y sociedad en el Río de Almería: de la época islámica a la cristiana (siglos XV y XVI).* Almería: Instituto de Estudios Almerienses.

Steiger, Arnold. 1967. "Arabismos." En *Enciclopedia Lingüística Hispánica*, vol. 2, 93–126. Madrid: CSIC.

TLHA = Alvar Ezquerra, Manuel. 2000. *Tesoro léxico de las hablas andaluzas.* Madrid: Arco/Libros.

Walsh, John. 1967. *The Loss of Arabisms in the Spanish Lexicon.* PhD diss., University of Virginia.

Chapter 10

Cultured borrowing of verbs: the case of the Spanish -*ir* conjugation

Christopher J. Pountain

Queen Mary University of London

Summary

The historical morphology of the highly defective -*ir* class of verbs in Modern Spanish has to date been studied primarily from the point of view of the inherited verbs which belong to it. However, the class was significantly extended by the cultured borrowing of a large number of other verbs, many, but not all, of which, as prefixal forms of inherited stems, were partially modelled on existing verbs. Not only did these cultured borrowings reinforce an anomalous morphological set which was showing signs of losing the productivity it had once displayed, but they created new anomalies. This study shows the importance of paying attention to the impact of cultured borrowings not only on the lexicon of the Romance languages, but also on their structural features.

Resumen

El estudio de la morfología histórica de los verbos españoles en -*ir*, conjugación sumamente defectuosa, se suele enfocar en los verbos patrimoniales que la constituyen. Pero esta clase se amplió por la incorporación de gran número de cultismos, muchos de los cuales, si bien no todos, siguieron el modelo de los verbos existentes. Estos cultismos no solo respaldaron una clase morfológica anómala que mostraba síntomas de perder la productividad que había tenido, sino que también crearon nuevas anomalías. Este estudio demuestra la importancia de prestar atención al impacto que han tenido los cultismos no solo en el léxico de las lenguas románicas sino también en sus características estructurales.

Keywords

Spanish morphology, Lexical borrowing, Latin.

1 The historical morphology of -*ir* verbs

The -*ir* class of verbs in Modern Spanish is a highly defective conjugation morphologically. A significant problem for historical morphology has been the creation of three radical-changing patterns, which are illustrated in Figure 10.1. The /e/ of stressed stems may diphthongise to /ie/, as in radical-changing verbs deriving from the short/open /ɛ/ of Latin in the -*ar* and -*er* conjugations (type *sentir*, E~IE~I), or it may raise to /i/ (type *pedir*, E~I), the latter being a phenomenon which occurs in neither of the other conjugations. The /e/ also raises to /i/ atonically in forms which have an inflection beginning with a yod (/j/) (*pidió*). There is also a small hybrid category of verbs (all cultured borrowings)[1] of the type *adquirir*, I~IE~I, which appear to diphthongise like *sentir* in the first person present stem despite having /i/ atonically throughout. There have been many attempts to reconcile and explain the processes of diphthongisation, metaphony and analogy which have fashioned this situation, based, naturally enough, on inherited vocabulary (e.g. Malkiel 1966, López Bobo 1998, Montgomery 1985, Penny 2002), but that is not my primary purpose here.

---

[1] I use the term "cultured borrowing" to denote words of Latin (or Greek, via Latin) origin which do not appear to be directly inherited from Latin but to be borrowed in much the same way as other adstrate loanwords. Although these words were at first undoubtedly characteristic of educated discourse (reflected in such designations as Eng. *learnèd*, Fr. *savant* and the Spanish term *cultismo*, some have now diffused to such an extent that they are among the commonest words in the modern Romance languages and are not restricted to, or even characteristic of, formal registers: this is why I have rejected terms such as *cultismo* and the traditional contrast between *learnèd* and *popular*, which may carry such implications (see also Clavería Nadal, this volume). Cultured borrowings are identifiable according to three principal criteria (which may not all be present in the case of any one word): (a) failure to undergo the expected sound changes, with minimal phonetic adaptation to the host language, (b) a relatively late date of first attestation in the textual record, typically in the works of authors who are known to have favoured the introduction of such borrowings, (c) preservation of a Classical Latin meaning, which is often, especially at first, abstract or specialised in nature.

	E~IE~I	E~I	I~IE~I
atonic	sentir	pedir	adquirir
tonic	siento	pido	adquiero
atonic before inflection in /j/	sintió	pidió	adquirió

Figure 10.1. Radical change in the Spanish -*ir* conjugation

Despite this complexity, or more likely, I will be arguing, as a contributory factor towards it, the -*ir* conjugation was at one time very productive, and in particular the default home for many inherited verbs of the Latin rhizotonic 3rd conjugation in -*ĕre* (like *pedir* < *pĕtĕre*), a conjugation-type which is today completely absent in both Spanish and Portuguese. A number of reasons for this have been proposed. Menéndez Pidal (1962: 285) hypothesises that the presence of a yod (/j/) in the 1st person singular of the present (e.g. *fŭgĭo* (*fŭgĕre*)) encouraged analogy with the -*ĭo* that was a regular feature of the same form in -*īre* verbs (e.g. *sentĭo* (*sentīre*)). Another seems to have been the strong association of verbs of the -*er* conjugation with stative lexical aspect, which even resulted in the migration of dynamic aspect verbs of the Latin -*ēre* conjugation to the Castilian -*ir* category, e.g. Lat. *complēre* > Sp. *cumplir*; the -*ir* conjugation hence received dynamic aspect verbs from the rhizotonic conjugation in -*ĕre*, e.g. Lat. *parĕre, spargĕre* > Sp. *parir, esparcir*. The -*ir* conjugation also seems to have been particularly receptive to verbs with a high stem vowel, e.g. Lat. *dīcĕre, scrībĕre* > Cast. *decir, escribir* (Penny 2002, 1055). Yet apart from the influx of inherited verbs from these various sources, the conjugation becomes unproductive: Menéndez Pidal (1962, 286) describes it as "enteramente estéril para la producción de nuevos verbos", which henceforward would be assimilated into the majority -*ar* conjugation. (In French, by contrast, a large number of borrowed rhizotonic verbs are assimilated into the first, or -*er*, conjugation, e.g. Lat. *discŭtĕre* > Sp. *discutir*, Fr. *discuter*.)

The exceptions are, of course, cultured borrowings, many of which are etymologically or analogically related to existing -*ir* verbs and so join the conjugation on that account, and as a result have generally been overlooked.

While many of these verbs are essentially regular apart from the orthographical adjustments required by Spanish spelling conventions (for example *coincidir, concluir, concurrir, discutir, existir, prohibir, restringir*), others belong to the radical-changing types identified above (thus *transferir* is an E~IE~I type and *repetir* an E~I type). All except those in *-venir* have regular future stems modelled on the infinitive, and this extends to verbs which have etymologically related but non-identical inherited forms: thus while *querer* has the irregular future stem *querr-*, the cultured borrowings in *-quirir* and *-querir* have *-quirir-* and *-querir-* (*adquirirá, requerirá*).

The formation of past participles also shows a high degree of analogical regularity. In present-day Spanish, all culturally borrowed *-ir* verbs have regular past participles in *-ido* with the exception of those in *-scribir*, which have followed the inherited verb *escribir* to form their past participles in *-scrito* (Lat. *-scriptu(m)*). Many, if not the majority, however, had irregular past participle / supine forms in Latin, e.g. Sp. *permitido* but Lat. *permissu(m)*, Sp. *dividido* but Lat. *dīvīsu(m)*. Some Latin irregular forms have yielded adjectival cultured borrowings in their own right: Lat. *exactu(m) (exĭgĕre)* > Sp. *exacto*, Lat. *distinctu(m) (distinguĕre* > Sp. *distinto*. The question arises as to how far the cultured borrowings from such irregular forms acted as past participles in Spanish: for all the cases I have examined, while the irregular forms can act as adjectives and form part of apparent verbal paraphrases, especially with *ser*, *estar* and *quedar*, they never combine with the auxiliaries *haber* or *tener* to form perfects. The examples in (1a–e) show the pattern for *electo* and *elegido*: although *elegido* is also able to participate in passive paraphrases, it is the unique possibility with the *haber* auxiliary (e):

(1)
- a. los que han de seer **electos** pora obispos. & ordenados pora clerigos (*CORDE*: Alfonso X, *Primera Partida*. British Library Ms. Add. 20787, 1256-1263).
- b. ¿Cómo y no consideráis que está **electo** gobernador? (*CORDE*: Miguel de Cervantes Saavedra, *Segunda parte del ingenioso caballero don Quijote de la Mancha*, 1615).
- c. con lo que quedó **electo** por contralto de esta Sta. Iglesia el referido Andrés Cerrato (*CORDE*: Anon., *Documentos sobre música en la catedral de Sigüenza*, 1600–1713).
- d. e tantos muyt **electos** varones et florescientes causlleros perdio Roma la hora por aquesta guerra ciudadana (*CORDE*: Juan Fernández de Heredia, *Traducción de la Historia contra paganos, de Orosio. Valencia, Pontificia (Patriarca), olim Corpus C ...*, 1376–1396).
- e. Este Rey don alfonsso fue **electo** en discordia por enperador de alemaña & por que los mas delos electores le aujan **elegido** & tenjan la boz del

ynperio por el partio para ella a Resçibir el ymperio enla qual yda fizo grandissimas espenssas & a la fin fallose ende burlado. (*CORDE*: Pablo de Santa María, *Suma de las coronicas de España*, 1454).[2]

2 The presence of cultured borrowings in the *-ir* conjugation

The scale of the overall impact of such cultured borrowings can be appreciated by the statistics derivable from the frequency list of Davies and Davies (2017), who list 164 verbs in *-ir* among the 5,000 most frequent words in modern Spanish. Of these 164, 67 can be considered inherited words while the other 97, the overwhelming majority, for one reason or another, are likely cultured borrowings from Latin, whether directly or via other Western European languages.

While there is obviously not space to justify the cultured status of each of these 67 individually, some general indications of the problems in categorising these words as cultured borrowings is clearly in order.

2.1 Verbs which have stems identical to existing inherited words

A particular problem is the status of verbs which have stems which are identical to existing inherited words and where there are no phonetic changes distinguishing the inherited developments from their adoption as cultured borrowings in compounds. I think here of the compounds of *escribir*, *partir*, *regir*, *sentir*, *sumir*, *venir* and *vivir*. For example, of the compounds of *partir*, only *impartir*, though not described as such by Corominas and Pascual (1980–1991, IV, 414), is likely to have been a cultured borrowing: they characterise it as a "término forense" (but it is absent from *CODEA+*), and it makes its first appearance in *CORDE* in what may be regarded as a more general context, indicating its wider diffusion, in the sixteenth century:

(2)

Y porque Sant Pedro aún estaba dudoso si a los muy idólatras y muy pecadores se había igualmente de **impartir** e comunicar la doctrina christiana (*CORDE*: Fray Bartolomé de las Casas, *Apologética historia sumaria*, 1527–1550).

---

[2] I follow the dating given by CORDEMÁFORO (Rodríguez Molina and Octavio de Toledo y Huerta 2017).

2.2 Doublet developments

In just one or two cases, there is evidence of a doublet development of a Latin source, which increases my confidence in the cultured nature of the form which is formally closest to Latin. Thus the cultured borrowing *elegir* and the inherited form *esleír~esleer* from Lat. *elīgĕre*, with the same or very similar meaning, are both found in the thirteenth century (3a–b), after which *elegir*, to be taken as the cultured borrowing, gains the ascendant (Figure 10.2):

(3)
    a. Mandamos que en Leon é en nas oltras cibdades que ayan juizes **elegidos** que rrevilguen los plitos de todo el poblo (*CORDE*: Anon., *Concilio de León*, c 1250).
    b. E antes [que] sepa el mancebo aborrecer el mal e **esleer** el bien, sera la tierra dexada (*CORDE*: Almerich, *La fazienda de Ultra Mar*, c 1200).

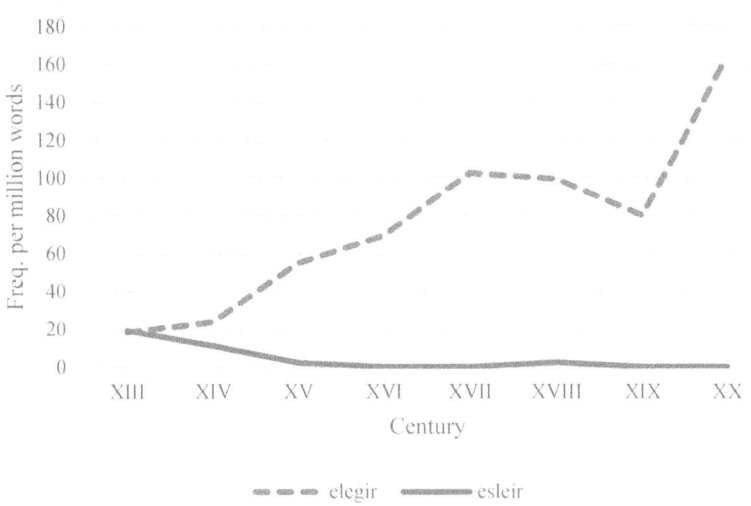

Figure 10.2. Competition between *elegir* and *esleír* in Spanish (*CDE*)[3]

2.3 Secondary evidence

The Romance textual record may also occasionally offer valuable secondary evidence[4] of cultured borrowing status. The history of *presidir* and its related

---

[3] Based on a moderated search of all anticipated inflected forms and variant spellings.

forms is particularly problematic, since *praesidens*, the present participle of *praesidēre* and the origin of Sp. *presidente*, is amply attested in documents which were still being written in the Latin way (4a), and must have been familiar to at least the cultured élite. But in this case there is secondary evidence that, however familiar *presidens* may have been, it was not recognised as part of the vernacular, as can be clearly seen in (4b), from the Alfonsine corpus. Similarly, when Juan Fernández de Heredia uses *president(e)* (4c), he glosses it, again as *adelant(r)ado*. And it is the same author who in fact provides the first attestation of the verb *presidir* (4d)

(4)
    a.   Actum est hoc era MXX septima, **presidente** in Sancto Iohanne Transmiro abbate, et in Aragone Oriolo episcopo (*CORDE*: Anon., *Privilegio de confirmación [Documentos correspondientes al reinado de Sancho Ramírez]*, 1090).
    b.   Et por que estos que ellos ordenauan de poner ally avrian de andar en los fechos delante los otros omnes de las tierras llamaron los en su latin ***presides*** & *perfectos* que dizen en el lenguaje de castilla tanto commo adelantados commo fueron en espanna afraneo & petreo & labieno & acçio varo & otros (*CORDE*: Alfonso X, *General Estoria. Quinta parte*, a 1284) (my italics).
    c.   Pilato, adelantrado o **president**, el qual auia pronunciado la sentencia de la condapnacion contra Ihesu Xristo (*CORDE*: Juan Fernández de Heredia, *Traducción de la Historia contra paganos, de Orosio. Valencia, Pontificia (Patriarca), olim Corpus C ...,* 1376–1396).
    d.   & apres el rey autari fizo paç por .iij. anyos con esmaragdo patriçio. qui la ora **presidie** en rauena (*CORDE*: Juan Fernández de Heredia, *Gran crónica de España, I. Ms. 10133 BNM*, 1385).

2.4 Chronological gaps in attestation

Another methodological problem in the classification of words as cultured borrowings is the chronology of their attestation. There may be a considerable gap between the first attestation of a word and its subsequent appearances. *Intuir*

---

[4] In the sense of Bloomfield (1944). On the nature of secondary evidence derivable from corpora, see Pountain and García Ortiz (2019).

is attested once in the fifteenth century in Villena (5a) and once in the sixteenth century in *CDE* (5b), but subsequent attestations are not until 1900 (5c):

(5)
a. Aquí la profética dotrina mostró cuándo mejor podrié reposadamente **intuir** las maravillas del soberano Bien (*CORDE*: Enrique de Villena, *Exposición del Salmo "Quoniam videbo"*, 1424).
b. No puede, aunque sea en su persona un santo, dejar de **intuir** en ellos malos humores, tomándose todos licencia de perpetrar los vicios que o ella hace o de ellas se creen y publican (*CDE*: Tomás de Mercado, *Summa de tratos y contratos*, 1545).
c. Prefiero la pampa sentida e **intuida** por quien nació en ella a vistosas montañas de oro, no más que con artificio construidas (*CORDE*: Miguel de Unamuno, *15: a Francisco Soto y Calvo [Epistolario inédito]*, 1900).

While this confirms the cultured status of *intuir* in Villena and Mercado, where it must be seen as an ephemeral borrowing which did not at the time further diffuse, in its later manifestation it seems more likely to have been a back-formation from *intuición* (Corominas and Pascual 1980–1991, III, 460–1) than a cultured borrowing as such. *Intuición*, together with *intuitivo*, was only very sporadically attested in the seventeenth and eighteenth centuries, but became firmly embedded in the nineteenth century, while *intuir* embeds only much more recently: Figure 10.3 shows the relative chronology of the three words.

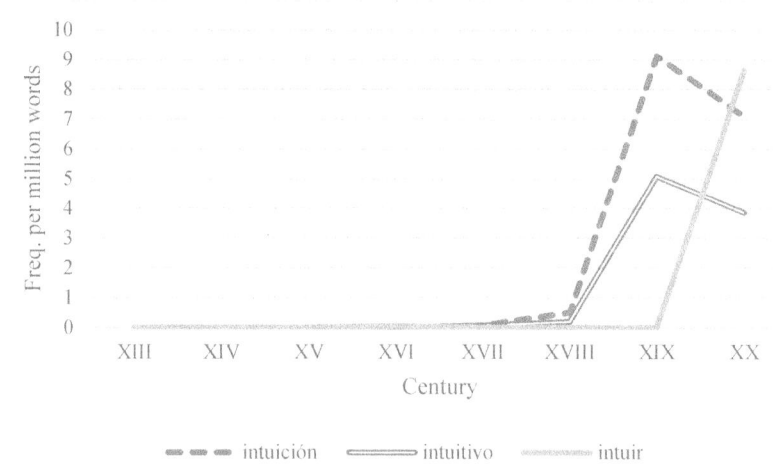

Figure 10.3. *Intuir, intuición, intuitivo* in *CDE*

2.5 Verbs which are formally similar do not necessarily appear at the same time

Of crucial relevance to my assessment of the impact of borrowed *-ir* verbs is the observation that verbs which are formally similar do not necessarily appear at the same time. The family of verbs in *-vertir* is instructive in this regard. The first attestation of *convertir*, today the commonest of these, in a clearly Romance form (6) is early enough to cast doubt on it being a cultured borrowing at all:

(6)
    A .vii. migeros de Capharnaum, contra meridie, es Cesarea Palestina, e alli **convertio** sant Peydro a Cornelius Centurio e lo babtizo (*CORDE*: Almerich, *La fazienda de Ultra Mar*, c 1200).

Moreover, Lat. *convertĕre* must have been very familiar from a religious context. In addition to the meaning of 'convert (to a religion)' it has the more general meaning, also strongly associated with religion, of 'turning (to or away from)'. *Advertir* and *divertir*, however, are more clearly cultured borrowings, appearing for the first time in the fifteenth century in Villena (7a–b)

(7)
    a. Viniendo a la segunda parte, buelve las palabras a los familiares del padre e suyos, diziéndoles paren bien mientes a lo que dezir les quiere, rindiéndoles dóçiles, porque eran muchos e de diversos juizios e convenía **advertir** de un acuerdo a lo que les dixesen más que si a tina persona fuese fablado (*CORDE*: Enrique de Villena, *Traducción y glosas de la Eneida. Libros I–III*, 1442).

    b. En esto significa cuántos embolvimientos la prosperidat busca para fazer perder el tiempo a los prosperados en banas cosas, porque non puedan **divertir** su entendimiento a lo complidero a su spiritual salud, diuturnando la ignorançia en aquéllos (*CORDE*: Enrique de Villena, *Traducción y glosas de la Eneida. Libros I–III*, 1442).[5]

---

[5] I again follow the dating given by CORDEMÁFORO (Rodríguez Molina and Octavio de Toledo y Huerta 2017).

Invertir seems to be a relatively late addition to the *-vertir* group, and, as can be seen from Figure 10.4, shows a less steep upward profile which only begins in the eighteenth century.

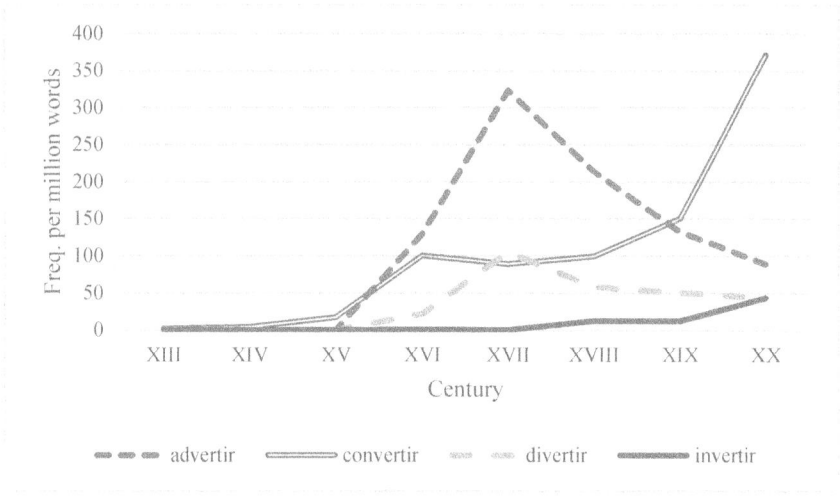

Figure 10.4. *-vertir* verbs in *CDE*

The first convincing example in *CORDE* (8a) is from the mid-sixteenth century in the meaning of 'to invest'. In the seventeenth century, the meaning of 'to reverse', now arguably its primary meaning, becomes common (8b).

(8)
    a. suplicamos a V. M. sea servido de mandar que la dicha bula de redenpcion de cautivos se predique y publique y que haya la cuenta que es razon y se requiere en la limosna que della se uviere para que no se **invierta** ni gaste ni pueda gastar en otra cosa aunque sea muy piadosa (*CORDE*: Anon., *Cortes de Toledo de 1559 que comenzaron el 11 de diciembre de 1559 y concluyeron el 19 de noviembre ...*, 1559–1560).

    b. todo cuanto yo hice se **invirtió** y que hoy está la cosa en el estado primero (*CORDE*: Anon., Carta del Licenciado Hernando de Ribera dando cuenta a su Majestad del estado del negocio, sobre la ..., 1616).

The process of addition to a set of formally related verbs can therefore be gradual; expansion of such sets nevertheless clearly reinforces conjugational patterns.

3 Patterns of assimilation

3.1 Assimilation to inherited verbs

All the compounds of *escribir, partir, regir, sentir, sumir, venir* and *vivir* are totally assimilated into the inflectional paradigm of the corresponding inherited verb. Thus, for example, *provenir* follows the E~IE~I pattern of *venir* (*provenir, proviene, provino*), as well as its irregular first person singular present stem (*provengo*) and its irregular future stem (*provendré*). Here, then, cultured borrowings simply significantly increase the class-membership of irregular verbs (in this and subsequent lists, the number in square brackets is the frequency ranking of the verb according to Davies and Davies 2017):

- Based on *escribir*: *describir* [1272], *inscribir* [3553], *suscribir* [3944] (also *adscribir, circunscribir, prescribir, proscribir, rescribir, transcribir*)
- Based on *partir*: *impartir* [3924]
- Based on *regir*: *dirigir* [390]
- Based on *sentir*: *asentir* [4711], *presentir* [4210]
- Based on *sumir*: *asumir* [1208], *consumir* [1820], *presumir* [4255], *resumir* [3028]
- Based on *venir*: *intervenir* [1552], *prevenir* [3080], *provenir* [2383] (also *a(d)venir, desavenir, circunvenir, contravenir, devenir, evenir, revenir, sobrevenir, subvenir*)
- Based on *vivir*: *convivir* [3789], *revivir* [4520], *sobrevivir* [1908]

3.2 Assimilation on the basis of formal parallelism

There are also cases of assimilation on the basis of formal parallelism.

3.2.1 *adherir*

The Latin etymon of *adherir* (*adhaerēre*) belonged to the Latin second, *-ēre*, conjugation. It is one of only a very few such verbs to be borrowed into the *-ir* class (others are the verbs in *-hibir*: *exhibir* < Lat. *exhĭbēre* and *prohibir* < Lat. *prŏhĭbēre*), which may be a testimony to the gravitational pull of the *-ir* class in medieval Castilian. *Adherir* is extremely infrequent until the eighteenth century (Figure 10.5), although it is attested in *CORDE* as early as fifteenth century (9a).

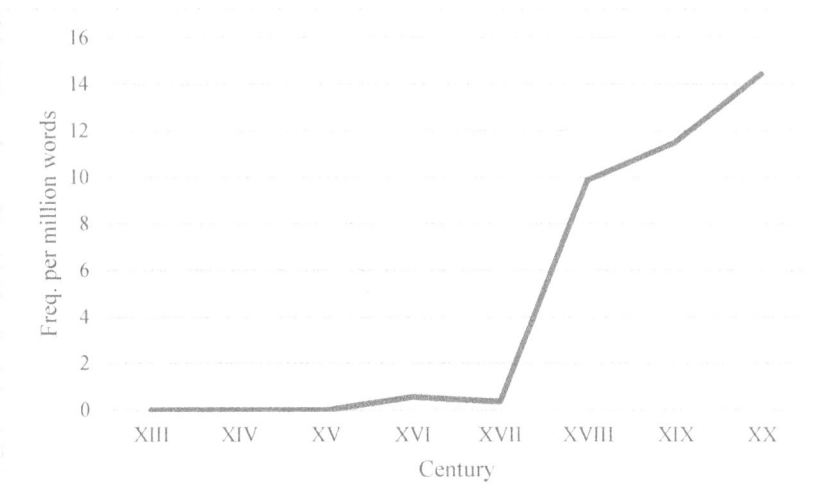

Figure 10.5. *adherir* in *CDE*

It seems that *adherir* is subject to morphological variation initially. When Cartagena uses it, as in (9a), it can be seen that the tonic /e/ apparently undergoes no radical change to /ie/, though when the present stem is next met, which is not until the seventeenth century, it does display the diphthong (9b). While the preterite stem in finite forms always shows a change to /i/, the generally earlier attested gerund sometimes retains /e/ (9c):

(9)
    a. La terçera manera de pensar es quando **adhere** omne a la una parte por razones que le paresçen ser sufiçientes (*CORDE*: Alfonso de Cartagena, *El Oracional*, a 1456).
    b. y asi ese se **adhiere** á la Iglesia, donde vienen á morir (*CORDE*: Juan de Solórzano y Pereira, *Política indiana*, 1648).
    c. De manera que no sólo no se ha de procurar división entre los compañeros de un cargo; pero aun quando el favor del pueblo la introduxere, **adheriendo** parte a uno, y parte a otro, como suele acontecer, y sin culpa suya han de cuydar de no parecer autores, ni cabeças de la parcialidad, tratándose más familiarmente, y con mayores demostraciones de amistad para ahogar con ellas la llama, antes que el ayre popular la levante en alto (*CORDE*: Fray Juan Márquez, *El gobernador cristiano*, 1612 – a 1625).

Adherir has ultimately followed the E~IE~I radical-changing pattern of *herir* (*hiero, hirió*), though etymologically there is no lexical relationship between these two verbs (*herir* 'to wound' is an inherited development of Lat. *ferīre* 'to strike (to kill)'). It is therefore likely that this pattern only becomes established at a relatively late date.[6]

Similar observations might be made about *impedir* (Lat. *impĕdīre*), which from the first seems to follow inherited *pedir* (< Lat. *pĕtĕre*) with an E~I radical-changing pattern.

3.3 The creation of new derivational types

Yet new derivational types are also created.

3.3.1 The *-quirir* class of verbs

Verbs of the *-quirir* class are especially interesting in that, as already noted, they form a distinctive radical-changing class I~IE~I. The reason usually adduced for this (cf. Butt and Benjamin 2011, 175) is that the older form of the infinitive was *-querir*, and indeed *requerir*, the first of these verbs to be attested, has preserved the /e/ into the modern language, so making *requerir* part of the E~IE~I radical-changing class. However, there is evidence of variation (10a–b), as also for *adquirir* and *inquirir* (10c–d).

(10)
    a. E dizen que Alixandre solia **requerir** el su regno él por sí mesmo, por que non querie creer el mal fecho que le dizíen de algunos, de aquí fasta que él lo viese por sí (*CORDE*: Anon., *Bocados de oro*, a 1250).
    b. Senyor dixo el / yo so uenido aqui de part de mi hermano & mia. & semblantment de part delos pueblos lusitanos & Jllurgitanos por **requirir** & demandar la uuestra misericordia & merçet por razon dela falta que nos hauemos fecho contra uos (*CORDE*: Juan Fernández de Heredia, *Gran crónica de España*, I. Ms. 10133 BNM, 1385).
    c. los coraçones delos prínçipes non son que religados & **adqueridos** / por oro. del qual **adquirir** & ganar / aquella gent es muyt glota &

---

[6] *Adherir* shows no radical change in the *-nte* form *adherente*, however (contrast *hiriente* from *herir*).

cobdiçiosa (*CORDE*: Juan Fernández de Heredia, *Gran crónica de España*, I. Ms. 10133 BNM, 1385).

d. Segundamente, le aconseja non quiera más preguntar de lo que le fuere mandado, ne **inquerir** por cuál razón, por cuanto la perfecçión de la religión está en obedesçer sin contienda e cumplir lo mandado, non preguntando por qué ne **inquiriendo** en su voluntad (*CORDE*: Enrique de Villena, *Traducción y glosas de la Eneida. Libros I–III*, 1442).[7]

In the case of *adquirir* and *inquirir*, it is unlikely that the /e/ was an input to diphthongisation; it should also be noted that the Latin verbs were formed in -*quīrĕre* (in this case, the Latin derivative is distinct from the simple verb, *quaerĕre*, which as the inherited verb *querer* did show the expected diphthongisation of /ae/ to /ie/ in *quiero*, etc.). Analogy of *adquirir* and *inquirir* with *requerir* is a possible scenario, assuming a greater similarity when these verbs also could end in -*querir*; but latterly a different subclass has been created as a result of different resolutions of the Preterite endings (*adquirí, adquirió* but *requerí, requirió*).

Here, then, cultured borrowing effectively introduces further complication into the -*ir* conjugation class with *adquirir* (and *inquirir*) having created a further subclass.

3.3.2 -*vertir*

In fact, there is evidence of ongoing variation within the -*ir* class in which the impact of a cultured borrowing is also of relevance. Verbs in -*vertir* do not follow the model of the inherited simple verb *verter* but are assimilated to the E~IE~I radical-changing pattern of the -*ir* conjugation. However, there is variation both in some -*vertir* verbs and, perhaps rather more surprisingly, in *verter* itself, which suggests the closely felt morphological and semantic relatedness of all these verbs. *Verter*, while radical-changing to /ie/ under stress (e.g. first person singular present *vierto*), maintains /e/, as is characteristic of the -*er* conjugation, in the third person singular and plural of the preterite (*vertió, vertieron*) and the gerund (*vertiendo*). But there is some evidence of a tendency to follow the -*vertir* pattern and change /e/ to /i/ in

---

[7] I again follow the dating given by CORDEMÁFORO (Rodríguez Molina and Octavio de Toledo y Huerta 2017).

these forms (so *virtió, virtieron, virtiendo*, as also a corresponding infinitive *vertir*).[8] Maintenance of the /e/ is the majority situation: *CORPES XXI* records 518 instances of forms in /e/ as against only 11 of forms in /i/. *Verter* also has a relatively uncommon derivational form *reverter*, with which *revertir* forms a doublet development with a different meaning: *reverter* is defined by *DLE* as "rebosar o salir de sus términos o límites", while *revertir* is "volver al estado o condición que tuvo antes". None the less, there is an observable tendency for *revertir* to follow *(re)verter* in the preterite (11):

(11)
> En los medios de comunicación es frecuente encontrar este verbo conjugado de manera regular en las formas que cambian la "e" de la raíz por una "i": "El incremento se **revertió** en parte en el 2015", "El fallo **revertió** la decisión adoptada el pasado viernes por tres jueces" o "Tres goles en tres balones colgados **revertieron** el marcador" (https://www.lavanguardia.com/vida/201 80509/443450227197/fundeu-bbva-de-revertir-revirtio-no-revertio.html, accessed 12 August 2019).

(It is pointed out that these verb forms should be *revirtió* and *revirtieron*.) This may be the result of *revertir* having extended its meaning to that of "to reverse", which is the case of all the examples given in (11). (Such extension of meaning is a characteristic of what in Pountain (2018) I have called *cultismos de éxito* or successfully embedded cultured borrowings.)

In this case, therefore, cultured borrowing has created structural variation and instability.

4 Conclusions

The cultured borrowing of verbs in *-ir* has obviously had a lexical impact on Spanish which I have not investigated here; in this respect, their borrowing has clearly been propitiated by the existence of established models (however, although I have been paying attention here to borrowings which are a transparent combination of prefix and stem, several borrowed *-ir* verbs actually include verbs which, while they appear to be prefixal forms, lack a

---

[8] This infinitive form, which is puristically censured (*DPD*, http://lema.rae.es/dpd/?key=verter), yields forms such as first person plural present *vertimos* instead of standard *vertemos*.

lexicalised Spanish stem).⁹ What has in effect happened is that the available vocabulary of Spanish has come more and more to replicate that of Latin. What I hope to have demonstrated is that cultured borrowings played a significant part in strengthening a conjugation type which had become unproductive and which was in many respects morphologically anomalous; in fact, they reinforced the anomalies and even created new ones. The historical morphology of this class of verbs has been primarily considered to date on the basis of inherited words, but I would maintain that the impact of cultured borrowings cannot be neglected, since, as already seen, it has created tensions which are still being worked out in the ongoing dynamics of the language. All of this goes to show that, so far from cultured borrowings being marginal to the history of Spanish, they are a most important characteristic of its *Ausbau* development (Kloss 1967) and its present-day structure, and that their impact can go far beyond the purely lexical.

References

Corpora

CDE = Davies, Mark. 2002–. *Corpus del Español: 100 million words, 1200s–1900s*. Accessed 19 September 2019. http://www.corpusdelespanol.org.

CODEA+ = Sánchez-Prieto Borja, Pedro (coord.). n.d. *Corpus de Documentos Españoles Anteriores a 1700*. Accessed 20 September 2019. http://demos.bitext.com/codea.

CORDE = Real Academia Española. n.d. *Banco de datos (CORDE). Corpus diacrónico del español*. Accessed 20 September 2019. http://www.rae.es.

CORPES XXI = Real Academia Española. n.d. *Banco de datos (CORPES XXI). Corpus del español del siglo XXI*. Accessed 20 September 2019. https://www.rae.es/recursos/banco-de-datos/corpes-xxi.

---

⁹ *Invadir* [2053], *impedir* [1030], *aplaudir* [3407], *decidir* [368], *definir* [1052], *diluir* [4570], *disminuir* [1745], *dividir* [1385], *elegir* [561], *exigir* [854] and *restringir* [4290]: there are no forms *vadir*, *plaudir*, *cidir*, *finir*, *luir*, *minuir* or *vidir*. This is sometimes also the case of verbs which appear to form an extensive morphological group (*aludir* [3627]: cf. *coludir*, *deludir*, *eludir*, *iludir*; *discutir* [1310], *percutir*, *repercutir*): there are no verbs *ludir* or *cutir*.

Bibliographical references

Bloomfield, Leonard. 1944. "Secondary and Tertiary Responses to Language." *Language* 20: 45–55.

Butt, John, and Carmen Benjamin. 2011. *A New Reference Grammar of Modern Spanish*, 5th ed. London / New York: Routledge.

Corominas, Joan, and José Antonio Pascual. 1980–1991. *Diccionario crítico etimológico castellano e hispánico,* 6 vols. Madrid: Gredos.

Davies, Mark, and Kathy Hayward Davies. 2017. *A Frequency Dictionary of Spanish. Core Vocabulary for Learners*, 2nd ed. London: Routledge.

DLE = Asociación de Academias de la Lengua Española. 2014–. *Diccionario de la lengua española*, 23rd ed. Madrid: Espasa. Accessed 20 September 2019. http://www.rae.es/obras-academicas/diccionarios/diccionario-de-la-lengua-espanola.

DPD = Real Academia Española. 2005. *Diccionario panhispánico de dudas.* Madrid: Real Academia Española / Asociación de Academias de Lengua Española. Accessed 20 September 2019. https://www.rae.es/recursos/diccionarios/dpd.

Kloss, Heinz. 1967. "*Abstand*-Languages and *Ausbau*-Languages." *Anthropological Linguistics* 9: 29–41.

López Bobo, María Jesús. 1998. *El vocalismo átono en la conjugación castellana: etapa medieval y clásica.* Oviedo: Departamento de Filología Española.

Malkiel, Yakov. 1966. "Diphthongization, Monophthongization, Metaphony: Studies in Their Interaction in the Paradigm of the Old Spanish -IR Verbs." *Language* 42 (2): 430–472.

Menéndez Pidal, Ramón. 1940. *Manual de gramática histórica española*, 6th ed. Madrid: Espasa-Calpe.

Montgomery, Thomas. 1985. "Sources of Vocalic Correspondences of Stems and Endings in the Spanish Verb." *Hispanic Linguistics* 2: 99–114.

Penny, Ralph. 2002. "Procesos de clasificación verbal española: polaridad de vocales radicales en los verbos en *-er* e *-ir*." In *Pulchre, bene, recte. Estudios en homenaje al Prof. Fernando González Ollé*, edited by Saralegui Platero and Casado Velarde, 1053–70. Pamplona: EUNSA / Gobierno de Navarra, Depto de Educación y Cultura.

Pountain, Christopher J. In press. "Los cultismos de cada día." In *Actas del XI Congreso Internacional de Historia de la Lengua Española, Lima, 6–10 de agosto de 2018.*

Pountain, Christopher J., and Isabel García Ortiz. 2019. "La investigación de las voces cultas a través de los corpus históricos." *Revista de Historia de la Lengua Española* 14: 47–76.

Rodríguez Molina, Javier, and Octavio de Toledo y Huerta, Álvar. 2017. "La imprescindible distinción entre texto y testimonio: el *CORDE* y los criterios de fiabilidad lingüística." *Scriptum Digital* 6: 5–68.

Chapter 11

The Impact of New Contacts on an Old Pattern: the Modifier–Modified Order in the Formation of Italian Compounds

Alessandro Carlucci

University of Bergen

Summary

In Italian endocentric noun + noun compounds such as *capostazione* 'station master', the modified element precedes its modifier. Traditionally, the opposite order of modification was only found in a few remnants (e.g. *terremoto* 'earthquake', from Latin *terrae mōtus*), in learnèd formations (often part of relatively homogenous international terminologies, e.g. *gasdinamica* 'gas dynamics') and in compounds formed under the influence of foreign models (*ferrovia* 'railway'). But in recent years many scholars have claimed that the modifier–modified order (also referred to as "right-headed compounding") is expanding beyond its traditional limits, and some have specifically attributed this expansion to English influences (the normal compounding pattern in English is with the modified element following its modifier). By exploring the history of a particularly important type of Italian compounds displaying the modifier–modified order, this Chapter addresses some of the problems involved in defining and verifying the actual expansion of this order of modification, and it clarifies the role to be assigned to contact with English.

Resumen

En italiano, en los sustantivos compuestos N + N como *capostazione* 'jefe de estación', el elemento modificado precede a su modificador. Tradicionalmente, se encontraba el orden contrario tan solo en algunos restos (p.ej. *terremoto* del lat. *terrae mōtus*), en formaciones cultas (en muchos casos términos internacionales, p.ej. *gasdinamica* 'dinámica de gases') y en sustantivos compuestos acuñados bajo la influencia de modelos extranjeros (*ferrovia* 'ferrocarril'). Pero en años recientes muchos estudiosos han sostenido que el orden modificador–modificado (también denominado "right-headed compounding") ha rebasado sus límites tradicionales, y esta expansión ha sido atribuida a la influencia del inglés (siendo normal en inglés que el elemento modificado sigue a su modificador). Mediante la exploración de un tipo de sustantivo compuesto italiano muy importante que muestra el orden modificador–modificado, este capítulo trata algunos problemas que plantean la definición y comprobación de la expansión de este orden, y aclara el papel que desempeña el contacto con el inglés en esta tendencia.

Keywords

Italian morphology, Lexical borrowing, Lexical compounds, English, Latin.

1 Preliminaries

Since the establishment of historical linguistics in the nineteenth century, the development of this discipline has periodically been affected by influential proposals warning against an excessive emphasis on major written languages and calling for special attention to spoken varieties – especially rural varieties which are used for in-group communication in predominantly informal contexts. The Neogrammarians famously encouraged their colleagues to rejuvenate the bookish atmosphere of their study rooms by letting in the "clear air" of "the living dialects" (Brugmann and Osthoff, quoted in Seuren 1998, 91). These proposals (which often echoed Romantic feelings of fascination for surviving traditions and "popular" culture) were crucial for the advancement of Romance linguistics and dialectology; yet, they have also had limiting consequences. In particular, those working on language contact in Romance languages are for the most part convinced that the best objects of study are "dialectal varieties, especially linguistic islands surrounded by other languages, which are not subject to linguistic norms" (Sala 2013, 236). As a result, the application of up-to-date concepts from contact linguistics to languages with a history of codification, institutional support and written use in a wide range of formal contexts is a relatively underdeveloped scholarly enterprise.

A connected, widely accepted principle is that contact only leads to significant change when it involves large-scale, prolonged human proximity and/or mobility. Sala (2013) refers to this situation of widespread bilingualism and regular speaker interaction as "direct contact" and states that its results are "generally much more important than in indirect contact" (p. 188). This view leads to overlooking or downplaying the influence that the international languages of intellectual, economic and religious life (whether "living" or "dead" languages) exert through indirect, or "learnèd" (Thomason 2001), contact. In fact, elite bilingualism, the study of "foreign" or "classical" languages, and the circulation of texts without large-scale speaker interaction play an especially important role in the history of standardised, socially prestigious varieties.[1] Moreover, as suggested for instance by Crystal (2012) and McLaughlin (2011), the importance of indirect contact has increased thanks to globalisation (which favours passive familiarity with international languages) and the emergence of the Internet (including its automatic or semiautomatic forms of translation).

Finally, another assumption remains dominant especially among Romance linguists, namely that contact and internal development are best studied as alternative causes of change. Ever since the nineteenth century, great scholarly efforts have been directed at deciding whether particular changes in the history of Romance varieties were due to endogenous or xogenous causes : Sala (2013) offers a comprehensive review. More recently, theorists of language contact and change have moved away from monocausal approaches by stressing that change often results from the mutually reinforcing combination of exogenous and endogenous factors (see especially Thomason 2004; 2010). However, given the conventional preference for monocausality, it is no surprise that the vast majority of existing research on contact as a cause of change is devoted to single combinations, i.e., to the influence of language A on language B at a particular moment in time. Very little research has been devoted to the combined, asynchronous influences of multiple languages (A, C, D) on the diachronic development of a grammatical structure of B.

In this Chapter I intend to define an open question in the history of Italian as a relevant case for a multicausal study of language change. The question concerns a particular feature of Italian word-formation, namely the order in

---

[1] See Pountain's (2011, 607-610) critical discussion of the insufficient attention paid, in Romance linguistics, to the particular "forces acting on [the historical development] of an *Ausbau* language" (p. 607).

which the modifier and the modified element are combined within compounds. In particular, I will explore the role that language contact has played in the diachronic expansion of the compounding pattern in which the modifier *precedes* the modified element. The modifier is the element that reduces, or specifies, the potential reference of the modified element (see Bauer 2017). In referring to the modificational structure of compounds, I will also use the abbreviations "MR" for the modifier and "MD" for the modified element.

2 Brief review of the literature

Apart from surviving in a few products of Latin word-formation (Lat. *caprifŏlĭum* > It. *caprifoglio* 'honeysuckle'), the MR–MD order was traditionally typical of what is called "cultured" (*colta*), "learnèd" (*dotta*) or "neoclassical" (*neoclassica*) compounding (*composizione*) in Italian linguistics. Iacobini (2015) opts for "neoclassical compounding" and gives the following definition: "the word-formation pattern which uses combining forms [...] taken from Latin and Ancient Greek with the particular aim of coining technical and scientific terms" (Iacobini 2015, 1662), such as *etnologia* 'ethnology' or *termometro* 'thermometer'. However, it has repeatedly been claimed that the MR–MD order is increasingly spreading beyond neoclassical compounding, and is gaining ground against the opposite order, which is also present in Italian, as shown by *capostazione* 'station master' (modified elements in bold for clarity). Radimský (2013) has substantiated this claim with regard to noun + noun compounds. He argues that, although the MR–MD order "has been developing as a direct continuation of learnèd compounding patterns", it is currently "breaking the two traditional limits of the learnèd compounding, since it ceases to combine only a set of compound elements of learnèd origin on one hand, and it begins to produce a significant number of non-terminological compounds on the other hand" (Radimský 2013, 48).

This change in the productivity of the MR–MD pattern has often been attributed to language contact, especially to the influence of the English language. According to De Mauro (2002[1963]), the expansion of the MR–MD order is due to multiple factors, especially the "pressure of Greek or Greek-inspired models traditionally present in technical terminologies, and of German and Anglo-Saxon models" (p. 224). Klajn (1972), Dardano (1986), Lepschy and Lepschy (1999), Pulcini (2002), Bisetto (2003 and 2004), Beccaria (2006) and Renzi (2012) all mention the MR–MD order in their discussions of English influences. Pulcini writes that "[t]he order of the elements of English compounds (*determinans* + *determinatum*) violates the syntagmatic order of Italian which usually places the modifying element on the right of the modified one" (2002, 160). Beccaria observes that MR–MD compounds "contrast with the internal structure of Italian", where "the 'head' comes first, followed by the modifier" (Beccaria 2006, 188),[2] and Renzi stresses the "cultured nature [*natura colta*]" (2012, 74) of the MR–MD pattern. Similarly, Scalise and Bisetto (2008, 128) view the MD–MR order as the core Italian pattern, and the opposite order as a peripheral contact-induced innovation. Iacobini (2015) links the expansion of the MR–MD order to the influence of "modern foreign languages" (p. 1671), especially of "English borrowings" (p. 1674). Other linguists have gone further by speaking of a "proliferation" of MR–MD compounds (Berruto 2012, 124 n. 27), and by including this change in progress in alarmed accounts of the allegedly disruptive impact that English influences are having on Italian (see e.g. Giovanardi 2015). According to Sullam Calimani (2003, 12), the ongoing expansion of MR–MD compounding "seems to mark a turning point in the process of formation of Italian compounds, which might eventually become like what is seen in Germanic languages".

3 An exploratory study

In order to test these views I need, first of all, to distinguish between different types of compounds displaying the MR–MD order. My discussion in the following pages is limited to endocentric subordinative compounds in which two independent nouns, or an independent noun and a nominal bound formative, have been combined to form a noun, as in English [[*station*]+[*master*]]$_N$ or [[*photo-*]+[*synthesis*]]$_N$, and it constitutes a pilot version of a larger study which

---

[2] It is common practice to speak of "right-headed compounds" with reference to what are here called "modifier-modified compounds". I prefer the latter label because the notion of a compound head (It. *testa*, Fr. *tête*) is less obvious, and less univocally understood, than it might seem at first. In discussing the impact of language contact on the recent development of French compounding, Renner (2017) uses the phrase "semantic head [*tête sémantique*]" (see also Renner 2018, 4: "semantically right-headed nominal compounds"); yet Bauer (2017, 37) posits that "a 'centre' is a semantic notion, while a 'head' is a grammatical one". In his book, Bauer shows that the question of headedness in compounds is a complex and problematic one. An Italian example is worth adding to his discussion. While it is generally agreed that *calcio scommesse* 'illegal bets on football results' is an example of the MR-MD order (and it is, indeed, frequently cited as such), referring to it as a right-headed compound raises the problem of why the compound is masculine singular: if feminine plural *scommesse* is the head, it should transmit its grammatical properties to the entire compound.

I have recently undertaken as part of a research project on the role of language contact in the history of Italian.³ The first of the three groups I have identified supports the view of the MR–MD order as a peripheral pattern in Italian, and it does so both structurally and sociolinguistically. The compounds under (1) are formed by combining bound formatives (*biblio-*, *-logo*, etc.) and/or independent words of "learnèd" origin – that is, by using material that Italian borrowed from Latin or Greek (sometimes through the mediation of French or other modern languages).⁴ Although these compounds have become increasingly common, for the most part they remain typical of technical terminologies and special varieties of Italian:

(1)
bibliologia 'book studies, book history'
discopatia 'disc disease'
fisiologo 'physiologist'
fotografo 'photographer'
gasdinamica 'gas dynamics'
ideologo 'ideologue'
psicologo 'psychologist'
pneumonectomia 'pneumonectomy'
radiofonia 'radio broadcasting'
radioterapia 'radiotherapy'
xenofobo 'xenophobe'

---

³ This project is funded by the Department of Foreign Languages at the University of Bergen.
⁴ In Romance historical linguistics, the terms "learnèd" and "popular" are often used in a way which implicitly conflates a structural distinction and a sociolinguistic one (see Pountain 2011, 628). From a structural point of view, independent words and bound morphemes are "learnèd" if they display semantic and especially phonological properties which suggest that they were not directly transmitted but were in fact borrowed from Latin (see also footnote 7, below). This sense of the term is defined and applied, for instance, by Maiden (1995, see especially p. 84). From the point of view of language variation, "learnèd" points instead towards Latinate lexical material and grammatical patterns which have been used by an educated elite in elevated registers or specialist contexts. While in many cases the two points of view are compatible, Tesi (2007, 15-19) stresses the existence of words which qualify as learnèd in one sense but not in the other.

The MR–MD order is also found in compounds which are not linked to technical terminologies: *internet-caffè* 'Internet café', *telequiz* 'game show', *web-sondaggio* 'web survey'. For the purposes of the present Chapter, however, these compounds can be said to constitute a subtype of group 1, in the sense that they are still formed by combining two etymologically non-native lexemes. In this case, the source languages include Turkish (*caffè*), French (*sondaggio*) and English.

In the other two groups, by contrast, either or both of the elements that form each compound are "popular" or inherited lexemes (some of them formally adjusted by means of a linking -*i*, as in *funivia*, from *fune* 'rope' + *via* 'way', or by deletion of the final vowel, as in *puttan-tour*). Type 2 consists of compounds in which one of the elements is native:

(2)
>*acquapark* 'water park'
>*acqua-scooter* 'water scooter, jet-ski'
>*arteterapia* 'art therapy'
>*astronave* 'spaceship'
>*bimbocard* 'discount pass for children'
>*calcio crack* 'financial collapse in the world of football' (Iacobini 2015, 1673)
>*computer grafica* 'computer graphics'
>*piano-bar* 'piano bar'
>*puttan-tour* 'prostitute(-viewing) tour'[5]
>*scuolabus* 'school bus'
>*telegiornale* 'television news'

During the last fifty years or so, mixed compounds of this type have been created in large numbers in the language of advertising, newspapers and young people (see especially Klajn 1972, 175–76; Dardano, Frenguelli and Perna 2000; Iacobini 2015), but not all of them have become established.

The third group is probably the least numerous, but it is important because it consists of compounds in which both elements can be considered native:

---

[5] On this practice, see Crowhurst and Eldridge (2020). The word was recorded by Lanza (1974, 80).

(3)
> *acquascivolo* 'water slide'
> *agopuntura* 'acupuncture'
> *calciomercato* 'football transfer market'
> *calcio scommesse* 'illegal bets on football results'
> *cartamodello* 'paper pattern'
> *filovia* 'trolley-bus line'
> *fruttivendolo* 'fruit vendor, greengrocer'
> *funivia* 'cableway'
> *vetroresina* 'fibreglass'

In (2) the MR–MD pattern still retains a partial connection to a particular lexical stratum, which is perceived by speakers as "foreign" (*card*, *crack*) and/or identified by etymologists as "borrowed" (*astro-*, *tele-*, *terapia*). In the examples under (3), however, the MR–MD pattern is unconditionally applied to inherited lexical items – which in contact linguistics is a sign that a borrowed pattern is no longer restricted to the periphery of the recipient language, but has instead been more deeply integrated into its morphological structures (see Gardani 2018).[6] As a preliminary attempt at establishing when this development took place and what role (if any) contact with English had in favouring it, I have decided to focus on the earliest attestations of compounds which can reasonably be assigned to type 3.

In fact, deciding which compounds belong to this type is not a straightforward task, and especially the choice between types 2 and 3 appears to be a matter of degree in some cases. This is because, in the Romance languages, the question of what counts as inherited lexical material is itself irreducible to a neat dichotomy between native and non-native items.[7] In the Italian case, in particular, some

---

[6] According to Gardani (2020), proper morphological borrowing can only be said to have taken place when borrowed formatives or patterns apply to "native (or nativised) lexemes of the recipient language" (p. 103).

[7] A relatively restricted meaning (often close to the original Latin meaning) and the absence of regular sound changes (e.g. retention of [kt], which in the transition from Latin to Italian became [t:]) are traditionally considered as the main properties of Latinisms, and, as such, have long been used as criteria for identifying them. Philological and chronological considerations can also be helpful in deciding between borrowing and direct transmission. Yet the picture is complicated by "semilearnèd" words and other problematic cases. See Pountain (2011, 628-639).

early borrowings from Latin and other languages are already common in medieval texts, where they appear to have been phonologically and morphologically adapted as well as semantically transformed. At the same time, some words which did not undergo all the expected sound changes were probably never borrowed at all: they survived throughout the transition from Latin to Italian, but their pronunciation was influenced by Latin models. For instance, where should *bancogiro* 'credit transfer' and *vetrocemento* 'concrete blocks containing glass panels' be placed? According to etymological criteria, they might have to be treated as type 2 compounds, given that *banco* 'counter, bank' is ultimately of Germanic origin,[8] and that *cemento* 'cement' is usually considered a "learnèd" variant (cf. Lat. *caementum*).[9] By the time they were used to form compounds, however, these words had largely been nativised and were essentially the same as those in (3). The same can be said of frequently-used modern borrowings such as *turismo* (from Eng. *tourism*, via French), found in *pescaturismo* 'fishing tourism'.

In order to obtain a sufficiently representative sample, I have avoided applying overly restrictive criteria.[10] Compounds such as *bancogiro*, *vetrocemento* and *pescaturismo* have therefore been added to my sample. I have also included a particular subtype of compounds in which the modified element is a bound formative, *-vendolo* 'trader, vendor', characterised by the presence of the suffix *-olo* (as in *fruttivendolo*). My sample also includes a series of compounds with *capo-* as a modifying element, even though a few of these *compounds* (especially *capomastro* 'master builder') may be interpreted

---

[8] See *Lessico Etimologico Italiano* (henceforth *LEI*), s.v. **panc*, where the emergence of a financial meaning is, however, specifically identified as an Italo-Romance innovation.

[9] The "popular" continuants of late Lat. *cimentum* are It. *cimento*, Fr. *ciment*, Sp. *cimiento*, with which It. *cemento*, Fr. *cément*, Sp. *cemento* form doublets. I am grateful to Chris Pountain for suggesting these comparisons (see *LEI*, s.v. *caementum/cimentum*, for further evidence and discussion).

[10] The selection of my material has been facilitated by a number of richly-documented scholarly works – most notably Micheli (2020), but also earlier works by Tollemache (1945), Benedek (1978), Dardano, Frenguelli and Perna (2000), Grossman and Rainer (2004), Dardano (2009) and Iacobini (2015). For establishing the dates of the first recorded occurrences of the selected compounds, I have used etymological dictionaries (Cortelazzo and Zolli 1999; *LEI*; Nocentini 2010) as well as the *Grande dizionario della lingua italiana*, the *Grande dizionario italiano dell'uso*, the *Tesoro della lingua italiana delle Origini*, the *Vocabolario Treccani on line*, and *Google Books*.

as coordinative formations ('someone who is a master *and* a builder') rather than subordinative ones (in this particular example, coordination seems to be suggested by the doubly inflected plural *capimastri*, while the variant *capomastri* supports a subordinative analysis). Finally, I have included compounds containing elements which, although originating from learnèd bound formatives, have become independent nouns with a new meaning, such as *foto* 'photograph, picture' (< *fotografia* 'photography') < *foto-* 'light'. On the other hand, I have excluded commercial names (e.g. *Scarpamondo* 'shoe world', an Italian company that began to open large shoe stores in the early 1990s) and compounds formed with the name of a public figure as the modifier and *pensiero* '(way of) thinking' as the modified element (*Agnelli- pensiero*, etc.), because these are often occasional formations (and are not normally recorded in dictionaries). They share this ephemeral status with some type 2 compounds; nonetheless, as remarked by Renzi (2012, 87), the *pensiero* subtype has been productive for decades and is therefore worth mentioning.

Except for the requirement of displaying the MR–MD order, compounds have been randomly selected for all the other variables that will be discussed below. I have thus produced a sample of 89 compounds.[11] In Figure 11.1, they are arranged according to the date of their earliest recorded occurrences:

---

[11] Here is the full list: *acquaparco* (1991), *acquascivolo* (1990), *acquedotto* (1342), *agopuntura* (1805), *animavversione* (1348), *apicoltura* (1847), *astronave* (1955), *autolavaggio* (1983), *autonoleggio* (1941), *autoparco* (1939), *autoricambi* (1966), *autorimessa* (1927), *autoscuola* (1950), *autostazione* (1961), *autostrada* (1924), *bachicoltura* (1865), *bancogiro* (1879), *banconota* (1849), *borgomastro* (1527), *cabinovia* (1963), *calcio scommesse* (1980), *calciomercato* (1967), *cannocchiale* (1610), *capitombolo* (1546), *capocannoniere* (1916), *capocarceriere* (1854), *capocenso* (1338), *capocomico* (1798), *capocuoco* (1830), *capogiro/capogirlo* (1363), *capolavoro* (1715), *capoluogo* (1771), *capomastro/capomaestro* (second half of the thirteenth century), *capomaglio* (1310), *capomorbo* (second half of the fourteenth century), *capopurgio* (first half of the fourteenth century), *caposoldo* (1280), *caprifico* (1340), *caprifoglio* (first half of the fourteenth century), *cartamodello* (1958), *cartamoneta* (1788), *casa-base* (1967), *castrocampo* (second half of the fourteenth century), *erbivendolo* (1835), *ferrovia* (1852), *filodiffusione* (1958), *filovia* (1917), *fotomodello* (1967), *fotoromanzo* (1956), *fotostoria* (1990), *fruttivendolo* (1780), *funivia* (1942), *gattafodero* (second half of the fourteenth century), *lanavendolo/lanovendolo* (1298), *lattivendolo* (1869), *madrelingua* (1810), *madrepatria* (1774), *manrovescio* (1440), *maremoto* (1891), *metanodotto* (1942), *mondovisione* (1962), *motocalcio* (1935), *motogiro* (1963), *motoraduno* (1935), *motoricambi* (Fochi 1966),

The Impact of New Contacts on an Old Pattern 201

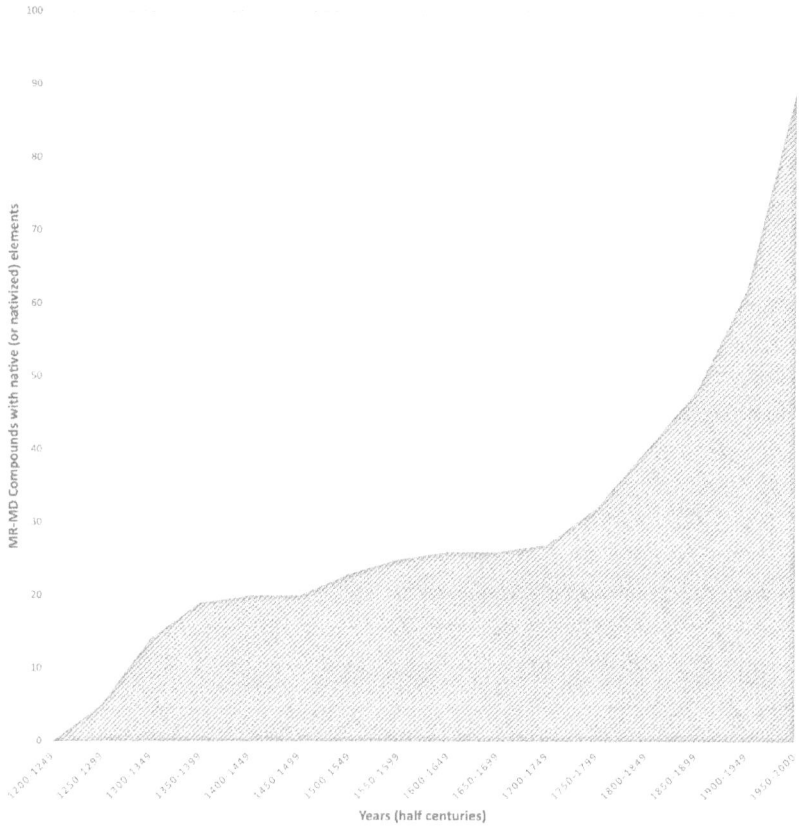

Figure 11.1. Type 3 compounds according to the period of their first recorded occurrence

Apart from minor differences, a claim is essentially shared by all those who have considered the diachronic development of MR–MD compounding in Italian – namely that modern contacts have boosted this pre-existing word-formation pattern. The chronological distribution of the compounds in my sample supports

---

motorimessa (1963), *nocepesca* (second half of the sixteenth century), *nocepesco* (second half of the sixteenth century), *panicuocolo* (1342), *pannotendolo* (first half of the fourteenth century), *pennivendolo* (1904), *pescaturismo* (1998), *pescivendolo* (1360), *pollicoltura* (1880), *pollivendolo* (1872), *pornodivo* (1988), *postagiro* (1926), *postemastro* (first half of the sixteenth century), *puttangiro* (Lanza 1974), *seggiovia* (1948), *spazionave* (1988), *spazioporto* (1974), *straccivendolo* (1838), *terratremolo* (second half of the thirteenth century), *terremoto* (1294), *vetrocemento* (1936), *vetromattone* (1978), *vetroresina* (1983), *viadotto* (1837).

this claim. The number of MR–MD compounds grows especially in the thirteenth and fourteenth centuries. This first growth is probably due to the fact that the extant texts preserve the first written attestations of compounds which had been inherited from Latin or formed under the influence of Latin models (I shall return to this point). The productivity of the MR–MD pattern seems to be quite low from the fifteenth century until the first half of the eighteenth century. The number of these compounds increases again from the late eighteenth century and especially in the twentieth century, during a period of growing internationalisation (or, as it is usually called today, "globalisation") in the economic, political and cultural life of Western societies. My data, however, do not support the attribution of a special role to contact with English: this language only began to marginalise other international languages (especially French) within Italian society, and to exert a substantial influence on Italian lexical and grammatical structures, after the Second World War (Cartago 1994; Sullam Calimani 2003; Bonsaver, Carlucci and Reza 2019). If English had been the dominant source for the expansion of the MR–MD pattern, the number of MR–MD compounds would be expected to increase more sharply and consistently in the second half of the twentieth century (see Figure 11.2 below). In sum, English should be considered as one of the exogenous sources (not as *the* source) for the change in question.

If the data presented in Figure 11.1 are broken down, it is found that only a portion of the Italian MR–MD compounds in my sample can be traced back to Latin antecedents, or have likely models in English, French or German (see Figure 11.3). Some of them can be regarded as having been formed in other languages, before being "borrowed" into Italian without adaptation of the direction of modification between the two formative elements.[12] Examples include *terremoto* 'earthquake' (cf. Lat. *terrae mōtus*), *capoluogo* (cf. Fr. *chef-lieu*) and *ferrovia* 'railway', a calque of German *Eisenbahn* and/or English *railway* (in Figure 11.3, 'Multiple sources' identifies *ferrovia* and *cartamoneta*

---

[12] I use the term "borrowing" in its "broad sense" (Kuteva 2017, 165) – i.e., as a general term including not only cases in which the phonetic substance of the source-language model is replicated (Ger. *Espresso* < It. *espresso*, It. *pub* < Eng. *pub*, often called "loanwords"), but also cases where only the structure and meaning of the model are replicated (It. *fine settimana* < Eng. *weekend*, usually referred to as a "calque"). See also Matras's (2009) comprehensive discussion of "matter" and "pattern" replication, and Renner's (2018) recent article on "structural", as opposed to "material", borrowing. Note the adapted direction of modification in *fine settimana* (MD-MR), compared to the Germanic MR-MD order in *weekend*.

'paper money', which have more than one likely model language). *Pescivendolo* 'fishmonger' and *panicuocolo* 'baker' are instead compounds of Latin origin which survived in cultured registers of Italo-Romance; that is, they were not borrowed from Latin but "inherited through learnèd transmission [*ereditati dal latino per trafila dotta*]" (Micheli 2020, 95). Their overall number (25 out of 89 randomly selected compounds) suggests morphological change, in that it confirms that the expansion of the MR–MD order is not an exclusively lexical phenomenon due to the survival, and increasing borrowing, of compound words with this internal order of modification.[13]

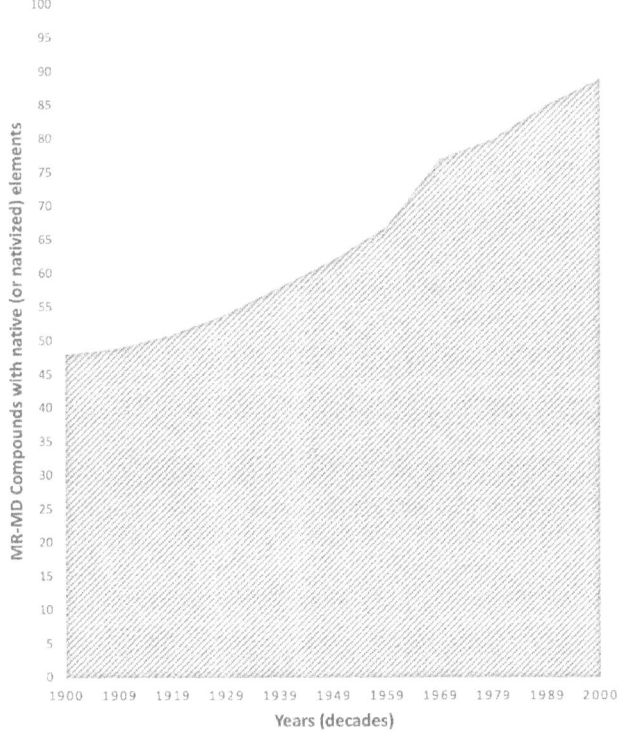

Figure 11.2. Type 3 compounds by decade (1900–2000)

---

[13] The extension of an existing pattern (including an increase in its productivity) is considered a typical form of contact-induced change by authors such as Thomason (2001, 70-71, 88-90) and Matras (2009, 239), who discuss it alongside more radical forms of change (such as the loss of an existing pattern or the addition of a new pattern).

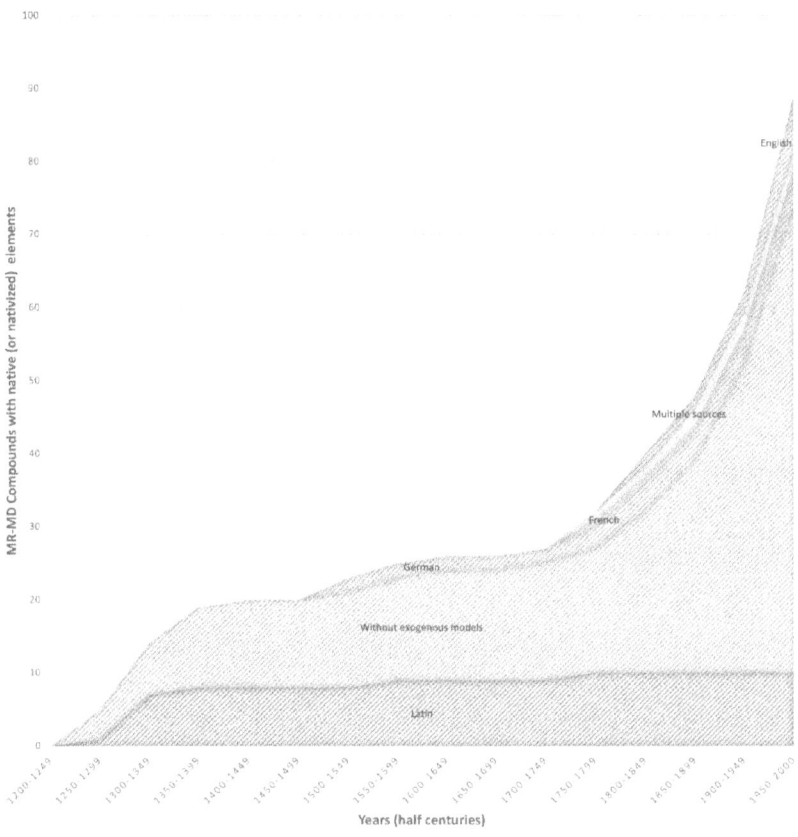

Figure 11.3. Type 3 compounds by century and likely model language

Finally, my exploratory study confirms that neatly separating the role of language contact from that of internal factors is not always possible (nor desirable, if one wishes to do justice to the complexity of a language's history). A detailed discussion of the mechanisms underlying the emergence and expansion of MR–MD compounding is beyond the scope of this Chapter. The interaction between lexical borrowing and internal factors can nonetheless be sketched out. Compared to words such as the names of the days (*lunedì* < Lat. *lūnae dĭe* 'day of the moon', etc.), whose morphological complexity had generally become opaque in the Middle Ages, *terremoto*, *pescivendolo*, etc. would seem to have retained a greater ability to be interpreted as compounds ('movement of the earth', etc.), at least by some speakers. Since then, the tendency to segment some words in this way has operated regardless of whether they were inherited or borrowed words; and the resulting analysis has been replicated analogically in the creation of new compound words (see also the nineteenth-century cases briefly discussed by Cortelazzo and Zolli 1999, s.v. *coltivare*). The fact that speakers have been doing this for a long-drawn period of centuries is typical of diachronic developments involving analogy (see Gaeta 2010). The internal structure of *terremoto, ferrovia*, etc. may have initially been opaque to speakers who were not familiar with the ancestor/source language; however, their interpretation as compounds would eventually take root, as shown by the emergence of paradigmatic series: *pescivendolo, lanovendolo* 'wool trader' (discussed along these lines by Micheli 2020, 95–96), and later also *erbivendolo* 'greengrocer', *pennivendolo* 'dishonest journalist, hack' (literally 'pen-seller'); *terremoto, maremoto* 'seaquake'; *ferrovia, funivia, cabinovia* 'cableway with small (usually two-seater) cars' (see Grossman and Rainer 2004, 42–43). Most likely, the whole process has also been supported by the presence of the MR–MD order in neoclassical and terminological compounding: compounds such as those listed under (1) (*bibliologia*, etc.) have long been associated with prestigious varieties of Italian, due to their vitality in scientific and intellectual discourse, and have themselves been on the rise since the beginning of the twentieth century (see Sobrero 2000; Iacobini 2015).[14]

4 In lieu of a conclusion

In the particular case explored in this Chapter, language contact appears to have contributed to changing the productivity of a word-formation pattern. Based on the evidence reviewed above, this contribution should be considered as a by-product of lexical borrowing. More research is needed in order to determine whether language contact contributed to the expansion of the MR–MD pattern also through direct transfer of this word-formation pattern. It may be possible to put forward this additional argument, if future research shows that: (a) the frequency of MR–MD compounds has been consistently higher in translations, or in other (oral or written) texts which were produced under the influence of "foreign" or "classical" languages, compared to texts produced in predominantly monolingual settings; (b) the former texts also contain many of

---

[14] At the same time, according to Iacobini, "acceptance of compound words from Germanic languages (esp. English)" was one of the factors contributing to the migration of neoclassical compounds into "common usage" (2015, 1668-69).

the earliest occurrences of Italian MR–MD compounds that do not have antecedents in those languages.

In any case, it should be pointed out that the languages to which this influence has been attributed have historically been used by relatively small sectors of the Italian-speaking community, and probably by even smaller numbers of bilinguals regularly interacting with speakers of Latin, German, French or English. Pountain argues against considering Latin as the prototypical "dead" language which could only influence Romance languages through written texts: during the Middle Ages, and even later, Latin "continued to be used fluently in certain sectors of Romance-speaking societies, and so was in many respects a living and dynamic language" (Pountain 2011, 628). Beyond religious organisations and socio-cultural elites, however, the relationship with Latin in medieval Italy varied from passive familiarity to complete ignorance (later, the incomprehensibility of "latinorum" for the average person became almost proverbial).[15] This brings me back to the distinction between direct and indirect contact, and to the priority traditionally accorded to the former, which I mentioned at the beginning of this Chapter. Although my preliminary exploration of the development of Italian MR–MD compounding does not warrant general conclusions, it does suggest that the results of indirect contact need not be as insignificant as is often assumed.

Bibliographical references

Bauer, Laurie. 2017. *Compounds and Compounding*. Cambridge: Cambridge University Press.

Beccaria, Gian Luigi. 2006. *Per difesa e per amore: La lingua italiana oggi*. Milan: Garzanti.

Benedek, Nándor. 1978. "Sostantivi composti nell'italiano contemporaneo." *Lingua nostra* 39(4): 117–121.

Berruto, Gaetano. 2012. *Sociolinguistica dell'italiano contemporaneo*, 2nd ed. Rome: Carocci.

Bisetto, Antonietta. 2003. "Da *formattare* a *calcio mercato*: l'interferenza dell'inglese sull'italiano contemporaneo." In Sullam Calimani 2003, 87–99.

---

[15] A fourteenth-century Roman chronicle relates that "ordinary merchants and many other good people […] do not understand Latin" (Campanelli 2013, 89). See also Carlucci (forthcoming).

Bisetto, Antonietta. 2004. "L'influsso dell'inglese sul lessico e la morfologia dell'italiano: osservazioni teoriche." In *L'italiano delle traduzioni*, edited by Giuliana Garzone and Anna Cardinaletti. Milan: Franco Angeli, pp. 49–64.

Bonsaver, Guido, Alessandro Carlucci, and Matthew Reza, eds. 2019. *Italy and the USA: Cultural Change through Language and Narrative*. Oxford: Legenda.

Campanelli, Maurizio. 2013. "The Preface of the Anonimo Romano's *Cronica*: Writing History and Proving Truthfulness in Fourteenth-Century Rome." *The Mediaeval Journal* 3(1): 83–106.

Carlucci, Alessandro. Forthcoming. "Opinions about Perceived Linguistic Intelligibility in Late-Medieval Italy." *Revue Romane*.

Cartago, Gabriella. 1994. "L'apporto inglese." In *Storia della lingua italiana*, edited by Luca Serianni and Pietro Trifone, vol. 3, 721–750. Turin: Einaudi.

Cortelazzo, Manlio and Paolo Zolli. 1999. *Dizionario etimologico della lingua italiana*, 2nd ed. Bologna: Zanichelli.

Crowhurst, Isabel and Adam Eldridge. 2020. "'A Cathartic Moment in a Man's Life': Homosociality and Gendered Fun on the *Puttan Tour*." *Men and Masculinities* 23(1): 170–193.

Crystal, David. 2012. *English as a Global Language*, 2nd ed. Cambridge: Cambridge University Press.

Dardano, Maurizio. 1986. "The Influence of English on Italian." In *English in Contact with Other Languages*, edited by Wolfgang Viereck and Wolf-Dietrich Bald, 231–252. Budapest: Akadémiai Kiadó.

Dardano, Maurizio. 2009. *Costruire parole: La morfologia derivativa dell'italiano*. Bologna: Il Mulino.

Dardano, Maurizio, Gianluca Frenguelli and Teresa Perna. 2000. "L'italiano di fronte all'inglese alle soglie del terzo millennio." In *L'italiano oltre frontiera*, edited by Serge Vanvolsem et al., vol. 1, 31–55. Florence: Cesati.

De Mauro, Tullio. 2002. *Storia linguistica dell'Italia unita*, 7th ed. Rome: Laterza. First published 1963.

Fochi, Franco. 1966. *Lingua in rivoluzione*. Milan: Feltrinelli.

Gaeta, Livio. 2010. "Analogical Change." In *The Bloomsbury Companion to Historical Linguistics*, edited by Silvia Luraghi and Vit Bubenik, 147–160. London: Bloomsbury.

Gardani, Francesco. 2018. "On Morphological Borrowing." *Language and Linguistics Compass* 12(10): 1–17.

Gardani, Francesco. 2020. "Morphology and Contact-Induced Language Change." In *The Oxford Handbook of Language Contact*, edited by Anthony Grant, 96–122. Oxford: Oxford University Press.

Giovanardi, Claudio. 2015. "Un bilancio delle proposte di traduzione degli anglicismi dieci anni dopo." In *La lingua italiana e le lingue romanze di fronte agli anglicismi*, edited by Claudio Marazzini and Alessio Petralli, 64–85. Florence: Accademia della Crusca.

Grossmann, Maria and Franz Rainer. 2004. *La formazione delle parole in italiano*. Tübingen: Niemeyer.

Iacobini, Claudio. 2015. "Foreign Word-Formation in Italian." In *Word-Formation: An International Handbook of the Languages of Europe*, edited by Peter Müller, Ingeborg Ohnheiser, Susan Olsen and Franz Rainer, vol. 3, 1660–1679. Berlin: De Gruyter.

Klajn, Ivan. 1972. *Influssi inglesi nella lingua italiana*. Florence: Olschki.

Kuteva, Tania. 2017. "Contact and Borrowing." In *The Cambridge Handbook of Historical Syntax*, edited by Adam Ledgeway and Ian Roberts, 163–86. Cambridge: Cambridge University Press.

Lanza, Cesare. 1974. *Il mercabul: Il controlinguaggio dei giovani*. Milan: SugarCo.

Lepschy, Anna Laura and Giulio Lepschy. 1999. "Anglismi e italianismi." In *L'amanuense analfabeta e altri saggi*, 169–182. Florence: Olschki.

Maiden, Martin. 1995. *A Linguistic History of Italian*. London: Longman.

Matras, Yaron. 2009. *Language Contact*. Cambridge: Cambridge University Press.

McLaughlin, Mairi. 2011. *Syntactic Borrowing in Contemporary French: A Linguistic Analysis of News Translation*. Oxford: Legenda.

Micheli, Silvia. 2020. *Composizione italiana in diacronia: Le parole composte dell'italiano nel quadro della Morfologia delle costruzioni*. Berlin: De Gruyter.

Nocentini, Alberto. 2010. *L'etimologico. Vocabolario della lingua italiana*, with the assistance of Alessandro Parenti. Florence: Le Monnier.

Pountain, Christopher J. 2011. "Latin and the Structure of Written Romance." In *The Cambridge History of the Romance Languages*, edited by Martin Maiden, John Charles Smith and Adam Ledgeway, vol. 1, 606–59. Cambridge: Cambridge University Press.

Pulcini, Virginia. 2002. "Italian." In *English in Europe*, edited by Manfred Görlach, 151–167. Oxford: Oxford University Press.

Radimský, Jan. 2013. "Position of the Head in Italian N–N Compounds: The Case of 'Mirror Compounds'." *Linguistica Pragensia* 23(1): 41–52.

Renner, Vincent. 2017. "*Fan zone, webradio, infobulle*: les noms composés ont-ils perdu la tête?" In *Les anglicismes: Des emprunts à intérêt variable? Actes du colloque OPALE*, 321–28. Montreal: Office québécois de la langue française.

Renner, Vincent. 2018. "Structural Borrowing in Word-Formation: An Exploratory Overview." *SKASE: Journal of Theoretical Linguistics* 15(2): 2–12.

Renzi, Lorenzo. 2012. *Come cambia la lingua: L'italiano in movimento*. Bologna: Il Mulino.

Sala, Marius. 2013. "Contact and Borrowing." In *The Cambridge History of the Romance Languages*, edited by Martin Maiden, John Charles Smith and Adam Ledgeway, vol. 2, 187–236. Cambridge: Cambridge University Press.

Scalise, Sergio and Antonietta Bisetto. 2008. *La struttura delle parole*. Bologna: Il Mulino.

Seuren, Pieter. 1998. *Western Linguistics: An Historical Introduction*. Oxford: Blackwell.

Sobrero, Alberto. 2000. "Lingue speciali." In *Introduzione all'italiano contemporaneo. La variazione e gli usi*, edited by Alberto Sobrero, 237–277. Rome: Laterza. First published 1993.

Sullam Calimani, Anna-Vera, ed. 2003. *Italiano e inglese a confronto: Problemi di interferenza linguistica*. Florence: Cesati.

Tesi, Riccardo. 2007. *Storia dell'italiano: La formazione della lingua comune*. Bologna: Zanichelli.

Thomason, Sarah. 2001. *Language Contact: An Introduction*. Edinburgh: Edinburgh University Press.

Thomason, Sarah. 2004. "Contact as a Source of Language Change." In *The Handbook of Historical Linguistics*, edited by Brian Joseph and Richard Janda, 686–712. Oxford: Blackwell.

Thomason, Sarah. 2010. "Contact Explanations in Linguistics." In *The Handbook of Language Contact*, edited by Raymond Hickey, 31–47. Oxford: Blackwell.

Tollemache, Federigo. 1945. *Le parole composte nella lingua italiana*. Rome: Rores.

Chapter 12

Los cultismos en una novela dialogada del siglo XVI: un estudio de sociolingüística histórica

Rocío Díaz-Bravo y Gael Vaamonde

Universidad de Granada

Resumen

El texto literario *Retrato de la Loçana andaluza* (*RLA*) fue compuesto en Roma por Francisco Delicado (1524) y publicado en Venecia (1530?). En su Retrato, el autor intenta retratar la lengua hablada de sus personajes de diverso origen geográfico y social, teniendo en cuenta diferentes variedades discursivas. Por tanto, *RLA* es una fuente ideal para el estudio de la variación lingüística en el español del siglo XVI.

En este capítulo se ha llevado a cabo un análisis de los cultismos en *RLA*, basado en la metodología de la sociolingüística histórica. Se han aplicado las siguientes variables: el nivel educativo de los personajes (culto, letrado y analfabeto) y el tipo discursivo (considerando su posición en el *continuum* existente entre la inmediatez y la distancia comunicativas). Con objeto de realizar un análisis automático, hemos desarrollado un nuevo recurso: *Lozana Digital*, el cual permite una investigación léxica cuantitativa.

Entendemos por "cultismos" préstamos tomados directamente del latín (incluidos aquellos incorporados del griego al latín). Delicado usó un número llamativo de cultismos para caracterizar a sus personajes cultos (especialmente, aquellos que representan su *alter ego*: Silvano y Auctor), como *agricultura, animosíssimos, archiospital, omnipotente, sacristía, salutífera*, etc. Asimismo, los cultismos son más frecuentes en textos más cercanos o afines a la distancia comunicativa, mientras que su frecuencia es significativamente menor en los textos pertenecientes al polo de la inmediatez comunicativa.

En definitiva, con este estudio basado en corpus pretendemos realizar una contribución a la investigación de los cultismos en la literatura española del Siglo de Oro.

Summary

The literary text *Retrato de la Loçana andaluza* (*RLA*) was composed by Francisco Delicado in Rome (1524) and published in Venice (1530?). In his *Retrato* ('portrait'), the author intends to portray the spoken language of his characters from various geographical and social backgrounds, taking into account different discourse varieties. Therefore, *RLA* is an ideal source for the study of linguistic variation in sixteenth-century Spanish.

In this paper, a historical sociolinguistic analysis of learnèd borrowings in *RLA* is conducted. The following variables were applied: the educational level of characters (learnèd, literate and illiterate) and discourse type (considering its position in the *continuum* between communicative immediacy and distance). In order to conduct automatic linguistic analysis of this literary book, a new digital resource has been developed, *Lozana Digital*, which enables quantitative lexical research.

By "learnèd borrowings" (*cultismos*) we refer to words that were borrowed directly from Latin (including Greek borrowings into Latin). Delicado used a striking number of learnèd borrowings to portray his learnèd characters (notably, those representing his *alter ego*: Silvano and Auctor), such as *agricultura, animosísimos, archiospital, onmipotente, sacristía, salutífera*, etc. Furthermore, cultured borrowings are more frequent in the texts characterised or closer to the communicative distance, while its frequency is significantly lower in those texts belonging to the communicative immediacy.

Ultimately, with this corpus-based study we aim to make a contribution to the research of learnèd borrowings in Spanish Golden-Age literature.

Keywords

Lexical borrowing, Latin, Historical sociolinguistics, Corpus, Spanish Golden-Age literature.

1 Introducción

El *Retrato de la Loçana andaluza* (en adelante, *RLA*) fue escrito en Roma (1524) por Francisco Delicado y publicado en Venecia de manera anónima, posiblemente en 1530. En esta obra literaria su autor pretende retratar la lengua hablada de sus variados personajes (139, según el estudio de Díaz-Bravo 2019a, 191–198), desde una perspectiva geográfica y social, y teniendo en cuenta diferentes variedades o tipos discursivos. Por tanto, *RLA* es una fuente ideal para el estudio de la variación lingüística del español del siglo XVI (Díaz-Bravo 2019b, 1197). Por otra parte, Delicado —humanista, corrector de imprenta en Venecia y autor polígrafo que escribe en español, italiano y latín— posee la conciencia lingüística característica de un autor literario y cercana a la de un gramático del Siglo de Oro (Díaz-Bravo 2019c).

En este capítulo presentamos un estudio de los cultismos en *RLA*, siguiendo un enfoque propio de la sociolingüística histórica. Partimos de la hipótesis de que Delicado usa un mayor número de cultismos para la caracterización de los personajes cultos y de los textos menos afines a la inmediatez comunicativa (por ejemplo, narraciones), que él mismo escribe como autor literario.

En este estudio, entendemos por "cultismos" préstamos del latín (incluidos los préstamos del griego al latín), normalmente denominados así porque se considera que fueron introducidos en la lengua receptora por una élite culta (Pountain 2011, 628). Siguiendo a Pountain (2020, 177), lo definiremos de la siguiente manera:

> "Para nosotros el cultismo es simplemente un préstamo del latín que se reconoce generalmente por constituir una excepción a los cambios fonéticos esperados, por aparecer por primera vez en una fecha relativamente tardía, muchas veces en obras de autores conocidos por su afán de introducir tales préstamos, o en registros especializados o técnicos del idioma, y por pertenecer a un campo semántico más bien intelectual y abstracto, en el que mantiene su significado latino."

De este modo, se han considerado cultismos[1] palabras como, por ejemplo, *agricultura, concubina, fábula, filosofía, mérito, patria* o *salutífera*, mientras que se han excluido voces que no cumplen alguno de los criterios expuestos en la cita anterior:

---

[1] Para la identificación de cultismos en *RLA*, se han consultado diccionarios latinos (fundamentalmente, Lewis y Short 1879) y del español (*NTLLE, DLE*), etimológicos (Corominas y Pascual 1980–1991), corpus diacrónicos del español (*CORDE* y *CDE*), así como obras especializadas en cultismos (Bustos Tovar 1974, Clavería 1991).

a. Ausencia de cambios fonéticos propios de la evolución del latín al castellano: por ejemplo, se han descartado formas que presentan reducción del grupo consonántico culto -*CT*- en *letores, manifatura* o *senetud*.
b. Fecha de aparición relativamente tardía: se han excluido términos cuya primera fecha de aparición (según el *CORDE*) se documenta en los orígenes del idioma (*causa*) o en la primera mitad del siglo XII (*candela, ventura*).
c. Significado generalmente abstracto: se han descartado palabras que no poseen un significado abstracto, como el caso de *cámara* 'habitación' o *secreta* 'letrina'.

2 Descripción del corpus y variables de análisis (sociolingüística histórica)

RLA es una obra literaria de gran riqueza para la realización de estudios de sociolingüística histórica como el que se presenta en este capítulo, debido, principalmente, a la variedad de personajes y de tipos discursivos.

Por una parte, el libro posee una estructura compleja, pues el *Retrato* propiamente dicho (la novela dialogada) está precedido y seguido por paratextos que representan diversos tipos discursivos, como epístolas y textos epilogales (véase Díaz-Bravo 2019b, 1197). El *Retrato*, a su vez, está dividido en tres partes y en sesenta y seis mamotretos en los que ocurre la trama. La protagonista, la prostituta Lozana, entabla conversación con personajes de diversa procedencia geográfica y condición social en espacios públicos, privados e íntimos. A través de los diálogos conocemos elementos de la vida cotidiana de la Roma de aquella época.

Delicado se sirve del recurso literario de la mímesis de la oralidad para la caracterización de sus personajes (Díaz-Bravo 2010, 2019a, 2019b), incluidos los personajes cultos. En *RLA* encontramos personajes con diferentes niveles educativos: analfabetos, letrados (en su sentido arcaico: 'que sabe leer', *DLE*, s.v.) y cultos, así como personajes cuyos datos no son suficientes para descifrar su nivel de educación. Su distribución aparece recogida en la Figura 12.1:

Nivel educativo	N° de personajes	Porcentaje
culto	13	9.35
letrado	8	5.76
analfabeto	62	44.60
desconocido	56	40.29
TOTAL	139	100.00

Figura 12.1. Distribución de personajes según el nivel educativo

Recabar dicha información sobre cada personaje resulta una tarea compleja. No obstante, el nombre de los personajes, con frecuencia, constituye un dato clave para la interpretación de su condición social. Así, muchos tienen como nombre el oficio que desempeñan, lo cual sirve para identificar su nivel educativo (cf. Díaz-Bravo 2010, 186–189). En el caso de los personajes cultos (todos hombres), encontramos médicos (Físico/Médico, Médico —Arresto—, Cirúgico), abogados (Notario, Jurista, Cursor), clérigos (el cardenal Monseñor), nobles (la alta nobleza: Enbaxador, Comendador y Coronel), así como el autor y sus amigos (Autor/Auctor y Silvio/Conpañero, Silvano). Silvio es quien le da noticias de Lozana a Autor por primera vez; sus intervenciones se limitan al mamotreto XXIV. Debe destacarse el hecho de que cuando el autor pretende retratar el modo de hablar de un personaje por una característica concreta, suele resaltar ese rasgo. Por ello, al retratar a Silvano como un personaje culto, lo presenta como un buen lector:

(1)

LOÇANA: Mi señor, no sea mañana ni el sábado, que terné priessa, pero sea el domingo a çená y todo el lunes, porque quiero que me leáys, vos que tenéys graçia, las coplas de Fajardo y la comedia Tinalaria y a Çelestina, que huelgo de oýr leer estas cosas muncho. SILUANO: ¿Tiénela vuestra merçed en casa? LOÇANA: Señor: velda aquí. Mas no me la leen a mi modo, como haréys vos. (*Lozana Digital*, fol. 38r).

La Figura 12.2 presenta un resumen de los personajes cultos en *RLA*:

alter ego de Delicado (3)	Silvio/Conpañero Silvano Autor/Auctor
médicos (3)	Físico/Médico Médico (Arresto) Cirúgico
abogados (3)	Notario Jurista Cursor
clérigos (1)	Monseñor
nobles (3)	Enbaxador Comendador Coronel

Figura 12.2. Personajes cultos en *RLA*[2]

---

[2] Nótese que el nombre asignado a algunos personajes cultos es un cultismo, en concreto: *Auctor, Físico, Médico, Notario* y *Cursor*.

Por otra parte, *RLA* presenta una gran riqueza discursiva, pues encontramos numerosos tipos textuales situados gradualmente en diversos puntos del *continuum* existente entre el polo de la inmediatez y de la distancia comunicativas (Koch y Oesterreicher 2007), como se resume en la Figura 12.3:

Grupos de variedades discursivas	Variedades discursivas
Grupo oral (polo de la inmediatez comunicativa)	Interacción oral prototípica[3]
	Narración oral
Grupo intermedio oral (cercano a la inmediatez comunicativa)	Diálogo argumentativo
	Diálogo expositivo
	Diálogo narrativo
	La reproducción oral del discurso referido en estilo directo
Grupo intermedio escrito (cercano a la distancia comunicativa)	Aparte
	Monólogo
	Epístola
Grupo escrito (polo de la distancia comunicativa)	Narración – títulos
	Narración
	Exposición
	Argumentación

Figura 12.3. Variedades discursivas en *RLA*, adaptado de Díaz-Bravo (2010, 239; 2019b, 1197)

3 Metodología

Todos los datos ofrecidos en este trabajo se han obtenido a partir de *LD*. *Lozana Digital* (Díaz-Bravo y Vaamonde 2019, en adelante *LD*), un recurso electrónico que combina una edición digital de *RLA* con un corpus anotado y especialmente diseñado para realizar análisis lingüísticos de esta obra. Nos limitaremos a exponer algunas cuestiones técnicas de carácter general para centrarnos a continuación en los aspectos metodológicos que consideramos más relevantes para los intereses de este estudio. Entre estos aspectos, cobra especial importancia la marcación de la información lingüística y extralingüística que nos ha permitido obtener los resultados aquí presentados y

---

[3] Véanse Díaz-Bravo (2010: 221–27), Díaz-Bravo y Fernández Alcaide (2018: 362).

que pueden organizarse en tres subapartados: marcación de cultismos, tipo discursivo y nivel educativo de los personajes.

3.1 Cuestiones generales

Prácticamente toda la información que permite generar la edición digital y el corpus lingüístico de *LD* está almacenada en un único archivo electrónico. Este archivo contiene la transcripción del texto de *RLA*, basada en la edición crítica de Díaz-Bravo (2019), así como la marcación en lenguaje XML-TEI de diferentes aspectos textuales y metatextuales de la obra.

Tanto para la visualización de la edición digital como para la creación y explotación del corpus, *LD* utiliza la plataforma TEITOK (Janssen 2014), un sistema web especialmente pensado para ver, crear y editar corpus a partir de datos estructurados en lenguaje XML-TEI. TEITOK genera un corpus lingüístico que permite realizar búsquedas basadas en la información previamente marcada en lenguaje XML-TEI. En el nivel textual, la unidad básica es el *token* (*i. e.* palabras y signos de puntuación), que TEITOK marca automáticamente con el elemento <tok>. A partir de aquí, el sistema permite aplicar diferentes herramientas automáticas, como son un normalizador ortográfico, un etiquetador morfosintáctico y un lematizador, y genera un resultado que es almacenado en el propio archivo XML mediante atributos del elemento <tok> (@nform, @pos y @lemma, respectivamente). Por ejemplo, la expresión *Gente contra gente, terremotos, hambre, pestilencia* (folio 53v, línea 1) sería procesada en TEITOK del modo siguiente:

```
1   <tok lemma="gente" pos="NCFS000">Gente</tok>
2   <tok lemma="contra" pos="S">contra</tok>
3   <tok lemma="gente" pos="NCFS000">gente</tok>
4   <tok lemma="," pos="Fc">,</tok>
5   <tok pos="NCMP000" lemma="terremoto">terremotos</tok>
6   <tok lemma="," pos="Fc">,</tok>
7   <tok nform="hambre" lemma="hambre" pos="NCFS000">hanbre</tok>
8   <tok lemma="," pos="Fc">,</tok>
9   <tok nform="pestilencia" lemma="pestilencia" pos="NCFS000">pestilençia</tok>
```

Figura 12.4. Fragmento *tokenizado* y anotado en *LD. Lozana Digital*

Nótese que, una vez procesado el texto de esta forma, se puede obtener información de diferente tipo: una lista con los lemas más frecuentes del corpus, el conjunto de sustantivos comunes de género masculino o las variantes ortográficas de la palabra *hambre*, por citar algunos ejemplos. A ello cabría sumar cuanta información textual y metatexual se haya decidido marcar previamente en el archivo XML. En otras palabras, aumentar la marcación en el archivo XML supone aumentar la información que es importada al corpus lingüístico, lo que se traduce, en definitiva, en mayores opciones de búsqueda.

3.2 Marcación de cultismos

Entre la información con la que hemos enriquecido nuestros datos, la marcación de cultismos constituye un aspecto clave en nuestro estudio. Una vez decidida la noción de cultismo se procedió a rastrear los casos atestiguados en *RLA*. En términos de XML, esta información se marcó mediante un atributo @lform (*learnèd form*) asociado al *token* correspondiente. Por ejemplo, la expresión *le sean notorios los sacros derechos* (folio 54r) se marcaría del modo siguiente:

```
<tok lemma="le" pos="PP3CSD">le</tok>
<tok lemma="ser" pos="VSSP3P0">sean</tok>
<tok lemma="notorio" pos="NCMP000" lform="notorios">notorios</tok>
<tok lemma="el" pos="DA0MP0">los</tok>
<tok lemma="sacro" pos="AQMP00" lform="sacros">sacros</tok>
<tok lemma="derecho" pos="NCMS000">derechos</tok>
```

Figura 12.5. Marcación de cultismos en *LD. Lozana Digital*

Nótese que los *tokens notorios* y *sacros* incluyen un atributo @lform cuyo valor, en ambos casos, repite la forma transcrita en el original. De esta manera, queda constancia del carácter de cultismo de ambas formas para que esta información sea potencialmente recuperable en el corpus.

3.3 Marcación del tipo discursivo

Como ya se ha mencionado previamente, en este trabajo se analiza la distribución de cultismos en *RLA*. Para explicar esta distribución se han considerado fundamentalmente dos variables: el tipo o segmento discursivo en que aparece el cultismo y el nivel educativo del personaje que lo utiliza. Para el análisis de la primera variable, se ha partido de la clasificación recogida en la Figura 12.6, de modo que todo fragmento en la obra está asociado a una (y solo una) de las siguientes categorías, anteriormente mencionadas.

Tipo discursivo		Código
Argumentación		(A)Arg
Exposición		(E)Exp
Narración	Narración	(N)Narr
	Títulos	(N)Tit
Epístola	Epístola	(C)For
Monólogo	Monólogo	(M)Mon
	Aparte	(M)Ap
Diálogo	Interacción oral prototípica	(D)Iop
	Diálogo argumentativo	(D)Arg
	Diálogo expositivo o descriptivo	(D)Exp
	Diálogo en función narrativa — Reproducción oral del discurso referido en estilo directo	(D)Ned
	Diálogo en función narrativa — Narración oral	(D)Nor
	Diálogo en función narrativa — Diálogo narrativo	(D)Narr

Figura 12.6. Marcación de tipos discursivos en *LD. Lozana Digital*, clasificación adaptada de Díaz-Bravo (2010, 110)

Para la marcación de los tipos discursivos se utilizó el elemento <seg> combinado con los atributos @type y @subtype, como se muestra en el siguiente ejemplo, cuya marcación XML se ha simplificado por razones de claridad (folio 50v, líneas 43–45):

```
<seg type="D" subtype="Iop">
No aya vuestra merçed miedo que yo jamás lo descubra.
</seg>

<seg type="D" subtype="Narr">
Señora, bien que me veys ansí solo no só de los ýnfimos de mi tierra, mas la honrra me costriñe, que, si pudiese, querría salir con vna apuesta que con otros hize, y es que, si venía a Roma con dinero, que ordenaua mi Robusto de bacalario. [...]
</seg>
```

Figura 12.7. Marcación de tipos discursivos en *LD. Lozana Digital*

Al tratarse de un diálogo entre dos personajes, ambos segmentos están marcados con el código D, como muestra el atributo @type. No obstante, el primero de ellos constituye un caso de interacción oral prototípica (Iop), mientras que el segundo se ha tratado como diálogo narrativo (Narr), como se aprecia en el atributo @subtype.

3.4 Marcación de los rasgos de personajes

La segunda variable que se ha tenido en cuenta en este estudio está relacionada con el nivel educativo de cada personaje. En *LD*, las intervenciones de los personajes se han marcado con un elemento <sp> (*speech*), que consta de diferentes atributos para dar cuenta de los rasgos esenciales asociados a ese personaje, a saber: nivel educativo (@educ), estatus social (@stratum), género (@sex) y lugar (@place). Por tanto, simplificando nuevamente la marcación XML por razones de claridad, el fragmento anterior quedaría del modo siguiente (Figura 12.8):

```
1   <sp educ="analfabeto" stratum="no privilegiado" sex="mujer" place="Cordoba" who="#lozana">
2       <seg type="D" subtype="Iop">
3       No aya vuestra merçed miedo que yo jamás lo descubra.
4       </seg>
5   </sp>
6
7   <sp educ="letrado" stratum="noble" sex="hombre" place="desconocido" who="#porfirio">
8       <seg type="D" subtype="Narr">
9       Señora, bien que me veys ansí solo no só de los ynfimos de mi tierra, mas la
10      honrra me costriñe, que, si pudiese, querría salir con vna apuesta que con otros
11      hize, y es que, si venía a Roma con dinero, que ordenaua mi Robusto de
12      bacalario [...]
13      </seg>
14  </sp>
```

Figura 12.8. Marcación de los rasgos de personajes en *LD*. *Lozana Digital*

4 Resultados y análisis

Se han contabilizado un total de 401 ocurrencias de formas cultas en *LD* (*i. e.* *tokens*), que se distribuyen en 225 palabras diferentes (*i. e.* tipos). Se han descartado del recuento aquellas formas cultas que presentan más de 10 ocurrencias en el corpus,[4] pues en tales casos se ha entendido que su frecuencia de uso en la obra era un indicio de su difusión en la época, como se ha comprobado al consultar la frecuencia por siglos en el *CDE*.

De los 401 cultismos registrados, 258 aparecen en boca de algún personaje y, por tanto, podrían ser interpretados como un recurso caracterizador. El resto de

---

[4] Se trata de palabras como *contento* o *médico*. Siguiendo el criterio de una frecuencia mayor a 10 ocurrencias, también se ha eliminado del recuento la palabra *mamotreto* (Wislocka Breit, en prensa, estudia este cultismo y lo interpreta como 'cartapacio' en *RLA*), incluida en el título de cada uno de los 66 mamotretos del Retrato, así como *máxime*, con 17 ocurrencias, pues hemos concluido que se trata de una palabra característica del idiolecto de Delicado, usada en boca de cualquier personaje y en diversas variedades discursivas.

Los cultismos en una novela dialogada del siglo XVI

los cultismos (143) se distribuye en pasajes no dialogados ni monologados de la obra. Los primeros admiten una distribución por personaje, tal como se muestra en la Figura 12.9:

Nombre del personaje	N° de cultismos	Porcentaje	Porcentaje acumulado
Lozana	107	41.47	41.47
Silvano	50	19.38	60.85
Autor	18	6.98	67.83
Rampín	10	3.88	71.71
Médico (Arresto)	9	3.49	75.20
Valijero	8	3.10	78.30
Divicia	7	2.71	81.01
Sagüeso	4	1.55	82.56
Otros	45	17.44	100.00
TOTAL	258	100.00	100.00

Figura 12.9. Distribución de cultismos por personaje

Como se puede apreciar, más del 80% de los cultismos identificados en la obra se reparten entre siete personajes, lo que sugiere que, de ser cierto que las formas cultas constituyen un recurso literario del autor para caracterizar a sus personajes, su explotación se circunscribe a un número reducido de personajes; más precisamente, y de manera muy significativa, a Auctor y a Silvano, que representan el *alter ego* del propio Delicado. Recordemos que Silvano es presentado como un buen lector y que la lengua es uno de los recursos más poderosos para caracterizar a los personajes en una obra literaria (Bubnova 1987, 182). La siguiente intervención de Silvano ilustra un número elevado de cultismos (destacados en negrita) como forma de caracterización de este personaje:

(2)

SILUANO: **Finalmente**, es vna felice **patria** donde, siendo el rey, **personalmente** mandó despeñar los dos ermanos Carauajales, ombres **anímosíssimos**, acusados **falsamente** de tiranos, la **cuia sepultura** o **mausoleo** permanece en la capilla de Todos Santos, que antiguamente se dezía la Santa Santorum, y son en la dicha capilla los huesos de **fortíssimos** reyes y animossos maestres de la dicha orden de Calatraua. (*LD*, fols. 37v–38r).

En este fragmento encontramos, además, otros de los recursos usados por Delicado para caracterizar a sus personajes cultos (Díaz-Bravo 2019a, 19–20): adverbios terminados en -*mente* (*finalmente, personalmente, falsamente, antiguamente*), el sufijo superlativo -*ísimo* y su paradigma (*animossísimos, fortíssimos*), el relativo *cuyo* y su paradigma (*cuia*) y la lengua latina (en este caso, se observa el latinismo morfológico *Santorum*, cuyo sufijo marca el genitivo plural). Se trata de un pasaje en que Delicado, a través del personaje Silvano, demuestra sus conocimientos históricos sobre la Peña de Martos (Jaén, Andalucía), patria chica del autor, descrita con elogios hiperbólicos.

Por otro lado, Lozana es el personaje que utiliza un mayor número de formas cultas con acusada diferencia con respecto al resto (107), pues es también el personaje que tiene una mayor presencia en la obra. Asimismo, es llamativo que Rampín (pareja/criado de Lozana), el personaje con un mayor número de *tokens* en la obra tras Lozana, sea el cuarto personaje en el empleo de cultismos (10 en total), así como que otros personajes analfabetos como la vieja prostituta Divicia (jubilada) y el vagabundo Sagüeso aparezcan entre los ocho personajes que usan más cultismos, con 7 y 4 ocurrencias, respectivamente. En la Figura 12.10 se ofrece el número total de *tokens* del corpus, distribuidos por personaje:

Nombre del personaje	N° de *tokens*	Porcentaje	Porcentaje acumulado
Lozana	33620	47.79	47.79
Rampín	5019	7.13	54.92
Autor	2962	4.21	59.13
Valijero	1786	2.54	61.67
Silvano	1711	2.43	64.10
Lavandera	1521	2.16	66.26
Compañero Valerián	1285	1.83	68.09
Judío	1053	1.49	69.58
Sagüeso	1021	1.45	71.03
Divicia	976	1.39	72.42
Otros	19402	27.58	100.00
TOTAL	70356	100.00	100.00

Figura 12.10. Distribución de *tokens* por personaje

Para la interpretación de estos datos, no resulta casual el extenso diálogo que tiene lugar entre Loçana, Divicia y Sagüeso en la tercera parte, en el que Delicado de nuevo intenta demostrar sus conocimientos sobre diversos temas (la historia y peligros del Río Tíber o el origen de la sífilis) y alabar la ciudad en la que reside (Roma) y su pueblo (la Peña de Martos), como ilustra (3). En este diálogo narrativo sobre el origen de la plaga del mal francés 'sífilis', Divicia usa seis cultismos (destacados en negrita), entre los que se incluyen dos adjetivos terminados con el sufijo superlativo *-ísimo* y un participio de presente (*yncontinente*).

(3)

    LOÇANA: [...] Dime, Diuçia, ¿dónde començó o fue el prinçipio del mal francés? DIUÇIA: En Rapolo, vna villa de Génoua, y es puerto de mar, porque allí mataron los pobres de San Lázaro y dieron a saco los soldados del rei Carlo **christianíssimo** de Françia aquella tierra y las casas de San Lázaro, y vno que vendió vn colchón por vn ducado, como se lo pusieron en la mano, le salío vna buuua ansí redonda como el ducado, que por esso son redondas. Después aquel lo pegó a quantos tocó con aquella mano y luego **yncontinente** se sentían los dolores **acerbíssimos** y **lunáticos**, que yo me hallé allí y lo vi; que por esso se dize "el Señor te guarde de su ira", que es esta **plaga**, que el **sexto** ángel deramó sobre casi la metad de la tierra. (*LD*, fol. 43r).

La Figura 12.11 incluye el número de cultismos usados por personajes cultos. Además de los datos comentados anteriormente, debemos destacar la presencia de los tres médicos que aparecen en *RLA* (Médico Arresto, Físico y Çirúgico), así como de Silvio, amigo del Autor/Auctor.

Personajes cultos	N°
Silvano	50
Autor	18
Médico (Arresto)	9
Físico	3
Silvio	2
Cirúgico	1

Figura 12.11. Distribución de cultismos por parte de personajes cultos

En cualquier caso, y más allá del análisis de personajes concretos, resulta interesante agruparlos por nivel educativo. De esta forma, podemos comprobar si la presencia de formas cultas es más acusada en personajes con un alto nivel educativo, y viceversa, si en personajes analfabetos desciende el número de cultismos. La Figura 12.12 muestra esta distribución, contabilizando nuevamente solo los 258 cultismos que aparecen en boca de algún personaje, esto es, en pasajes dialogados o monologados de la obra. La primera columna informa sobre el nivel educativo de acuerdo con la clasificación expuesta anteriormente. La segunda columna informa sobre el número total de *tokens* registrados en el corpus. La tercera columna informa sobre el número total de *tokens* marcados como cultismo. La cuarta y última columna ofrece el porcentaje de cultismos por nivel educativo de los personajes:

Nivel educativo	N° de *tokens*	N° de cultismos	Porcentaje
culto	6783	83	1.22
letrado	2550	7	0.27
analfabeto	50898	140	0.28
desconocido	10125	28	0.28
TOTAL	70356	258	0.37

Figura 12.12. Distribución de cultismos según el nivel educativo de los personajes

Por ejemplo, se registran 6783 *tokens* en boca de personajes cultos, de los cuales se identifican 83 cultismos. Por tanto, el porcentaje de cultismos en personajes cultos representa un 1,22% respecto al total de *tokens*. La tabla muestra claramente que la frecuencia relativa de cultismos en personajes cultos es la más alta, mientras que la frecuencia relativa de cultismos en letrados y analfabetos es prácticamente idéntica. Este hecho sugiere que Delicado utiliza las formas cultas para caracterizar a personajes cultos, pero no a personajes letrados, en donde la presencia de cultismos resulta casi testimonial.

Para comprobar si existe una asociación estadísticamente significativa entre el uso de cultismos y el nivel educativo resulta adecuado agrupar los datos de la tabla anterior en una tabla de contingencia como la que se ofrece a continuación (Figura 12.13). En esta tabla se comparan únicamente los datos relativos a personajes cultos frente a personajes analfabetos. La prueba del chi-cuadrado confirma que existe una asociación estadísticamente significativa entre ambas variables:

	Cultismos	No cultismos	TOTAL
personajes cultos	83	6700	6783
personajes analfabetos	140	50758	50898
TOTAL	223	57458	57681

χ^2= 139.847, valor p < 0.001

Figura 12.13. Cultismos y no cultismos en personajes cultos y analfabetos

La segunda variable que nos proponemos analizar en este estudio tiene que ver con el tipo discursivo en que se distribuyen los cultismos. Se espera que las formas cultas tengan una mayor presencia dentro de la obra en aquellos tipos discursivos más próximos a la distancia comunicativa, y que su uso se vea reducido en los tipos discursivos más próximos a la inmediatez comunicativa. Para analizar esta segunda variable se ha podido utilizar el total de cultismos registrados en la obra (401), puesto que toda la obra está organizada en tipos discursivos. La Figura 12.14 muestra la distribución de cultismos en función de cuatro bloques fundamentales, de acuerdo con la clasificación expuesta en la Figura 12.3 (§2):

Tipo discursivo	N° de *tokens*	N° de cultismos	Porcentaje
grupo I escrito	5843	72	1.23
grupo II intermedio escrito	5451	82	1.50
grupo III: intermedio oral	22250	170	0.76
grupo IV: oral	45292	77	0.17
TOTAL	78836	401	0.50

Figura 12.14. Distribución de cultismos según el tipo discursivo

Por ejemplo, se registran 5843 *tokens* en segmentos discursivos que fueron clasificados dentro del bloque grupo I, de los cuales se han identificado 72 cultismos. Por tanto, el porcentaje de formas cultas localizadas en segmentos discursivos del grupo I representa un 1.23% respecto al total de *tokens* contabilizados en dicho grupo. Los datos de esta tabla indican claramente que la frecuencia relativa de cultismos en los grupos I y II, que son los más próximos a la distancia comunicativa, es mayor que la frecuencia relativa de cultismos en los dos grupos restantes, más próximos a la inmediatez comunicativa. Los datos sugieren, por tanto, que Delicado tiene en cuenta el tipo discursivo a la hora de utilizar formas cultas, restringiendo su uso cuando el tipo de discurso está más estrechamente relacionado con la dimensión de lo hablado (*i. e.* interacción oral prototípica y narración oral).

De nuevo, agrupamos los datos de la tabla anterior en una tabla de contingencia para comprobar si existe una asociación estadísticamente significativa entre el uso de cultismos y el tipo discursivo (Figura 12.15). Hemos fusionado los datos correspondientes a los grupos I y II en una única fila, y lo mismo con los datos relativos a los grupos III y IV. Obtenemos de esta forma una tabla de 2x2 con una variable independiente (el tipo discursivo) que adopta dos valores: distancia e inmediatez comunicativa. La prueba del estadístico chi-cuadrado confirma nuevamente que existe una asociación estadísticamente significativa entre ambas variables:

	Cultismos	No cultismos	TOTAL
Distancia comunicativa (Grupos I y II)	154	11140	11294
Inmediatez comunicativa (Grupos III y IV)	247	67295	67542
TOTAL	401	78435	78836

$\chi^2 = 190.383$, valor $p < 0.001$

Figura 12.15. Cultismos y no cultismos en discursos de distancia e inmediatez comunicativas

En cualquier caso, en la interpretación de los datos también debemos tener en cuenta que se trata de una oralidad fingida o elaborada (Del Rey Quesada 2019), pues nos encontramos ante un texto literario en el que "es el autor del texto, o sea, la conciencia lingüística del autor, la que selecciona ciertos rasgos lingüísticos considerados característicos de la lengua hablada" (Oesterreicher 2004, 756).

Por otra parte, en ocasiones, el cultismo se usa con una finalidad cómica, como en el siguiente ejemplo:

(4)
    DIUIÇIA: ¡Calla, puta de quis vel qui! LOÇANA: ¡Y tú puta de tres **quadragenas** menos vna! (*LD*, fol. 42v).

Con estas palabras irónicas usadas en un breve fragmento de interacción oral prototípica, Lozana llama 'vieja' a la prostituta Divicia, "'puta de tres cuarentenas menos una', o sea 'de ochenta años'" (Joset y Gernert 2007, 266).

5 Conclusiones

Este estudio consiste en un análisis de los cultismos en el *Retrato de la Loçana andaluza* siguiendo un enfoque de sociolingüística histórica y teniendo en cuenta las siguientes variables: nivel de educación de los personajes y tipo discursivo. Somos conscientes de que el número de cultismos con respecto al corpus es reducido, pero su estudio arroja resultados interesantes. El total de *tokens* correspondiente tanto a personajes cultos como a textos de la distancia comunicativa es bastante inferior al de personajes analfabetos y al de fragmentos de inmediatez comunicativa, respectivamente.

No obstante, fijándonos en las frecuencias relativas, se ha demostrado que las dos variables estudiadas son estadísticamente significativas. En cuanto al nivel educativo de los personajes, es fundamental destacar que —con la excepción de Lozana, cuyo número de *tokens* se corresponde con casi la mitad de la totalidad de la obra— Auctor y su amigo Silvano, presentado explícitamente como un buen lector conocedor de obras literarias de la época, usan el mayor número de cultismos tanto en datos absolutos como relativos. Con respecto a las variedades discursivas, destaca la escasa cantidad de cultismos (en términos de frecuencia relativa) en las variedades más afines a la inmediatez comunicativa, es decir, la interacción oral prototípica y la narración oral, frente a un número mayor de cultismos en el resto de variedades, especialmente en los grupos de la distancia comunicativa (entre los que se incluyen las epístolas, narraciones y textos epilogales del autor).

En definitiva, con este trabajo pretendemos realizar una aportación al estudio de los cultismos en la literatura del siglo XVI desde una perspectiva de la sociolingüística histórica.

Referencias bibliográficas

Bubnova, Tatiana. 1987. *F. Delicado puesto en diálogo: las claves bajtinianas de «La Lozana andaluza»*. Ciudad de México: Universidad Autónoma de México.

Bustos Tovar, José Jesús. 1974. *Contribución al estudio del cultismo léxico medieval (1140–1252)*. Madrid: Anejo XXVIII del *Boletín de la Real Academia Española*.

CDE = Davies, Mark. 2002–. Corpus del Español: 100 million words, 1200s–1900s. Fecha de consulta marzo 2020. http://www.corpusdelespanol.org.

Clavería Nadal, Gloria. 1991. *El latinismo en español*. Barcelona: Universitat Autònoma de Barcelona.

CORDE = Real Academia Española. Banco de datos (CORDE). Corpus diacrónico del español. Fecha de consulta marzo de 2020. http://www.rae.es.

Corominas, Joan, y José Antonio Pascual. 1980–1991. *Diccionario crítico etimológico castellano e hispánico*. Madrid: Gredos.

Del Rey Quesada, Santiago. 2019. "Variantes de la oralidad elaborada en la segunda mitad del siglo XIX: dos traducciones coetáneas de «Los Cautivos» de Plauto." *Oralia: Análisis del discurso oral*, 22.2: 283–326.

DLE = Asociación de Academias de la Lengua Española. 2014–. *Diccionario de la lengua española*, 23ª ed. Madrid: Espasa. Fecha de consulta marzo de 2020. https://dle.rae.es.

Díaz-Bravo, Rocío. 2010. *Estudio de la oralidad en el «Retrato de la Loçana andaluza» (Roma, 1524)*. Málaga: Universidad de Málaga.

Díaz-Bravo, Rocío. 2019a. *Francisco Delicado, «Retrato de la Loçana andaluza»: Estudio y edición crítica*. Cambridge: Modern Humanities Research Association (vol. 56).

Díaz-Bravo, Rocío. 2019b. "Study of Medial and Conceptional Orality in the Retrato de la Loçana andaluza." *Bulletin of Hispanic Studies*, 96:10, 1191–1217.

Díaz-Bravo, Rocío. 2019c. "La conciencia lingüística del autor andaluz Francisco Delicado." En *Quan sabias e quam maestras: Disquisiciones de lengua española*, editado por Diana Esteba Ramos, Manuel Galeote, Livia C. García Aguiar, Pilar López Mora y Sara Robles Ávila, 139–156. Málaga: Universidad de Málaga.

Díaz-Bravo, Rocío, y Gael Vaamonde. 2019. LD. Lozana Digital. Granada: Universidad de Granada. Fecha de consulta marzo de 2020. http://corpora.ugr.es/lozana/.

Díaz-Bravo, Rocío, y Marta Fernández Alcaide (2018). "La oralidad en el siglo XVI. Lo literario y lo privado (I). Marcadores discursivos." Bulletin of Hispanic Studies, 95, 357–381.

Gernert, Folke, y Jacques Joset (eds.). 2013. *La Lozana andaluza*, edición de Folke Gernert y Jacques Joset. Madrid: Real Academia Española / Barcelona: Galaxia Gutenberg, Círculo de Lectores, Biblioteca Clásica de la Real Academia Española, vol. 22.

Janssen, Maarten. 2014. TEITOK. A Tokenized TEI environment. Fecha de consulta marzo de 2020. http://teitok.corpuswiki.org/site/index.php.

Koch, Peter, y Wulf Oesterreicher. 2007 [1990]. *Lengua hablada en la Romania: español, francés, italiano*. Traducido por Araceli López Serena, *Gesprochene Sprache in der Romania, Französisch, Italienisch, Spanisch* [Tubinga: Max Niemeyer Verlag]. Madrid: Gredos.

Lewis, Charlton Thomas and Charles Short. 1879. *A Latin Dictionary*. Oxford: Clarendon Press. Fecha de consulta marzo de 2020. https://www.latinitium.com/latin-dictionaries.

NTLLE = Real Academia Española and Asociación de Academias de la Lengua Española. 2001. *Nuevo Tesoro Lexicográfico de la Lengua Española*. Fecha de consulta marzo de 2020. http://ntlle.rae.es/ntlle/SrvltGUILoginNtlle.

Oesterreicher, Wulf. 2004. "Textos entre inmediatez y distancia comunicativas. El problema de lo hablado escrito en el Siglo de Oro." En *Historia de la lengua española*, editado por Rafael Cano Aguilar, 729–769. Barcelona: Ariel.

Pountain, Christopher J. 2011. "Latin and the Structure of Written Romance." En *The Cambridge History of the Romance Languages. Volume I: Structures*, editado por Martin Maiden, John Charles Smith y Adam Ledgeway, 606–659. Cambridge: Cambridge University Press.

Pountain, Christopher J. 2020. "Mi «último» saludo: historia de un préstamo culto." En *Contigo aprendí: estudios en homenaje al profesor José Luis Caramés Lage*, editado por Carmen Escobedo de Tapia, Jorge Luis Bueno Alonso y Carolina Taboada Ferrero, 177–203. Oviedo: Universidad de Oviedo.

Wislocka Breit, Bozena (en prensa). "La inesperada carrera de *mamotreto* en la lengua española." *Revista de Historia de la Lengua Española.*

Chapter 13

Magic, witches and magicians in a semantic and etymological perspective in European languages

Ingmar Söhrman

Göteborgs Universitet

Summary

The human need to influence and transform nature and reality is one of the oldest activities known. The activity itself has mystic, religious and traditional aspects and its performers have been seen as a resource, often scary and doubtful – but needed. It is quite clear that there have been many cultural and linguistic connections between the Romance cultures and the Germanic and Slavic ones, often based on Roman and Greek perceptions of these lexemes.

This Chapter will try and link these cultural and linguistic connections together and explain what is common and what is unique to each language and also comment on the variety of concepts such as 'sorcerer', 'wizard', 'witch' and 'magician' and how and why they have become parts of the different European languages. There is also a gender perspective. How have female magicians been looked upon in comparison to male ones? What are the differences? And how do are these lexemes used with reference to modern illusionists? What semantic changes have taken place recently?

And finally, how have people connected these lexemes to nature and religion and how are these words used today? Are there semantic changes or do the notions remain the same? How are these concepts used nowadays in fantasy literature and magic entertainment? Have they semantically changed these words? What are the linguistic and semantic connections between these words in different languages, and how are they related?

Resumen

La necesidad humana de influir y transformar la naturaleza y la realidad es una de las actividades más antiguas que conocemos. La actividad misma tiene aspectos de carácter místico, religioso y tradicional a la vez que se ha considerado a los que practican la magia como un recurso dudoso que con frecuencia da miedo – pero que también se necesita. Queda claro que ha habido muchas conexiones culturales y lingüísticas entre las culturas románicas y las germánicas y eslavas, que muchas veces se basan en la percepción romana y griega de estos lexemas.

En este capítulo la intención es intentar conectar estos contactos culturales y lingüísticos y explicar lo que es común y lo que es único en cada idioma y también comentar la gran variedad de conceptos como 'hechicero', 'brujo', 'bruja' y 'mago' y cómo y por qué estas palabras se han transformado en partes lexicales constituyentes de diferentes lenguas europeas. Hay además una perspectiva de género. ¿Cómo se han visto las magas en comparación con los magos? ¿Cuáles han sido las diferencias? Y ¿cómo usamos estos lexemas con referencia a los ilusionistas modernos? ¿Cuáles han sido los cambios semánticos recientes?

Y, finalmente, estos lexemas ¿cómo se han conectado con la naturaleza y con la religión, y cómo se usan hoy en día? ¿Existen cambios semánticos o se conservan los sentidos antiguos? ¿Cómo se usan hoy en la literatura fantástica y en los espectáculos de entretenimiento? ¿Han cambiado semánticamente? ¿Cuáles son las conexiones entre estas voces en diferentes lenguas y cómo están relacionadas?

Keywords

Semantic change, Lexical borrowing, Indo-European languages, Magic.

1 Magic and witchcraft

Humans try to create a world that fits them, and therefore they need to be able to influence, shape and transform their environment and thereby nature. Obviously, magic is one way of doing this, and it is also one of the oldest known human activities (Bates 2002). The activity itself has mystic, religious and traditional aspects, and its performers have been seen as a human resource, often a scary and a doubtful one, but necessary for community life. As Dell

(2018, 7) puts it, "There is no culture on Earth that does not contain within it some form of magic" (see also Stanmore, 2019, and for a more extensive perspective Hubert and Mauss, 1950).

Although there can be a relation between magic and religion, in more intellectualised hermetic religious activities (Dell 2018, 8) there has existed (and still exists) a rejection, especially from the established churches, of mystic religions and beliefs (Hutton 2017, 282–285). However, this bond is stronger in shamanistic nature-orientated religious beliefs. In a very general way it can be said that while religion depends on deities that can be benign and listen to prayers, and thus intervene in human life, and is also there for the benefit of many, magic is based on ritual power where the wizards or witches achieve something through perlocutionary and supernatural means without any divine interference and often for their own good or for a specific person or a restricted group of people (Dell 2018, 811). This could be simplified by saying that any rite which is not part of an organised cult is magic (Hubert and Mauss 1950, 16), but in some cults this is difficult to uphold: for example, in voodoo and other shamanistic beliefs.

It is also quite clear that there have been many cultural and linguistic connections between Romance cultures and beliefs and Germanic and Slavic ones, which are often based on Indo-European, Roman and Greek perceptions of these "magic" concepts and their linguistic realisations, i.e. the corresponding lexemes, but the origin of magic and its vocabulary goes much further back, possibly to the dawn of mankind, although nothing is known about this until ancient societies had developed written comments and texts that were transferred to new generations.

One example that captures the eye is that the abilities to read and write were related early on to magic and the practitioners of this "power". In many ancient religions, the God of scripture and reading was also the God of magic, whether these texts were Runic (Arries 2019, 253–294) or Latin, or in other languages. In any case the texts were incomprehensible to the vast majority of people, and therefore a text *per se* could be seen as a mysterious and magical tool for good or bad.

A result of this conceptual duality is that the Latin word *grammatica* in French not only turned into *grammaire* (> Eng. *grammar*) but also into *grimoire* 'a book of (black) magic and spells' (Rey 1992). This meant that the ability to read and write a particular language (mainly Latin, since most texts were written in Latin at that time) gave the person who knew how to read and write this language a special prestige (and caused envy). Furthermore, Latin texts were incomprehensible for most people and thus possibly psychologically even more related to magic secrets. Therefore, it is striking that these two words, which came from the same Latin lexeme, have such different meanings. Fr. *grimoire* appeared in the fourteenth century (it also yields the seldom-used Sp. *grimorio*). In French, the meaning was extended also to signify 'difficult or incomprehensible book or speech' (Rey 1992). In the nineteenth century it was imported into English with the meaning of 'magic book' (Rey 1992). It is also interesting to see that this word has not spread into other Romance languages (with the exception of Spanish), as is often the case. However, there is a possibility that it is linked to *grimaud* 'student; unpleasant person' (also present in Occitan, meaning 'sorcerer; devil': see de Fourvière 1973) but this seems far-fetched, and the origin of *grimaud* is probably connected to the name *Grimwald* (Rey 1992).

This Chapter will show the cultural and linguistic links pertaining to magic and explain what is common and what is unique to each language and culture; it will also comment on the variety of concepts such as 'sorcerer', 'wizard', 'witch' and 'magician', and how and why they are represented in different European languages. There is not space here to present an exhaustive study covering all European languages and all synonyms and semantically related lexemes, but, nevertheless, the intention is to be precise and reasonably thorough in order to evoke the reader's interest and stimulate further research in the field.

There is also a gender perspective: how have female magicians been looked upon in comparison to male ones? What are the differences between languages, cultures and religions in this respect? I will also include some vocabulary used to refer to entertainers and illusionists (see *La Magia en la BNE*, 2011) through history.

This study is based on Buck (1949), which led me to look for more lexemes that are available in etymological and other dictionaries listed in the bibliography. As it is reasonably easy to find the different instances in these dictionaries, I have not given the page references. All these dictionaries are found in the first part of the bibliography.

2 Different kinds of magicians

Before discussing the words and their etymologies, I must differentiate between several kinds of magicians as a basic cultural background for my purposes. As can be seen, there are two totally different kinds, the "real" magicians and the entertainers, and while there are two or three main varieties of the "real" ones, the illusionists (entertainers) can be divided into many subvarieties (great illusions, stage magic, mentalism, close-up magic, etc.: see Daniel 2013); but that is not really my concern here. However, some main categories can be distinguished, which apply to both male and female practitioners (cf. Hutton 2017, 279):

(1)

Real magicians: people who believe or pretend that they have magic powers, mostly claim to have a special relation to nature (such as shamans, etc.), supernatural forces, gods and/or demons. In many legends they can also transform themselves to animals or humans if they are demons (such as different kinds of *succubi* and *incŭbi*; cf. Rom. *strigoi* and *zmeu*; see Niculae 2017).

  a. *Good ones* (white magic), who try to defend people, help and often heal them, such as Merlin, Gandalf, Polgara, etc. In this category are also wise women and men (medicine women/men) who in bad times can be considered witches or sorceresses and are therefore dangerous just because they feel different and do things most people cannot do.

  b. *Bad ones* (black magic), who serve or are supposed to serve dark forces, such as Morgana le Fay, Voldemort, Circe, Loki and Sidonia von Borck, a typical witch who was burnt for her supposed activities in the seventeenth century.

  c. A third category would be the *seers* or *future-tellers* who look into the future and tell the person who pays them for a vision. They are mainly neutral, not good nor evil. Such were the Greek *oracles* and Norse *Mimir* and *norns*. Eng. *oracle* derives from Lat. *ōrāculum,* from *ōrāre* 'to pray, plead', which has derivatives in many languages (Rey 1992), now mainly used in a metaphoric sense. Oracles are supposed to speak for the gods or to be able to see the future in other ways.

(2)   *Illusionists*, entertainers, who do not seriously claim that they have special powers.[1] There are also testimonies of the existence of this kind already from Antiquity. To this category belong artists such as Paul Daniels, David Copperfield and Juan Tamariz. For many years, women were "just" assistants: it is only recently that there have been more and more excellent female illusionists.

What is interesting is to see how people have connected lexemes that refer to these activities and the practitioners of the different kinds of magic to nature and its forces and linked them to religion throughout history and to see how these words are used today. Are there any semantic changes, or do the notions remain the same through time?

One field where "real" magic remains today is, of course, in literature. An interesting question is how these concepts are used nowadays in fantasy literature, films, games and magic entertainment? How have these words changed semantically? This is not the place to go into the field of the uses of magic, but I will look at the semantic content of words for magic and its few practitioners today as well as those in the past.

3 The origin of *magic* and its practitioners

In Indo-European there must have existed a word **keudes* 'magic force'. In Old Church Slavonic there is a word *čudo* 'miracle, wonder', and this still exists in modern Slavic languages, cf. Russian чудо 'miracle' and Polish *cud*. This word also exists in Greek as κῦδος but with the meaning of 'glory, renown' (Buck 1949; Menge and Gütling 1954); however, Benveniste (1969, part 2, 57ff.) suggests that in Homer this word meant 'the magic force, the irradiation of power a god can bestow upon a king or hero'.

Another lexical option is Indo-European **soito* 'sorcery' (Menge and Gütling 1954), reflexes of which are not uncommon in Indo-European languages (Buck 1949): this is supposed to be the origin of Welsh *hud* 'magic' (where Indo-European /s/ became /h/). In Old Norse there is the word *seið*, cf. Swedish *sejd* 'magic (Hellquist 1957; cf. §5). This is mainly used for future-telling and evil magic to hurt one's enemies. In Old English there is a word

---

[1] This is the reason why so many illusionists were annoyed by Uri Geller, who for many years claimed that he had real magic power.

ælfsiden 'elf magic; fever' that seems to have the same root. This morpheme, *s(e)jd*, may be related to the verb 'bind' in Old Norse *seiðr* and Old English *sāda* 'band, cord'; 'something that binds together'. There is also a vague possibility that it could be related to *-set* in the word *nesset* 'magic' in Tocharian A (Menge and Güthling 1954; Benveniste 1969, vol. 2, 57ff.).

A semantically more interesting lexeme is IE *$*h_xolu$ or *$*alu$ 'spell'. It seems that this is the origin of Hittite *alwanzātar* 'magic', *alwanzena* 'magician' and the feminine counterpart *alwanzenas SAL-za*[2] 'a Sumeric *SAL* woman', i.e. 'witch'. The corresponding verb is *alwanzahh-* 'bewitch' and the poor victim is *alwanza-*.[3] In Greek there is a lexical correspondence: ἀλύω 'to be beside oneself: be bespelled'. This could possibly be related to Scandinavian Runic *alu*, ᚨᛚᚢ,[4] for some kind of 'magic spell'. It seems clear that it meant some kind of charm, although its exact meaning is disputed (MacLeod 2006, 24, 101, 109). In Old Norse there is *Ölrún*, which is formed from *runa* 'letter; secret' and a prefix that could be *alu-* or *ali-*. The meaning of this prefix is debated. However, there is a possibility that it is related to Germanic, Baltic and Slavic words for 'beer'. Brewing is an ancient art, and the brewer was considered a master, who possibly possessed magic in order to get the right flavour. One has only to compare Old English *ealu*, Modern English *ale*, Swedish *öl*, Lithuanian and Latvian *alus*, (Hellquist 1957, II; Barnhart 1995; Buck 1949) and Finnish *olut*.

In Old Persian,[5] Avestan, *yātav-* means both 'magic' and 'magician' but the feminine *pairika-* only means 'witch'. There are thus two different roots, and they are also found in Middle Persian, but differentiating *jādūgīh* 'magic' from *jādūg* 'magician' while also maintaining the root *parig* 'witch'. Also, in Modern Persian these lexemes continue, *jādū* 'magic' and *jādūgar* 'magician'. There are also *sehr* 'magic' and *sehrbāz* 'magician'. In Middle Persian *kundāgīh* means 'magic' and 'astrology' and *kēd* means both 'magician' and 'soothsayer', which

---

[2] Capitals are used for Sumeric logograms but they should be read as if they were written in Hittite. This is a frequent phenomenon in Hittite texts.

[3] I would like to thank Prof. Folke Josephson very much for his kindness in sharing these Hittite and Sumeric examples with me.

[4] These runes are also found on a Merovingian sword found in Saint-Dizier 2002 and now preserved in its museum.

[5] I am very grateful to Dr Judith Josephson who kindly provided me with these Persian lexemes.

shows how strongly these activities were associated in people's minds. This last stem is probably related to the above discussed *keudes*.

Semantically, it can be seen that in many languages the magic action is called a deed or work. As already seen, the word for 'magic' in Avestan was *yātav*, but there were also *kṛtyā* 'deed', especially a magic one, and *māyā* 'supernatural power, magic'. As will be made clear below, the verb used with magic in the languages that are dealt with here is 'to do', and, as the magic transformation is supposed to happen when the magician says the word, it is in most cases a perlocutionary speech act, with the natural words for 'deed' and 'do' connecting with this verbal performance.

However, the words for 'magic' and 'magician' that dominate today come from Lat. *magia, magica ars* and *magus* (originally Gk. μάγος), often through other languages. In Greek 'magic' was called μαγία and more often μαγεία, but in Modern Greek the accent has moved to the first syllable as in Ibero-Romance languages, μάγια (mágia), (Menge and Gütling 1954; cf. Buck 1949).

In Sanskrit there is *māyā* 'magic' and *māyāvin* 'magician' and *māyāvinī* 'witch'.[6] In Greek this word is often used as a derogatory name for Persian priests (μάγος / plural μάγοι) and it becomes *magūs* in Persian. They were considered (Zoroastrian) sorcerers and not "real" (i.e. Greek) priests.

This lexeme comes from the name of prince Magog or a people (this is debated) named after the legendary prince, Magog, who was imprisoned with Gog by Alexander the Great according to legend and gave the name to the Iranian *magoi* (see Georgius Monachus 1904, I, 11, mid-ninth century; cf. Hult 2019, 40).

Later, i.e. during the Middle Ages, Spanish-Arabic travellers called the Vikings *madjus* (Retsö 2018), probably from *Magog*, an interesting semantic change, possibly because of the fact that they also came from the "non-civilised" North and were thus excluded from the "civilised" world, as Magog had once been.

However, most languages have used this same lexeme, but, of course, as a Latin borrowing, since Latin was the dominant language, being the language of the church and science, the words *magia* and *magica ars* are found in different transformed manifestations in many languages and cultures.

---

[6] For the Sanskrit examples I am once again in debt to Prof. Folke Josephson's kind help.

4 Romance languages

Lat. *magia* is the origin of most modern Romance representations of this notion. Fr. *magie* appears in the mid-sixteenth century (Rey 1992), and the other Romance languages follow the same model. At this time *magie* is semantically divided and contained more the meaning of 'necromancy' than 'magic' (Wagner 1939: 26). Lerch (1934, 18–27) sees Fr. *magique* as a learnèd form of Lat. *(ars) magica*.

In the First Part of Cervantes's *Don Quijote* (1605), there is Sp. *magia* with the stress on the first syllable as in Modern Spanish and in Cat. *màgia*, and similar lexemes are found more or less at the same time in the other Romance languages: Rom. *magie*, It. *magia*, Pg. *magia* and *mágica*, Occ. *magio*[7] and *mascarie* (Taupiac 1992, de Fourvières 1973), though the latter refers mainly to black magic. In Dolomitic Ladin the same lexeme is used but with different spellings in the different varieties *magia* (Badiot, Ghërdeina), *magìa* (Fascian, Fodom) and *majia* (Ampezzan) (Valentini 2002). Surselvan differs (see §§4.1 and 4.2), while the other Romansh varieties use *magia*.

4.1 Latin and Celtic origins

Most Western Romance languages use words for 'witch' similar to Sp. *bruja*: Pg. *bruxa*, Cat. *bruixot* or *bruixa* (which is also a most probable origin of Sard. *bruscia* and possibly also Aragonese *broxa*), Gasc. *broucho*, and Occ. *brèicho* (Corominas 1954–57; Rey 1992).

However, the etymology of this word is very uncertain, and it is first found in the fourteenth century (Corominas and Pascual 1980–1991). It could be Celtic *bruskja* 'rain lightly; blowing a cold wind', but semantically this does not really make sense. Neither does the suggestion that the Engadin (a South Eastern Romansh variety; cf. Söhrman 1999; 2005a; 2005b) *brüscha* 'a thin snow cover' and similar forms in Northern Italian, would be the origin, as some have suggested. Corominas and Pascual (1980–1991) suggest a possible Celtic origin **vroiksā* 'she who goes through the heather with the devil' or 'pagan woman, enemy of the Christians' as the origin of Cat. *bruixot* and thereby all the other similar Romance words. This seems more plausible than Hubschmid's idea (1952) of dialectal Catalan *bruixò* and *calabruix* 'hot wind'

---

[7] Final *o* is mostly pronounced [a] in modern Occitan.

indicating a 'magic user', i.e. a 'witch', and blaming that person for causing this wind.

In French, *sorcière* 'witch' is the feminine form of the word *sorcier*, and a *sorcier* is considered inferior to and darker than the later Latin import *magicien,* which did not appear until the end of the fifteenth century (Wagner 1939, 26). There is a geocultural difference, as the *sorcier* was more associated with the village magician and the production of magic potions (Wagner 1939, 38), while *devin* is the prestigious seer in the towns (Wagner 1939, 27–29) and *magicien* is more associated with ghosts and revenants and with predictions by communication with the dead, so therefore closer to necromancy and to the art of the devils (Wagner 1939, 37–38, 142–145). Bodin (1580) says that the *sorcier* is one who tries to achieve something by deliberately using diabolic means. Together with the *sorcier* whose magic is called *sorcellerie* there is also *enchanteur*, evidently specialising more in spells, but at the same time this term is more general and seems to have been used more frequently before the introduction of *magicien* (Wagner 1939, 149). The feminine form of *enchanteur* is *enchanteresse*, and less often *enchanteuse*, just as *devineresse* is more frequent than *devineuse* (see below). It is also quite clear that the semantic content of these lexemes has changed as time has gone by, and there may also be geographical and cultural differences: I will not explore this further here, but they are nowadays more synonymous than they used to be, possibly due to a lack of need for separation now that the belief in these magic practitioners has lost its importance for most people. However, the lexemes *magicien* / *magicienne* are also used for illusionists today while *sorcier* and *sorcière* are still mainly used for the practitioners of dark arts.

In Spanish and other Ibero-Romance languages there is the feminine form *maga* for 'witch', and quite often this word is used for modern women illusionists, which *bruja* is not. There is also a masculine form, *brujo*, in Spanish, but it refers to the man who practises witchcraft and not a more traditional magician (Corominas and Pascual 1980–1991).

People who do magic have often been called by names that derive from words for *magic*. However, this is far from the whole truth. *Magus* is thus the origin of most Romance representations of 'magician', and Sp. *mago* (Corominas and Pascual (1980–1991) is first found in a text from the thirteenth century by Gonzalo de Berceo (1195–1264). In French there has been competition between *mage* and *magicien* since the fifteenth century (Wagner 1939, 26). Nowadays *illusioniste* also exists and *mage* seems more serious and refers to magic powers. Sp. *mago* is well established, as is *ilusionista*, as are Cat. *màgic* (noun and adjective) and *ilusionista*.

Apart from Fr. *magicien* and *sorcier* there is also *prestidigitateur* 'illusionist' (Hladik 1974), a late word, the earliest text in which it is found being from 1823. However, its etymology is interesting since it is formed by two elements, from two different languages, neither of which is French: It. *presto* 'quick' (borrowed as Fr. *preste*, ultimately < Late Lat. *praestus*) + Lat. *dĭgĭtus* 'finger', followed by the agentive suffix -*a* and the suffix -*teur* 'doer, maker' (i.e. 'the one with quick, nimble fingers'). 'Magic' is *prestidigitation* (Rey 1992). This word also exists in It. *prestidigitazione*, but, despite the probable Italian origin of the first morpheme, it does not appear in Italian until fifteen years later, and the compound lexeme must therefore most probably have been created in France. However, in Latin there is a noun *praestigīae* (fem.pl.) 'illusion', which was used also in more "modern" texts such as the *Ars magica* by Francesco Giovanni di Dio Staidel (1750) (*In terris apparuit quando ars magica & scholæ **præstigiarum** incæperunt sordescere*). There are similar words in the Romance languages as Fr./Eng. *prestige*, like It. *prestigio* 'illusion' from the fourteenth century and thus Lat. *prestigia(e)* must have been instantly comprehensible.

The seer is related to the magic world as a person who could help people to choose the right or most advantageous way. The official Roman priest (Lat. *augur*) who read the future from the way birds flew and behaved was highly respected, and although this morpheme has been kept as a learnèd word in many languages (Fr. *augure* (c.1150) and *augureor* (1213) (Rey 1992); Sp. *augur*), it does not really belong to common usage today, with the exception of Italian (even though here, semantically, it has become a fond greeting, and *auguri* from the related Lat. *augŭrĭum* 'prediction, divination' now means 'greetings', as well-wishing could be seen as some kind of benevolent magic; the noun *augure* refers only to a Roman seer). There are other lexemes that took its place, such as Pg. and Sp. *vidente* and Fr. *voyant*. Romanian has another word, *ghicitor*, of unknown origin, and Catalan and Italian use *endevinador* and *indovino* respectively, both from a hypothesised Latin verb *indivinare. Less frequent is It. *veggente* which corresponds to the French and Spanish words. In French there is also the lexeme *devin/devineresse* which comes from Lat. *divinus* 'godly', although the feminine form *devineresse* corresponds to a lost **devineur,* and there was a time during the Middle Ages when there also existed *devine* and *devineuse* (Rey 1992). Lexemes such as

Sp. *vidente* and It. *veggente* are both feminine and masculine, while all other words for women future-tellers in Romance languages (Fr. *voyante,* Rom. *ghicitoare* , Cat. *endivinadora* and It. *indovina*) are feminine forms of the same morphemes that are used for their male counterparts.

In Sursilvan there are both *divinader* and *striun* and their corresponding feminine forms *divinadra* and *stria* (Vieli and Decurtins 1980). The first of these lexemes obviously has the same origin as Fr. *devineur*; *striun*, however, is the common word for 'magician', and this shows how semantically close these words for different kinds of magic users can be. Nevertheless, since 'seer' is not the prime topic of this Chapter I will comment on words for seers only in a few cases.

'To perform or do magic' is rendered explicitly in Romance languages: Pg. *fazer magia,* Sp. *hacer magia* , Cat. *fer màgia,* Fr. *faire (des tours de) magie; pratiquer la magie (blanche/noire),* It. *fare (le) magie* and Rom. *a face magie.*

However, Portuguese and Romanian go one step further as the noun related to the verb for 'do' in these languages takes on the semantics of 'magic' or 'spell', as can be seen in Rom. *fapt* 'fact, deed', from *a face* 'do'. Thus, Pg. *fazer* gives the noun *feitiço* 'magic', which clearly comes from Lat. *factīcĭus* . This Portuguese lexeme has given Fr. *fétiche* and Eng. *fetish* (the latter possibly through French in the seventeenth century), and the meaning has changed into something that protects its owner through magic. Originally, this is how Europeans labelled "pagan" religious objects in America (Rey 1992). Nowadays, the magic part of this sememe has weakened but not entirely disappeared: it signifies something that has an attraction or protection in the eyes of the wielder. Rom. *fapt* 'deed' can also mean 'magic', as can be seen in the following examples: *a face de fapt* 'do of a deed = do magic (in order to get someone's love)', and if the magic needs to be very strong, the spell to be pronounced was *faptul cel mare* 'the greatest deed' or *faptul pe cap de om* 'the deed on a man's head' (Ciorănescu 2002).

In medieval Central European cultures, the singers of poetry were called *joglars* (from Lat. *ioculārius*) in southern France, but further north they were known as *trobadors,*[8] and they often had other competences, as can be seen from English *juggler.* How often they dealt with magic performances is hard to

---

[8] A word with a much-disputed origin.

say, but in Germanic languages there are several lexemes that originate from *joglar* (see §5).

Another Latin-French lexeme that has influenced Germanic vocabulary is Fr. *conjurer* from Lat. *cum* + *iūro* 'swear', but that has achieved further semantic development in the Germanic languages: it originally meant 'to swear; make a pact with; to achieve something magic', but it has achieved the meaning 'to pronounce spells' (cf. §5).

4.2 Slavic and Greek influences

In Romanian there are also a Slavic loanword, *vrăjitor*, 'one who emits spells, magician' (Ciorănescu 2002; Vinereanu 2009) and *vrăji* (sing. *vrajă*) or *blesteme* 'spells', the latter being a Greek loanword 'speak profane, i.e. false' (Barnhart 1995, cf. Eng. *blasphemy*: the Slavic origin is *vraža* 'enchantment; curse' (cf. Polish *wróg*; and see also §7).

Nevertheless, in some Romance languages the originally Greek lexeme *strix* has become the generic lexeme. The origin of Gk. στρίγλα 'harpy, hellcat' is στριξ 'owl' (Menge-Gütling 1954). In Greek culture and elsewhere in Europe the owl was connected with magic and dark forces, especially witches (Hutton 2017, 67–72), being a big bird that moves around mainly at night and hoots in a way that may have been perceived as threatening; in Greek mythology it was sometimes confused with a bat (*ibid.*). In Antiquity owls were reputed to suck blood from children, and during the Middle Ages, female seers were supposed to have a relationship with the devil and the owl (*ibid.*). Saint Isidore (560–636 CE) described this "horrible" bird in his *Etymologiae* (Lindsay 2011). Latin imported this word for 'owl', and *strix* (Colonna 1997) thus gave It. *strega* 'witch', in addition to its meaning as a spiced liquor (which may have been associated with witchcraft). This etymon has also entered Polish, where it gives *strzyga*, but there it focuses semantically on blood-sucking, as it means 'vampire'.

In Sursilvan (a North Western Romansh variety) there does not only exist the lexeme *magia* but also *striegn* for 'magic', and in Friulan (Faggin 1985) *striege* is also used for 'magic', though there is also the lexeme *magie* (Vieli and Decurtins 1980). In Romanian folklore there are *strigoi*, a kind of vampire that sucked the lifeforce from humans (Evseev 1998: 444–445). In Sursilvan *striegn* is the most used word and could be seen as the hypernym; *cudisch da striegn* means 'magic book', and 'magician' is thus *striun*.

In Italian there is another religious lexical import that has come to mean 'witch, old hag', *befana*, which is a contracted derivative of Lat. *Epiphănĭa* 'Epiphany' (Colonna 1997). When written with a capital (*Befana*), it refers to an old woman who comes along at Epiphany handing out sweets to children.

5 Germanic languages

In the Germanic languages Lat. *magia* is also found as the origin of modern words such as Eng. *magic* (*wizardry* and *witchcraft*[9] also mean 'magic'), Germ. *Magie*, Danish and Swedish *magi*. With the exception of Icelandic, the word *magi* is used in all Scandinavian languages. However, the Latin word came to the Germanic languages through French, as in English, where there are *magus* 'man skilled in magic' from Latin plural *magi* and *magic* from Fr. *magique* (Barnhart 1995).

In Icelandic the lexeme *seið*, is used, and this word is found in other Scandinavian languages too such as *sejd* in Swedish (Hellquist 1957). It focuses on future telling and has a close relation with the forces of nature. The greatest wielder of this magic was Odin, but otherwise it seems to have been an art practised mostly by women. This lexeme might be related to Lithuanian *saitas* 'magic' (Hellquist 1957).

In Scandinavian languages the word *magi* is high register, and the old lexemes that were and still are used are mainly related to the horrible mythological creature *troll*, which is some kind of ogre, and a magician is called *trollkarl* 'magician' (*karl* 'man') and *trollkonstnär* in Swedish, *tryllekunstner* (cf. *konstnär, kunstner* 'artist') in Danish and Norwegian, referring to modern illusionists; but *trollkarl* may also refer to a "true" magician in Swedish, especially when referring to ancient times, legends and fantasy literature. The words ending in *kunstner* or *konstnär* are gender-neutral and indicate the performer but not the practitioner. However, in German the word for the performer is similar, *Zauberkünstler* (again, *künstler* 'artist'), with a feminine form, *Zauberkünstlerin*, but *Zauberer* and (less frequently) *Magier* are the masculine words for the practitioner, while the female

---

[9] Remember that Harry Potter and his friends went to Hogwarts School of Witchcraft and Wizardry. There does not seem to be any difference between the two arts. They are synonyms in the books, but elsewhere there are sometimes differences, mainly due to the gender of the practitioner.

practitioners are called *Zauberin* and *Magierin*. Today *Zauberer* is also used for an illusionist, as is *Zauberkünstler*, together with the corresponding feminine forms (Kluge 2011).

In Old High German 'to do magic' is *zoubar*, and in Middle High German *zoubar*, *zaubern* (cf. *Zauberei* 'magic'), and in Middle Low German *tover*, *tober* from Germanic **taubrá-* (Kluge 2011), as in Old Norse *taufr* 'red chalk', associated with 'red pigment; red lead', referring to the red-tinted magic runes on holy stones[10] (but "unclear" according to Buck 1949), and in Dutch 'magician' is *tovernaar* or *magiër* (Kruyskamp 1961; Beets and Muller 1900).

Many illusionists in Scandinavia prefer these *troll* words to *magiker* which also exists in Scandinavian languages meaning 'magician', but the latter has a more lugubrious and foreign sense.

The origin is possibly a semantic change from 'making somebody a troll' to 'enchant'; Swedish *trolla*, Norwegian and Danish, *trylle*, but in Icelandic another word is used, *galdr*, *galdur*, 'incantation', 'spell'. *Galdur* is a '(magic) song' often sung in a pitched voice, which is connected to Anglosaxon *begalan* 'enchant' and Old German *galan* 'sing (magic) songs'. In Swedish the verb *gala* 'crow' is the song of a cockerel. Whether it has anything to do with English *gale* (earlier *gaile*) is unknown, but it is not altogether impossible since a storm makes noise when it is blowing (Hellquist 1954; Hannesson 1984). From this word derives *galdramaður* 'magician'.

The Icelandic word *töfra* is connected to Old Norse *taufr* and Middle Low German *tōver* and Dutch *toverkunst,* earlier *tooverkunst* (Beets and Muller 1900) 'magic'; thus, Dutch *betovering* means 'magic, but in Dutch there also exists the word *magie*. In Icelandic a magician could also be called or *töframaður* < *töfra* 'enchant' based on the same root. However, these *taufr* words mainly refer to black magic (Hannesson 1984; Hellquist 1957).

In the Netherlands the inhabitants of the town Schiedam are sometimes called *tovenaars* and those in Belgian Idegem *toveraraars* because of the witchcraft trials that took place there. These ethnonyms are derogatory (Kruyskamp 1961).

---

[10] Could this be the reason why texts and pictures on rune stones and rock carvings are always filled out in red?

Magic as entertainment is called *trolleri* in Swedish and *trylleri* in Danish and Norwegian, while *magi* is the "real" magic as well. In Dutch there are *goochelarij, goochelkunst, gegoochel* (Beets and Muller 1900) and thus, a magician/illusionist and also seer is a *goochelaar,* from Old High German *gougulâri,* which comes in turn from Fr. *jogleor* Occ. *joglar* and Lat. *ioculārius* (Beets and Muller 1900). In many medieval cultures the singers of poetry were called by borrowings from Occ. *joglar* (see §4.1).

It is always difficult to draw any strict lines between the semantic content of all these words, as the different magic activities became confused at medieval markets, where many presented themselves as "real" magicians with a show, or were jugglers who combined this activity with magic; the border between magic and medicine was also not very clear at this time (and this is still sometimes the case).

As in the Romance languages, witches were called something different from "just" the feminine form of the word for 'magician'. Eng. *witch*, earlier *wiche*, (feminine of *wicca*) probably has another origin, *wicca*, which is based on *witan* in Gothic, Old Saxon and Anglo-Saxon, and Modern English *wit*, which means 'know' and is also related to 'see' as in Latin *vidēre* and Gk εἴδω. Nowadays *wicca* is used by modern pagan religion and pagan witchcraft (Dell 2018, 373–374) and *witch* is never used for modern female illusionists, only in fiction and the Wicca religion.

Germ. *Hexe* and Danish and Norwegian *heks* come from Germanic *hag* / Scandinavian *hage* 'enclosed pasture', although this is not undisputed (Hellquist 1954–57). It has to do with English *hedge* and *hag,* before 1200 probably *hagge. Hexe* possibly refers to demons who rode the fence in order to achieve something from the farmer (energy) or the animals (milk, blood etc.). In Swedish *häxa* appears in the seventeenth century, when the witchcraft trials started, and it is probably a loanword from Low German *hex*, as are the Danish and Norwegian words. *Hag* is possibly related to Dutch *kaai* (Beets and Muller 1900) and comes from Middle Low German *kâje* (Kluge 2011), which is a loanword from Fr. *quai* 'embankment', deriving from Celtic (cf. Welsh *cae* 'enclosure' (Evans and Thomas 2002) and Middle Breton *quae* 'hedge'), in turn possibly from Indo-European *kag^{u}h* 'rider of the fence'. Semantically it is close to the Germanic root *mar,* medieval Dutch *mare* or *maer* (Rey 1992) as in English *nightmare*, Swedish *mardröm* (*dröm* 'dream') and Fr. *cauchemar*. The original meaning might be 'crush', but its origin is dubious. In Swedish one can be 'ridden by the *mara*', a creature which sucks out energy (cf. Rom.

strigoi, see §4.2). However, the semantic and morphological resemblance to Old Slavic *mora* 'witch' indicates a more widespread usage of this lexeme.

Eng. *magician* is the established word, but there are also *conjurer/conjuror*, *sorcerer* and *wizard* (from *wicca*: see Wicca.nu). The activity is sometimes called *conjuring*. The word *conjurer* came from French and originally from Lat. *con* (< *cum* 'with') + *iurare* 'swear (an oath or a spell)'. Fr. *conjurer* originally meant 'to swear; make a pact with; to achieve something magic' (cf. §4.1). In English this word appears in the fourteenth century, but in French it is three hundred years older, and originally meant 'to achieve holy power', hence 'to pronounce spells' and thereby 'to prevent evil' (Rey 1992).

Eng. *warlock* is another word for 'magician' that is rarely used today, apart from occasional use in fantasy literature. It seems that the warlock originally was close to witches. The word is found already in Old English (before 900) as *wærloga* while the modern spelling is Scottish, spelt as *warlock* (earlier without a *c*) for the first time in 1685. The first element *war* 'covenant' is related to *wāer* 'true' and the second *loga* comes from *lēogan* 'lie'. It could thus mean 'a true liar' which would go well with the meaning 'scoundrel', which is also connected to *warlock*. Needless to say, that the lexeme *war* is not related to the first part of *werewolf* 'manwolf' (here *were-* 'man' is connected to Lat. *vir* 'man').

6 Celtic

In the Celtic languages there are remains of the old Druid religion and there are several words related to Eng. *druid* such as Old Irish *druidecht*, but and its synonym *aimmitecht*. *Druidecht* is clearly related to this priesthood that the Christians perceived as pagan sorcerers. In Modern Irish the corresponding words are *draoidheacht* and its synonym *pisedog*. 'Druid' is *draoi*, which nowadays also means 'magician, wizard and trickster' *Pisedog* has an unknown etymology. *Druidecht* and *draodeaicht* mean magic with reference to the old druids and their religion (Buck 1949). The semantic differences between these words are not very clear.

Breton *breou* has an interesting semantic development as its origin is Fr. *bref* or *brevet* 'letter, document' which metaphorically has come to indicate 'spell, incantation' (Hemon 1974; Buck 1949). I mentioned earlier the Welsh lexeme *hud* (Buck 1949; Evans and Thomas 2002), but in Welsh there are also other words such as *cyfaredd* and *dewiniaeth* for 'magic'; 'magician' is a *dewin* or *swynwr* and 'witch' is *dewines* or *gwiddon*. It seems very likely that these words are borrowings from Latin *dīvīnus,* and it can also be seen that, semantically, 'knowledge' is important, as in Welsh 'to know' is *gwybod*; *cyfarwydd* means 'skilled' and 'storyteller' (cf the closely related word *cyfaredd*, which means 'spell').

7 Balto-Slavic and Finno-Ugric

Latin influence is clear, since 'magic' in Lithuanian and Russian is магие, in Polish *magia*, in Czech *magie* (also *čarodějnitsví*) and in Serbian and Croatian *magija*, to take just a few representative examples. There is also Slavonic влушиба 'magic', In Russian волшебство and Bulgarian вълшебство and вълшебник 'magician' has a flavour of fairy tale, as it is in these stories that the word is mainly found nowadays, while Bulgarian магьосник 'magician', is derogatory (black magic, a qualifier for good painters or artists). In Old Slavonic влъхвъ means 'wise man, magician' and влъхвованье 'enchantment'. This very root is also used in Russian волшебник 'magician' from Old Slavic волшебный 'enchanter', as well as колдун, маг, and there is also чародей, based on the Old Slavonic stem *čar-* related to Sanskrit *kr̥* 'to do' (cf. §3), which is found in many other Slavic languages such as Polish *czarodziej* and *czary*, Czech *čary* 'enchantment'. They all refer to a "real" magic as do Croatian *magija, čarolija* or *čar* 'magic'. *Mađioničar* means both '(real) magician' and 'illusionist' in modern Croatian, and in Serbian there is *čarobnost* 'enchantment' (Tsyganenko 1970, Fasmer 2009, Shurbanova 2007).

The witch is often related to knowledge, and Old Slavonic вѣд (vjat) 'know' (cf. Lat. *video*) is thus the origin of Bulgarian вещица, Croatian *vještica,* Polish *wiedźma* and Russian ведьма 'witch'. In Polish there are also the variants *szeptucha ~ szeptunka* 'witch' and the masculine equivalent *szeptun*, from the verb *szeptać* 'to mumble', which must refer to the incantation of spells.

Lat. *magus* has its role in Slavic lexicons, but mainly there are two Slavic roots that dominate: *volsj-* and *čar-*.

As the Slavic root *vrag* 'enemy' was introduced into Romanian vocabulary, it developed the final occlusive into a stem-final fricative (*vrag* > *vrajă*), and with a semantic change to 'enchantment; curse'. Until the seventeenth century *vrajă* also meant 'destiny, luck', and in Polish there are idioms such as *zły wróg* 'bad luck' y *rzucać wróżę* 'foresee'; also *wróżyć* and *wróżka* 'fairy' and *wróżbit* 'seer'.

An interesting Scandinavian connection is the Old Norse word *vala* (Hellquist 1957) or *völva* 'seer' (Arries 2019, 158–167) from *vǫlr* 'staff-carrier'. They were a special highly esteemed group of prestigious seers with a special mythological function connected to their magic staffs. Comparing this word with Slovene *vôłhva* and Finnish *velho* 'magician' and *velho naisesta* 'witch' (*naisen* 'woman'; see Cantell 2008) as well as Estonian *võlu* 'enchantment', *võlur* 'magician' and *võlumine* 'magic' (Eesti-inglise sõnaraamat 2001), a striking similarity can be seen. The relationship between Scandinavian and the Finno-Baltic languages is obvious, but the Slovene connection is more questionable, though intriguing. It has also come into contemporary usage in Icelandic as the word created to signify 'computer': *tölva*, from *tala* 'speak, talk' + *völva* (foreign loanwords are avoided in Icelandic).

There is an interesting semantic and morphological development that has led to words such as Russian and Bulgarian фокусник, 'illusionist', and there is also илюзионист, but I will focus on the first lexeme фокус 'magic trick' in Bulgarian and правя фокуси 'to do magic' (Tsyganenko 1970; Fasmer 2009; Shurbanova 2007).

The word *fokus* could be seen as a Latin borrowing from *focus*, but it is actually *hokus-pokus* that is supposed to be a parody of the Latin words *hoc est corpus* used in the Eucharist. The German transmission into Slavic languages had its phonological consequences as German /h/ does not correspond to a Slavic /h/ and /h/ has therefore been substituted by /f/. Consequently, there are Bulgarian and Russian (фокус-покус), the traditional 'spell', which is also the base for фокусник 'illusionist'. In some Slavic languages (for instance Polish) *hokus-pokus* also exists as a spell in performances, but it is probably a later loan where the original /h/ has been kept.

8 Albanian

In Albanian, Latin influence is evident in *magji*, 'magic'. *magjistar* and *magjibërës* 'wizard'. In the latter it is a translation of 'magic doer', since *bëj* means 'to do' (Kalogjere 2003).

There is another inherited Albanian word, *trillim* 'lie, fiction' and also *marifet* 'nimble one' (cf. sleight of hand and also the Greek lexeme ταχυδακτυλουργίες (Kostallari 1980; see also §9).

9 Modern Greek

In Modern Greek 'do magic' is κάνω μαγικά as in English *to do* (or *perform*) *magic*. There also exists the interesting saying κάνω μαγικά μεταφορικά 'to do (metaphorical) magic', and one can also say κάνω ταχυδακτυλουργίες, the latter being a derogatory word for 'magician'. Its origin is τάχυς 'quick' + δάχτυλος 'finger', ταχυδαχτυλουργός ('nimble' (= 'magician') and also 'pickpocket' (Beekes 2009). This could be compared to Germ. *Taschenspieler*, literally 'pocketplayer' but meaning 'inept illusionist' or just a derogatory word for 'illusionist' (cf. Swedish *taskspelare*, an obvious loanword from German with the very same meaning).

In Classical Greek φαρμακίς meant 'witch, poisoner'. Medicine and poison were close, so magic is also called φαρμακεία and also often meaning 'poison'. In Modern Greek φαρμάκωμα means 'poisoning', but today μάγισσα is used for 'witch' and μάγος is 'magician' (Beekes 2009).

This magical usage of words connected to pharmacy has given some interesting results in other languages. Magicians in Romanian fairy tales are usually called *fermecător* or a woman *fermecătoare* from the word *farmec* which means 'witchcraft', and in Romani *farmakatarkas* 'witch' (Lee 2011).

10 A minor digression: the Wise Men from the East

The Three Wise Men, or Magi, are called magicians in most Romance languages. As already seen, wisdom and magic have been closely related in people's minds for thousands of years. In Spanish they are called *los Reyes Magos* (Matthew 2,1), in Catalan *els Reis Mags*, in Italian *i Re Magi* and in French *les Rois Mages*. Dolomitic Ladin combines the Romance and the Germanic expressions *i magi dal urient*, while Surselvan follows the Germanic model 'Wise men' (see below): *i sabis digl orient*.

In Romanian, instead of using the commonly used *rege* 'king' they are called *cei trei crai de la răsărit* 'the three kings from the east' using a Slavic loanword *crai* 'king (in a fairy tale or deck of cards)' (Vinereanu 2009). *Crai* comes from Old Slavonic *kralĭ* as in Russian король, Bulgarian *крал* from an older *кралят* (Fasmer 2009; Shurbanova 2007). This word is also found in Albanian *kralj* and may come from the name *Karl*, i.e. *Charlemagne*. Another explanation is that it comes from Greek κρείων 'king, ruler', such as Homer's κρείων Ἀγαμέμνων 'king Agamemnon' (Beekes 2009).

In modern Albanian another word for 'king', *mbret*, is used, and this is a reduced form of Latin *imperator*, and was the word used for king Zog (1895–1961, reigned 1928–1939).

In Germanic languages the Wise Men are not magicians and sometimes kings, Eng. *the Wise Men / three Kings from the East,* Ger. *Die drei Weisen / Königen aus dem Morgenlande*, and also *Magi* (cf. Rubens' painting *The Adoration of the Magi*); in Swedish they are never kings: Sw. *de tre vise männen* (*från Österland*), although this last directional indication sounds old-fashioned nowadays.

11 Finally, some conclusions

Magic is thus an old human activity which has gone through conceptual and semantic changes, but it remains a part of human life. Many lexemes have spread not only to closely related languages but also to others, and semantically there are no hard borders; however, each one of these words is closely related semantically to others in the same language and also in neighbouring languages.

The connection between different words for magic practitioners is seldom clear, and nowadays they are often seen as synonyms. These terms are now used in literature and by illusionists who for some reason prefer one word to another, but earlier, as has been pointed out, words such as *sorcerer, wizard, witch* and *magician* have referred to different kinds of magic users, which has to do with peoples' changing beliefs and the fact that "real" magicians have vanished from most European cultures. The blending of references to practitioners and performers is very old, and the two categories cannot always be distinguished, but nowadays performers are much more common with the magic shows on TV and elsewhere; they use the traditional lexical heritage which is part of the illusion that is being created.

The bond between language and culture is very clear, since the lexemes refer to local or regional beliefs and ideas about the "other world". It is also interesting that women are more often concerned with nature magic and therefore also with healing. Although there are no absolute semantic gender restrictions, female practitioners are often referred to by lexemes other than male-referring ones, even in Romance, but seldom in Slavic languages where female nouns are constructed by changing the suffix (e.g. Surselvan *divinader / divinadra* and Polish *szeptunka* 'witch' and the male equivalent *szeptun*. This latter case is interesting as it shows that, if the practitioners fulfil the same kind of magic, the nouns that refer to these arts come from the same lexical root. The gender perspective is clearer shown by the fact that men and women have often dedicated themselves to different kinds of magic, although this has changed over time. In Greece the oracles and seers were often women, but in Rome the seers, such as augurs, were men.

A sad cultural reflection is that, during periods when there have been witchcraft trials, mostly women were convicted and burnt, while few male magicians suffered this fate.

The dominance of Greek and Roman cultures and languages is quite clear in the fact that most lexemes and concepts that refer to magic come from these languages, often from Latin to French and from there to different Germanic languages, while the Slavic world has taken more words from Greek. There is also a lexical link between Slavic and Germanic, mainly Scandinavian vocabulary, which should be investigated further. Many of these "loans" come from old Indo-European culture (cf. Buck 1949, v–xvii). The association of magic with knowledge is seen in such words as Eng. *witch, wizard* and Russian ведьма, which derive from the same IE root as Lat. *video* 'see', a concept semantically close to 'know'.

Several European languages have been spread around the world as the languages of conquering and colonising powers, leaving a vast vocabulary to the local languages, but these do not always bend to the dominant language in the area of magic, which shows how deep-rooted these notions are in different cultures. Neologisms do not enter so easily into these lexical fields. Thus, a good final example comes from Ecuatorian Kichwa/Quichua where the speakers have not borrowed *magia* from Spanish but use the lexeme *saillulai* from *saillu* 'real' and *shalana* 'change', i.e. 'change reality', which is a good description of magic.

References

Dictionaries

Barnhart, Robert K. 1995. *The Barnhart Concise Dictionary of Etymology.* New York: HarperCollins Books.

Beekes, Robert. 2009. *The Etymological Dictionary of Greek*, 2 vols. Leiden/Boston: Brill.

Beets, A., and J.W. Muller. 1900. *Wordenboek der nederlandse taal.* 's-Gravenhage: Martinus Nijhoff.

Buck, Carl Darling. 1949. *A Dictionary of Selected Synonyms in the Principal Indo-European Languages.* Chicago: University of Chicago Press.

Cantell, Ilse. 2008 [2000]. *Suomi ruotsi suomi sanakirja.* Helsingfors: Werner Söderström Osekeyhtiö.

Ciorănescu, Alexandru. 2002. *Dicționarul etimologic al limbii române.* București: Saeculum.

Colonna, Barbara. 1997. *Dizionario etimologico della lingua italiana. L'origine delle nostre parole.* Genoa: Newton & Compton Editori.

Corominas, Joan. 1954–1957. *Diccionario crítico etimológico de la lengua castellana.* Bern: Francke Verlag.

Corominas, Joan, and José A. Pascual. 1980–1991. *Diccionario crítico etimológico castellano e hispánico.* Madrid: Gredos.

Coromines,[11] Joan. 1983–1988. *Diccionari etimològic i complementari de la llengua catalana*, 8 vols. Barcelona: Curial edicions catalanes, Caixa de pensions "La Caixa".

de Fourvières, Xavier. 1973. *Lou pichot tresor.* Avignon: Aubanel.

Eesti-inglise sõnaraamat, 2001. Tallinn: TEA.

Evans, Harold Meurig, and William O. Thomas. 2002 [1958]. *Y Geiriadur Mawr / The Complete Welsh-English –English-Welsh Dictionary.* Ammanford: Gwasg Dinefur Press.

Faggin, Giorgio. 1985. *Vocabolario della lingua friulana*, 2 vols. Udine: del Bianco Editore.

Fasmer, Max (Фасмер, Макс). 2009 [1964–1973; first edition in German 1950–1958]. *Этимологический словарь русского языка.* Moscow: Biblio.

Hannesson, Jóhann, et al. 1984. *Ensk-íslensk orðabok.* Reykjavik: Örn og Örlygur.

Hellquist, Elof. 1957. *Svensk etymologisk ordbok,* Lund: Gleerups förlag.

Hemon, Roparz. 1974. *Dictionnaire français-breton.* Brest: Al Liamm.

Kalogjere, Damira. 2003. *Modern rječnik, englesko-hrvatski.* Zagreb: Naklada.

Kluge, Friedrich. 2011. *Etymologisches Wörterbuch der deutschen Sprache*, 25th ed. Berlin/Boston: De Gruyter.

Kostallari, Androkli. 1980. *Fjalor i gjuhës së sotme shqipe.* Tirana: Akademia e shkencave e RPS të shqipërisë.

Kruyskamp, Cornelis. 1961. *Groot woordenboek der Nederlandse taal.* 's-Gravenhage: Martinus Nijhoff.

---

[11] In his Catalan Joan Coromines has preferred to use the Catalan version of his name while he used the Castilian version in the Spanish dictionary.

Lee, Ronald. 2011. *Romani Dictionary, English-Kalderash*. Toronto: Magoria Books.
Menge, Hermann, and Otto Güthling. 1954 [1913]. *Enzyklopädisches Wörterbuch der griechischen und deutschen Sprache*. Berlin-Schöneberg: Langenscheidt.
Rey, Alain, dir. 2000. *Dictionnaire historique de la langue française*, 3 vols. Paris: Dictionnaires Le Robert.
Shurbanova, Daniela. (Шурбанова, Данела). 2007. *Нов учителен речник*. Sofia: Ernst Klett Sprachen.
Taupiac, Jacme. 1992. *Diccionari de mila mots*. Toulouse: Collègi d'Occitania.
Tsyganenko, Galina Pavlovna (Цыганенко, Галина Павловна). 1970. *Этимологический словарь руского языка*. Kiev: Издательсво "Радянськая Школа".
Valentini, Erwin, Matthias Stuflesser, Fabio Chiochetti, Nadia Chiochetti, and Daria Valentin. 2002. *Dizionar dl Ladin Standard*, Urtijei/Fascia/Val Badia/Bulzan: Servisc de Planificazion y Elaborazion dl Lingaz Ladin.
Vieli, Ramun, and Alexi Decurtins. 1980 [1975]. *Vocabulari tudestg-sursilvan*. Cuera: Ligia Romontscha.
Vinereanu, Mihai. 2009. *Dicționar etimologic al limbii române*. Bucharest: Alcor Edinpex SRL.

Other references

Arries, Javier. 2019. *Magia y religión nórdicas*. Barcelona: Luciérnaga.
Bates, Brian. 2002. *The Real Middle Earth. Magic and Mystery in the Dark Age*. London: Pan Books.
Benveniste, Émile. 1969. *Le vocabulaire des institutions indo-Européennes*, 2 vols. Paris: Éditions de Minuit.
Biblioteca Nacional de España. 2011. *La Magia en la BNE*, 2011. Madrid: Biblioteca Nacional de España.
Bodin, Jean. 1580. *De la démonomanie des sorciers*. Paris: Iacques du Puys.
Daniel, Noël. 2013. *Magic*. Cologne: Taschen.
Dell, Christopher. 2018 [2016]. *The Occult Witchcraft and Magic. An Illustrated History*. London: Thames & Hudson.
di Dio Staidel, Francesco Giovanni. 1750. *Ars magica*. Accessed 18 November 2020. https://play.google.com/store/books/details?id=rBNGAAAAcAAJ&rdid=book-rBNGAAAAcAAJ&rdot=1.
Evseev, Ivan. 1998. *Dicționar de magie, demonologie și mitologie românească*. Timișoara: Editura Amarcord.
Georgius Monachus, ed. C. De Boor. 1904 [831–842]. *Chronicon* I–II. Stuttgart: Teubner.
Hladik, Jean. 1974 [1967]. *Prestidigitation et illusionisme*. Paris: PUF.
Hubert, Henri, and Marcel Mauss. 1950. *Esquisse d'une théorie générale de la magie*. In *Sociologie et Anthropologie*, 1–141. Paris: PUF.

Hubschmid, Johannes. 1952. "Span. *bruja* 'Hexe' und Wörter für atmosfährische Erscheinungen." *Vox Romanica* 12: 112–119.

Hult, Karin. 2019. "Alexanderromanen." In *Alexander den store – en gränslös historia*, edited by Karin Hult and Gunhild Vidén, 25–46. Stockholm: Appell.

Hutton, Ronald. 2017. *The Witch. A History of Fear, from Ancient Times to the Present*. New Haven/London: Yale University Press.

Lerch, M.E.. 1934. "Les trois mages." *Le français moderne*, 2: 18–27.

Lindsay, W.M. 1911. *Isidori Hispalensis Episcopi Etymologiarvm sive originvm libri XX / recognovit breviqve adnotatione critica instrvxit W.M. Lindsay*, 2 vols. Oxford: Clarendon Press. Accessed 18 November 2020. http://penelope.uchicago.edu/Thayer/E/Roman/Texts/Isidore/home.html.

MacLeod, Mindy, and Bernard Mees. 2006. *Runic Amulets and Magic Objects*. Woodbridge: Boydell Press.

Niculae, Cornel-Dan. 2017. *Magia și Ființe Fantastice din Arhaicul Românesc. Leacuri și Remedii magice din Carpați*. Bucharest: Carpathia Rex.

Retsö, Jan. 2018. "The Reception in Early Arabic Writings". In Margaret Clunies Ross (ed.) *The Pre-Christian Religions of the North. Research and Reception Vol. I: From the Middle Ages to c. 1830,* pp. 81-89. Tournhout: Brepols.

Skutsch, Carl (ed.). 2005. *Encyclopedia of the World's Minorities*, 3 vols. New York/London: Routledge.

Söhrman, Ingmar. 1999. "Romansh." In *Dictionary of the Languages of Europe*, edited by Glanville Price, 388–393. Oxford: Oxford University Press.

Söhrman, Ingmar. 2005a, "Friulians." In Skutsch (ed.), 1, 471–473.

Söhrman, Ingmar. 2005b. "Romansh." In Skutsch, (ed.), 3, 1027–1028.

Söhrman, Ingmar. 2005c. "Switzerland." In Skutsch, (ed.), 3, 1160–1162.

Söhrman, Ingmar. 2017. *Den sanna historien om Dracula. Mannen – myten – legenden*. Eskilstuna: Vaktel.

Stanmore, Tabisha. 2019. "In medieval England magic was a service industry used by rich and poor alike." *The Conversation*, September 24, 2019. Accessed 18 November 2020. https://theconversation.com/in-medieval-england-magic-was-a-service-industry-used-by-rich-and-poor-alike-124009.

Wagner, Robert-Léon. 1939. *"Sorcier" et "magicien". Contribution à l'histoire du vocabulaire de la magie*. Paris: Droz.

Wicca.nu. Accessed 18 November 2020. http://www.wicca.nu/vadarwicca/wiccashistoria.html.

Index of topics

Albanian, 249
Alfonso X the Wise / el Sabio, 31, 136, 137, 140, 141, 142, 144, 145, 146, 147, 148, 149, 150, 151, 152
Alonso, Dámaso, 2–5, 19
Anglicisms, 73
anti-Latinism, 37
Arabism, 139, 143, 149, 157–68
Aragon, Crown of, 137
Argote de Molina, Gonzalo, 144, 150, 151
Aristotle, 31
attention, 104–5
Ausbau language, 193
Balto-Slavic languages, 248–49
Berceo, Gonzalo de, 135, 136, 137, 144, 146
bilingualism, 193
binomial, 28
Boccaccio, Giovanni, 31
Boethius, 31
borrowing, 2–7, 10, 195, 199, 202, 203, 204, 205
calque, 202
calquing, 34
Catalanism, 167
Celtic languages, 239–43, 247–48
chiasmus, 30
Cicero, 31
Cisneros, Cardinal, 159
colto (cultured), 194
combinación binaria (binary combination), 27
communicative distance (*distancia comunicativa*), 27, 32, 34
communicative immediacy (*inmediatez comunicativa*), 27, 212

competencia léxica (lexical competition), 160–61, 165
composición culta (cultured compounding), 91–106
composición semiculta (semicultured compounding), 94, 98, 99
composition, morphological, 96
composizione (compounding), 194
compounding, right-headed, 191, 195
compounds, noun, 191–206
contact, linguistic, 193
convergence, 33, 34–37, 45, 46
corpus, linguistic, 25, 26, 28, 29, 30–34, 30, 36, 37, 38, 41, 42, 45, 46, 55, 64, 67, 71, 73, 74, 75, 79, 80, 81, 83, 87, 104, 126, 127, 129, 130, 140, 149, 152, 157–68, 179, 211–27
cultismo (cultured borrowing), 1–20, 2–5, 7, 53–67, 72, 74, 78, 79, 81, 84, 86, 90–108, 117, 173, 174, 211–27
cultismo de éxito (successful cultured borrowing), 55, 187
cultured borrowing, 5, 7, 16, 18, 20, 117, 120, 122, 124, 125, 126, 132, 174, See cultismo, (palabra) culta, (mot) savant, (parola) dotta, (parola) colta, learnèd (borrowing), Latinism/latinismo.
de Meun, Jean, 31
de Quesne, Jean, 31
Delicado, Francisco, 211–27
derivation, morphological, 96
dictionaries, Spanish, 1–20
difference, 36
discourse analysis, 109

discourse tradition, 34
distancia comunicativa
  (communicative distance), 211,
  212, 216, 225, 226, 227
divergence, 33, 34–37, 45, 46
doblete (doublet), 109, 111, 115
don Juan Manuel, 150, 151
dotto (learnèd), 194
doublet, 29
Ecuatorian Kichwa/Quichua, 252
elaboration, linguistic, 27–47, 33,
  34, 47, 135, 138
embedding, 54
English as a Foreign Language
  (EFL), 132
English for Speakers of Other
  Languages (ESOL), 132
English, influence of, 194
epitaph, 112
Fernández de Heredia, Juan, 137,
  140, 141, 143, 144, 145, 148,
  150, 179
Finno-Ugric languages, 248–49
future-teller, 235
Gallicism, 139
Germanic languages, 244–47, 252
Gilliéron, Jules, 154
globalisation, 193
Góngora, Luis de, 3
Granada, Kingdom of, 157–68
Greek, 118, 121, 124, 131, 243–
  44, 252
  Ancient Greek, 118, 119
  Modern Greek, 118
Hellenism, 16
hetero-Latinism, 36, 43, 44, 46
Homer, 31
humanism, 132
hyper-Latinism, 35, 36, 41, 43, 44,
  46
hyper-position, 35
identity, 36
illusionist, 231, 234, 235, 236,
  240, 244, 245, 246, 251

inherited word, 2–5, 5, 7, 8, 9, 15,
  16, 19, 109, 117, 136, 137, 139,
  145, 173, 174, 175, 176, 177,
  178, 183, 185, 186, 188, 197,
  198, 202, 203, 204, 249, *See
  also palabra patrimonial.*
inmediatez comunicativa
  (communicative immediacy),
  211, 213, 216, 225, 226, 227
intensificación (intensification), 73,
  81
interference, linguistic, 34–37, 47
-ir , Spanish verbs in, 173–89
irony, 74
iterazione sinonimica (synonymous
  iteration), 27
language
  classical, 117–33
  lesser-studied languages, 131
  modern, 117–33
  official language, 118
  profane language, 118
  sacred language, 118
  spoken and written, 5
  universal language, 119
Latin, 118, 119, 121, 124, 125,
  131, 132
  Classical Latin, 118, 119
  Early Latin, 118
  Late Latin, 118
  Low Latin, 118
  Medieval Latin, 118
  Vulgar Latin, 118
Latini, Brunetto, 31
Latinism, 1–20, 35, 135, 136, 137,
  138, 139, 140, 141, 142, 143,
  144, 145, 146, 147, 148, 150,
  151, 152, 153, 154, 198
latinismo (Latinism), 2, 71–88,
  109, 115, 135, 136, 137, 222
learnèd, 1–20, 32, 136, 152, 174,
  193, 194, 196, 199, 200, 203,
  239, 241
  learnèd borrowing, 25–47, 212
  learnèd group, 7, 8, 9, 10, 19

letter *x*, Spanish, 10
léxico ampliado (extended lexicon), 7
léxico tradicional (inherited lexicon), 7
linguistic change, causes of, 193
litotes, 42
Livy, 31
magic, 231–52
 black magic, 235
 magic and gender, 234, 252
 white magic, 235
magician, 231, 234–36, 238, 240, 246
 female, 231, 234, 252
medicine, 53–67
memory, 104–5
Mena, Juan de, 31, 33, 36, 39, 45, 46
Mercado, Tomás de, 180
metaforización (metaphorisation), 65
Modern Greek, 249–50
moriscos, 160
morpholexical families, 17–19, *See also* derivation, morphological.
music, 112
Nebrija, Antonio de, 140, 141, 142, 143, 144, 149, 150, 151, 159
neoclassico (neoclassical), 194
Neogrammarians, 192
neologism, 1, 73, 93, 98, 99, 115, 116, 135, 136, 138, 139, 144, 151, 153, 154, 252
 typology, 94
neonimia, 95
neurocognitive approach to language, 104–5
obsolescence, lexical, 158, 168
orality, conceptual, 27
Oresme, Nicole, 31
orthoepy, 10
orthography, Spanish, 8

palabra culta (cultured borrowing), 53, 54, 55, 73, 115, 136, 191, 220, 221, 222, 223, 224, 225
palabra patrimonial (inherited word), 115, 136, 137
parallelism, 30
parasynonymy, 29
paratactic lexical groups, 27–47, 29
phonology, Spanish, 7, 8–17
play on words, 80–87
popular, 3, 5, 174, 196
popularisation, 55
prefixation, 96, 154
press, Spanish-language, 52–69
prestige, 99, 118, 153, 234
Proaza, Alonso de, 141
pseudoprefixes, 97
pseudosuffixes, 97
psycholinguistics, 93
Real Academia Española, 8
relatinisation, 6–7, 8, 137
religion, magic and, 233
remodelación (remodelling), 6
Renaissance, 118, 132
Retrato de la Loçana andaluza, 211–27
Romance languages, 234, 239–43, 243, 246, 250, 251
Sánchez de Arévalo, Rodrigo, 141
Sánchez de Vercial, Clemente, 150
Santillana, Marqués de, 137
savant (cultured), 174
scripturality, conceptual, 27
seer, 235, 240, 241, 242, 243, 248, 249, 252
semilearnèd, 32, 198
shaman, 233, 235
sintagma no progresivo (non-progressive syntagm), 28
Slavic languages, 236, 243–44, 252
snobbishness, 74
sorcerer, 231, 238, 247
spell, 240

spelling. *See* orthography
sports, 52–69
Strasbourg Oaths, 132
substitution, lexical, 157–68
suffixation, 96, 154
Synonymendoppelung, 27
synonymy, 28–30
TEITOK, 217
Terreros, Esteban de, 14–17
tipo discursivo (discourse type*)*,
    218–19, 225–26, 227
translation, 27–47, 193
transnational, 7, 121, 133
trans-position, 35
troll, 244
Valladolid, Alfonso de, 141
Viciana, Martín de, 161
Villena, Enrique de, 31, 33, 39, 41,
    141, 149, 150, 152, 180, 181
voodoo, 233
Wise Men from the East, 250–51
witch, 231, 233, 235, 243, 246,
    247, 248
witchcraft, 231–52, 240, 243, 245,
    246, 252
wizard, 231, 233, 234
wizardry, 244

Index of words in Romance languages, Latin, Greek, Arabic and English

Arabic words
almuxfíyyah, 163
tanqîya, 165
ṭarḥîn, 166
tarkím, 165
tarkīm, 165

Aragonese words
broxa, 239
débile, 137
difícile, 137
fácile, 137
mascar, 149
útile, 137

Aranese words
tarküm, 165

Asturian words
mazcar, 149

Catalan words
bruixa, 239
bruixò, 239
bruixot, 239
calabruix, 239
endevinador, 241
endevinadora, 242
fàcil, 139, 140
fenyer, 150
fingir, 150
fraguar, 148
ilusionista, 241
mag
    els Reis Mags, 250
màgia, 239
fer màgia, 242
màgic, 241
rabeu, 142

English words
accidence, 58
accident, 59, 60
ancient, 117, 124, 126, 127
class, 120
classic, 117, 120, 121, 122
classical, 117–33
conjurer, 243, 247
fetish, 242
foreign, 117, 126, 128, 131, 132
grammar, 233
juggler, 242
language, 117–33, 122
learnèd, 117, 124, 126, 127, 132
magic, 244
magician, 247
magus, 244
mode, 122
modern, 117–33
oracle, 235
predicament, 56
prestige, 241
pub, 202
railway, 202
signo, 60
sorcerer, 247, 251
symptom, 60, 66
symptomatic, 66
token, 60
tongue, 117, 118, 126, 128
vernacular, 117, 125, 126, 128
vulgar, 117, 124, 125, 126, 128, 132
weekend, 202

witch, 234, 251
witchcraft, 244
wizard, 247, 251, 252
wizardry, 244

French words
accidence, 58
accident, 59
augure, 241
augureor, 241
carecer, 40
cément, 199
chef-lieu, 202
ciment, 199
classique, 121
combination, 45
conferente, 40
conjecturer, 41
conjugation (conjugaison), 45
convier, 149
croix, 138
devin, 240, 241
devine, 241
devineresse, 240, 241
devineur, 241
devineuse, 240, 241
discuter, 175
domestique, 43
enchanteresse, 240
enchanteur, 240
enchanteuse, 240
end[i]eble, 140
entendre, 41
expedient, 35
fétiche, 242
grammaire, 233
grimaud, 234
grimoire, 233, 234
illusioniste, 240
inique, 42, 43
jogleor, 246
juste, 35
legier, 139
leuger, 139

mage, 240
  les Rois Mages, 250
magicien, 240
magicienne, 240
magie, 239
  faire (des tours de) magie, 242
  pratiquer la magie, 242
magique, 239, 244
médicaliser, 4
opportune, 41
pâle, 143
paroxysme, 16
pervers, 43
phalange, 44
poison, 145
prêcher, 148
preste, 241
prestidigitateur, 241
prestidigitation, 241
prestige, 241
profit, 43
rade, 142
rapide, 142
sorcellerie, 240
sorcier, 240
sorcière, 240
subside, 43
symptôme, 61, 66
testue, 44
trobador, 242
utile, 40
voyante, 242
ydonnne (idoine), 41

Friulan words
magìe, 243
striege, 243

Greek words
ἀγρο-, 99
αὐτο-, 99
-λόγος, 112
μαγεία, 238
μαγία, 238

μάγος, 238
οἰκο-, 112
στρίγλα, 243
στριξ, 243
σῠμβεβηκός, 57
συμπίπτω, 55
σύμπτωμα, 53–67
φαγο-, 99
χρονο-, 99

Genoese words
güechu, 116
prichar, 148

Gascon words
broucho, 239

Italian words
acquaparco, 200
acquapark, 197
acquascivolo, 198, 200
acqua-scooter, 197
acquedotto, 200
agevole, 139
Agnelli-pensiero, 200
agopuntura, 198, 200
animavversione, 200
apicoltura, 200
arteterapia, 197
astro-, 198
astronave, 197, 200
augure, 241
auguri, 241
autolavaggio, 200
autonoleggio, 200
autoparco, 200
autoricambi, 200
autorimessa, 200
autoscuola, 200
autostazione, 200
autostrada, 200
banco, 199
bancogiro, 199, 200
banconota, 200

befana, 244
bibliologia, 196, 205
bimbocard, 197
borgomastro, 200
cabinovia, 200, 205
calcio scommesse, 195, 198, 200
calcio-crack, 197
calciomercato, 198, 200
cannocchiale, 200
capitombolo, 200
capo-, 199
capocannoniere, 200
capocarceriere, 200
capocenso, 200
capocomico, 200
capocuoco, 200
capogirlo, 200
capogiro, 200
capolavoro, 200
capoluogo, 200
capomaestro, 200
capomaglio, 200
capomastro, 199, 200
capomorbo, 200
capopurgio, 200
caposoldo, 200
capostazione, 194
caprifico, 200
caprifoglio, 194, 200
cartamodello, 198, 200
cartamoneta, 200, 202
casa-base, 200
castrocampo, 200
cemento, 199
cimento, 199
computer grafica, 197
convidare, 149
croce, 138
discopatia, 196
erbivendolo, 200, 205
espresso, 202
etnologia, 194
facile, 139, 140
ferrovia, 200, 202, 205
filodiffusione, 200

filovia, 198, 200
fine settimana, 202
fisiologo, 196
foto-, 200
fotografia, 200
fotografo, 196
fotomodello, 200
fotoromanzo, 200
fotostoria, 200
fruttivendolo, 198, 199, 200
funivia, 197, 198, 200, 205
gasdinamico, 196
gattafodero, 200
grandezza, 37
ideologo, 196
indovina, 242
indovino, 241
internet caffè, 197
lanavendolo, 200
lanovendolo, 200, 205
lattivendolo, 200
leggero, 139
lunedì, 204
madrelingua, 200
madrepatria, 200
magia, 239
magie
   fare (le) magie, 242
magnitudine, 37
mago
   i Re Magi, 250
manrovescio, 200
maremoto, 200, 205
mensiero, 200
metanodotto, 200
mondovisione, 200
motocalcio, 200
motogiro, 200
motoraduno, 200
motoricambi, 200
motorimessa, 201
nocepesca, 201
nocepesco, 201
pàllido, 143
panicuocolo, 201, 203

pannotendolo, 201
pennivendolo, 201, 205
perpetuo, 44
pescaturismo, 199, 200, 201
pescivendolo, 201, 203, 204, 205
piano-bar, 197
pneumectomia, 196
pollicoltura, 201
pollivendolo, 201
pornodivo, 201
postagiro, 201
postemastro, 201
prestidigitazione, 241
presto, 241
psicologo, 196
pub, 202
puttangiro, 201
puttan-tour, 197
radiofonia, 196
radioterapia, 196
ratto, 142
Scarpamundo, 200
scuolabus, 197
seggiovia, 201
sempiterno, 44
spazionave, 201
spazioporto, 201
straccivendolo, 201
tele-, 198
telegiornale, 197
telequiz, 197
terapia, 198
termometro, 194
terratremolo, 201
terremoto, 201, 204, 205
turismo, 199
-vendolo, 199
vetrocemento, 199, 201
vetromattone, 201
vetroresina, 198, 201
viadotto, 201
web-sondaggio, 197
xenofobo, 196

Latin words

abstineo, 9
accepto, 9
accidens, 57, 58, 59
accidentia, 57, 58
accido, 58
acer, 102
addendum, 115
adhaerĕo, 183
adventans, 42
Alea iacta est, 77, 88
alma mater, 77, 79, 88
alter ego, 78, 88
anĭma, 36
annus horribilis, 77, 82, 84, 88
Ars gratia artis, 114
Audentes fortuna iuvat, 114
augur, 241
augŭrĭum, 241
auxīlĭum, 43
Ave, Caesar, morituri te salutant, 83, 86, 88
baptīzo, 147
caementum, 199
caprifŏlĭu, 194
Carpe diem, 77, 82, 88, 114
cătīnus, 163
-cidium, 99
cimentum, 199
clamo, 121
classĭcus, 117
classis, 121
coitus interruptus, 85, 88
complēo, 175
confĕrens, 40
coniecturo, 41
coniugātĭo, 45
coniurare, 247
conmandūco, 149
contendo, 43
contra natura, 80, 88
contra naturam, 80, 88
convito*, 149
convīvĭum, 149
copia, 144

cōpĭa, 44
cŏrōna, 137
crux, 138
cum laude, 77, 88
curriculum vitae, 115
cursus, 148
dēbĭlis, 140
dĕus, 138
dīco, 175
diffĭcīlis, 140
dĭgĭtus, 241
discŭto, 175
distinguo, 176
dīvĭdo, 176
divinus, 241
dīvīnus, 248
dīxī, 9
dŏmestĭcus, 43
dūrus, 137
effectum, 9
ēgrĕgĭus, 42
ēlegantĭa, 44
ēlĭgo, 147, 150, 178
Epiphănĭa, 244
exāmen, 9
excellens, 9
exercĕo, 9, 10
exercĭtus, 144
exhĭbĕo, 183
expĕdĭens, 35
extrēmus, 141
făbrĭco, 147
făcĭlis, 139, 140
factīcĭus, 242
factus, 9
fĕrĭo, 185
fingo, 147, 149, 150
fŭgĭo, 175
gĕmĭtus, 152
gĕmo, 147
gens, 148
grammatica, 233
grosso modo, 79, 88
Habemus papam, 85, 88
homo erectus, 84

homo sapiens, 84, 88
hŏstis, 144
ĭdōnĕus, 41
immortālis, 44
impĕdĭo, 185
in extremis, 78, 88
in situ, 76, 88
incŭbus, 235
indivinare (conjectural), 241
ĭnīquus, 42
insīpĭens, 40
instans, 9
ĭnultus, 29
invictus, 75, 78, 88
invīto, 135, 139, 147, 149
ioculārius, 242, 246
ipso facto, 112
iŭgum, 138
lectĭo, 9
lūnae dĭes, 204
magia, 238, 239, 244
magica (ars), 238, 239
Magister dixit, 85, 88
magnĭtūdo, 37
magus, 238, 240, 248
mastĭcare, 139
mastīco, 135, 139, 147
mea culpa, 75, 88
mĕdĭcīna, 148
mĕdĭcīna, 148
Mens sana in corpore sano, 77
misericordia, 114
mŏdernus, 117, 122
mŏdus, 122
modus operandi, 76
motu proprio, 76
mŭndus, 138
noctuas Athenas afferre, 114
nŭmquam, 138
nūtrio, 148
ŏcŭlus, 116
opportūnus, 41
ōrāculum, 235
parĭo, 175
pater, 76

permitto, 176
persona non grata, 79, 80
pĕto, 175, 185
-phăgus, 99
pīnus, 137
pŏtens, 42
pōtĭō, 145
praedĭco, 135
praedīco, 139, 148
praesidens, 179
praestigĭae, 241
praestus, 241
prīmārĭus, 145
prīmum, 145
primus inter pares, 75, 84, 88
prŏhĭbĕo, 183
promptus, 9
pugnum, 9
pūrĭtās, 144
pūrus, 137
quaero, 186
quartus, 145
quintus, 145
Quo vadis?, 83, 88
quŏtīdĭānus, 148
răpĭdus, 141, 142
rara avis, 74, 80, 88
rĕcĭto, 147
requiem, 76, 79, 82, 88
rŭgio, 148
rŭgītus, 151
scĕlĕrātus, 43
scrībo, 175
secundus, 145
sentĭo, 175
sextus, 146
signalis, 63
significo, 9
signum, 63
sine die, 75, 88
sollemnis, 9
spargo, 175
status quo, 78, 79, 88
stĕrĭlis, 142
strega, 243

Index of words

strix, 243
succŭbus (succŭba), 235
sui generis, 76, 88
summus, 36
superavit, 115
symptoma, 58, 59, 60, 61
Tarquinius, 167
terrae mōtus, 191, 202
tertārĭus, 145
tertĭus, 145
testūdo, 44
thalamus, 43
totus tuus, 83, 88
ultĭmus, 141
unda, 43
ūnĭcus, 141
urgens, 42
ūtĭlis, 141
Vade retro, 87, 88
vĕnēnum, 137
Veni, vidi, vici, 77, 83, 86, 88
vernācŭlus, 125
versus, 148
vestīgĭum, 41
via crucis, 75, 88
vidēre, 252
vīnum, 137
vir, 247
vulgāris, 124
vulgus, 124

Occitan words
brèicho, 239
esterle, 142
joglar, 242, 246
magio, 239
mascarie, 239
pozon, 145
prezicar, 148

Portuguese words
abundância, 44
acelerante, 42
bruxa, 239

derradeiro, 36
excelência, 44
extremo, 36
feitiço, 242
ignorante, 40
magia, 239
    fazer magia, 242
mágica, 239
meezinha, 148
ocorrente, 42
poridade, 144
puridade, 144
segredo, 144
sumo, 36
vidente, 241

Romanian words
crai
    cei trei crai de la răsărit, 250
fapt, 242
farmec, 250
fermecătoare, 250
fermecător, 250
ghicitoare, 242
ghicitor, 241
magie, 239
    a face magie, 242
rege, 250
strigoi, 235, 243, 247
zmeu, 235

Romansh words
brüscha, 239
divinader, 242, 251
divinadra, 242, 251
magia, 239
magìa, 239
magu
    i magi dal urient, 250
majia, 239
puschun, 145
sabi
    i sabis digl orient, 250
stria, 242

striegn, 243
striun, 242, 243

Sardinian words
preigare, 148
preikare, 148
rattu, 142

Spanish words
abdomen, 17
aberración, 17
aborígen, 17
abscisa, 17
absorción, 17
abstener, 9
ácaro, 17
accéssit, 17
accidente, 60, 63, 64
aceptar, 9, 10
acerbísimo, 223
acético, 17
acetilsalicílico, 18
ácido, 1, 17, 18
acrílico, 18
acústico, 17
addendum, 115
adherir, 183
adorar, 147, 148
adquirir, 174, 176, 185
adscribir, 183
advenir, 183
advertir, 181
agricultura, 213
agrio, 102
agro-, 99
agronegocios, 100, 101, 102
aína, 135, 139, 142
álbum, 7
albuminoideo, 17
alea iacta est, 77, 88
alma, 36
alma mater, 77, 79, 88
almofía, 158, 163, 164, 165, 168
alter ego, 78, 88

aludir, 188
amarillo, 143
anejo, 12, 14
anexación, 13
anexar, 13
anexidad, 13
anexión, 13
anexo, 12, 14
ánima, 36
animosísimo, 221, 222
annus horribilis, 77, 82, 84, 88
antiguamente, 222
antiguo, 117, 123, 124, 126, 129
aorar, 147, 148
aplaudir, 188
aprovechable, 141
árido, 142
arsénico, 18
asentir, 183
asumir, 183
atosigado, 15
augur, 241
auto-, 99
autodiagnóstico, 100, 101, 102, 103
automodelismo, 102
automóvil, 102
autorruta, 102
auxiliado, 15
auxiliar, 15
auxilio, 15
avenir, 183
ávido, 142
axis, 7
barbitúrico, 18
barro, 168
basuraleza, 94
batear, 147, 148
bautizar, 147, 148
benzoico, 17
bibliografía, 17
bicifobia, 95
bicóncavo, 17
bioeconomía, 95
bípede, 17

bórico, 17
bronquio, 17
bruja, 239
bruscia, 239
cabero, 140
cámara, 214
campus, 7
candela, 214
cápsula, 7
carbónico, 17
carcaj, 12
carpe diem, 77, 82, 88, 114
catorzeno, 146, 147
cemento, 199
-cidio, 99
cieno, 166, 168
cimiento, 199
cinquanteno, 146
cinqueno, 146
circunscribir, 183
circunvenir, 183
clase, 120
clásico, 117–33
clasificar, 17
cohesión, 17
coincidir, 175
coitus interruptus, 85, 88
cojear, 12
coludir, 188
complejo, 12, 13, 15
complexión, 14, 16
complexionado, 16
complexo, 12, 13
compulsivo, 17
concluir, 175
concubina, 213
concurrir, 175
consumir, 183
contender, 43
contento, 220
contravenir, 183
convergencia, 17
convertir, 181
converto, 181
convidar, 147, 149

convivir, 183
corona, 137
coso, 151
cosso, 151
cotidiano, 148
cristianísimo, 223
crono-, 99
cronófago, 100, 101, 102, 103
cruz, 138
cuadragésimo, 147
cuarentena, 146
cuarenteno, 146
cuarteno, 146
cuarto, 145
cum laude, 77, 88
cumplir, 175
currículo, 115
curriculum vitae, 115
curso, 148, 151
cúspide, 17
cutiano, 148, 150
cuyo, 221, 222
débil, 140, 141, 153
debilidad, 153
decámetro, 17
decena, 146
decidir, 188
décimo, 146
decimonono, 147
décimoquarto, 146
décimoquinto, 146
decimosexto, 147
decir, 175
déficit, 7
definir, 188
deflagración, 17
deludir, 188
denigración, 39
dentífrico, 17
derradero, 140
desavenir, 183
descolorado, 143
descolorido, 143
describir, 183
detergente, 17

devenir, 183
dezeno, 146
dicesseno, 146
diez y ocheno, 146
diez y seseno, 146
diez y seteno, 146
difícil, 140
dificultad, 153
digitígrado, 17
digno, 7
diluir, 188
Dios, 138
dirigir, 183
discutir, 175, 188
disminuir, 188
distinto, 176
divertir, 181
dividir, 176, 188
docena, 146
doseno, 145, 146
dozeno, 146
duodécimo, 146
duro, 137
ecológico, 112
efectividad, 17
efecto, 7, 9, 10
egregio, 41
ejecución, 16
ejecutar, 16
ejecutor, 16
ejecutorial, 16
ejercer, 10, 16
ejercicio, 16
ejercitar, 16
ejército, 11, 16, 135, 139, 144
elección, 150
electo, 150, 176
elegir, 147, 150, 176, 178, 188
eludir, 188
embidar, 149
emer, 152
enarrar, 35
endeble, 140
enfengir/enfingir, 150
enfeñir, 147, 149

envidar, 135, 139, 147, 149
epístola, 115
escosso, 142
escribir, 175, 177, 183
escudilla, 165
esleer, 147, 150, 178
esleír, 150, 178
esparcir, 175
espasmódico, 17
estadística, 17
estéril, 142
esterlas, 142
esterle, 142
evacuante, 17
evenir, 183
exacto, 176
exactus, 176
examen, 9, 10, 11, 16
examinador, 16
examinar, 16
excelente, 9
exención, 16
exento, 16
exequias, 11, 16
exercer, 9
exhibir, 183
exigir, 188
existir, 175
exótico, 11
éxtasis, 11
extranjero, 117, 126, 130, 131
fabricar, 147
fábula, 213
fácil, 140
facilidad, 153
falsamente, 221, 222
fango, 166
feble, 140
feñir, 149
festino, 142
filantropía, 17
filarmónico, 17
filosofía, 213
finalmente, 221, 222
fingir, 147, 150

fís(s)ico, 149
fis(s)igo, 149
flaco, 140
flojo, 12
fórceps, 17
fortísimo, 221, 222
fosforescencia, 17
fotografía, 17
fraguar, 147
fumigación, 17
gafo, 143
gaho, 143
gastroagenda, 95
gemer, 147, 152
gemido, 152
gemir, 147, 152
gente, 148, 152
glúteo, 17
grave, 140
grieve, 140
grimorio, 234
grosso modo, 79, 88
hecho, 9
hemisferio, 43
heñir, 150
herir, 185
hexasílabo, 17
hueste, 16, 135, 139, 144
idioma, 117, 118, 129, 130, 131
iludir, 188
ilusionista, 241
impartir, 177, 183
impedir, 185, 188
impermeable, 17
impugnación, 39
in extremis, 78, 88
in memoriam, 75, 88
in situ, 76
incontinente, 223
iniciación, 19
iniciador, 19
iniciadora, 19
inicial, 18
inicialar, 19
inicialista, 19

inicializar, 19
iniciar, 18
iniciático/ca, 19
iniciativo/a, 19
inicio, 19
inquirir, 185
insano, 43
inscribir, 183
instante, 9
internacional, 17
intervenir, 183
intuición, 180
intuir, 179
intuitivo, 180
inulto, 29
invadir, 188
invitar, 135, 139, 147, 149
ipso facto, 112
jabón, 11
jamuga, 11
jeringa, 11, 12
jofaina, 163, 165, 168
júnior, 7
lactación, 17
latente, 43
lección, 9, 10
lector, 214
lengua, 117, 118, 125, 126, 129, 130, 131
leproso, 143
lidiar, 115
ligero, 139, 142
límpido, 142
litigar, 115
liviano, 139
llano, 115
lodo, 166, 168
lujo, 16
lujoso, 16
lunático, 223
machorra, 142
magia, 239, 252
    hacer magia, 242
magister dixit, 85, 88
mago, 240, 241

los Reyes Magos, 250
malato, 143
mamotreto, 220
manifactura, 214
maña, 142
mañero, 142
mañoso, 142
mascar, 135, 139, 147, 149
masticar, 135, 139, 147, 149
mausoleo, 221
máxime, 220
me(t)ge, 149
mea culpa, 4, 75, 88
meandro, 4
meato, 4
mecánica, 4
mecánicamente, 4
mecanicismo, 4
mecanicista, 4
mediático, 4
mediatización, 4
medicalización, 4
medicalizar, 4
medicina, 4, 148, 149
médico, 4, 149, 220
medio, 4
melecina, 149
melezina, 148, 149
mérito, 213
mesiello, 143
misericordia, 114
moderno, 117–33
modo, 122
modus operandi, 76
motu proprio, 76
mudiar, 152
mugir, 152
mundo, 138
muriátrico, 17
narcoauto, 102
nauseabundo, 17
necrobiosis, 99
necroturismo, 99
nítido, 142
nítrico, 17

nodrecer, 147
nodrir, 147
nono, 146
noveno, 146
nunca, 138
nutrir, 147
óbito, 17
obstetricia, 17
obtener, 7
ochavo, 146
ocheno, 146
ochenteno, 146
octavo, 146
ojo, 116
ontología, 17
onzeno, 146
ostensible, 17
palidez, 153
pálido, 143, 153
parir, 175
paroxismo, 16
partir, 177, 183
páter, 76
patria, 213, 221
pedir, 174, 175, 185
percutir, 188
permitir, 176
persona non grata, 79, 80
personalmente, 221, 222
pino, 137
plaga, 223
plano, 115
pobre, 10
ponzoña, 144, 145
poridad, 144
posición, 10
postrero, 140
postrimero, 140
potente, 41
predicar, 135, 139, 148, 149
preigar, 135, 139, 148
preludiar, 17
prescribir, 183
presentir, 183
presidente, 179

presidir, 178
presto, 142
presumir, 183
prevenir, 183
primero, 145
primo, 145, 146
primus inter pares, 75, 84, 88
pro, 141
prohibir, 175, 183
prójimo, 12, 13, 14
pronto, 9, 142
proscribir, 183
provenir, 183
próximo, 12, 13, 14
proyectil, 17
pugilato, 17
puño, 9
puridad, 144
puro, 137
quartodécimo, 147
quatrodécimo, 146
querer, 176, 186
quincuagésimo, 147
quinto, 145
quinzeno, 146, 147
Quo vadis, 112
rabio, 141
rapidez, 153
rápido, 135, 139, 141, 142, 153
rara avis, 74, 80, 88
rastro, 41
raudo, 141
recitar, 147
reflejo, 15
regir, 177, 183
rehez, 139
relajación, 15
reloj, 12
remitente, 17
repercutir, 188
repetir, 176
requerir, 176, 185
réquiem, 76, 79, 82, 88
rescribir, 183
reseno, 146

restringir, 175, 188
resumir, 183
retentivo, 17
revenir, 183
reverter, 187
revertir, 187
revivir, 183
rogir, 151
roxicado, 15
rudimento, 17
rugir, 148, 151
ruido, 151
ruir, 148, 151
sabio, 117, 126, 129, 132
salutífera, 213
secreta, 214
secreto, 144
seductivo, 17
senectud, 214
sénior, 7
sentir, 174, 177, 183
señal, 63
séptimo, 146
séptimo décimo, 147
sepultura, 221
seseno, 146
sesenteno, 146
seteno, 146
setenteno, 146
sexto, 146, 223
siesta, 146
siesto, 146
siglación, 94
significar, 9
signo, 64
similitud, 40
sincericidio, 100, 102, 103
sinceridad, 103
sine die, 75, 88
sintaxis, 11
síntoma, 53–67, 64
sobrevenir, 183
sobrevivir, 183
solemne, 9, 10
solemnemente, 10

solemnizado, 10
solemnizar, 10
statu quo, 78, 79, 88
subvenir, 183
sui géneris, 76, 88
sulfúrico, 17
sumir, 177, 183
superávit, 115
suscribir, 183
symptoma, 62
tálamo, 43
tarquín, 158, 165–67, 168
tercero, 145
tercio, 145
típico, 17
tósigo, 15
tóssico, 145
tossigamiento, 145
tóssigo, 145
tossigoso, 145
toste, 142
tóxico, 15
toxicología, 15
toxicológico, 15
trans, 94
transcribir, 183
transferir, 175
trasero, 140
tredécimo, 146
treinteno, 146
treseno, 146
trezeno, 146
trigésimo, 147
túrbido, 142
ultimátum, 112, 115
último, 140, 141
undécimo, 146
único, 141
útil, 141, 153
vade retro, 87, 88
veintena, 146
veinteno, 146
veneno, 137, 144
venir, 177, 183
ventura, 214

vernáculo, 117, 125, 126, 130
versatilidad, 17
verso, 148, 151
verter / vertir, 186
veterinario, 17
vía crucis, 75, 88
vidente, 241
videoendoscopia, 95
viesso, 148, 151
vigésimo, 147
vino, 137
vitriólico, 17
vivir, 177, 183
vivo, 130
vulgar, 117, 124, 125, 126, 132
xilografía, 12
yemdo, 152
yente, 148, 152
yugo, 138
yuyu, 94
zaguero, 140
zoología, 17

www.ingramcontent.com/pod-product-compliance
Lightning Source LLC
Chambersburg PA
CBHW072124290426
44111CB00012B/1772